Richard Morris

Historical Outlines of English Accidence

Comprising Chapters on the History and Development of the Language. Second Edition

Richard Morris

Historical Outlines of English Accidence
Comprising Chapters on the History and Development of the Language. Second Edition

ISBN/EAN: 9783337203450

Printed in Europe, USA, Canada, Australia, Japan

Cover: Foto ©Thomas Meinert / pixelio.de

More available books at **www.hansebooks.com**

HISTORICAL OUTLINES

OF

ENGLISH ACCIDENCE.

HISTORICAL OUTLINES

OF

ENGLISH ACCIDENCE,

COMPRISING

CHAPTERS ON THE HISTORY AND DEVELOPMENT OF THE LANGUAGE, AND ON WORD-FORMATION.

BY THE

REV. RICHARD MORRIS, LL.D.

EDITOR OF HAMPOLE'S "PRICKE OF CONSCIENCE," "THE STORY OF GENESIS AND EXODUS," "AYENBITE OF INWYT," "OLD ENGLISH HOMILIES," ETC. ETC.
MEMBER OF COUNCIL OF THE PHILOLOGICAL SOCIETY,
LECTURER ON ENGLISH LANGUAGE AND LITERATURE IN KING'S COLLEGE SCHOOL.

SECOND EDITION

London:
MACMILLAN AND CO.
1872.

[*The Right of Translation and Reproduction is reserved.*]

LONDON:
R. CLAY, SONS, AND TAYLOR, PRINTERS,
BREAD STREET HILL.

PREFACE.

MANY writers on the structure and history of English, in spite of the plain evidence to the contrary, have regarded our language as one that has sprung up, comparatively speaking, within a very recent period. Some have dared to carry it as far back as Chaucer's time, because he has usually been spoken of as "the well of English undefiled." Others again, not so bold, have deemed it quite sufficient to date the rise of the English language from the time of the greatest of Elizabethan writers. By not regarding the earlier stages of our language as *English*, all the necessary helps to a rational treatment of its grammatical forms and idioms have been cast aside. The *Saturday Review* has, very rightly, raised its voice rather loudly against the absurdity of such a view, and has properly insisted upon the right of all periods to be designated as *English*,—the very oldest term for our language, and one that is identified with its earliest history and with the very best writers of all its periods, from Alfred the Great down to the present time. This outcry against an absurd nomenclature has been productive of good results, as is seen in the growing tendency that manifests itself nowadays to study the older stages of English, for the sake of the light they throw upon its later and more modern periods; and in very many of our public schools, the upper forms possess a very creditable acquaintance with some of our old English worthies, and are enabled by the knowledge they have thus acquired to get a satisfactory account of the peculiarities and anomalies of modern English.

The unsatisfactory state of most of our English Grammars is perhaps due to the limited knowledge of their writers,[1] and to their unwillingness to avail themselves of the help afforded by the remains of our early literature. English Grammar, without a reference to the older forms, must appear altogether anomalous, inconsistent, and, unintelligible. In Germany, the grammar of our language has been studied and treated scientifically, in the order of its historical development, by means of our early literature, and it has also been illustrated by the results of Comparative Philology. To the most recent of the German works on our language, that by Professor Koch —the most orderly and scientific English grammar yet written—I have been greatly indebted in the compilation of the present volume, especially for the chapters on word-

---

[1] I do not include Dr. Latham's English Grammars among the works of the numerous grammar-mongers here alluded to.

formation and the Appendices I. and II. I have also made much use of the lectures of Professor Max Müller on "The Science of Language," and those of Professor Whitney on "Language, and the Study of Language." I have, I hope, turned to good account the many old English works that have been issued from time to time by our Book Clubs, especially those published by the present Early English Text Society;[1] but the size of my book obliged me to admit only so many old English illustrations as were absolutely necessary for the full explanation of the forms under consideration. I have endeavoured to write a work that can be profitably used by students and by the upper forms in our public schools; a very elementary book formed no part of my plan. I hope, however, to have leisure to write a more elementary work than the present one, as well as to compile "Historical Outlines of English Syntax," as a supplement to this "Accidence."

To my own shortcomings I am fully alive, as I know from my experience as a teacher how difficult it is in linguistic matters to make one's statements plain and simple as well as accurate; I have, however, been more anxious to write a useful than a popular book, and for the convenience of English students I have sacrificed the *scientific* method of treating English adopted by Koch,

---

[1] It is the plain duty of every Englishman who can in any way afford it, to support this Society, and the Chaucer Society.

to the more *practical* one followed by Mätzner in his "Englische Grammatik." Koch commences with a hypothetical primitive Teutonic speech (*Grundsprache*), and traces our language chronologically through all its stages up to its present form.

In Appendix II. the reader will find an abstract (with some few additions) of Koch's historical scheme of the " Accidence," exhibiting the chief inflexional forms of the English language in its earlier stages. I have added comparative Tables of Adverbs, Prepositions, Conjunctions, and Interjections, and can vouch for their correctness only so far as my own reading goes. The classification is Koch's.

KING'S COLLEGE, LONDON,
December 1871.

GRAMMATICAL WORKS CONSULTED.

Lectures on the Science of Language. First and Second Series. By Max Müller. 1861—1864.

Comparative Grammar of the Sanskrit, Zend, Greek, Latin, &c. Languages, by Professor F. Bopp. Translated by B. Eastwick, F.R.S. Third Edition. London: 1862.

Compendium der vergleichenden Grammatik der Indo-germanischen Sprachen, von August Schleicher. Weimar: 1866.

Deutsche Grammatik, von Jacob Grimm. Göttingen: 1819—1840.

A Comparative Grammar of the Teutonic Languages, by James Helfenstein, Ph.D. London: 1870.

Families of Speech, by the Rev. F. W. Farrar, M.A., F.R.S. London: 1870.

Lectures on the English Language, by G. P. Marsh. London: 1861.

The Origin and History of the English Language, and of the Early Literature it embodies, by G. P. Marsh. London: 1862.

Historische Grammatik der Englische Sprache, von C. Friedrich Koch. 1863—1869.

Englische Grammatik, von Eduard Mätzner. Berlin: 1860—1865.

Wissenschaftliche Grammatik der Englishe Sprache, von Eduard Fiedler, 1 Bd. Zerbst: 1850. 2 Bd. von Dr. Carl Sachs. Leipzig: 1861.

The English Language, by R. G. Latham, M.D. 1855.

The Elements of the English Language, by Ernest Adams, Ph.D. 1870.

A Sanskrit Grammar for Beginners, by Max Müller. London: 1870.

A Grammar of the Anglo-Saxon Tongue from the Danish of Erasmus Rask, translated by Benjamin Thorpe. London: 1865.

A Comparative Grammar of the Anglo-Saxon Language, by Francis A. March. London: 1870.

Affixes in their Origin and Application, by S. S. Haldeman. Revised Edition. Philadelphia: 1871.

A Shakespearian Grammar, by E. A. Abbott, M.A. London: 1870.

Language, and the Study of Language. By W. D. Whitney. London: 1867.

Philological Essays, by the Rev. Richard Garnett. London: 1859.

Observations on the Language of Chaucer's Canterbury Tales, and Gower's Confessio Amantis, by F. J. Child. Boston.

My own schemes of the Grammar of the Old English Southern dialect will be found in the "Ayenbite of Inwyt," "Old English Homilies" (First Series), and "An Old English Miscellany;" of the East Midland, in the "Story of Genesis and Exodus," and "Old English Homilies" (Second Series);[1] of the West Midland, in "Early English Alliterative Poems"—(all published by the Early English Text Society); of the Northern, in Hampole's "Pricke of Conscience" (Philological Society).

---

[1] In the Press.

CONTRACTIONS.

Abs. and Achith. = Absalom and Achitophel.
Allit. = Alliterative Poems (ed. Morris).
Areop. = Milton's Areopagitica (ed. Arber).
Ayenbite = Ayenbite of Inwyt (ed. Morris).

B. and F. = Beaumont and Fletcher.
Boeth. = Boethius.

C. Tales = Canterbury Tales.
Compl. of L. Lyfe = Complaint of a Lover's Lyfe (attributed to Chaucer).
Confess. Amant. = Confessio Amantis (Gower).
Coriol. = Coriolanus.
Cosmog. = Cosmography (Earle).
Cymb. = Cymbeline.

Dan. = Danish.

E. E. Poems = Early English Poems (ed. Furnivall).
E. E. Spec. = Specimens of Early English (ed. Morris).

F. Q. = Faerie Queene.

Gen. and Ex. = Story of Genesis and Exodus (ed. Morris).
Ger. = German.
Gest. Rom. = Gesta Romanorum (Early English Version).
Goth. = Gothic.
Gr. = Greek.

Icel. = Icelandic.

Lat. = Latin.
Laȝ. = Laȝamon's Brut (ed. Madden).

Med. Lat. = Mediæval Latin.
Mel. = Anatomy of Melancholy (Burton).
Mid. H. G. = Middle High German.

O. E. = Old English.
O. E. Hom. = Old English Homilies (ed. Morris).
O. F. = Old French.
O. H. Ger. = Old High German.
O. N. = Old Norse.
Orm. = Ormulum (ed. White).
O. Sax. = Old Saxon.

P. L. = Paradise Lost.
P. of C. = Pricke of Conscience (ed. Morris).
P. of P. = Pastime of Pleasure (Hawes).
Pilgrimage = Pilgrimage of the Lyf of Manhode (ed. Aldis Wright).
Prov. E. = Provincial English.

Robt. of Gl. = Robert of Gloucester.

Sansk. = Sanskrit.
Shep. Cal. = Shepherd's Calendar.
Spec. E. E. = Specimens of Early English (ed. Morris).
Swed. = Swedish.

Tr. and Cr. = Troilus and Cressida.
Trist. = Lay of Sir Tristram (ed. Scott).

CONTENTS.

CHAPTER I.
	PAGE
FAMILIES OF LANGUAGES	1

CHAPTER II.
GRIMM'S LAW 13

CHAPTER III.
HISTORY OF THE ENGLISH LANGUAGE 27

CHAPTER IV.
OLD ENGLISH DIALECTS 41

CHAPTER V.
PERIODS OF THE ENGLISH LANGUAGE 48

CHAPTER VI.
PHONOLOGY 57

CHAPTER VII.

ORTHOGRAPHY . . . . PAGE 62

CHAPTER VIII.

ACCENT 74

CHAPTER IX.

ETYMOLOGY 79

CHAPTER X.

SUBSTANTIVES 82

CHAPTER XI.

ADJECTIVES 104

CHAPTER XII.

PRONOUNS 116

CHAPTER XIII.

VERBS 153

CHAPTER XIV.

ADVERBS 193

CHAPTER XV.

PREPOSITIONS 203

CHAPTER XVI.

CONJUNCTIONS 207

CHAPTER XVII.

INTERJECTIONS 209

CHAPTER XVIII.

DERIVATION AND WORD FORMATION 211

APPENDICES.

APPENDIX I. 251
APPENDIX II. 260
APPENDIX III. 337

INDEX 357

ERRATA.

Page 95, § 79, col. 7, *for* *mûs* read *mŷs*.

Page 128, footnote 1, dele from *We* to *beyond*, and add, *anent* = O.E. *anefent* = *on-efn*, *on-emn* = even with, against, &c.

Page 171, footnote 1. The theory of *Rückumlaut*, or a return to an original sound which has undergone *umlaut*, though adopted by most German philologists, cannot be defended. Mr. Sweet has, in the *Academy*, very clearly explained the apparent vowel-change in such *weak* verbs as *told*, *sold*, &c.

The Gothic *saljan*, to sell, represents the primitive form of the verb in which *umlaut* has not taken place, as it has in O. Eng. *sellan* (= *selian*). In the infinitive mood and present tense the suffix *i* dropped out after *umlaut* had taken place; but in the preterite *salde* (= *salide*), sold, the *i* dropped out without causing *umlaut*, so that the root-vowel was thus preserved.

Page 176, line 12, *for* § 283 *read* 282.

Page 228, line 8, *an-hungred* is not found in the oldest English, but is met with in subsequent periods.

Page 229, line 11, for *many* read *navy*.

HISTORICAL OUTLINES

OF

ENGLISH ACCIDENCE.

CHAPTER I.

FAMILIES OF LANGUAGES.

1. WORDS are articulate sounds used to express perception and thought. The aggregate of these articulate sounds, accepted by and current among any community, we call *speech* or *language*.

2. The language of the same community often presents local varieties; to these varieties we give the name of *dialects*.

3. Grammar treats of the words of which language is composed, and of the laws by which it is governed.

4. The science of Grammar is of two kinds: (*a*) **Descriptive Grammar**, which classifies, arranges, and describes words as separate parts of speech, and notes the changes they undergo under certain conditions.

(*b*) **Comparative Grammar**, which is based on the study of words, goes beyond the limits of Descriptive Grammar; that is, beyond the mere statement of facts. It analyses words, accounts for the changes they have undergone, and endeavours to trace them back to their origin. It thus deals with the growth of language.

Descriptive Grammar teaches us that the word *loveth* is a verb, indicative mood, &c. Comparative Grammar informs us, (1) that the radical part of the verb is *lov* (or *luf*), denoting desire (cp. Lat. *lubeo*); (2) that the suffix *-th* is a remnant of a demonstrative pronoun signifying *he, that*, of the same origin as the *-t* in *lube-t*.

5. Comparative Grammar has shown us that languages may be classified in two ways : (1) According to the peculiarities of their grammatical structure, or the mode of denoting the relation of words to one another ; (2) according to historical relationship.

6. The first mode of classification is called a *morphological* one. It divides languages into, (1) Monosyllabic or Isolating ; (2) Agglutinative ; (3) Inflectional or Polysyllabic.

These terms also represent three periods in the growth of languages —that is to say, that language, as an organism, may pass through three stages. (1) The monosyllabic period, in which roots are used as words, without any change of form.

In this stage there are no prefixes or suffixes, and no formally distinguished parts of speech.

The Chinese is the best example of a language in the isolating or monosyllabic stage.

"Every word in Chinese is monosyllabic ; and the same word, without any change of form, may be used as a noun, a verb, an adjective, an adverb, or a particle. Thus *ta*, according to its position in a sentence, may mean great, greatness, to grow, very much, very.

" We cannot in Chinese (as in Latin) derive from *ferrum*, iron, a new substantive *ferrarius*, a man who works in iron, a blacksmith ; *ferraria*, an iron mine, and again *ferrariarius*, a man who works in an iron mine ; all this is possible only in an inflected language." —MAX MULLER.

(2) The agglutinative period. In this stage two unaltered roots are joined together to form words ; in these compounds one root becomes subordinate to the other, and so loses its independence.[1] Cf. *man-kind*, *heir-loom*, *war-like*, which are agglutinative compounds. The Finnish, Hungarian, Turkish, the Tamul, &c., are agglutinative languages.

The Basque and American languages are agglutinative, with this difference, that the roots which are joined together have been abbreviated, as in the Basque *ilhun*, "twilight," from *hill*, dead + *egun*, day. In the Mexican language their compound terms are equivalent to phrases and sentences, *achichillacachocan*, "the place where people weep because the water is red ; " from *alt*, "water ; " *chichiltic*, "red ; " *tlacatl*, "man ; " and *chorea*, "weep."

It has been proposed to call these languages *polysynthetic* or *incorporating*. It is remarkable that most of these languages show that the people who speak them are deficient in the power of abstraction.

---

[1] Cp. Hungarian *var—at—andot—ta—tok* (= wait—and—will—have—you)= you will have been waited for.

(3) The inflectional period, in which roots are modified by prefixes or suffixes, which were once independent words. In agglutinative languages the union of words may be compared to mechanical compounds, in inflective languages to chemical compounds.

In most living languages we find traces of all these processes, and are thus enabled to see how gradually one stage leads to another. Take, for example, the following :—

    He is *like God* = monosyllabic.
    He is *God-like* = agglutinative.
    He is *God-ly* = inflectional.

Here the syllable *ly* = *like*, originally a word, has dwindled down to a formative element or suffix.

7. The classification of languages according to historical relationship is a *genealogical* one.

Historical relationship may be shown by comparing the grammar and vocabulary of any two or more languages; if the system of grammatical inflexions bear a close resemblance to one another, and if there be a general agreement in the employment of those terms that are least likely to have been lost or displaced by borrowed terms (such as pronouns, numerals, words denoting near relationship, &c.), then it may be safely asserted that such languages are related to one another.

Historical relationship, then, rests upon, (1) the similarity of grammatical structure; (2) the fundamental identity of roots.

8. Comparative Grammar teaches us that the English language is a member of a group of allied languages, to which the term Teutonic has been given.

The *Teutones* were a German tribe conquered by Marius : hence the terms *Teutonicus* and *Theoticus* were subsequently applied to all German-speaking people.

The Germans still call their language *Deut-sch*.[1]

The origin of the term is found in Old High German *diot*, people, *duit-isc*, national. In the oldest English *theod* and *theodisc* = people (cf. Umbrian Latin *tuticus*, from *tuta*, a city). The Teutons were *the people*, in contradistinction to the Romans and others, whom they called *Welsh*, or foreign.

The name *German* was probably given to the Teutons by some continental Keltic tribes. By some philologists the word German is said to mean howlers, shriekers (from Keltic *gairm-a*, to cry out), on account of their warlike shouts.

---

[1] *Dutch* is merely another form of the same word.

9. The **Teutonic** dialects may be arranged in three groups or subdivisions:—

(1) The Low German; (2) the Scandinavian; (3) the High German.

The English language is a Low German dialect, and is closely allied to the dialects still spoken on the northern shores and lowlands of Germany. This relationship is easily accounted for by the emigration of the Angles, Saxon, and other Low German tribes from the lowlands of Germany situate between the Rhine and Baltic coasts.

I. To the Low German division belong the following languages:—

(1) **Gothic**, the oldest and most primitive of the Teutonic dialects, of which any remains are known, was spoken by the Eastern and Western Goths, who occupied the province of Dacia, whence they made incursions into Asia, Galatia, and Cappadocia.

The oldest record of this dialect is found in the translation of the Bible by Bishop Ulphilas (born 318, died 388), the greater part of which has perished, though we still possess considerable portions of the Gospels and St. Paul's Epistles, some pieces of the Old Testament, and a small portion of a Commentary.

(2) **Frisian.** (a) *Old Frisian* as preserved in documents of the twelfth and thirteenth centuries; (b) *Modern Frisian*, still spoken in Friesland, along the coasts and islands of the North Sea between the Weser and the Elbe, and in Holstein and Sleswick.

The Frisian is more closely allied to English than the rest of the Low German languages.

(3) **Dutch.** (a) *Old Dutch* (as seen in documents from the thirteenth to the sixteenth century); (b) *Modern Dutch*, spoken in Holland and Belgium.

(4) **Flemish.** (a) *Old Flemish*, the language of the Court of Flanders and Brabant in the sixteenth century; (b) *Modern Flemish*.

(5) **Old Saxon**, or the Saxon of the Continent, spoken between the Rhine and Elbe, which had its origin in the districts of Munster, Essen, and Cleves.

There is a specimen of this dialect in a poetical version of the Gospels (of the ninth century), entitled the *Heljand* (O.E. *Heiland*) = the *Healer* or Saviour.

The Old Saxon is very closely related to English, and retains many Teutonic inflexions that have disappeared in other Low German dialects.

    (6) **English.** (*a*) Old English; (*b*) Modern English; (*c*) Provincial English; (*d*) Lowland Scotch.

    II. To the **Scandinavian** division belong the following tongues:—(1) Icelandic; (2) Norwegian; (3) Swedish; (4) Danish.

The Icelandic is the purest and oldest of the Scandinavian dialects. The Old Icelandic, from the eleventh to the thirteenth century, is often called Old Norse, a term that properly applies only to Old Norwegian.

Iceland was colonized by the Northmen, who established a Republic there, and were converted to Christianity A.D. 1000.

    III. To the **High German** division belongs Modern German, the literary dialect of Germany, properly the speech of the south-east of Germany, Bavaria, Austria, and some adjacent districts.

It is divided into three stages—

    (*a*) Old High German, comprising a number of dialects (the Thuringian, Franconian, Swabian, Alsacian, Swiss, and Bavarian), spoken in Upper or South Germany from the beginning of the eighth to the middle of the eleventh century.

    (*b*) Middle High German, spoken in Upper Germany from the beginning of the twelfth to the end of the fifteenth century.

    (*c*) Modern High German, from the end of the fifteenth century to the present time.

Luther ennobled the dialect he used in his beautiful translation of the Bible, and made the High German the literary language of all German-speaking people. The Low German dialects of the Continent are yielding to its influence, and, in course of time, will be wholly displaced by it.

10. If we compare English and modern German we find them very clearly distinguished from each other by regular phonetic changes:[1] thus a *d* in English corresponds to a *t* in German, as *dance* and *tanz*; *day* and *tag*; *deep* and *tief*; *drink* and *trink*. A *t* in English agrees with an *s* or *z* in German, as is shown by *foot* and *fuss*;

---

[1] See Grimm's Law, p. 13.

tin and *zinn*; *to* and *zu*; *two* and *zwei*; *water* and *wasser*. A German *d* is equivalent to our *th*, as *die* and *the*; *dein* and *thine*; *bad* and *bath*, &c.

Not only English, but all the remaining members of the Low German family, as well as the Scandinavian dialects, are thus distinguished from High German.

11. The Scandinavian dialects differ from the other members of the Teutonic family in the following particulars :—

(1) The definite article follows its substantive, and coalesces with it.

In O. Norse *inn* = ille ; *in* = illa ; *itt* = illud : hence *hani-nn*, the cock ; *giöf -in*, the gift ; *fat -it*, the foot.

In Swedish and Danish *en* (mas. fem.) and *et* (neut.) = the.

Swed.—Konung-*en*, the king. | bord-*et*, the table.
Dan.—Kong-*en*, ,, ,, | hjert-*et*, the heart.

(2) The reflex pronoun *sik* (O. N.), *sig* (Swed. and Dan.),[1] Lat. *se*, = *self*, coalesces with verbs, and forms a reflexive suffix : as O. N. *at falla* = fall down, and *sik* = self, produce the reflexive (or middle) verb *at fallask*.

Sk is still further worn down to *st*, and when added to the verb renders it passive, as O. N. *at kalla*, to call ; *at kallast*, to be called.

In English we have borrowed at least two of these reflexive verbs ; namely, *bu-sk*, from the Icel. *bu-a*, to prepare, make ready, direct one's course, and *ba-sk* (= *bak-sk*) from Icel. *baka*, to warm, which is identical with Eng. *bake*.

12. Comparative Philology has also proved to us that the Teutonic dialects form a subdivision of a great family of related languages, to which the term **Indo-European** has been applied.

When we recollect that the Indo-European family comprehends nearly all the languages of Europe, and all those Indian dialects that

---

[1] From the following table it will be seen that *sik* is accusative:—

	O. Norse.	Swedish.	Danish.	Dutch.	German.	Latin.
Nom.	wanting	...	...	...	...	...
Gen.	sin	wanting	...	zijns	sein	sui
Dat.	ser	sig	sig	zich	sich	sibi
Acc.	sik	sig	sig	zich	sich	se

FAMILIES OF LANGUAGES.

have sprung from the old Hindu language (Sanskrit), the term is by no means an inappropriate one. It has been proposed, however, by eminent philologists, that the term Aryan should be used in its place. The word Aryan is a Sanskrit word, meaning *honourable, noble*. It was the name by which the old Hindus and Persians, who at a very early period had attained a high degree of culture and civilization, used to call themselves in contradistinction to the uncivilized races or non-Aryans of India whom they conquered.

Vestiges of the old name are found in Iran, Armenia, Herat, &c. There are two great divisions of the Indo-European family: A. European; B. Asiatic.

A. EUROPEAN DIVISION.

I. The **Teutonic Languages**, of which we have already spoken.

II. The **Keltic Languages**.
   (*a*) *Cymric Class.* — (1) Welsh; (2) Cornish (died out about the middle of sixteenth century); (3) Bas-Breton.
   (*b*) *Gadhelic Class.* — (1) Erse or Irish; (2) Gaelic, spoken in the Highlands of Scotland; (3) Manx (the dialect spoken in the Isle of Man).

III. The **Italic** or **Romanic Languages**.
   (*a*) Old Italian dialects, as the Oscan (of South Italy), the Umbrian (of N.E. Italy), Sabine.
   (*b*) The Romance dialects, which have sprung from the Latin. (1) Italian; (2) French; (3) Provençal; (4) Spanish; (5) Portuguese; (6) Rhæto-Romanic (or Roumansch), spoken in Southern Switzerland; (7) Wallachian, spoken in the northern provinces of Turkey (Wallachia and Moldavia).

The Wallachian is divided by the Danube into two dialects, the Northern and the Southern. It owes its origin chiefly to the Roman colonies sent into Dacia by Trajan.

IV. The **Hellenic Languages**.
   (1) Ancient Greek (comprising the Attic, Ionic, Doric, and Æolic dialects).
   (2) Modern Greek (comprising several dialects).

The *Albanian* dialect is a representative of the language spoken by the Illyrians, who probably occupied the Greek peninsula before the Hellenic tribes.

All that can be positively stated about it is that it belongs to the Indo-European family, and is closely related to Greek.

The Albanians inhabit part of the ancient Epirus and Illyrium. They call themselves Skipetars or mountaineers, and the Turks call them *Arnauts* (= *Arbanites*).

V. The Sclavonic Languages.

(*a*) South-east Sclavonic.

(1) Old Bulgarian (or Old Church Slavic) of the eleventh century.

(2) Russian ; (*a*) Russian Proper ; (*b*) Little Russian or Ruthenian.

(3) Illyric, comprising, (1) Servian ; (2) Kroatian ; (3) Slovenian (of Carinthia and Styria).

(*b*) Western Branch.

(4) Polish.

(5) Bohemian.

(6) Slovakian.

(7) Upper and Lower Sorbian (Lusatian dialects).

(8) Polabian (on the Elbe).

VI. The Lettic Languages.

(1) Old Prussian (the original language of N.E. Prussia).

(2) Lettish or Livonian (spoken in Kurland and Livonia).

(3) Lithuanian (spoken in Eastern Prussia).

The Turkish, Hungarian, Basque, Lappish, Finnish, and Esthonian do not belong to the Indo-European family.

B. Asiatic Division.

VII. The Indian Languages.

(1) Sanskrit (dead).

(2) Prakrit (Indian dialects, preserved in Sanskrit dramas).

FAMILIES OF LANGUAGES. 9

(3) 1, Pali (the sacred language of the Buddhists); 2, Cingalese, spoken in the Island of Ceylon.
(4) Modern Indian dialects descended from Sanskrit, as Hindī, Hindustanī, Bengalī, Mahrattī.
(5) Gypsy dialect. (The Gypsies are of Indian origin.)

Sanskrit is the oldest and most primitive of the existing Indo-European tongues.

VIII. The Iranian Languages.

(1) Zend (or Zand), the language of the Zoroastrians, preserved in the Zend-Avesta, or sacred writings of the old Persians, parts of which are at least a thousand years old.
(2) The cuneiform inscriptions of Darius and Xerxes and their successors (of the Achæmenid dynasty), the oldest of them being about five centuries before Christ.
(3) Pehlevi or Huzvaresh, the language of the Sassanian dynasty (A.D. 226–651).
(4) Parsi or Pazend, spoken in a more eastern locality than the Pehlevi, about the time of the Mohammedan conquest.
(5) Modern Persian, which differs but little from the Parsi, arose after the Mohammedan conquest. Its first great national work, *Shah-Nameh*, was written by Firdusi (died 1020).

The *Armenian*, *Ossetic* (spoken in the Caucasus), *Kurdish* (spoken by the mountaineers of the border land between Persia, Turkey, and Russia), *Afghan* (or *Pushto*), the language of *Bokhara*, are all clearly related to Sanskrit and Persian, but it has not yet been decided to which group they severally belong.

13. All the Indo-European languages are descended from one common stock; that is to say, all the Indo-European languages are dialects of an old and primitive tongue which no longer exists.

The people who spoke this tongue must have lived together as one great community more than three thousand years ago. Tradition, as well as the evidence of language, points to the north-eastern part of the Iranian table-land, near the Hindu-Kush mountains, as the original abode of this primitive people.[1]

---

[1] The Aryan people, as they called themselves in opposition to the *barbarian*, must have occupied a region of which Bactria may be regarded as the centre.

We must not suppose that they formed one strongly-constituted state, but were probably divided into distinct tribes, united solely by the general bond of race, by similarity of manners, religion, and language.

The language of the primitive Indo-Europeans had its local varieties or dialects, which were distinguished by certain euphonic differences; and these differences, after the Indo-European tribes left their ancient abode and separated, would become more marked, and other changes would take place, so that these dialects would assume the aspect of languages at first sight wholly unconnected.

By the aid of Comparative Philology we find that it is possible to classify and arrange the *phonetic differences* of the various Indo-European languages, and to reduce them to certain rules, so that we are enabled to determine what sound in one language corresponds to that of another.[1]

Philological research has found "that the primitive tribe which spoke the mother-tongue of the Indo-European family was not nomadic alone, but had settled habitations, even towns and fortified places, and addicted itself in part to the rearing of cattle, in part to the cultivation of the earth. It possessed our chief domestic animals —the horse, the ox, the sheep, the goat, and the swine, besides the dog; the bear and the wolf were foes that ravaged its flocks; the mouse and fly were already its domestic pests.

"The region it inhabited was a varied one, not bordering upon the ocean. The season whose name has been most persistent is the winter. Barley, and perhaps also wheat, was raised for food, and converted into meal. Mead was prepared from honey, as a cheering and inebriating drink. The use of certain metals was known; whether iron was one of these admits of question. The art of weaving was practised; wool and hemp, and possibly flax, being the materials employed. Of other branches of domestic industry little that is definite can be said; but those already mentioned imply a variety of others, as co-ordinate or auxiliary to them. The weapons of offence and defence were those which are usual among primitive peoples—the sword, spear, bow, and shield. Boats were manufactured, and moved by oars. Of extended and elaborate political organization no traces are discoverable; the people was doubtless a congeries of petty tribes, under chiefs and leaders rather than kings,

---

The primitive Aryan must have embraced nearly the whole of the region situated between the Hindu-Kush (Belurtagh), the Oxus, and the Caspian Sea; and perhaps extended a good way into Sogdiana, towards the sources of the Oxus and the Taxartes. (Pictet.)

[1] Rask first discovered, and Grimm afterwards worked out, the law which governs the permutation of consonants; hence it is always known as Grimm's Law.

and with institutions of a patriarchal cast, among which the reduction to servitude of prisoners taken in war appears not to have been wanting.

"The structure and relations of the family are more clearly seen; names of its members, even to the second and third degrees of consanguinity and affinity, were already fixed, and were significant of affectionate regard and trustful interdependence. That woman was looked down upon as a being in capacity and dignity inferior to man we find no indication whatever.

"The art of numeration was learned, at least up to a hundred; there is no general Indo-European word for 'thousand.' Some of the stars were noticed and named. The moon was the chief measurer of time.

"The religion was polytheistic, a worship of the personified powers of nature. Its rites, whatever they were, were practised without the aid of a priesthood."—WHITNEY.

14. Next to the Indo-European the most important family of languages is the Semitic, sometimes called the *Syro-Arabian* family, of which the chief divisions are as follows :—

> (*a*) The *Northern* or *Aramaic*, comprehending, (1) the Syriac (ancient and modern); (2) the *Assyrian* and *Babylonian*.
>
> (*b*) The *Central* or *Canaanitic*, including, (1) *Hebrew*, *Phœnician*, *Samaritan*, and *Carthaginian* or *Punic*.
>
> (*c*) The *Southern* or *Arabic*, comprehending, (1) Arabic and Maltese ; (2) *Himyaritic* (once spoken in the S.W. of the peninsula of Arabia), and the *Amharic* and other Abyssinian dialects ; (3) the *Ethiopic* or *Geëz* (the ancient language of Abyssinia).

It has not yet been shown that the Semitic languages, although inflectional, are historically connected with the Indo-European family.

It has not been decided whether the *Hamitic* family, containing, (1) the ancient Egyptian and Coptic ; (2) Galla ; (3) Berber; (4) Hottentot, &c., have any historical connection with the *Semitic*.

15. The other languages of the world fall into various groups.

> A.—The **Alatyan** or **Scythian**, comprehending, (1) Hungarian; (2) Turkish; (3) Finnish and Lappish ; (4) the Samoyed dialects ; (5) Mongolian dialects ; (6) Tungusian dialects (as Manchu).

B.—I. The *Dravidian* or *Tamulic* (including *Tamul, Telegu, Malabar, Canaries*). II. The languages of N.E. Asia (including the dialects of the *Corea*, the *Kuriles, Kamchatka*, &c.). III. *Japanese*, and dialect of *Loo-Ckoo*. IV. *Malay-Polynesian* or Oceanic languages (comprehending the dialects of *Malacca, Java, Sumatra, Melanesia*, &c.). V. The *Caucasian* dialects (*Georgian*, &c.).

C.—*South African dialects.*

A, B, and C are agglutinative in their structure, but have no historical connection with each other.

D.—I. *Chinese.* II. The language of *Farther India* (the *Siamese, Burmese, Annamese, Cambodian*, &c.). III. *Thibetan.*

These are monosyllabic or isolating in structure.

E.—I. *Basque.* II. The aboriginal languages of South America—all polysynthetic in structure.

CHAPTER II.

GRIMM'S LAW.

16. I. If the same roots or the same words exist in Sanskrit, Greek, Latin, Keltic, Slavonic, Lithuanian, Gothic,[1] and Old High German, then, wherever the Sanskrit or Greek has an *aspirate* the Gothic has the corresponding *flat* mute.

II. If in Sanskrit, Greek, &c., we find a *flat* mute, then we find a corresponding *sharp* mute in Low German, and a corresponding *aspirate* in High German.

III. If the six first-named languages show a *sharp* mute, the Gothic shows the corresponding *aspirate*, and Old High German the corresponding *flat* mute.

TABLE OF COMPARATIVE SOUNDS.

Sanskrit.	Greek.	Latin.	Gothic and Low Germ. Languages.	Old High German.	Modern High German.
bh *(h)	φ	f* (b)	b	p	p
dh (dh)	θ	f* (d, b)	d	t	t
gh (h)	χ	h, (f)	g	k	g
b	β	b	p	f	f
d	δ	d	t	z	s, z
g	γ	g	k	ch	ch
p	π	p	f, b	f, v	f
t	τ	t	th	d	d
k	κ	c	h*	h*	h

[1] *Gothic* is here taken as the best representative of the Low German and Scandinavian dialects, and Old High German of the other division of the Teutonic languages.   * Not always regular.

ILLUSTRATIONS OF GRIMM'S LAW.

I. Sansk. *bh*; Gr. φ; Lat. *f* (*b*); Goth. *b*; O. H. Ger. *p*.

Sanskrit.	Greek.	Latin.	Gothic.	O. H. Ger.	English.
bhanj (=bhranj), to break	ῥήγνυμι	frangere	brikan	prëchan (Ger. brechen)	break.
Zend. bar (=bhar) to bore	φάρος (plough)	forare	—	poran	bore.
bhratri	φρατήρ	frater	brôthar	pruoder (Ger. bruder)	brother.
bhri	φέρω	fero	baira	piru	I bear.
budhna (=bhudhna), depth	πυθμήν*	fundus	—	bodam	bottom.
bâhu (=bhâhu), arm	πῆχυς*	—	O.N. bog-r	buoc	el-bow.
banh (= bhanh), to grow	—	—	bag-m-s, tree	Ger. baum	beam.
bhaj (to bend)	φεύγω	fugio	biugan	Ger. beugen	bow (O. E. bugan).
—	φράσσω	—	bairgan	Ger. bergen	O.E. beorgan (to protect).
—	νεφέλη	nebula	nibls	nepal (Ger.nebel)	—

* Not quite regular.

bhi (to fear)	φηγός / φέβομαι	fagus	bôka	puocha / —	beech. / O.E. bevir, biver (shake).
bhram (to whirl)	βρέμω	fremo	—	—	O.E. breem (fierce), brim (edge).
bhrâj	φλέγω	fulgeo, flagro	—	—	bright (Prov. Eng. blunk, spark).
bhû	φύω	fu-i	—	pi-m (Ger. bi-n)	be (O.E. be-om).

II. Sansk. *dh*; Gr. θ (φ); Lat. *f* (*d*, *b*); Goth. *d*; O.H. Ger. *t*.

duhitri	θυγάτηρ	—	dauhtar	tohtar (Ger. tochter)	daughter.
dvâra (= dhvâra)	θύρα	fores	daur	tor	door.
—	θήρ (φήρ)	fera	dius	tior (Ger. thier)	deer.
dhâ	τίθημι	do in con-*do*, &c.	—	Ger. thun	do.
—	θέμις	—	dôms	—	doom.
dhû (to shake, blow)	θύω, θύελλα, θυμός	fumus, suf-fio	dauns (smell)	tunst (storm)	dust.
dhri (to support)	θρᾶνος (bench)	firmus	—	—	—
dhrish	θαρσεῖν	fortis	ga-daursan	tarran	dare, durst.

Sanskrit.	Greek.	Latin.	Gothic.	O. H. Ger.	English.
vadhu (wife)...... (cp. Zend. *vad*, to lead)	—	—	—	wette.........	wed, wife.
indh (to burn) ...	αἴθω.........	aestas, aedes	—	cit (fire).........	O.E. ad.
madhya............	μέσσος.........	medius	midja............	miti (Ger. mitte).	mid-dle, midst.
ruh (= rudh), to grow	—	—	—	ruota (Ger. rute).	rood, rod.
rudhira (blood)...	ἐρυθρός	ruber, rufus	—	rôt (Ger. roth) ...	red.

III. Sansk. *gh* (*h*) ; Gr. χ ; Lat. *h* (*f, g*) ; Goth. *g* ; O. H. Ger. *k*.

gharma............	θερμός	formus	—	—	warm.
ghas (to eat)......	—	hostis, hospes....	gasts	—	guest.
ghrishti (pig)	χοῖρος.........	—	O.N. gris	—	O.E. gris, grice, gris-kin.
—	χέω.........	—	giutan	Ger. giessen......	O.E. geotan (to pour, gutter).
hansa*............	χήν	anser (= hanser)	gans	kans (Ger. gans).	goose.
hari*............	χλόη	—	—	—	green.
haryāmi* (I love)	χαίρω............	gratus	-gairns (greedy)..	Ger. gern (gladly)	yearn.

Sanskrit	Greek	Latin	(Teutonic)	(German/Gothic)	(English/OE)
—	χόρτος	co-hors, hortus	garls (house)	karto (Ger. garten)	garden, yard orchard (= ort-yard)
hyas*	χθές	heri, hesternus	gistra	kēstar (Ger. gestern)	yester-day.
vah* (to carry)	ὄχος	trahere / vehere	dragan / vigs (way)	trakan / waggan (currus)	drag. waggon, wag. wain
—	εἴχω	—	aigan	eikan	owe (O. E. agan).
khan† (dig)	χαίνω	—	—	ginêm (I yawn)	yawn (O. E. gene).
nakha	ὄνυξ	—	nagls	Ger. nagel	nail (O. E. nagel).
stigh (to mount)	στείχω	—	steiga (I go up)	Ger. steigen	O. E. stigen (styc).

* *H has grown out of gh.*   † *kh originally gh.*

IV. Sansk. *b*; Gr. β; Lat. *b*; Goth. *p*; O. H. Ger. *f.**

Sanskrit	Greek	Latin	(Teutonic)	(German/Gothic)	(English/OE)
—	κάνναβις	—	—	hanaf (Ger. hanf)	hemp.
—	βραχύς, ἔμβρυχος	—	O.N. hanpr, praggan, to press	—	O. E. prangle. slip, sleep, limp.
lamb (to fall)	—	labor	—	—	—
kubja (crooked)	κύβος	cubare	lups	huf	hip, hump.

* *The initial b is rare in Teutonic words. In Sans., Gr., and Lat. b has been developed from other sounds*

V. Sansk. *d*; Gr. δ; Lat. *d*; Goth. *t*; O. H. Ger. *z* (Ger. *s*, *z*).

Sanskrit.	Greek.	Latin.	Gothic.	O. H. Ger.	English.
asru (= dasru)...	δάκρυ	lacruma (= dacruma)	tagr	zahar, zähre......	tear.
dah (to burn)....	δάφνη	lignum	—	—	—
dir..................	δύω	duo	twai	zuei (Ger. zwei)..	two, twain.
svid (to sweat) ...	ἱδρώς	sudare	sweitan	svizzan	to sweat.
das'an...............	δέκα	decem	taihun	zēhan (Ger. zehn)	ten, tithe.
dant..................	ὀδούς (-όντος) ...	dens	tunthus	zand (Ger. zahn).	tooth (O. E. toth = tonth).
swâdu	ἡδύς	suairs..............	sutis	suozi (Ger. süss).	sweet (O.E. swot).
ad.....................	ἔδειν	edere..............	itan	ĕzan (Ger. essen)	eat.
vid....................	εἴδειν, οἶδα	videre	witan	wizan (Ger. wissen)	wit (wot, wist).
dam	δαμάω	domare	tamjan	zëman, zëhmen...	tame.
dama (house) ...	δόμος	domus	timr (timber)....	Ger. zimmer......	timber.
druma (wood) ...	δρῦς, δόρυ, δένδρον	—	triu	—	tree.
dar (tear)	δέρω	—	tairan............	zëran	tear.
dis' (to show) ...	δείκνυμι	dico	teiha	teigōm (I show).	teach.
nida (nest).........	—	nidus..............	—	—	nest.
hridaya.............	καρδία	cor (cordis)	hairtô	hërza..............	heart.
kratu (power) ...	κράτος	—	hardus	harti	hard.
pâda	πούς (ποδός)	pes (pedis)	fōtus	vuoz (Ger. fuss)..	foot.

ud-a	ὕδωρ	unda	watô	wazar (Ger. wasser)	water.
—	ῥίζα, βρίζα	radix	vaurts	wurza	O.E. wort (herb, plant; cp. *colewort*, cabbage plant).

VI. Sanskrit, &c. *p*; Goth. *f*; O.H.Ger. *f(x, v)*.

panchan	πέμπε (πέντε)	quinque	fimf	vinf (Ger. fünf)	five.
saptan	ἑπτά	septem	sibun	sieben	seven.
pûrna	πλέος	plenus	fulls	Ger. full	full.
pitri	πατήρ	pater	fadar	vatar (Ger. vater)	father (O.E. fader).
upari	ὑπέρ	super	ufar	ubar (Ger. über)	over.
apa (away)	ἀπό	ab	af	aba	off, of.
pará (away)	παρά	per	fra-	far- (Ger. -ver)	from, fro.
pak (cook)	πέπτω	coquo	—	—	—
par (to bring over)	περάω, πόρος (passage)	porta (gate), ex-perior*	faran	varan (Ger. fahren)	fare.

* Cp. Lat. *periculum*; Ger. *gefahr*; Ger. *wohlgefahrt*; Gr. εὐπορία.

Sanskrit.	Greek.	Latin.	Gothic.	O. H. Ger.	English.
prî (to please, to love)	πραΰς	—	frijôn	freund, freuen (to be glad)	friend (O.E. freon, to love).
prath (to extend)	πλατύς	planus (= plat-nus)	—	—	flat.
pat-tra (wing), from pat, to fly	πτερόν, πέτομαι	penna (=pesna), peto	—	fedara (wing)	fea-ther (= feth-ther).
—	—	paucus	favs	fôh	few (O.E. fea-wa).
—	—	quercus (= per-cus)	—	foraha (Ger. föhre)	fir.
prach (ask)	—	precor	fraihnan, fragan	Ger. fragen	O.E. fregnan, frain.

VII. Sansk. *t* ; Goth. *th* ; O. H. Ger. *d*.

Sanskrit	Greek	Latin	Gothic	O. H. Ger.	English
tvam	τύ	tu	thu	du	thou (O.E. thú).
tam (acc.)	τόν	is-tum, ta-lis, ta-m	tha-na	d-ên (Ger. den)	the (thi-s, tha-t).
tri	τρεῖς	tres	threis	dri (Ger. drei)	three.

antara	ἕτερος	alter	anthar	andar (Ger. an-der)	other (= on-ther)
—	ταλάω	tolero	thulan	dolan (Ger. dul-den)	thole (suffer).
tan (stretch)	τείνω	tendo	thanja (extendo).	Ger. dehnen	—
tanus (thin)	—	tenuis	O.N. thunnr (thin)	dunni (Ger. dünn, thin)	thin.
tu (be powerful)	ταΰς (great)	totus, tutus, Umb. tuta (city)	thiuda (people)	diot	O.E. thede.
trish	τέρσομαι	torreo	thairsan	Ger. dursten	to thirst.

VIII. Sansk. *k*; Gr. κ; Lat. *c*, *qu*; Goth. *h* (*g*); O. H. Ger. *h* (*g*).

kapâla	κεφαλή	caput	haubith	houpit (Ger. haupt)	head (O.E. heafod, hevcd).
kas (= kva)	πός, κό-s	quis	hva-s	wër (Ger. wer)	who (O.E. hwa).
pas'u	ποῦ	pecus	faihu	Ger. vieh	fee (O.E. feoh), cattle.
kala (time)	καιρός δκ-ός = ὀ-πός, gen. of ὄψ	—	hweila (awhile)	—	while.
karsh (to draw)	—	oc-ulus	—	ouga (Ger. auge)	eye (O.E. eáġe, eghe).
kâs (to cough)	—	accerso	—	huosto	hearse, harrow. husky, hoarse (O.E. has).

Sanskrit.	Greek.	Latin.	Gothic.	O. H. Ger.	English.
kalya (healthy)	καλός	—	hails	Ger. heil	whole, heal (O.E. hál, hol.)
hrid (= krid)	καρδία	cor (cordis)	—	—	heart.
s'vas'ura	ἑκυρός	socer	swaihra	Ger. schwager	O. E. sweor.
s'âlâ* (house)	καλία	cella, domicilium	haims (village)	Ger. heim	hall.
s'i (to lie)	κεῖμαι	quies, civ-is	—	—	home (O.E. hám.)
—	κλέπτω, κλέπτης	clepo	hliftus (thief)	—	shop-lifter (O.E. lift, to steal.)
—	στίζω	in-stigare	stikan	Ger. stecken	stick.
s'van	κύων, κυνός	canis	hunths	hund	hound.
s'veta (white)	—	—	hweits	huiz	white wheat.

* The Sanskrit s' has been developed from an original guttural.

IX. Sansk. j (g); Gr., Lat. g; Gothic k; O. H. G. ch.

jnâ	γνῶμι	gnosco	kunnan	Ger. kennen, können	ken, con, know.
	—	—	kan	chan	can.

Sanskrit	Greek	Latin	Gothic/O.Sax./O.N.	OHG/German	English
jâti...	γένος...	genus...	kum...	chuni...	kin.
—	γόνος (offspring).	—	O. Sax. kind...	Ger. kind...	child.
jânu...	γόνυ...	genu...	kniu...	chniu...	knee.
janî (mother)...	γυνή...	—	qino, qens...	chena...	queen.
janaka (father)...	—	—	—	chuninc (Ger. könig)	king (O.E. cyning).
ah-am...	ἐγώ...	ego...	ik...	ih (Ger. ich)...	I (O.E. ic, ich).
—	—	nodus (= gnodus)	O.N. knûtr...	Ger. knote...	knot.

17. No satisfactory explanation has yet been given of this permutation of consonants throughout the Indo-European family of languages, "nevertheless we have no reason to believe it of a nature essentially different from the other mutations of sound[1] of equally arbitrary appearance, though of less complication and less range, which the history of language everywhere exhibits."—WHITNEY.

The changes of sounds just noticed have arisen from what Max Müller terms *dialectic growth*. Even in the history of our own language we find traces of similar changes, as *vat*, in wine-vat, is the old Southern English form for the Northern *fat*, a vessel.

In the dialects of the South of England, we may still hear dirsh = *thrush ;* drash = *thrash*.

The aspirate dental *th* has become *s* in the third person singular of verbs, as *he loveth* = *he loves*. But this was once a dialectical peculiarity.

18. There are other changes that must not be confounded with the permutations coming under Grimm's Law : the chief are those that arise from an endeavour to make the work of speaking easier to the speaker, to put a more facile in the stead of a more difficult sound or combination of sounds, and to get rid of what is unnecessary in the words we use.

"All articulate sounds are produced by effort, by expenditure of muscular energy, in the lungs, throat, and mouth. This effort, like every other which man makes, he has an instinctive disposition to seek relief from, to avoid ; we may call it laziness, or we may call it economy—it is in fact either the one or the other—according to the circumstances of each separate case ; it is laziness when it gives up more than it gains ; economy when it gains more than it abandons." —WHITNEY.

These wearing down processes are often called euphonic [2] changes Max Müller terms them the results of phonetic decay.

Thus, as he remarks, nearly all the changes that have taken place in our own language within the last eight centuries come under this class of changes.

(1) Softening of gutturals at end of words, as *silly* from *sǽlig* *godly* from *godlic* = godlike, *barley* from *bær-lic*.

---

[1] All letter-change must be based upon physiological grounds.
[2] The seat of euphony is in the vocal not in the acoustic organs.
[3] *bar* = O.E. *bere* = barley, cp. Lat. *far; -ley* = O.E. *-lic* (as in garlick, hemlock) = plant.

In *laugh, cough*, &c. the guttural is represented by a labial aspirate (cp. O.E. *thof* = though ; *thruf, thurf* = through). A similar change is seen in Lat. *frio, frico*, as compared with Gr. χρίω, Sansk. *gharsh*, to rub; Lat. *formus*, warm; Sansk. *gharma*, and Gr. θερμός.

Trough is pronounced in some parts as *troth*, just as we hear children saying *fum* for *thumb*, and *nuffing* for *nothing*. The Russians put *f* regularly for *th*, turning Theodore into *Feodor* or *Fedor* (cp. Gr. θήρ, Lat. *fera*, Eng. *deer*).

In *dough* and *plough* (also in *dry, buy*, O.E. *drige, bugge*) the guttural sound is altogether lost, just as it is in many Sanskrit words, as *mah* for *magh*, to become great; *duh* for *dugh*, to milk, &c. (cp. *anser* for *hanser* = *ghanser*, Gr. χήν).

G has been softened down to *j* in *ridge, edge, bridge*, &c. from O.E. *rigg, egg, brigg*.

In *bat* and *mate* a *t* supplies the place of an original *k* (cp. O.E. *bak* = bat, *make* = mate, *fette* = *fechche* = fetch, *scratte* = *scrachche* = scratch).

(2) Softening of initial gutturals, as *child* for *cild*, &c.

(3) Substitution of *d* for *th*, as *burden* for *burthen, murder* for *murther*, &c.

(4) Loss of letters, as *woman* for *wif-man* (cp. *goody* for *goodwife*, *huzzy* for *huswife*), *lord* for *hláford*, *king* for *cyning, mole* for *moldwarp, stranger* for *estrangier* (Fr.) = *extraneus* (Lat.), &c. (cp. loss of *n* before *th* in English words, *tooth* for *tonth, mouth* for *munth*, &c).

(5) Insertion of letters, *b, d*, as *slumber* for *slumer-ian, thumb, limb*, for *thum, lim* (cp. *number* from *numerus*, and the insertion of *p* after *m* in Latin), *thunder* for *thuner, hind* for *hine* (cp. *souns* for *soun*, from Lat. *sonus;* and *cinder, tender*, from Lat. *cinis, tener;* Gr. γαμβρός for γαμρός ; and Goth. *hund-s*, Eng. *hound*, Lat. *canis;* Gr. ἄνδρες for ἄυρες).

It must be recollected that certain letter-changes are brought about under the influence of neighbouring sounds, as English *cob-web* for O.E. *cop-web*, where the influence of *w* has changed the *p* into a *b ; orchard* = O.E. *ort-yard* = *ort-geard:* so we find in the sixteenth century *goujeer* for *good year*.

When two consonants come together the first is often assimilated to the second, or the second to the first, thus *d* or *t* + *s* will become *s*, as O.E. *god-sib* has become *gossip.* So *gospel, grunsel, foster* = *god-spel, ground-sel, fodster; chaffare* = *chapfare; cup-board* is pronounced *cubboard;* Lat. *ad-fero* = *affero,* &c. ; *puella* = *puerella,* &c.

When two dentals come together, the first is sometimes changed into a sibilant, as *mot-te* = *moste* = most, and *wit-te* = *wiste* = wist (cp. Lat. *hest* from O.E. *hat-an,* to command; *missus* for *mittus* from *mitto; esum* = *edtum* from *edo*).

Sometimes *s* becomes *st,* as O.E. *whiles* = *whilst, hoise* = *hoist,* &c.

When two consonants come together, the first is made like the second or the second similar to the first,[1] as *wept* = *weeped, kembd* and *kempt* = *kembed* = combed; so we have *clotpoll* and *clodpoll* (cp. Lat. *scriptus* = *scrib-tus*). To a similar principle must be ascribed the loss of the guttural sound of *h* or *gh* before *t;* thus *might* (= *mihth*), *night* (= *nihth*) : cp. It. *otto* for *octo.*

---

[1] In other words the only combination of mutes are *flat* + *flat* and *sharp* + *sharp.*

CHAPTER III.

HISTORY OF THE ENGLISH LANGUAGE

19. WE must bear in mind, (1) that English is a member of the Indo-European family; (2) that it belongs to the Teutonic group; (3) that it is essentially a Low German dialect; (4) that it was brought into Britain by wandering tribes from the Continent; (5) that we cannot use the terms English or England in connection with the country before the middle of the fifth century.

20. According to the statements of Bede, the Teutonic invaders first came over in A.D. 449, and for about 100 years the invasion may be said to have been going on. In the course of time the original Keltic population were displaced by the invading tribes, who became a great nationality, and called themselves Ænglisc or English. The land they had won they called Ængla-land (the land of the Angles) or England.

Bede makes the Teutonic invaders to consist of three tribes—Angles, Saxons, and Jutes. The Saxons, he tells us, came from what was known in his time as the district of the Old Saxons, the country between the Elbe and the Eider.

The Angles came from the Duchy of Sleswick, and there is still a district in the southern part of the duchy, between the Slie and the arm of the Baltic, called the Flensborg Fiorde, which bears the name *Angeln*.

Bede places the Jutes to the north of the Angles, that is, probably the upper part of Sleswick or South Jutland.

There were no doubt a considerable proportion of Frisians from Greater and Lesser Friesland. Bede mentions the Frisians (Fresones) among the natives from whom the Angles were descended.

The settlements are said to have taken place in the following order:—

    I. Jutes, under Hengest and Horsa, who settled in KENT and the Isle of Wight and a part of Hampshire in A.D. 449 or 450.

II. The first division of the Saxons, under Ella (Ælle) and Cissa, settled in SUSSEX, in 477.

III. The second body of Saxons, under Cerdic and Cynric, in WESSEX, in 495.

IV. The third body of Saxons in ESSEX, in 530.

V. First division of the Angles, in the kingdom of EAST ANGLIA (Norfolk, Suffolk, Cambridgeshire, and parts of Lincolnshire and Northamptonshire).

VI. The second division of the Angles, under Ida, in the kingdom of Beornicia (situated between the Tweed and the Firth of Forth), in 547.

Two other kingdoms were subsequently established by the Angles —*Deira* (between Tweed and Humber), and *Mercia*,[1] comprehending the Midland counties.

Teutonic tribes were known in Britain, though they made no settlements before the coming of the Angles. In the fourth century they made attacks upon the eastern and south-eastern coast of this island, from the Wash to the Isle of Wight, which, on that account, was called "*Littus Saxonicum*," or the Saxon shore or Saxon frontier; and an officer known as the Count of the Saxon Shore (*Comes Littoris Saxonici per Britannias*) was appointed for its defence. These Teutonic invaders were known to the Romans and Celts by the name of *Saxons;* and this term was afterwards applied by them to the Teutonic settlers of the fifth century, who, however, never appear to have called themselves Saxons, but always Ænglisc or English.

21. The language that was brought into the island by the Low-German settlers was an *inflected* speech, like its congener, modern German. It was, moreover, an *unmixed* language, all its words being English, without any admixture of foreign elements.

The Old English borrowed but very few words from the original inhabitants. In the oldest English written language, from the ninth to the end of the eleventh century, we find scarcely any traces of Keltic words.

In our old writers, from the thirteenth century downwards, and in the modern provincial dialects, we find more frequent traces of words of Keltic origin, and a few still exist in modern English.

22. The English were converted to Christianity about A.D. 596, and during the four following centuries many Latin words were

---

[1] *Mercia* — march or frontier. In Southern and West Mercia the people were of Saxon origin; the others came of an Anglian stock.

introduced by Roman ecclesiastics, and by English writers who translated Latin works into their own language.

This is called the Latin of the *Second period*. What is usually designated the Latin of the *First period* consists of words that have had no influence upon the language itself, but are only to be found in names of places, as *castra*, a camp, in Don-caster, Chester, &c.

23. Towards the end of the eighth century the Northmen of Scandinavia (*i.e.* of Denmark, Norway, and Sweden), who were then without distinction called Danes, ravaged the eastern coast of England, Scotland, the Hebrides, and Ireland.

In the ninth century they gained a permanent footing in England, and subdued the kingdoms of Northumbria, East Anglia, and Mercia.

In the eleventh century Danish sovereigns were established on the English throne for nearly thirty years.

Chronologically the facts are as follows :—

In 787 three ships of Northmen appeared and made an attack upon the coast of Dorsetshire.

In 832 the Danes ravaged Sheppey in Kent.

In 833 thirty-five ships came to Charmouth in Dorsetshire, and Egbert was defeated by the Danes.

In 835 the Welsh and Danes were defeated by Egbert at Hengestesdun.

In 855 the Danes wintered in Sheppey.

In 866 they wintered in East Anglia.

In 868 they got into Mercia as far as Nottingham, and in 870 they invaded East Anglia.

In 871 the eastern part of Wessex was invaded by the Danes.

In 874 the Danes entered Lincolnshire.

In 876 they made settlements in Northumbria.

In 878 Alfred concluded a treaty with Guthorm or Guthrum, the Danish chief, and formally ceded to the invaders all Northumberland and East Anglia, most part of Essex, and the north-east part of Mercia.

In 991 the Norwegians invaded the east coast of England and plundered Ipswich; they were defeated at the battle of Maldon. Before 1000 the Danes had settled in Cumberland.[1]

In 1013 Svein, King of Denmark, conquered England; and between the years 1013 and 1042 a Danish dynasty ruled over England.

---

[1] For an admirable account of the Danish invasions see Dr. Freeman's *Old English History for Children*, pp. 91—239.

24. The Danish and English are allied tongues, and consequently there is an identity of roots, so that it is by no means an easy matter to detect the Danish words that have found their way into English.

In the literature of the tenth and eleventh centuries we find but few traces of Danish, and what little there is occurs in the scanty literature of Northern English, and not in the dominant English of the South. We know, too, that in the north and east of England the Old English inflections were much unsettled by Danish influence, and that in the thirteenth and fourteenth centuries nearly all the older inflections of nouns, adjectives, and verbs had disappeared, while in the south of England the old forms were kept up to a much later period, and many of them have not yet died out.

There are numerous traces of Scandinavian words—(1) in the local nomenclature of England; (2) in Old English literature of the north of England; (3) in the north of England provincial dialects.

In modern English they are not so numerous. It may be sufficient for the present to say that there are a few common words of undoubted Danish origin, as *are, till, until, fro, fro*ward, *ill, bound* (for a place), *busk, bask,* &c.

25. The next great event that affected the English language was the Norman invasion in 1066, by which French became the language of the Court, of the nobility, of the clergy, of literature, and of all who wished for or sought advancement in Church or State.[1]

An old writer tells us that gentlemen's children were taught French from their cradle; and in the grammar-schools boys were taught to construe their Latin into French. Even uplandish men (or rustics) tried to speak French in order to be thought something of, so low did the English and their language fall into disrepute.

In the universities Latin or French was ordered to be used. French was employed in the courts of law, and the proceedings of Parliament were recorded in French.

---

[1] To the Normans we owe most of the terms pertaining to (1) feudalism and war, (2) the church, (3) the law, and (4) the chase.

(1) Aid, arms, armour, assault, banner, baron, battle, buckler, captain, chivalry, challenge, duke, fealty, fief, gallant, hauberk, homage, lance, mail, march, soldier, tallage, truncheon, tournament, vassal, &c.

(2) Altar, Bible, baptism, ceremony, devotion, friar, homily, idolatry, interdict, piety, penance, prayer, preach, relic, religion, sermon, scandal, sacrifice, saint, tonsure.

(3) Assize, attorney, case, cause, chancellor, court, dower, damages, estate, fee, felony, fine, judge, jury, mulct, parliament, plaintiff, plea, plead, statute, sue, tax, ward.

(4) Bay, brace, chase, couple, copse, course, covert, falcon, forest, leash, leveret, mews, quarry, reynard, rabbit, tiercet, venison.

The great mass of the people, however, clung to their mother-tongue, and from time to time there arose men who thought it a meritorious work to write in English, for the benefit of the "unlered and lewed," who knew nothing of French.

It must be recollected that the Norman invaders did not carry on an exterminating war against the natives as the Saxons did against the Keltic inhabitants, nor were they superior in numbers to the English; and therefore, as might be expected, there came a time when the two races—the conquering and the conquered—coalesced and became one people, and the language of the majority prevailed. While this was taking place French became familiar to the English people, and very many words found their way first in the spoken and then in the written language. But after this coalescence of the two races Norman-French became of less and less importance, and at last ceased to be spoken.

In 1349 boys ceased to learn their Latin through the medium of French, and in 1362 (the 36th year of Edward III.) it was directed by Act of Parliament that all pleadings in the law courts should henceforth be conducted in English, because, as is stated in the preamble to the Act, French was become much unknown in the realm.

Norman-French had suffered too by being transported to English soil, and in the thirteenth and fourteenth centuries had become a mere provincial dialect, in fact a corrupt sort of French which would no longer pass current as the "French of Paris."

These changes were brought about by political circumstances, such as the loss of Normandy in King John's reign, and the French wars of Edward III. (1339), which produced a strong anti-Gallican feeling in the minds of both Anglo-Normans and English.

26. We have seen that Norman-French is sprung from the Latin language brought into Gaul by the Romans. It has, however, preserved (1) some few Keltic words borrowed from the old Gauls;[1] (2) many Teutonic terms introduced by the Franks, who in the fifth century conquered the country, and imposed their name upon the country and language;[2] (3) a few Scandinavian words brought into the language by the Northmen who settled in Normandy in the tenth century.

But the Norman-French was essentially a Latin tongue, and it added to English another Latin element, which is usually called the *Latin of the third period.*

27. From the revival of learning in the beginning of the sixteenth century up to the present time we have introduced a large number

---

[1] As *vassal, varlet,* &c.   [2] *Marshal, seneschal, guile,* &c.

of words from Latin. These have been called the *Latin of the fourth period*.

28. Greek words have also found their way into the language, but have been borrowed more sparingly than Latin.

The Latin element, then, comes to us either *indirectly* or *directly*. That introduced by the Norman-French comes *indirectly*, and has in very many instances undergone great change in spelling. Latin words of the fourth period are borrowed direct from the Latin, and have not suffered much alteration. A few examples will make this clear:—

Latin introduced by Norman-French.	Latin borrowed directly from the Latin.	Latin.
balm	balsam	balsamum
caitiff	captive	captivus
coy	quiet	quietus
feat	fact	factum
fashion	faction	factio
frail	fragile	fragilis
lesson	lection	lectio
penance	penitence	pœnitentia
sure	secure	securus
trait	tract	tractus

Compare, too, *ancestor* and *antecessor*; *sampler* and *exemplar*; *benison* and *benediction*; *chalice* and *calyx*; *conceit* and *conception*; *constraint* and *construction*; *defeat* and *defect*; *forge* and *fabric*; *malison* and *malediction*; *mayor* and *major*; *nourishment* and *nutriment*; *poor* and *pauper*; *orison* (prayer) and *oration*; *proctor* and *procurator*; *purveyance* and *providence*; *ray* and *radius*; *respite* and *respect*; *sir* and *senior*; *surface* and *superficies*, *treason* and *tradition*.

Loyal and *legal*; *privy* and *private*; *royal* and *regal*; *strait* and *strict*.

Aggrieve and *aggravate*; *couch* and *collocate*; *construe* and *construct*; *esteem* and *estimate*; *paint* and *depict*; *purvey* and *provide*; *rule* and *regulate*.

A few words from the Greek have suffered similar change, as *frenzy*, *blame* (cp. *blaspheme*), *fantom* (cp. *fantasm*), *story* (cp. *history*).

29. Our language has naturalized miscellaneous words from various sources besides those already mentioned.

(1) *Hebrew.*—Abbot, amen, cabal, cherub, jubilee, pharisaical, Sabbath, seraph, Shibboleth.

(2) *Arabic.*—Admiral, alchemy, alkali, alcohol, alcove, alembic, almanac, amulet, arrack, arsenal, artichoke, assassin, atlas,

azure, bazaar, caliph, chemistry, cotton, cipher, dragoman, elixir, felucca, gazelle, giraffe, popinjay, shrub, syrup, sofa, sherbet, talisman, tariff, tamarind, zenith, zero.

Arabia exercised powerful influence upon European culture in the Middle Ages. Many words in the above list, as admiral, artichoke, assassin, popinjay, &c., have come to us through one of the Romance dialects.

(3) *Persian.*—Caravan, chess, dervish, emerald, indigo, lac, lilac, orange, pasha, sash, shawl, turban, taffety.

(4) *Hindu.*—Calico, chintz, dimity, jungle, boot, muslin, nabob, pagoda, palanquin, paunch, pundit, rajah, rice, rupee, rum, sugar, toddy.

(5) *Malay.*—(Run) a-muck, bantam, gamboge, orang outang, rattan, sago, verandah; tattoo and taboo (Polynesian); gingham (Java).

(6) *Chinese.*—Caddy, nankeen, satin, tea, mandarin.

(7) *Turkish.*—Caftan, chouse, divan, fakir, janissary, odalisk, saloop, scimitar.

(8) *American.*—Canoe, cocoa, hammock, maize, potato, skunk, squaw, tobacco, tomahawk, wigwam, yam.

(9) *Italian.*—Balustrade, bandit, brave, bust, canto, carnival, charlatan, domino, ditto, dilettante, folio, gazette, grotto, harlequin, motto, portico, scaramouch, stanza, stiletto, stucco, studio, tenor, umbrella, vista, volcano, &c.

(10) *Spanish.*—Alligator, armada, cargo, cigar, desperado, don, embargo, flotilla, gala, mosquito, punctilio, tornado, &c.

(11) *Portuguese.*—Caste, commodore, fetishism, palaver, porcelain, &c.

(12) *French.*—Aide-de-camp, accoucheur, accouchement, attaché, au fait, belle, bivouac, belles-lettres, billet-doux, badinage, blasé, bon mot, bouquet, brochure, bonhomie, blonde, brusque, busk, coif, coup, début, débris, déjeuner, dépôt, éclat, élite, ensemble, ennui, etiquette, entremêts, façade, foible, fricassée, goût, interne, omelet, naïve, naïveté, penchant, nonchalance, outré, passé, persiflage, personnel, précis, prestige, programme, protégé, rapport, redaction, renaissance, recherché, séance, soirée, trousseau.

(13) *Dutch.*—Block, boom, boor, cruise, loiter, ogle, ravel, ruffle, scamper, schooner, sloop, stiver, yacht, &c.

(14) *German.*—Landgrave, landgravine, loafer, waltz, cobalt, nickel, quartz, felspar, zinc.

30. Taking the actual number of words from a good English dictionary, the sum total will be over 100,000. Words of classical origin are calculated to be about twice as numerous as pure English words ; hence some writers, who have only considered the constituent parts of our *vocabulary*, have come to the conclusion that English is not only a mixed or composite language, but also a Romance language. They have, however, overlooked the fact that the *grammar* is not mixed or borrowed, but is altogether English.

We must recollect that in ordinary conversation our vocabulary is limited, and that we do not employ more than from three to five thousand words, while our best writers make use of about twice that number.

Now it is possible to carry on conversation, and write numerous sentences, without employing any borrowed terms ; but if we endeavour to speak or write without making use of the native element (grammar or vocabulary), we shall find that such a thing is impossible. In our talk, in the works of our greatest writers, the English element greatly preponderates.

31. It will be interesting as well as useful to be able to distinguish the English or Low German elements from the Romance terms.

Pure English are—

I. 1. Demonstrative adjectives (a, the, this); pronouns (personal, relative, demonstrative, &c.) ; numerals.
   2. All auxiliary and defective verbs.
   3. Prepositions and conjunctions.
   4. Nouns forming their plural by change of vowel.
   5. Verbs forming their past tense by change of vowel.
   6. Adjectives forming their degrees of comparison irregularly.

II. 1. Grammatical inflections, as—
   (*a*) Plural suffixes (-s and -en) and ending of possessive case.
   (*b*) Verbal inflections of present and past tenses, of active and passive participles.
   (*c*) Suffixes denoting degrees of comparison.

III. 1. Numerous suffixes—
   (*a*) Of Nouns, as *-hood, -ship, -dom, -th (-t), -ness, -ing, -ling, -kin, -ock*.
   (*b*) Of Adjectives, as *-ful, -ly, -en, -ish, -some, -ward*.
   (*c*) Of Verbs, as *-en*.
   2. Numerous prefixes, as *a, al, be, for, ful, on, over, out, under*.

IV. Most monosyllabic words.

V. The names of the elements and their changes, of the seasons, the heavenly bodies, the divisions of time, the features of natural scenery, the organs of the body, the modes of bodily actions and posture, the commonest animals, the words used in earliest childhood, the ordinary terms of traffic, the constituent words in proverbs, the designation of kindred, the simpler emotions of the mind, terms of pleasantry, satire, contempt, indignation, invective, and anger, are for the most part unborrowed.[1]

Of English Origin.

I. Heaven, sky, welkin, sun, moon, star, thunder, lightning, fire, weather, wind, storm, blast, cold, frost, heat, warmth, cloud, dew, hail, snow, ice, rime, rain, hoarfrost, sleet, time, tide, year, month, day, night, light, darkness, twilight, dawn, morning, evening, noon, afternoon, winter, spring, summer, harvest.

II. World, earth, land, hill, dale, ground, bottom, height, water, sea, stream, flood, ebb, burn, well, spring, wave, waterfall, island.

III. Mould, sand, loam, clay, stone, gold, silver, lead, copper, tin, iron, quicksilver.

IV. Field, heath, wood, thicket, grove, tree, alder, ash, beech, birch, elm, fir, oak, lime, willow, yew, apple, pear, plum, berry, crop, corn, wheat, rye, oats, barley, acorn, sloe, bramble, nut, flax, grass, weed, leek, wort, moss, reed, ivy, clover, flax, bean, daisy, foxglove, honeysuckle, bloom, blossom, root, stem, stalk, leaf, twig, sprig, spray, rod, bow, sprout, rind, bark, haulm, hay, straw, ear, cluster, seed, chaff.

Of Romance Origin.

Firmament, meteor, planet, comet, air, atmosphere, season, autumn, hour, minute.

Mountain, valley, river, rivulet, torrent, cascade, fountain, undulation.

Brass, mercury, names of precious stones.

Forest, poplar, pine, fruit, cherry, apricot, juice, grape, grain, onion, carrot, cabbage, pea, flower, pansy, violet, lily, tulip, trunk, branch, &c.

---

[1] Rogers in *Edinburgh Review*, April 1859.

Of English Origin.

V. Hare, roe, hart, deer, fox, wolf, boar, marten, cat, rat, mouse, dog, hound, bitch, ape, ass, horse, mare, nag, cow, ox, bull, calf, neat, sheep, buck, ram, swine, sow, farrow, goat, mole.

VI. Bird, fowl, hawk, raven, rook, crow, stork, bittern, crane, glede, swan, owl, lapwing, starling, lark, nightingale, throstle, swallow, dove, finch, sparrow, snipe, wreh, goose, duck, hen, gander, drake.

VII. Fish, whale, shark, eel, herring, lobster, otter, cockle.

VIII. Worm, adder, snake, bee,' wasp, fly, midge, hornet, gnat, drone, humble-bee, beetle, chafer, spider, grasshopper, louse, flea, moth, butterfly, ant, maggot, frog, toad, tadpole.

IX. Man, woman, body, flesh, bone, soul, ghost, mind, blood, gore, sweat, limb, head, brain, skull, eye, brow, ear, mouth, lip, nose, chin, cheek, forehead, tongue, tooth, neck, throat, shoulder, arm, elbow, hand, foot, fist, finger, toe, thumb, nail, wrist, ankle, hough, sole, shank, shin, leg, knee, hip, thigh, side, rib, back, womb, belly, navel, breast, bosom, barm, lap, liver, maw, sinew, skin, fell, hair, lock, beard, whiskers.

Of Romance Origin.

Animal, beast, squirrel, lion, tiger, mule, elephant, &c.

Eagle, falcon, heron, ostrich, vulture, mavis, cock, pigeon.

Salmon, sturgeon, lamprey, trout.

Serpent, lizard, alligator.

Corpse, spirit, perspiration, countenance, stature, figure, palate, stomach, moustache, palm, vein, artery, intestines, nerves.

III.] HISTORY OF THE ENGLISH LANGUAGE. 37

Of English Origin.

X. Horn, neb, snout, beak, tail, mane, udder, claw, hoof, comb, fleece, wool, feather, bristle, down, wing, muscle.

XI. House, yard, hall, church, room, wall, wainscot, beam, gable, floor, roof, staple, door, gate, stair, threshold, window, shelf, hearth, fireside, stove, oven, stool, bench, bed, stall, bin, crib, loft, kitchen, tub, can, mug, loom, cup, vat, ewer, kettle, trough, ton, dish, board, spoon, knife, cloth, knocker, bell, handle, watch, clock, looking-glass, hardware, tile.

XII. Plough, share, furrow, rake, harrow, sickle, scythe, sheaf, barn, flail, waggon, wain, cart, wheel, spoke, nave, yoke.

XIII. Weeds, cloth, shirt, skirt, smock, sack, sleeve, coat, belt, girdle, band, clasp, hose, breeches, drawers, shoe, glove, hood, hat, stockings, ring, pin, needle, weapon, sword, hilt, blade, sheath, axe, spear, dart, shaft, arrow, bow, shield, helm, saddle, bridle, stirrup, halter.

XIV. Meat, food, fodder, meal, dough, bread, loaf, crumb, cake, milk, honey, tallow, flesh, ham, drink, wine, beer, ale, brandy.

XV. Ship, keel, boat, wherry, hulk, fleet, float, raft, stern, stem, board, deck, helm, rudder, oar, sail, mast.

Of Romance Origin.

Palace, temple, chapel, tabernacle, tent, chamber, cabinet, parlour, closet, chimney, ceiling, front, battlement, pinnacle, tower, lattice, table, chair, stable, garret, cellar, furniture, utensils, goblet, chalice, cauldron, fork, nap (-kin), plate, carpet, tapestry, mirror, curtain, cutlery.

Coulter.

Garment, lace, buckle, pocket, trousers, dress, robe, costume, pall, boot, cap, bonnet, veil, button, target, gauntlet, mail, harness, arms.

Victuals, provender, flour, lard, grease, butter, cheese, beef, veal, pork, mutton, roast, boiled, broiled, fry, bacon, toast, sausage, pie, soup, spirits.

Vessel, galley, prow.

Of English Origin.

XVI. Father, mother, sister, brother, son, daughter, husband, wife, bride, godfather, stepmother.

XVII. Trade, business, chapman, bookseller, fishmonger, &c.; pedlar, hosier, shoemaker, &c.; outfitter, weaver; baker, cooper, cartwright, fiddler, thatcher, seamstress, smith, goldsmith, blacksmith, fuller, tanner, sailor, miller, cook, skinner, glover, fisherman, sawyer, groom, workman, player, wright.

XVIII. King, queen, earl, lord, lady, knight, alderman, sheriff, beadle, steward.

XIX. Kingdom, shire, folk, hundred, riding, wardmote, hustings.

XX. White, yellow, red, black, blue, brown, grey, green.

XXI. Fiddle, harp, drum.

Of Romance Origin.

Family, grand (-father), uncle, aunt, ancestor, spouse, consort, parent, tutor, pupil, cousin, relation, papa, mamma, niece, nephew, spouse.

Traffick, commerce, industry, mechanic, merchant, principal, partner, clerk, apprentice, potter, draper, actor, laundress, chandler, mariner, barber, vintner, mason, cutler, poulterer, painter, plumber, plasterer, carpenter, mercer, hostler, banker, servant, journey(man), labourer.

Title, dignity, duke, marquis, viscount, baron, baronet, count, squire, master (mister), chancellor, secretary, treasurer, councillor, chamberlain, peer, ambassador, captain, major, colonel, lieutenant, general, ensign, cornet, sergeant, officer, herald, mayor, bailiff, engineer, professor, &c.

Court, state, administration, constitution, people, suite, treaty, union, cabinet, minister, successor, heir, sovereign, renunciation, abdication, dominion, reign, government, council, royal, loyal, emperor, audience, state, parliament, commons, chambers, signor, party, deputy, member, peace, war, inhabitant, subject, navy, army, treasurer.

Colour, purple, scarlet, vermilion, violet, orange, sable, &c.

Lyre, bass, flute, lute, organ, pipe, violin, &c.

III.] HISTORY OF THE ENGLISH LANGUAGE. 39

XXII. All words relating to art, except *singing* and *drawing*, are of Romance origin.

XXIII. Familiar actions, feelings, qualities, are for the most part unborrowed.

Of English Origin.
Talk, answer, behave, bluster, gather, grasp, grapple, hear, hark, listen, hinder, walk, limp, run, leap, &c. &c.

Of Romance Origin.
Converse, respond, reply, impel, prevent, direct, ascend, traverse, &c.

XXIV. The names of special action, qualities, &c., are mostly pure English; general terms are Latin, as—

Warmth, flurry, mildness, heat, wrath, &c.

Impression, sensation, emotion, disposition, temper, passion, &c.

Even, smooth, crooked, high, brittle, narrow, &c.

Equal, level, curved, prominent, fragile, &c.

32. The Romance element has provided us with a large number of synonymous terms by which our language is greatly enriched, as—

benediction	and	blessing
commence	,,	begin
branch	,,	bough
flour	,,	meal
member	,,	limb
gain	,,	win
desire	,,	wish
purchase	,,	buy
gentle	,,	mild
terror	,,	dread
sentiment	,,	feeling
labour	,,	work
flower	,,	bloom
amiable	,,	friendly
cordial	,,	hearty

33. Sometimes we find English and Romance elements compounded. These are termed Hybrids.

I. *Pure English words with Romance suffixes:*—

Ance. Hindr-*ance*, further-*ance*, forbear-*ance*.
Age. Bond-*age*, cart-*age*, pound-*age*, stow-*age*, tonn-*age*.
Ment. Forbode-*ment*, endear-*ment*, atone-*ment*, wonder-*ment*.
Ry. Midwife-*ry*, knave-*ry*, &c.
Ity. Odd-*ity*.

Let.
Et. } Stream-*let*, smick-*et*.
Ess. Godd-*ess*, shepherd-*ess*, huntr-*ess*, songstr-*ess*.
Able. Eat-*able*, laugh-*able*, read-*able*, unmistake-*able*.
Ous. Burden-*ous*, raven-*ous*, wondr-*ous*.
Ative. Talk-*ative*.

II. *Romance words with English endings:*—

Ness. Immense-*ness*, factious-*ness*, savage-*ness*, with numerous others formed from adjectives in *ful*, as merci-ful-*ness*, use-ful-*ness*, &c.
Dom. Duke-*dom*, martyr-*dom*.
Hood. False-*hood*.
Rick. Bishop-*rick*.
Ship. Apprentice-*ship*, sureti-*ship*.
Kin. Nap-*kin*.
Less. Use-*less*, grace-*less*, harm-*less*, and many others.
Full. Use-*ful*, grate-*ful*, bounti-*ful*, merci-*ful*, and numerous others.
Some. Quarrel-*some*, cumber-*some*, venture-*some*, humour-*some*.
Ish. Sott-*ish*, fool-*ish*, fever-*ish*, brut-*ish*, slav-*ish*.
Ly. Round-*ly*, rude-*ly*, savage-*ly*, and innumerable others.

III. *English words with Romance prefixes:*—

En, Em. *En*-dear, *en*-thral, *em*-bolden.
Dis. *Dis*-belief, *dis*-burden.
Re. *Re*-kindle, *re*-light, *re*-take, *re*-seat.

IV. *Romance words with English prefixes:*—

Be. *Be*-siege, *be*-cause, *be*-powder.
Under. *Under*-value, *under*-act, *under*-price.
Un. *Un*-stable, *un*-fortunate, and very many others.
Over. *Over*-turn, *over*-value, *over*-rate, *over*-curious.
For. *For*-pass, *for*-prise, *for*-fend.
After. *After*-piece, *after*-pains.
Out. *Out*-prize, *out*-faced.
Up. *Up*-train.

CHAPTER IV.

OLD ENGLISH DIALECTS.

34. BEFORE the Norman Conquest we find evidence of *two* dialects, a Southern and a Northern.

The Southern was the literary language, and had an extensive literature; in it are written the best of our oldest English works. The grammar of this dialect is exceedingly uniform, and the vocabulary contains no admixture of Danish terms.

The Northern dialect possesses a very scanty literature. An examination of existing specimens shows us, (1) that this dialect had grammatical inflections and words unknown to the Southern dialect; (2) that the number of Danish terms are very few.

Some writers think that these differences are due to the original Teutonic tribes that colonized the north and north-east of England. As these tribes are designated by old writers Angles, in contradistinction to the Jutes and Saxons, this dialect is called Anglian.

The chief points of grammatical difference between the Northern and Southern dialects are:—

(1) The loss of *n* in the infinitive ending of verbs, as,

N. *cuoetha* = S. *cwethan*, to say.
N. *drinc-a* = S. *drinc-an*, to drink.

(2) The first person singular indicative ends in *u* or *o* instead of *e*, as,

N. *Ic getreow-u* = S. *getreow-e*, I believe, trow.
N. *Ic drinc-o* = S. *drinc-e*, I drink.

(3) The second person singular present indicative often ends in *-s* rather than *-st*, and we find it in the second person singular perfect indicative of weak verbs—

N. *ðu ge plantad-es* = S. *ge plantod-est*, thou hast planted.

(4) The third person sing. frequently ends in *s* instead of *th*.

N. *he gewyrces* = S. *gewyrcath*, he works.
N. *he onsæces* = S. *onsæcath*, he denies.

(5) The third plural present indicative and the second person plural imperative often have *-s* instead of *-th*.
   N. *hia onfoas* = S. *hi onfoath*, they receive.

(6) The occasional omission of *ge* before the passive participle.
   N. *hered* = S. *geherod*, praised.
   N. *bledsed* = S. *gebletsod*, blessed.

(7) Occasional use of active participle in *-and* instead of *-end*.
   N. *drincande* = S. *drincende*, drinking.

(8) The use of *aren* for *syndon* or *synd* = *are* (in all persons of the plural).

In nouns we find much irregularity as compared with the Southern dialect.

(9) Plurals end in *a, u, o,* or *e,* instead of *-an*.[1]
   N. *heorta* = S. *heortan*, hearts.
   N. *witeg-u* = S. *witegan*, prophets.
   N. *ego* = S. *eagan*, eyes.
   N. *nome* = S. *naman*, names.

(10) *-es* is sometimes found instead of *-e* as the genitive suffix of feminine nouns.

(11) *the* and *thio* are sometimes found for *se* (masc.) and *seo* (fem.) = the.

(12) The plural article *tha* sometimes occurs for the demonstrative pronoun *hi* = they.

We see that 10, 11, 12, are really changes towards modern English.

35. After the Norman Conquest dialects become much more marked, and in the thirteenth and fourteenth centuries we are able to distinguish three great varieties of English.

(1) The Northern dialect, which was spoken in Northumberland, Durham, and Yorkshire, and in the Lowlands of Scotland.

(2) The Midland dialect, spoken in the whole of the Midland shires, in the East Anglian counties, and in the counties to the west of the Pennine chain; that is, in Cumberland, Westmoreland, Lancashire, Shropshire.

---

[1] In the Southern dialect words belonging to this declension had *n* in the oblique cases of the singular, but this is dropped in the Northern dialect.

(3) The Southern dialect, spoken in all the counties south of the Thames; in Somersetshire, Gloucestershire, and in parts of Herefordshire and Worcestershire.

It is not difficult to distinguish these dialects from one another on account of their grammatical differences.

The most convenient test is the inflection of the verb in the present plural indicative.

(4) The Southern dialect employs *-eth*, the Midland *-en*, as the inflection for all forms of the plural present indicative.

The Northern dialect uses neither of these forms, but substitutes *-es* for *-eth* or *-en*.[1]

The Northern dialect has its imperative plural in *-es*; the Southern and Midland dialects, in *-eth*.

EXAMPLES.

Plural Pres. Up-steg*hes* (up-go) hilles and feldes down-ga*s* (down-go).[2]
Thir (these) kinges rid*es* forth thair rade (road).[3]
And gret fisch*es* et*es* the smale (small).[4]
The mar thou drink*es* of the se
The mare and mar(e) threst*es* ye.[5]
Now we wyn and now we tyn (lose).[6]

Imp. Oppen*es* (open) your yates (gates) wide.[7]
Ga*is* (go) he said, and spir*s* (inquire) welle gern (earnestly).
Cum*s* (come) again and tel*s* (tell) me.[8]

Plural Pres. We habbe*th* (have) the maystry.[9]
Childern leue*th* Freynsch and construe*th* and lurne*th* an (in) Englysch.[10]

Imp. Luste*th* (listeneth) . . . late*th* (let) me speke.[11]
Adrawe*th* ʒoure (your) suerdes (swords).[12]

Plural Pres. Loverd we ar-*en* (are) bothe thine.[13]
Loverd we shol*en* the wel fede.[14]
And thei that fall*en* on the erthe, dy*en* anon.[15]

Imp. Do*th* awei ʒoure ʒatus (gates) and be*th* rerid out ʒee everlastende ʒatis.[16]

---

[1] We do not find *-s* often in the first person. Often all inflections are dropped in the plural, as in modern English.
[2] *Specimens of Early English*, p. 91. [3] Ib. p. 129. [4] Ib. p. 152.
[5] Ib. p. 154. [6] Ib. p. 178. [7] Ib. p. 88. [8] Ib. p. 130.
[9] Ib. p. 342. [10] Ib. p. 339. [11] Ib. p. 36. [12] Ib. p. 66.
[13] Ib. p. 47. [14] Ib. p. 48. [15] Ib. p. 202. [16] Ib. p. 94.

36. The Midland dialect, being widely diffused, had various local forms. The most marked of these are : (1) the Eastern Midland, spoken in Lincolnshire, Norfolk, and Suffolk; (2) the West Midland, spoken in Cumberland, Westmoreland, Lancashire, Cheshire, Shropshire.

The East Midland conjugated its verb in the present singular indicative like the Southern dialect—

    1st pers. hop-*e*   I hope.
    2nd ,,   hope-*st*   thou hopest.
    3rd ,,   hop-*eth*   he hopes.

The West Midland, like the Northern, conjugated its verb as follows :—

    1st pers. hope.[1]
    2nd ,,   hop-*es*.
    3rd ,,   hop-*es*.

37. There are many other points in which these dialects differed from one another.

(i.) The Southern was fond, as it still is, of using *v* where the other dialects had *f*, as *vo* = *fa* = foe ; *vinger* = finger. In the old Kentish of the fourteenth century we find *z* for *s*; as *zinge* = to sing; *zede* = said.

(ii.) It preferred the palatal *ch* to the guttural *k* in many words,[2] as—

    riche = Northern *rike* = kingdom.
    zech =   ,,   *sek* = sack.
    crouche =   ,,   *croke* = cross.

(iii.) It often had *ō* and *u* where the Northern dialect had *ā* and *i*, as—

    hul = Northern = *hil*.
    put =   ,,   = *pit*.
    bōn =   ,,   = *bān* = bone.
    lōf =   ,,   = *lāf* = loaf.
    ōn (oon) ,,   = *ān* = one.

In its grammar the Southern was still more distinctly marked.

(*a*) It preserved a large number of nouns with plurals in *n*, as *sterren* = stars, *eyren* = eggs, *kun* = kine, &c. The Northern dialect had only about four of these plurals, namely, *eghen*(=eyes), *hosen, oxen,* and *schoon*(=shoes).

---

[1] The Northern dialect has *s* occasionally in the first person.
[2] This softening serves to explain many of the double forms in modern English, as *ditch* and *dike, pouch* and *poke, church* and *kirk, nook* and *notch, bake* and *batch,* &c.

(b) It kept up the genitive of feminine nouns in *e*,[1] while the Northern dialect employed only the masculine suffix *s*, as in modern English.

(c) Genitive plurals in -*ene* [2] are very common, but do not occur at all in the Northern dialect.

(d) Adjectives and demonstrative pronouns retained many of the older inflections, and the definite article was inflected. Many pronominal forms were employed in the South that never existed in the North, as *ha* (*a*) = he; *is* = them; *is* = her.

(e) Where the older language had infinitives ending in -*an* and -*ian*, the Southern dialect had -*en* or -*e* and -*ie*.[3] The Northern dialect had scarcely a trace of this inflection.

(f) Active participles ended in -*inde* (*ynde*); in the North in -*ande* (*and*).[4]

(g) Passive participles retained the old prefix *ge* (softened down to *i* or *y*[5]); in the North it was never used.

(h) It had many verbal inflections that were unknown to the Northern dialect, as -*st* (present and past tenses), -*en* (plural past indicative), -*e* (second person plural past indicative of strong verbs).

(1) The Northern dialect had many plural forms of nouns that were wholly unknown to the Northern dialect, as —*Brether* = brethren, *childer* = children, *ky* = cows (kine), *hend* = hands.

(2) *That* was used as a demonstrative as at present, without reference to gender. In the Southern dialect *that* was often the neuter of the definite article.

(3) *Same* (as *the same*, *this same*) was used instead of the Southern *thilke*, modern *thuck*, *thick*, or *thucky*.

(4) *Thir*, *ther* (the plural of the Scandinavian article), the these, was often used.

(5) The pronominal forms were very different. Thus instead of the Southern *heo* (*hi*, *hii*) = she, this dialect used *sco*, *scho*, the older form of our *she*. It rejected the old plural pronouns of the third person, and substi-

---

[1] *Soule fode* = soul's food; *senne nede* = sin's need.
[2] *apostlene fet* = apostles' feet; *Gywene will* = Jews' will.
[3] *Lovie* (= *lufian*), to love; *hatie* (= *hatian*) to hate; *tellen*, *telle* = to tell.
[4] *singinde*, N. *singand* = singing.
[5] *y-broke* = *ybroken* = broken; *i-fare* = *ifaren* = gone.

tuted the plural article, as *thai, thair, thaim* (*tham*), instead of *hi* (*heo, hü*), *heore* (*here*), *heom* (*hem*) ; *ures, yhoures, thairs,* quite common then as now, were unknown in the South.

6. *At* = to was used as a sign of the infinitive mood; *sal* and *suld* = *schal* and *schuld*.

7. The Northern dialect had numerous Scandinavian forms, as—

hethen, hence	=	Southern	*henne*
thethen, thence	=	,,	*thenne*
whethen, whence	=	,,	*whennes*
sum	=	,,	*as*
fra	=	,,	*fram* = from
til	=	,,	*to*
by	=	,,	*tun* = town
minne	=	,,	*lesse* = less
plogh	=	,,	*sulȝ* = plough
nefe (*neve*)	=	,,	*fust* = fist
sterne	=	,,	*sterre* = star
bygg	=	,,	*bere* = barley
low	=	,,	*ley* = flame
werre	=	,,	*wyrse* = worse
slik	=	,,	*swich* = such
gar	=	,,	*do.*
&c.		&c.	&c.

38. The East Midland dialect had one peculiarity that has not been found in the other dialects, namely, the coalescence of pronouns with verbs, and even with pronouns, as—

caldes = *calde* + *es* = called them
dedes = *dede* + *es* = put them
hes = *he* + *es* = he + them
get = *ge* + *it* = she + it
mes = *me* + *es* = one (Fr. on) + them.

The West Midland dialect had its peculiarities, as *ho* = she ; *hit* = its ; *shyn* = shuln (plural).

39. We must bear in mind that the Midland dialect was the speech that was most widely spread, and, as we might expect, would be the one that would gradually take the lead in becoming the standard language. There were, as we have seen, many varieties of the Midland dialect, but by far the most important of these was the East Midland. As early as the beginning of the thirteenth

century it began to be cultivated as a literary dialect, and had then thrown off most of the older inflections, so as to become, in respect of inflectional forms and syntactical structure, as simple as our own.

In this dialect Wicliffe, Gower, and Chaucer wrote, as well as the older and well-known authors, Orm and Robert of Brunne. It was, however, Chaucer's influence that raised this dialect to the position of the standard language. In Chaucer's time this dialect was the language of the metropolis, and had probably found its way south of the Thames into Kent and Surrey.

At a later period the Southern dialect had so far retreated before it as to become *Western* rather than *Southern;* in fact, the latter designation was applied to the language which had become the standard one.

George Puttenham, writing in 1589, speaks of three dialects—the Northern, Western, and Southern. The Northern was that spoken north of the Trent; the Southern was that south of the Trent, which was also the language of the court, of the metropolis, and of the surrounding shires; the Western, as now, was confined to the counties of Gloucestershire, Somersetshire, Wiltshire, &c.[1]

---

[1] "Our maker (poet) therefore at these dayes shall not follow Piers Plowman, nor Gower, nor Lydgate, nor yet Chaucer, for their language is now out of use with us: neither shall he take the termes of Northern-men, such as they use in dayly talke, whether they be noble men, or gentlemen, or of their best clarkes, all is a matter; nor in effect any speach used beyond the river of Trent, though no man can deny but that theirs is the purer English Saxon at this day, yet it is not so courtly nor so current as our *Southerne English* is, no more is the far Westerne man's speach: ye shall therefore take the usual speach of the Court, and that of London and the shires lying about London within lx myles, and not much above. I say not this but that in every shyre of England there be gentlemen and others that speake but specially write as good Southerne as we of Middlesex or Surrey do, but not the common people of every shire, to whom the gentlemen and also their learned clarkes do for the most part condescend, but herein we are already ruled by th' English dictionaries and other bookes written by learned men."

CHAPTER V.

PERIODS OF THE ENGLISH LANGUAGE.

40. ALL living languages, in being handed down from one generation to another, undergo changes and modifications. These go on so gradually as to be almost imperceptible, and it is only by looking back to past periods that we become sensible that the language has changed. A language that possesses a literature is enabled to register the changes that are taking place. Now the English language possesses a most copious literature, which goes as far back as the end of the eighth century, so that it is possible to mark out with some distinctness different periods in the growth or history of our language.

I. *The English of the First Period.*

(A.D. 450—1100.)

(*a*) The grammar of this period is *synthetic* or inflectional, while that of modern English is *analytical*.[1]

(*b*) The vocabulary contains no foreign elements.

(*c*) The chief grammatical differences between the oldest English and the English of the present day are these:—

(1) *Grammatical Gender.*—As in Latin and Greek, gender is marked by the termination of the nominative, and also by other case endings. Substantives and adjectives have three genders—masculine, feminine, and neuter.

(2) *Declensions of Substantives.*—There were various declensions, and at least five cases (nominative, accusative, genitive, dative, and ablative or instrumental), distinguished by various endings.

(3) The *Definite Article* was inflected, and was also used both as a demonstrative and a relative pronoun.

(4) *Pronouns* had a dual number.

---

[1] Cp. O.E. *drincan* with "to drink."

(5) The infinitive of *Verbs* ended in *-an*, the dative infinitive in *-anne* (*-enne*).
(6) Only the dative infinitive was preceded by the preposition *to*.
(7) The present participle ended in *-ende*.
(8) The passive participle was preceded by the prefix *ge-*.
(9) Active and passive participles were declined like adjectives.
(10) In the present tense plural indicative the endings were, (1) *-ath ;* (2) *-ath ;* (3) *-ath*.
(11) In the present pl. subjunctive they were *-on*, *-on*, *-on*.[1]
(12) In the preterite tense plural indicative the endings were *-on* (sometimes *-an*).
(13) The second person singular in the preterite tense of weak verbs ended in *-st*, as *lufode-st* = thou loved-est ; the corresponding suffix of strong verbs was *-e*, as—
    æt-e, thou atest or didst eat.
    slep-e, thou slept-est.
(14) The future tense was supplied by the present, and *shall* and *will* were not usually tense auxiliaries.
(15) *Prepositions* governed various cases.

II. *The English of the Second Period.*
(A.D. 1100 to about 1250.)

41. Before the Norman Conquest the English language showed a tendency to substitute an analytical for a synthetical structure, and probably, had there been no Norman invasion, English would have arrived at the same simplification of its grammar as nearly every other nation of the Low German stock has done. The Danish invasion had already in some parts of the country produced this result ; but the Norman invasion caused these changes, more or less inherent in all languages, to take place more rapidly and more generally.

The first change which took place affected the *orthography;* and this is to be traced in documents written about the beginning of the twelfth century, and constitutes the only important modification of the older language.

This change consisted in a general weakening of the terminations of words.

i. The older vowel endings, *a, o, u,* were reduced to *e*.

---
[1] *-en* is an earlier form of this suffix.

This change affected the oblique cases of nouns and adjectives as well as the nominative, so that the termination

an	became	*en*.[1]		*ra, ru*	became	*re.*
as	,,	*es.*		*ena*	,,	*ene.*
ath	,,	*eth.*		*on*	,,	*en.*
um	,,	*en.*[1]		*od, ode*	,,	*ed, ede.*

ii. *C* or *k* is often softened to *ch*, and *g* to *y* or *w*.

To make these changes clearer, we give—

(1) A portion of Ælfric's homily, "*De Initio Creaturæ*," in the English of the first period ; (2) the same in the English of the beginning of the twelfth century; and (3 and 4) the same a few years later.[2]

1. An anginn is ealr*a* þing*a*, þæt is God Ælmightig.
2. An anginn is ealr*a* thing*en*, þæt is God Almightig.
3. An angin is alr*æ* ðing*æ*, þæt is God almihtiʒ.
4. *   *   *   *   *   *
5. One beginning is ther*e* of all things, that is God Almighty.

1. He is ordfrum*a* and ende : he is ordfrum*a* forði þe he wæs æfre.
2. He is ordfrum*a* and ænde : he is ordfrum*e* for þan þe he wæs æfre.
3. He is ordfrum*a* and ende : he is ordfrum*e* for þi ðe he wæs æfre.
4. [He is] hordfruma and ænde : he is ord for he wes efre.
5. He is beginning and end : he is beginning, for-that that he was ever.

1. He is ende but*an* ælcere geendunge, for ðan þe he bið æfre unge-endod.
2. He is ænd*æ* abut*en* ælcere geændunge, for þan þe he byð æfre unge-ændod.
3. He is ende buton ælcere endunge, for þan ðe he bið æfre unʒe-endod.
4. He is ænde buton ælcere ʒiendunʒe . . . . . .
5. He is end without any ending, for-that that he is ever unended.

1. He is ealr*a* cyning*a* cyning, and ealra hlaford*a* hlaford.
2. He is ealra king*ene* kinge, and ealra hlaford*e* hlaford.

---

[1] *n* sometimes disappears.
[2] Examples 3 and 4 were probably written in different parts of England before 1150.

v.] PERIODS OF THE ENGLISH LANGUAGE. 51

   3. He is alræ kynge kyng, and alre lafordæ laford.
   4. Heo is alra kingene king, and alra hlaforden hlaford.
   5. He is of all kings King, and of all lords Lord.

   1. He hylt mid his mihte heofanas and eorðan and ealle.
   2. He healt mid his mihte heofonas and eorðan and ealle.
   3. He halt mid his mihte heofenæs and eorðan and alle.
   4. He halt mid his mihte hefene and eorðe and alle.
   5. He holdeth with his might heavens and earth and all.

   1. Gesceafta butan geswince.
   2. Gesceafte [buten] geswynce.
   3. Isceafte buton swinke.
   4. Ʒesceafte buton Ʒeswince.
   5. Creatures without swink (toil).

The next example is given, (1) in the oldest English; (2) in that of 1100; (3) in that of about 1150.

   1. Twelf unþeawas syndon on þyssere worulde to hearme
   2. Twelf unðeawes synden on þyssen wurlde to hearme
   3. Twelf unþeawes beoð on þissere weorlde to hermen
   4. Twelve vices are there in this world for harm

   1. Eallum mannum gif hi moton ricsian and hi alecgað
   2. Eallen mannen gyf heo moten rixigen and heo alecged
   3. Alle monnen Ʒif hi moten rixian and hi alleggað
   4. To all men, if they might hold sway, and they put down

   1. Rihtwisnysse and þone geleafan amyrrað and mancynn
      gebringað
   2. Rihtwisnysse and þone geleafe amerreð and mancynn
      gebringeð
   3. Rihtwisnesse and þene ileafan amerrað and moncun bringeð
   4. Righteousness and (the) belief mar, and mankind bring

   1. Gif hi moton to helle.
   2. Gyf heo moten to helle.
   3. Ʒif hi motan to helle.
   4. If they might to hell.

From 1150 to 1200 numerous grammatical changes took place, the most important of which were—

   1. The indefinite article an (a) is developed out of the numeral. It is frequently inflected.

2. The definite article becomes þe, þeo, þe, (þat), instead of se, seo, þæt.¹
    It frequently drops the older inflections, especially in the feminine.
    We find þe often used as a plural instead of þa or þo.
3. Nominative plural of nouns end in -en (or e) instead of a or u, thus conforming to plurals of the n declension.
4. Plurals in -es sometimes take the place of those in -en (-an), the genitive plural ends in -ene or -e, and occasionally in -es.
5. The dative plural (originally -um) becomes e and en.
6. Some confusion is seen in the gender of nouns.
7. Adjectives show a tendency to drop certain case-endings :—
    (1) The genitive singular masculine of the indefinite declension.
    (2) The genitive and dative feminine of the indefinite declension.
    (3) The plural -en of the definite declension frequently becomes e.
8. The dual forms are still in use, but less frequently employed. The dative him, hem, are used instead of the accusative.
9. New pronominal forms come into use, as ha=he, she, they ; is=her ; is=them; me=one.
10. The n in min, thin, are often dropped before consonants, but retained in the plural and oblique cases.
11. The infinitive of verbs frequently drops the final n, as smelle=smellen, to smell ; herie=herien, to praise. To is sometimes used before infinitives.
12. The gerundial or dative infinitive ends often in -en or -e instead of -enne (-anne).
13. The n of the passive participle is often dropped, as icume =icumen=come.
14. The present participle ends in -inde, and is frequently used instead of the gerundial infinitive, as to swiminde=to swimene=to swim.
15. *Shall* and *will* began to be used as tense auxiliaries of the future.

---

¹ Traces of *se* and *si* are found in the Kentish dialect of the thirteenth century.

The above remarks apply chiefly to the Southern dialect. In the other dialects of this period (East and West Midland) we find even a greater simplification of the grammar. Thus to take the Ormulum (East Midland) we find the following important changes:—

(a) The definite article is used as at present, and *that* is employed as a demonstrative irrespective of gender.

(b) Gender of substantives is almost the same as in modern English.

(c) *-es* is used as the ordinary sign of the plural.

(d) *-es*, singular and plural, has become the ordinary suffix of the genitive case.

(e) Adjectives, as in Chaucer's time, have a final *e* for the older inflections, but *e* is chiefly used, (1) as a sign of the plural, (2) to distinguish the definite form of the adjective.

(f) The forms *they, theirs,* come into use.

(g) Passive participles drop the prefix *i* (*ge*), as *cumen* for *icumen*.

(h) The plural of the present indicative ends in *-en* instead of *-eth*.

(i) *Arn = are,* for *beoth*.

In an English work written before 1250, containing many forms longing to the West Midland dialect, we find—

(a) Articles and nouns and adjectives as in the Ormulum.

(b) The pronoun *thai* instead of *hi* or *heo* = they; *I* for *Ic* or *Ich*.

(c) Passive participles frequently omit the prefix *i*.

(d) Active participles end in *-ande* instead of *-inde*.

(e) Verbs are conjugated in the indicative present as follows:—

Singular.	Plural.
(1) luv-e	(1) luv-en
(2) luv-es	(2) luv-en
(3) luv-es	(3) luv-en

(f) Strong and weak verbs are conjugated after the following manner in the past tense:—

		Singular.	Plural.	
Weak.	(1)	makede	makeden	= made
	(2)	makedes	makeden	,,
	(3)	makede	makeden	,,
Strong.	(1)	schop	schop-en	= created, shaped
	(2)	schop	schop-en	,, ,,
	(3)	schop	schop-en	,, ,,

Here we see two important changes : (1) -*es* for -*est* in second person of weak verbs ; and (2) the dropping of *e* in strong verbs.

From 1150 to 1250 the influence of Norman-French begins to exhibit itself in the *vocabulary* of the English language.

III. *The English of the Third Period.*
(A.D. 1250—1350.)

42. (1) The article still preserves some of the older inflections, as: (1) the genitive singular feminine ; (2) the accusative masculine ; (3) the plural þo (the nominative being used with all cases of nouns).

(2) Nouns exhibit much confusion in gender—words that were once masculine or feminine becoming neuter.

(3) Plurals in -*en* and -*es* often used indiscriminately.

(4) The genitive -*es* becomes more general, and begins to take the place—(1) of the older -*en* and -*e* (in old masculine and neuter nouns); and (2) of -*e* in feminine nouns.

(5) The dative singular of pronouns shows a tendency to drop off; *mi*-self and *thi*-self often used instead of *me-self* and *the-self*.[1]

(6) Dual forms of the personal pronouns dropped out of use shortly before 1300.

(7) A final *e* used, (1) for the sign of plural of adjectives ; and (2) for distinguishing between the definite and indefinite declensions.

(8) The gerundial infinitive terminates in -*en* and -*e*.

(9) The ordinary infinitive takes *to* before it.

(10) Some few strong verbs become weak. Present participles in -*inge* begin to appear about 1300.

French words become now more common, especially towards the end of this period.

In ten pages of Robert of Gloucester, Marsh has calculated that four per cent. of the vocabulary is Norman-French.

IV. *The English of the Fourth Period.*
(A.D. 1350—1460.)

43. In this period the Midland dialect has become the prevailing one. Northern and Southern words still retain their own peculiarities.

---

[1] We sometimes find *miself* as well as *meself* in Laȝamon.

The following are the chief points to be noted:—
1. The plural article, *tho* = the, those, is still often used.
2. The *-es* in plural and genitive case of substantives is mostly a separate syllable.
3. The pronouns are:
    I for the older *Ic* (*Ich* sometimes occurs).
    sche for the older *heo*.
    him, them, whom, used as datives and accusatives.
    oures, youres, heres, in common use for *oure, youre, here*.
    thei (they) in general use instead of *hi* (*heo*).
    here = their.
    hem = them.
4. The plurals of verbs in the present and past indicative end *-en* or *-e*. .
    The imperative plural ends in *-eth*.
    -est often used as the inflection of the second person singular preterite of strong and weak verbs.
    The infinitive mood ends in *-en* or *-e*; but the inflection is often lost towards the end of the fourteenth century.
    The present participle ends usually in *-ing* (*inge*).
    The passive participle of strong verbs ends in *-en* or *-e*.

The termination *-e* is an important one.
1. It represents an older vowel ending, as *nam-e* = *nam-a*, *sun-e* = *sun-u*; or the termination *-an, -en*, as *withute* = *with-utan*.
2. It represents various inflections, and is used—
    (a) As a mark of the plural or definite adjective (adjectival *e*), as *smalë* fowles; the *gretë* see.
    (b) As a mark of adverbs, as *softë* = softly. (Adverbial *e*.)
    (c) As a mark of the infinitive mood, past tense of weak verbs and imperative mood. (Verbal *e*.)
    Him *thoughtë* that his hertë *woldë brekë*. (Chaucer.)

Towards the end of this period the use of the final *e* becomes irregular and uncertain, and the Northern forms of the pronouns, *their, theirs, them*, come into use in the other dialects.

V. *The English of the Fifth Period.*
(A.D. 1460 to present time.)

44. There are really two subdivisions of this period —
(1) 1460 to 1520.
(2) 1520 to present time.

From 1460 to 1520 there is a general dearth of great literary works, but there were two events in this period that greatly affected the language, especially its vocabulary—

(1) The introduction of printing into England by Caxton.
(2) The diffusion of classical literature.

For some peculiarities of Elizabethan English see Abbott's "Shakespearian Grammar."

CHAPTER VI.

PHONOLOGY.

Letters.

45. LETTERS are conventional signs employed to represent sounds. The collection of letters is called the Alphabet; from Alpha and Beta, the names of the first two letters of the Greek alphabet.

The alphabet has grown out of the old pictorial mode of writing. The earliest written signs denoted concrete objects; they were pictorial representations of objects, like the old Egyptian hieroglyphics.

Then single sounds were afterwards indicated by parts of these pictures.

The alphabet which has given rise to that now in use among nearly all the Indo-European nations, was originally syllabic,[1] in which the consonants were regarded as the substantial part of the syllable, the vowels being looked upon as altogether subordinate and of inferior value. Consequently the consonants only were written, or written in full—the accompanying vowel being either omitted, or represented by some less conspicuous symbol.

Such is the construction of the ancient Semitic alphabet—the Phœnician, from which have sprung the Hebrew, Syriac, Arabic, Sanskrit, Greek, and Latin alphabets.

The oldest English alphabet consisted of twenty-four letters. All except three are Roman characters. þ (thorn) and ƿ (wên) are Runic letters; Ð ð is merely a crossed *d*, used instead of the thorn; *i* and *j*, as well as *u* and *v*, were expressed by the same character.

---

[1] A pure syllabic alphabet is one whose letters represent syllables instead of articulations; which makes an imperfect phonetic analysis of words, not into the simple sounds that compose them, but into their syllabic elements; which does not separate the vowel from its attendant consonant or consonants, but denotes both together by an indivisible sign. One of the most noted alphabets of this kind is the Japanese. (See Whitney, p. 465.)

46. The *spoken* alphabet must be distinguished from the *written* alphabet.

The sounds composing the spoken alphabet are produced by the human voice, which is a kind of wind instrument, in which the vibratory apparatus is supplied by the *chordæ vocales* or vocal chords (ligaments that are stretched across the windpipe), while the outer tube, or tubes, through which the waves of sound pass, are furnished by the different configurations of the mouth.

The articulating organs, or *organs of speech*, are the tongue, the cavity of the fauces, the lips, teeth, and palate, and the cavity of the nostrils, which modify the impulse given to the breath as it arises from the larynx, and produce the various vowels and consonants that make up the spoken alphabet.

47. **Vowels** are produced by the vibrations of the vocal chords.

The pitch or tone of a vowel is determined by the vocal chords, but its quality depends upon the configuration of the mouth or buccal tube.

For the formation of the three principal vowels we give the interior of the mouth two extreme positions. In one we round the lips and draw down the tongue, so that the cavity of the mouth assumes the shape of a bottle without a neck, and we pronounce *u*. In the other we narrow the lips and draw up the tongue as high as possible, so that the buccal tube represents a bottle with a very wide neck, and we pronounce *i* (as in French and German). If the lips are wide open, and the tongue lies flat and in its natural position, we pronounce *a*.

Between these three elementary articulations there is an indefinite variety of vowel sounds.

A, i, u are by philologists called the primitive vowels, and from them all the various vowel sounds in the Aryan languages have been developed.

There are two steps in the early development of these sounds—(1) the union of *a* with *a*; (2) the union of *a* with *i* and *u*.

Primitive.	1st gradation.	2nd gradation.
1. *a* .	. *a + a = â* .	. *âa = â*.
2. *i* .	. *a + i = ai (ê)*	. *a + ai = âi*.
3. *u* .	. *a + u = au (ô)*	. *a + au = âu*.

Thus it is seen that *long* vowels are of secondary formation.

Sometimes a full vowel is weakened into a thin one, as *a* into *i* or *u* (Sanskrit, Greek, Latin, &c.).

In O.E. and in most of the Teutonic dialects, *a* is weakened into *e*, *i* into *e*, and *u* into *o*.

Sometimes a simple vowel is broken into two, as *garden* into *gearden* ; cp. Lat. *castra*, O.E. *ceaster*, English *chester;* thus in O. E. *a* is broken into *ea (ia)*; *i* to *eo (io, ie)*.

Sometimes a vowel in one syllable of a word is modified by another in the following syllable—*o* is affected by *i* and the sound *e* is produced, and this change remains even when the modifying vowel has been lost: as Eng. *feet*, compared with Goth. *fōtjus*, Old-Sax. *fōti*, shows that the original form must have been *fēti*.

When *i* is followed by *a* it becomes *e*, as O.E. *help-an*, to help, from the root *hilp*, help; and *u* followed by *a* becomes *o*: thus from the root *bug* (Old-Eng. *bugan*), to bend is formed *boga*, a bow.

48. **Diphthongs** arise when, instead of pronouncing one vowel immediately after another with two efforts of the voice, we produce a sound *during* the change from one position to the other that would be required for each vowel. If we change the *a* into the *i* position and pronounce a vowel, we hear *ai* as in *aisle*. If we change the *a* into the *u* position and pronounce a vowel, we hear *au* as in *how*. Here too we find many variations, and the less perfect diphthongs, such as *oi*, &c.

49. **Consonants** fall under the category of noises.

(*a*) Some are produced by the opening or closing of the organs of speech, in which the breath is stopped and cannot be prolonged. These are called *mutes* or *checks*, as G, K, D, T, &c.

If the breath is stopped and the veil is withdrawn that separates the nose from the pharynx, we obtain the *nasals* N, NG, M.

(*b*) If the breath be not wholly stopped, but the articulating organs are so modified as to allow the sound to be prolonged, then we get continuous consonants, called *breaths* or *spirants*, as H, TH, F, S, &c.

l and *r*, which belong to this class, are called *trills*, and are produced by a vibration of certain portions of the mouth (tongue or uvula).

(*c*) The consonants may be classified according to the organs by which they are produced, as *gutturals* (k, g, ch), *palatals* (ch, j), *linguals* (sh, zh), *dentals* (t, d, th, dh), *labials* (p, b, f, v).

(*d*) Those sounds produced by a greater effort of the vocal organs are called *sharp*, as *p, f, t*, &c.; if produced by a less effort, they are called *flat*, as *b, v, d*.

(*e*) The following table contains the consonants in the English alphabet, arranged according to a physiological plan :—

	Breaths or Spirants.			Mutes or Checks.			
	SHARP.	FLAT.	TRILLED.	SHARP.	FLAT.	NASAL.	
1. Glottis	h (*aspirate*)	..	..	..	..	..	Aspirate.
2. Root of tongue and soft palate	ch (in Scotch *loch*).	..	..	k	g	ng	Gutturals.
3. Root of tongue and hard palate	..	y (*yea*)	..	ch (*church*)	j (*judge*)	..	Palatals.
4. Tip of tongue and teeth ..	..	..	..	t	d	n	Dentals.
5. Tongue and edge of teeth ..	th (*breath*)	th (*breathe*)	..	..	..	..	Dentals.
6. Tip of tongue and teeth ..	s (*sin*)	z (*rise*)	l	..	..	..	Sibilants.
7. Tongue reversed and palate ..	sh (*sharp*)	zh (*pleasure*)	r	..	..	..	Sibilants.
8. Lower lip and upper teeth ..	f	v	..	..	..	..	Labials.
9. Upper and lower lips	..	..	..	p	b	m	Labials.
10. Upper and lower lips rounded ..	hw (*which*)	w (*with*)	..	..	..	..	Labials.

50. From this table of consonants we have omitted (1) *c*, because, when used before a *consonant* or *a, o, u*, it has the sound of *k*, and when used before *e, i, y*, it has the sound of *s* (in *rice*); (2) the soft sound of *g* (in *gem*), because this is represented by *j*; (3) *q*, because this is equivalen to *kw*; (4) *x*, because it is equivalent to *ks* or *gs*.

51. *On the Number of Elementary Sounds in the spoken English Alphabet.*

In addition to the *twenty-four* consonants already enumerated we have *fourteen* single vowels and *five* diphthongs, making altogether *forty-three* sounds.

1. *a* in *gnat*.
2. *a* in *pair, ware*.
3. *a* in *fame*.
4. *a* in *father*.
5. *a* in *all*.
6. *a* in *want*.
7. *e* in *met*.
8. *e* in *meet*.
9. *i* in *knit*.
10. *o* in *not*.
11. *o* in *note*.
12. *oo* in *fool, rude*.
13. *oo* in *wood, put*.
14. *u* in *nut*.
15. *i* in *high*.
16. *i* in *aye*.
17. *oi* in *boil*.
18. *ow* in *how*.
19. *ew* in *mew*.

CHAPTER VII.

ORTHOGRAPHY.

52. ORTHÖEPY deals with the proper pronunciation of words; Orthography with the proper representation of the words of the spoken language. The one deals with words as they are pronounced, the other with words as they are written.

A perfect alphabet must be based upon phonetic principles, and (1) every simple sound must be represented by a distinct symbol; (2) no sound must be represented by more than one sign.

(*a*) The spoken alphabet contains forty-three sounds, but the *written* alphabet has only twenty-six letters or symbols to represent them: therefore in the first point necessary to a perfect system of orthography the English alphabet is found wanting.

The alphabet, as we have seen, is *redundant*, containing three superfluous letters, *c*, *q*, *x*, so that it contains only twenty-three letters wherewith to represent forty-three sounds. So that it is both imperfect and redundant. Again, the five vowels, *a*, *e*, *i*, *o*, *u*, have to represent no less than thirteen sounds (see § 51).

The same combinations of letters, too, have distinct sounds, as *ough* in bough, borough, cough, chough, hough, hiccough, though, trough, through, Sc. sough; *ea* in beat, bear, &c.

(*b*) In regard to the second point, that no sound should be represented by more than one sign, we again find that the English alphabet fails. The letter ō (in *note*) may be represented by *oa* (boat), *oe* (toe), *eo* (yeoman), *ou* (soul), *ow* (sow), *ew* (sew), *au* (hautboy), *eau* (beau), *owe* (owe), *oo* (floor), *oh* (oh!). The alphabet is therefore *inconsistent* as well as *imperfect*.

Many letters are silent, as in *psalm*, *calf*, *could*, *gnat*, *know*, &c.

(*c*) The English alphabet is supplemented by a number of double letters called *digraphs* (*oa*, *oo*, &c.), which are as inconsistently employed as the simple characters themselves.

(*d*) Other expedients for remedying the defects of the alphabet are—

ORTHOGRAPHY.

(1) The use of a final *e* to denote a long vowel, as *bite, note,* &c. But even with regard to this *e* the orthography is not consistent : it will not allow a word to end in *v,* although the preceding vowel is short, hence an *e* is retained in *live, give,* &c.

(2) The doubling of consonants to indicate a short vowel, as *folly, hotter,* &c.

It must be recollected that the letters *a, e, i, o, u,* were originally devised and intended to represent the vowel sounds heard in *far, prey, figure, pole, rule,* respectively. In other languages that employ them they still have this value.

During the written period of our language the pronunciation of the vowels has undergone great and extensive changes at different periods, while the spelling has not kept pace with these changes, so that there has arisen a great dislocation of our orthographical system, a divorcement of our written from our spoken alphabet. The introduction of foreign elements into the English language during its written period has brought into use different, and often discordant, systems of orthography[1] (cp. *ch* in *church, chivalry, Christian,* &c.). In addition to this there are peculiarities of the orthographical usages of the Old-English dialects.

53. The following letter-changes are worth recollecting :—

LABIALS—B, P, F, V, W.

B. This letter has crept into many words, as O.E. *slumer-ian,* = slum*b*er ; *thum-a* = thum*b*; *lim* = lim*b.*

Cp. *humble* from *humilis, number* from *numerare.*

B has changed to—

(1) *p* in *gossip,* from O.E. *godsib; purse* from O.Fr. *borse* (cp. *bursar, disburse*) ; *apricot,* Fr. *abricot.*[2]

(2) To *v* in *have* from O.E. *habban, heave* from O.E. *hebban.*

(3) To *m* in *summerset* = Fr. *soubresaut.*

P. *P* is represented by—

(1) *b* in *lobster* = O.E. *loppestre; dribble* from *drip, drop*=O.E. *dropian, cobweb* = O.E. *copweb.*

(2) *v* in *knave* = O.E. *cnapa.*

It is often inserted between *m* and *t,* as *empty* = O.E. *emtig* (cp. *gleam* and *glimpse, semoster* and *seamster*) ; *tempt* = O.Fr. *tenter,* Lat. *tentare.*

---

[1] Whitney.   [2] We sometimes find in O.E. *apricock* = apricot.

F. An *f* frequently becomes *v*, as *vat, vetches, vixen* = *fat, fetches, fixen.*

Cp. *five* and *fifty*, *twelve* and *twelfth.*

F has disappeared from many words, as *head, lord, hawk, hath, woman* = O.E. *heáfod (heved), hláford (loverd), hafoc, hafath (hafth), wifman (wimman).*

Cp. O.Fr. *jolif,* O.E. *jolif* = jolly.

The O.E. *efeta,* an *eft,* has become (1) *evet;* (2) *ewt;* (3) *newt* (the *n* belongs to the indefinite article).

V in some Romance words represents *ph,* as *vial* = phial, O.E. *visnomy* = *physiognomy.*

It has been changed to (1) *w* in *periwinkle* = Fr. *pervenche,* Lat. *perivinca;* (2) to *m* in *malmsey* = O.E. *malvesie,* from O.Fr. *malvoisie.*

W. This letter has disappeared in—

    ooze = O.E. *wos.*
    lisp = O.E. *wlisp.*
    four = O.E. *feower.*
    soul = O.E. *sawl, sawul.*
    lark = Scotch *laverock,* O.E. *lawerce.*
    ought = O.E. *a-wiht (auht, oht).*
    tree = O.E. *treow.*
    knee = O.E. *cneow.*

W has crept into *whole* and its derivatives = O.E. *hal (hol)* ; so *whoop,* O.E. *hoop* (Fr. *houper).*

HW has become *wh,* as—

    who = O.E. *hwa.*
    whelp = O.E. *hwelp.*
    &c. &c.

The *w* has disappeared in certain combinations (*tw, thw, sw*), as—

    tusk = O.E. *twisc (tusc).*
    thong = O.E. *thwang (thwong).*
    sister = O.E. *swister (swuster).*
    such = O.E. *swilc (swuch).*

DENTALS—D, T, TH.

D. *D* has sometimes become—

(1) *t,* as   clot = *clod.*
            abbot = O.E. *abbad (abbod).*
            etch = *eddisc* = O.E. *edisc.*
            partridge = O.Fr. *perdrix,* Lat. *perdix.*

(2) *th*, as (*a*) O.E. *hider, thider, hwider* have become *hither, thither, whither;* (*b*) Lat. *fides,* O. Fr. *feid* = faith.

It has disappeared from—

    gospel   = O.E. *godspel.*
    answer   = O.E. *and-swærian (answerian).*
    woodbine = O.E. *wudu-bind.*

It has crept into—

    thunder   = O.E. *thunor.*
    hind   = O.E. *hina (hine).*
    lend   = O.E. *læn-an (lene).*
    round (to whisper) = O.E. *runian (runen, rounen).*
    gender   = O.Fr. *genre;* Lat. *genus.*
    sound   = O.E. *soun;* Lat. *sonus.*
    riband (ribbon)   = Fr. *ruban.*
    jaundice   = Fr. *jaunisse* (cp. *tender* from Lat. *tener*).

T. *T* is sometimes represented by *d*, as—

    proud   = O.E. *prut.*
    bud   = Fr. *bout.*
    diamond = Fr. *diamant.*
    card   = Fr. *carte;* Lat. *charta.*

It has become *th* in *author* (Lat. *auctor*) and *lant-horn* [1] (Lat. *laterna;* Fr. *lanterne*).

It has fallen away (before *s*) in *best* = O.E. *betst, last* = O.E. *latst;* Essex = *Eastsexan (Estsex).*

At the end of a word it has disappeared in—

    anvil   = O.E. *anfilt.*
    petty   = Fr. *petit.*
    dandelion = Fr. *dent de lion.*

It has crept in (*a*) after an *s*, as in *bchest* = O.E. *behæs;* also in *amongst, against, midst, amidst, whilst, betwixt,* and O.E. *onest, alongst, anenst,* &c.

    (*b*) in tyrant   = O.Fr. *tiran;* Lat. *tyrannus.*
    parchment = O.Fr. *parchemin.*
    cormorant   = Fr. *cormoran.*
    ancient   = O.Fr. *ancien.*
    pheasant   = O.Fr. *phaisan.*

---

[1] A corrupt spelling arising from a mistaken etymology.

Th has sometimes become—
- (1) *d*, as murder = O.E. *myrthra*.
  - could = O.E *cuthe* (*couthe, coude*).
  - fiddle = O.E. *fithele*.
  - dwarf = O.E. *thweorh* (*dwergh*).
  - Bedlam = *Bethlehem*.
- (2) *t*, as theft = O.E. *theofth*.
  - nostril = O.E. *nas-thyrlu* (*nosthirles*).
- (3) *s*, as love-s = *love-th*.

Th has disappeared in—
- Norfolk = O.E. *North-folc*, &c.
- worship = O.E. *weorthscipe* (*worthshipe*).

SIBILANTS—S, Z, SH.

S is closely allied to *r*, and even in the oldest English we have traces of the interchange in—

forlorn = *forloren* = *forlosen* (lost).
frore (Milton) = *froren* = *frosen* = frozen.
O.E. *gecoren* (*ycorn*) = *chosen*.
Cp. O.E. *isern* = *iren* = iron.

We often write *c* for an older *s*, as—
- mice = O.E. *mys*.
- pence = O.E. *pens, pans*.
- once = O.E. *ónes* (*ons*).
- hence = O.S. *hennes* (*hens*).

Sc has in many cases been softened down to *sh* (O.E. *sch*), as—
- shall = O.E. *sceal* (*scal*).
- shame = O.E. *scamu*.
- fish = O.E. *fisc*.

It is often preserved before *a, o, r*.

For *sc* and *sp* we frequently find by metathesis *cs* and *ps*, as—
- hoax = O.E. *husc*.

So for *ask* we find *axe* = O.E. *axien* = *acsian* = *ascian*.
In O.E. we find *clapsed* = clasped, *lipsed* = lisped.

In Romance words, **s** has passed into—

(1) *sh*, as cash = O. Fr. *casse, chasse;* Lat. *capsa.*
        radish = Lat. *radix.*
        nourish = O. E. *norysy, norice,* Lat. *nutrire,* O. Fr. *nurir.*

Cp. *blandish* (Lat. *blandiri,* O. Fr. *blandir*), *cherish* (O. Fr. *cherir*), *flourish* (Lat. *florere*), *perish* (Lat. *perire,* O. Fr. *perir*).

(2) To *-ge*, as cabbage = Fr. *cabus,* Lat. *cabusia.*
              sausage = Fr. *saucisse,* Lat. *salsisia.*

(3) To *x* (from mistaken etymology), as pickaxe = O. E. *pikois.*

French *s* (Lat. *t*) has become *sh*, as—

        fashion = O. Fr. *faceon, fazon,* Lat. *factio.*
        anguish = Fr. *angoisse,* Lat. *angustia.*

In some words *s* has disappeared—

    riddle = O. E. *ræd-else* (Ger. *rathsal*).
    pea = O. E. *pisa,* O. Fr. *peis,* Lat. *pesum.*
    cherry = O. E. *cirse,* Fr. *cerise,* Lat. *cerasus.*
    hautboy = Fr. *hautbois.*
    relay = Fr. *relais.*
    noisome = *noise-some,* from O. Fr. *noise* = Lat. *nausea,* or *noxa.*
    puny = Fr. *puisne.*

In a few words *s* has intruded, as—*s-melt, s-cratch, s-creak, s-quash, s-queeze, s-neeze, i-s-land* = O. E. *ea-land, igland;* aisle = Fr. *aile; demesne = demain,* O. Fr. *domaine, demeine* = Lat. *dominium.*

Z was not known in the oldest English, and through the influence of Norman-French it has taken the place of an older *s*, as—

        dizzy = O. E. *dysig.*
        freeze = O. E. *freosan.*

It also stands for a Fr. *c* or *s*, as hazard, lizard, buzzard, seize.

Z has intruded in *citizen* = Fr. *citoyen.*
It has changed to *g* in *ginger* (Lat. *zinziber,* O. E. *gingivere*).

GUTTURALS—K, G, CH, H.

K. (1) *c* (*k*) has become *ch*.

In Old-English before the Conquest *c* was always hard, but under Norman-French influence *c* (before *e, i, ea, eo*) has been changed to *ch;* as O.E. *cele, cese, cin, cild* have become *chill, cheese, chin, child; ceorl, ceaf* have become *churl, chaff.*

A final *c* has sometimes changed to *ch*, as O.E. *dic* to *dich; hwilc* to *which*. Sometimes the *ch* has disappeared, as O.E. *Ic = Ich = I; anlic = onlich = only; æferælc = everech = every, berlic = berlich = barley.*

In a few instances *c* has become first *ch* and then *j*, as—

jaw = chaw.
ajar = achar (on the turn), from O.E. *cerran*, to turn.
knowledge = O.E. *knowlech, knowlach = cnawlac.*

(2) In some Romance words *c* has become—

   (*a*) *ch*, as cherry = Fr. *cerise*, Lat. *cerasus.*
             chives = Fr. *cive.*
             coach = Fr. *carosse*, Lat. *carocium.*

   (*b*) *sh*, as shingle = O.Fr. *cengle*, Lat. *cingulum.*

   (*c*) *g*, as flagon = Fr. *flaçon.*
             sugar = Fr. *sucre.*

(3) *C* (followed by *t*) has sometimes become *gh*, as—

         delight = O.Fr. *deliter*, Lat. *delectare.*
         straight = O.Fr. *streit*, Lat. *strictus.*

G. In all words of English origin initial *g* is always hard, even before *e, i, y*, as *gave, give, go, get*, &c.

G has been softened (1) to *i, y, e, a*, as—

      O.E. *genoh* = enough.
           gelic = alike.
           hand-geweorc = handiwork.
           fæger = fair.
           hægel = hail.
           twegen = twain.
           wæga = way.

(2) To *w*—   O.E. *lagu*   = law.
             sage   = saw.
             maga   = maw.
             dagian = dawn.
             fugol = fowl.
             sorg (*sorh*) = sorrow.
             mearg = marrow.
             gealga = gallow(s).

Sometimes it is lost in the root and makes its appearance in the derivatives, as *dry* and *drought*, *slay* and *slaughter*, *draw* (drag) and *draught*.

It has disappeared in—
    if   = O.E. *gif*.
    icicle = O.E. *ís-gicel*.
    lent   = O.E. *lengten* (*lencten*).

It has been softened to
(1) *ge* (= *j*) in singe = O.E. *be sengan* (*sengen*).
              cringe = O.E. *cringan* (to die).
              Roger = O.E. *hrodgar*.

(2) to *ch* in orchard = O.E. *ort-geard* (*ortyard*) = herb-garden.

Gc (*Gg*) has often become *j* (*dg*)—
    edge   = O.E. *ecg* (*egg*).
    bridge = O.E. *brycg* (*brigge*).
    ridge = O.E. *hrycg* (*rigge*).

In Romance words *g* often disappears, as—
    master = O.E. *maister* = O.Fr. *maïstre*, Lat. *magister*.
    disdain = O.Fr. *desdaigner*, Lat. *disdignare*.

Sometimes *g* becomes *w*, as : wafer = O.Fr. *gauffre*, *goffre*, Lat. *gafrum*, cp. *wastel-brede* in Chaucer = cake-bread (Fr. *gâteau*).

G has crept into the following words—
    ·foreign   = O.Fr. *forain*, Lat. *forensis*.
    feign   = O.Fr. *feindre*.
    sovereign   = O.Fr. *soverain*, Lat. *superanus*.
    impregnable = Fr. *imprenable*.

Ch did not exist in the oldest English. In foreign words *c* was substituted for it, as O.E. *arcebiscop* = archbishop.

Through French influence *ch* came to represent a Latin *c*, as Lat. *cambiare*, O.Fr. *cangier*, *changier*, change. Cp. chapter, chapel, chamber, chief, &c.

Ch in many Romance words has been changed—
(1) To *dg*, as cartridge = Fr. *cartouche*.
(2) To *sh*, as parish = Fr. *paroisse*, Lat. *parochia*.
fetish = Fr. *fétiche*.
caboshed = Fr. *caboche*.
(3) To *tch*, as butcher = Fr. *boucher*.
dispatch = O.Fr. *depescher*.

H. This letter has disappeared from many words, especially before *l*, *n*, *r*, as—
it = O.E. *hit*.
loaf = O.E. *hlaf*.
lade = O.E. *hladan*.
neck = O.E. *hnecca*.
ring = O.E. *hring*.

In the following words *h* has intruded, as *wharf*, *whelk*, *whelm*.

It has fallen away from many words, as—
tear = O.E. *taher*, *tær*.
fee = O.E. *feoh*, *feo*.
&c. &c.

It has become *gh* in—
thigh = O.E. *theoh*.
high = O.E. *heah*.
nigh = O.E. *neah*.
though = O.E. *theah*.
knight = O.E. *cniht*.
wrought = O.E. *wrohte*.
&c. &c.

In some words *h* has become first *gh* and then *f*, as—
draft }
draught } = O.E. *droht* (*draht*).
enough = O.E. *genoh*.
laugh = O.E. *hleahhan*.
&c. &c.

In ilk, O.E. *eohl*, *h* has become changed to *k*.

We have both sounds side by side in—
candle and chandler.
carnal and charnel-(house).
cattle and chattel.

LIQUIDS—L, M, N, R.

L. In some Romance words *l* has been weakened to *u*, as—
  hauberk (O.Fr. *halberc, halbert*).
  auburn (Lat. *alburnum*).

In O.E. we find *assaut, maugre, paume, caudron, soudier*, &c.

L has disappeared in the following English words:—
  each   = O.E. *ælc (elch)*.
  which   = O.E. *hwylc (whilc, whilch)*.
  such   = O.E. *swylc (swilch, swulche, sulche)*.
  as   = O.E. *ealswa (also, alse, ase)*.
  England = O.E. *Engle-lond (Engelond)*.

L has become—
  (1) *r*, in lavender = Lat. *lavendula*.
           sinoper = Lat. *sinoplum*.
           colonel (pron. *kurnel*) = *coronel* (Spanish).

  In O.E. we find *brember* and *bremel* = bramble.

  (2) *n*, in postern = O.Fr. *posterle, posterne*; Lat. *posterula*.

L has intruded into the following words:—
  could   = (O.E. *cuthe, coude*).
  myrtle   = Lat. *myrtus*.
  manciple = O.Fr. *mancipe*; Lat. *mancipium*.
  participle = Lat. *participium*.
  principle = Lat. *principium*.
  syllable = Lat. *syllaba*.

M. *M* has been lost in some of the oldest English words, as—
  five = O.E. *fíf* (Goth. *fimf*).
  soft = O.E. *softe*; Germ. *sanft = samft*.

M is sometimes weakened to *n*, as—
  ant   = (O.E. *æmete*), emmet.
  count   = O.Fr. *cumte*; Lat. *comes*.
  renowned = O.E. *renowned*; Fr. *renommé*.
  noun   = Fr. *nom*; Lat. *nomen*.
  count   = O.Fr. *conter*; Lat. *computare*.
  ransom = O.Fr. *raancon*; Lat. *redemptio*; O.E. *ramson*.

M is sometimes changed to *b*, as *marblestone* = O.E. *marmanston*.

N. In the oldest English we find the loss of *n* before *f*, *th*, *s*, and the vowel lengthened in consequence, as—

  goose = (*gons*), cp. Germ. *gans*.
  tooth = (*tonth*), cp. Goth. *tunthus*; Germ. *zahn*.
  other = (*onther*), cp. Goth *anthar*; Germ. *ander*.

Cp. *us* with Germ. *uns*, and *could* (coud) with *can*.

It has disappeared from many adverbs and prepositions, as—

  beside = O.E. *bisidan*.
  before = O.E. *beforan*.
  within = O.E. *withinnan*.

It has also been lost in other words, as—

  ell   = O.E. *eln*.
  eve   = O.E. *æfen*.
  game = O.E. *gamen*.
  mill   = O.E. *mylen* (*miln*).
  eleven = O.E. *andlifum*.
  Thursday = O.E. *thunres-dæg* (*thunresdæi*).
  agnail = O.E. *ang-nægl*.
  yesterday = O.E. *gestran-dæg*.
  fortnight = O.E. *feowertene-niht* (*fourteniht*).

It has dropped from the beginning of a few words, as—

  adder = O.E. *næddre* (*nadder*).
  apron = O.Fr. *naperon*.

N has intruded in a few words, as—

  newt = *an ewt*.
  nag = Dan. *ög*; O.-Sax. *ehu* (cp. Lat. *equa*).

In Old-English we find *noumpere* = umpire (= Lat. *impar*); *nouch* = *ouche* (Fr. *oche*), *nounce* (= *uncia*). Shakespeare has *nuncle*, *naunt*.

It has sometimes crept into the body of a word, as—

  nightingale = O.E. *nihtegale*.
  messenger = O.E. *messager* (O.Fr. *messagier*).
  passenger = O.E. *passager* (O.Fr. *passagier*).
  popinjay = O.E. *popigay* (O.Fr. *papigai*).

At end of words we find an inorganic *n*, as *bittern* = O.E. *butore*, Fr. *butor* : *marten* = O.E. *mearth*.

ORTHOGRAPHY.

N has become (1) *m* in—

    smack   = O.E. *snacc* (boat), Fr. *semaque*.
    hemp   = O.E. *hanep*.
    lime (tree) = O.E. *lind*.
    tempt   = O.Fr. *tenter*, Lat. *tentare*.
    comfort = O.Fr. *confort*, Lat. *confortare*.
    venom   = Lat. *venenum*.
    vellum   = Fr. *velin*.
    megrim = Fr. *migraine*.

(2) *l* in flannel, formerly *flannen*.

R sometimes represents a more original *s*, as—

    ear = O.E. *eare*, Goth. *auso*.
    iron = O.E. *isen*, *iren*, Goth. *eisarn*.

It has disappeared from some few words, as—

    speak = O.E. *spræcan*.
    pin   = O.E. *preon*.
    palsy = O.E. *palasie*, Fr. *paralysie*, Gr. *paralysis*.
    cockade = O.Fr. *cocart*.

R has intruded into the following words:—

    groom (bridegroom) = O.E. *guma* (*gome*).
    hoarse = O.E. *hôs*.
    partridge = Fr. *perdrix*, Lat. *perdix*.
    cartridge = Fr. *cartouche*.
    corporal = Fr. *caporal*.
    culprit = Lat. *culpa*.

CHAPTER VIII.

ACCENT.

54. **Accent** is the stress of the voice upon a *syllable* of a word. Syllabic accent is an etymological one, and in oldest English it was upon the root and not upon the inflectional syllables.

By the Norman Conquest a different system of accentuation was introduced, which towards the end of the twelfth century began to show itself in the written language.

"The vocabulary of the French language is derived, to a great extent, from Latin words deprived of their terminal inflexions. The French adjectives *mortal* and *fatal* are formed from the Latin *mortalis* and *fatalis*, by dropping the inflected syllable; the French nouns *nation* and *condition*, from the Latin" accusatives *nationem, conditionem*, "by rejecting the *em* final. In most cases the last syllable retained in the French derivatives was prosodically long in the Latin original; and either because it was also accented or because the slight accent which is perceivable in the French articulation represents temporal length, the stress of the voice was laid on the *final* syllable of all these words. When we borrowed such words from the French, we took them with their native accentuation; and as accent is much stronger in English than in French, the *final* syllable[1] was doubtless more forcibly enunciated in the former than in the latter language."
—MARSH.

French accentuation even affected words of pure English origin, and we find in Robert of Gloucester *wisliche* (wisely) for *wis'liche*; *begynnyng'*, *endyng'*, &c.; and Chaucer rhymes *gladnes'se* with *distres'se*, &c.

Spenser's accentuation exhibits the influence of French accent. Thus he rhymes *blowes* with *shallowes*, *things* with *tidings*, &c.

"A straunger in thy home and *ignoraunt'*,
Of Phaedria', thine owne *fellow servaunt'.*"
F. Q. ii. 6. 9.

---

[1] The syllables that were accented in O.E. words of Fr. origin are: -ace, -age, -ail (-aille), -ain, -ance, -ence, -ant, -ent, -ee, -ey, -e, -eis, -el, -er, ere, -esse, -ice, -ise, -ie, -if, in, ine, -ite, -ion, -cion, -tion, -sion, -ment, -on, -our, -or, -ous, -te, -tude, -ure.

"A work of rich entayle and curious mould,
Woven with antickes and wild *imagery'*,
And in his lap a masse of coyne he told,
And turned upsidowne, to feede his eye
And covetous desire with his huge *threasury'*."
F. Q. ii. 7. 4.

"Hath now made thrall to your *commandëment*."
F. Q. ii. 10. 59.

Shakespeare and Milton retain many words accented upon the final syllable which are now accented according to the Teutonic method, as *aspéct, convérse, accéss*, &c.

As early as Chaucer's time an attempt was made to bring the words of French origin under the Teutonic accentuation, and in the "Canterbury Tales" we find *mor'tal, tem'pest, sub'stance;* and many words were pronounced according to the English or French accentuation, as *pris'on* and *prison', tem'pest* and *tempest'*.

In the Elizabethan period we find a great tendency to throw the accent back to the earlier syllables of Romance words, though they retained a secondary accent at or near the end of the word, as *na"ti'on, sta"ti'on*.

In many words a strong syllable has received the accent in preference to a weak one, as Fr. *ac'cepta'ble*, Lat. *ac'cepta"bilis*, has become not *ac"cept'able* but *accept"able*.

I. Many French words still keep their own accent, especially—

(1) Nouns, in *-ade, -ier (eer), -é, -ee,* or *-oon, -ine (-in),* as— *cascadé, crusadé,* &c. ; *cavalier', chandelier',* &c. ; *gazetteer', pioneer',* &c. (in conformity with these we say *harpooneer', mountaineer'); legateé, payeé,* &c. ; *balloon', cartoon',* &c. ; *chagrin', violin',* &c. ; *routiné, mariné,* &c.

Also the following words—*cadet', brunetté, gazetté, cravat', canal', control', gazellé, amateur', fatigué, antiqué, police',* &c.

(2) Adjectives (*a*) from Lat. adj. in *us,* as *august', benign', robust',* &c. ; (*b*) in *-ose,* as *morosé, verbosé,* &c. ; (*c*) *-esque,* as *burlesqué, grotesqué,* &c.

(3) Some verbs, as—*baptizé, cajolé, caress', carousé, chastisé, escapé, esteem',* &c. &c.

II. Many Latin and Greek words of comparatively recent introduction keep their original form and accent, as—*auro'ra, coro'na, colos'sus, ide'a, hypoth'esis,* &c.

III. Some few Italian words keep their full form and original accent, as *mulat'to, sona'ta, tobac'co, volca'no.*

Shortened forms lose their original accent, as *ban'dit, mar'mot,* &c.

55. In many words mostly of Latin origin a change of accent makes up for the want of inflectional endings, and serves to distinguish (*a*) a noun from a verb, (*b*) an adjective from a verb, (*c*) an adjective from a noun—

(*a*) aug'ment   to *augment'.*
     tor'ment   to *torment'.*
     &c.   &c.

(*b*) ab'sent   to *absent'.*
     fre'quent   to *frequent'.*

(*c*) a *com'pact*   to *compact'.*
     an *ex'pert*   to *expert'.*
     &c.   &c.

It occurs in some few words of Teutonic origin, as *o'verflow* and to *overflow', o'verthrow* and to *overthrow',* &c.

56. The accent distinguishes between the meanings of words, as—

to *con'jure* and to *conjure'.*
in'cense and to *incense'.*
Au'gust and *august'.*
min'ute and *minute'.*
su'pine and *supine.*

57. Influence of Accent.

Accent plays an important part in the changes that words undergo.

Unaccented syllables are much weaker than accented ones, and we find unaccented syllables dropping off—

(*a*) At the beginning of words (*Aphæresis*).
(*b*) At the end of words (*Apocope*).
(*c*) The accent causes two syllables to blend into one (*Syncope*).

EXAMPLES.

(*a*) bishop   = Lat. *episcopus.*
     reeve   = O.E. *ge-refa.*
     squire   = O.Fr. *escuier* (Lat. *scutarius*).

spy = O. Fr. *espier*.
story = O. Fr. *estoire* (Lat. *historia*).
stranger = O. Fr. *estranger* (Lat. *extrancus*).
ticket = O. Fr. *eticquette*.
dropsy = O. E. *ydropesie* (Gr. *hydropsis*).

A few double forms are sometimes found, as—*squire* and *esquire*, *strange* and *estrange*, *state* and *estate*, *spy* and *espy*, *spital* and *hospital*, *sport* and *disport*, *sample* and *example*, &c.

(*b*) name = O. E. *nama*.
riches = O. E. *richesse*.
chapel = O. E. *chapelle*.
&c. &c.

(*c*) brain = O. E. *brægen*.
church = O. E. *cyrice*.
French = O. E. *frencisc*.
hawk = O. E. *hafoc*.
head = O. E. *heafod*.
mint = O. E. *mynet*.
crown = Lat. *corona*.
comrade = Fr. *camarade*.
palsy = Gr. *paralysis*.
sexton = *sacristan*.
proxy = *procuracy*.
parrot = Fr. *perroquet*.

In compounds we find the same principle at work, and their origin is obscured :—

daisy = O. E. *dæges eage* (day's eye).
elbow = O. E. *eln-boga* (arm-bending).
gossip = O. E. *god-sibb* (God-related).
harbour = O. E. *here-berga* (*herberwe*), *i.e.* protection for an army.
habergeon (hauberk) = O. E. *heals-berga* (protection for the neck).
Lammas = O. E. *hláf-messe* (loaf-mass).
neighbour = O. E. *neáh-búr* (near-dweller).
nostril = O. E. *nose-thyrel* (nose-hole).
orchard = O. E. *ort-geard* (herb-garden).
sheriff = O. E. *scire-geréfa* (shire-reeve).
threshold = O. E. *thresc-wold* (thresh-wood, *i.e.* wood beaten or trodden by the foot = door-sill).
woman = O. E. *wífman* (= wife-man).

leman = O.E. *leof-man* (lief-man, dear-man, sweetheart).
constable = Lat. *comes stabuli*.
curfew = O.Fr. *cuevre-feu*.
kerchief = O.Fr. *cuevre-chief*.

In proper names we have numerous instances :—

(a) Names of places :—
Canterbury = O.E. *Cant-wara-burh* (= town of the men of Kent).
York = O.E. *Eofor-wic* (Everwich, Everwik).
Windsor = O.E. *Windles-ofra* (Wyndelsore).
Sunday = O.E. *Sunnan-dæg*.
Thursday = O.E. *Thunres-dæg*.

(b) Names of persons :—
    Bap   = Baptist.
    Ben   = Benjamin.
    Gib   = Gilbert.
    Hal   = Harry.
    Taff   = Theophilus.
    Wat   = Walter.
    Bess, Bet = Elizabeth.
    Meg, Madge = Margaret.
    Maude = Magdalen.
    Dol   = Dorothy.
Cp.   cab   = cabriolet.
    bus   = omnibus.
    consols = consolidated annuities.
    chum   = chamberfellow, &c.
    rail   = railway.
    tramway = Outram way.

CHAPTER IX.

ETYMOLOGY.

58. Etymology treats of the structure and history of words; its chief divisions are *inflexion* and *derivation*.

Words denote the *attributes* or *relations* of things, and are of two kinds: (1) those significant of quality; (*a*) of material things, as *sweet, bright,* (*b*) of acts, as *quick, slow,* &c.; (2) those indicative of position (relating to time, space, &c.), as *here, there, then, I, he.*
The first are called *notional* words, the second *relational* words.

A *root* or *radical* is that part of a word which cannot be reduced to a simpler or more original form. Roots are classified into—

(*a*) *predicative,* corresponding to *notional* words.
(*b*) *demonstrative,* corresponding to *relational* words.

Inflexions are shortened forms, for the most part, of *demonstrative,* sometimes of *predicative* roots. Hence all inflexions were once *significant.*

59. THE PARTS OF SPEECH, OR LANGUAGE, are—

I. Inflexional.
- 1. Noun (Substantive, Adjective).
- 2. Verb.
- 3. Pronoun.

II. Indeclinable words, or particles.
- 4. Adverb.
- 5. Preposition.
- 6. Conjunction.
- 7. Interjection.

60. Nouns[1] include—

(1) Abstract substantives, like *virtue,* which denote the *qualities* of things simply, significative only of mental conceptions.

(2) Concrete substantives, in which a *single* attribute stands synecdochically for many.[2]

---

[1] Fr. *nom,* Lat. *nomen,* from *gnosco* = that by which anything is known.
[2] Cp. *wheat,* which originally signified *white.*

(3) Adjectives, *i.e.* attributes used as descriptive epithets; being sometimes simple, as *black, white,* &c., sometimes compound words, as *sorrowful, godlike, friendly.*

In Greek and Latin all adjectives have distinctive terminations, which were originally separate words. Most of these terminations have a *possessive* signification; others denote similarity, &c., analogous to our *-like, -ful, -less;* and in all cases they do not so much belong to the *attribute* as to the *subject.* The termination puts the word in condition to be joined to some substantive.

61. The Verb was originally nothing more than a noun combined with the oblique case of a personal pronoun; so that in *am*—

$a = as =$ existence.
$m = $ of me, &c.

62. Pronouns are attributes of a peculiar kind, not permanently attached to certain objects or classes of objects; nor are they limited in their application. "Only one thing may be called the *sun;* only certain objects are *white;* but there is nothing which may not be *I* and *you* and *it,* alternately, as the point from which it is viewed.

"In this universality of their application as dependent upon relative situation merely, and in the consequent capacity of each of them to designate any object which has its own specific name besides, and so, in a manner, to stand for and represent that other name, lies the essential character of the Pronoun. The Hindu title, *sarvarnâ-man,* 'name for everything,' 'universal designation,' is therefore more directly and fundamentally characteristic than the one we give them, *pronoun,* 'standing for a name.'"—WHITNEY.

63. Adverbs are derivative forms of nouns, adjectives, or pronouns. Thus, our adverbial suffix *-ly* was originally *-lice* = the ablative or dative case of an adjective ending in *-lic*=like, the adverbial ending *-ment* of Romance words is the Latin ablative *mente,* "with mind" (Fr. *bonnement* = kindly = *bonâ mente,* "with kind intent").

Many relational adverbs are formed from demonstrative pronouns, as *he-re, hi-ther, whe-n,* &c.

64. Prepositions were once adverbial prefixes to the verb, serving to point out more clearly the direction of the verbal action: by degrees they detached themselves from the verb and came to belong to the noun, furthering the disappearance of its *case*-endings, and assuming their office. The oldest prepositions can be traced to pronominal roots; others are from verbal roots.—WHITNEY.

65. **Conjunctions** are of comparatively late growth, and are either of pronominal original, or abbreviated forms of expression, as—

    else   = O.E. *elles*, a genitive of *el* = *alius*.
    unless = *on less*.
    least   = *thy læs* = *eð minus*.
    but   = *be out* = (O.E. *bi-utan*).
    likewise = *in like wise* (manner).
      &c.   &c.

CHAPTER X.

SUBSTANTIVES.

I. GENDER.

66. GENDER is a grammatical distinction, and applies to words only. Sex is a natural distinction, and applies to living objects. By personification we attribute sex to inanimate things, as "The Sun in *his* glory, the Moon in *her* wane."

The distinctions of gender are sometimes marked by different terminations, as *genitor, genitrix; dominus, domina.* This is called *grammatical* gender.

67. Loss of Grammatical Gender in English.—The oldest English, like Greek and Latin, and modern German, possessed grammatical gender.

mag-a,	a kinsman.	*mag-e,*	a kinswoman.
nefa,	a nephew.	*nefe,*	niece.
widuwa,	a widower.	*widuwe,*	a widow.
munec,	a monk.	*municen,*	a nun.
god,	a god.	*gyden,*	a goddess.
webbere,	a weaver.	*webb-estre,*	a webster.

So *freo-dom* (freedom) was masculine; *gretung* (greeting), feminine; and *cycen,* chicken, neuter.

Grammatical gender went gradually out of use after the Norman Conquest, owing to the following causes :—

(1) The confusion between masculine and feminine suffixes.

(2) Loss of suffixes marking gender.

(3) Loss of case inflections in the masculine and feminine forms of demonstratives.

68. Traces of grammatical gender were preserved much longer in some dialects than in others. The Northern dialects were the first to discard the older distinctions, which, however, survived in the Southern dialect of Kent as late at least as 1340.[1]

69. The names of males belong to the masculine gender.
The names of females to the feminine gender.
The names of things of neither sex are neuter.
Words like *child*, *parent*, of which, without a qualifying term, the gender is either masculine or feminine, are said to be of the common gender.

70. There are three ways of distinguishing the masculine and feminine in English :—

(*a*) By employing a different word for the male and female.

(*b*) By the use of suffixes.

(*c*) By composition.

71. Before the Conquest our language possessed many words answering to our "man."

The term "man" corresponded generally to the German *mensch*, person, and was not confined originally to the masculine gender; hence it occurs frequently in compounds with a qualifying term, as —*wif-man*,[2] woman; *leof-man*, sweetheart; *wæpned-man*,[3] man, male.

Other common words for "man" were *guma*, as in *bryd-guma* = bride-groom (Ger. *bräutigam*) = the bride's man;[4] *gum-mann*; *beorn*; *carl*,[5] our *churl*; *wer*[6] (man and husband).

72. **I. Different words for the masculine and feminine.**

FATHER.   MOTHER.
BROTHER.   SISTER.

Father (O.E. *fæder*) is cognate with Lat. *pa-ter*, Gr. πατήρ = one who feeds or supports. Cp. *pa-sco*, *fee-d*, *fa-t*, &c.

---

[1]   "Therthe schok, the sonne dym becom
        In *thare tyde*."—SHOREHAM.
Here the inflection of the demonstrative shows that *tyde* is feminine.

"Be thise virtue the guode overcomth alle his vyendes *thane* dyevel, *the* wordle, and *thet* vless."—AYENBITE. *Dyevel* is masculine; *wordle* feminine; and *vles* neuter.

[2] *Wif* = wife, is cognate with the Lat. *ux-or*, and originally signified 'one carried off.'

[3] *Wæpned-man* = a man armed with a weapon.

[4] Spenser has *herd-groom* = herdsman. *Guma* is cognate with Lat. *homo*.

[5] Spenser uses *carl* for an old man, a churl. In O.E. we have the compounds *carlman* and *carman* = male, man. Cp. Scotch *carlin*, an old woman.

[6] *Wer* cognate with Lat. *vir*.

Mo-ther (O.E. *môdor, moder*), Lat. *ma-ter*, contains a root *ma*, to produce, bring forth.
Bro-ther (O.E. *brothor*), Lat. *frater*, originally signified 'one who bears or supports,' from the verb *bear*, cognate with Latin *fero*.
Sis-ter (O.E. *sweostar, suster*) is cognate with Lat. *soror* (= *sos-tor*), and had perhaps originally the same signification as *mo-ther*.

The termination in all these words denotes the *agent*. In the primitive Aryan speech there was no distinct suffix used as a sign of gender.

PAPA. MAMMA.

These words are of Latin origin. Papa = father: cp. *pope*. Mamma = mother: cp. *mammal*.

SON. DAUGHTER.

Son (O.E. *su-nu*) = one brought forth, born (cp. *bairn*), from the root *su*, to bring forth; *daugh-ter* cognate with Gr. θυγάτηρ = milker, milkmaid, from root *duh* (*dugh*), to milk.

UNCLE. AUNT.

Uncle is from O.Fr. *uncle, oncle*, from Lat. *avunculus*.
Aunt from O.Fr. *ante*, Lat. *amita*. The O.E. word for uncle was (1) *eam* (*em*), Ger. *ohm* (*oheim*), (2) *fædera*. *Aunt* in the oldest English was *modrige*.

BOY. GIRL.

Boy is not found in the oldest English; it is of frequent occurrence in O.E. writers of the fourteenth century, by whom it is applied to men occupying a low position, to menial servants: it is therefore often used as a term of contempt. The term is probably of Teutonic origin, and is cognate with O.Du. *boeve*, Platt-Deutsch *bôw*, Swed. *bof*, Ger. *bube*, O.H.Ger. *puopo*.

The O.E. word for boy was *cnapa* (knave), Ger. *knabe*, whence *knave-child*, a boy.

Gir-l is a diminutive of a root *gir*, cognate with Platt-Deutsch *gör*, a little child.

In O.E. writers of the fourteenth century *girl* was of the common gender: thus Chaucer has '*yonge girles*' = young persons; and the O.E. expression *knave-girle* occurs in the sense of *boy*.

Wench is a shortened form of the O.E. *wenchel*, which in the "Ormulum" is applied to Isaac, and was originally a word of the common gender.

In a metrical version of the Old and New Testaments of the fourteenth century, in the Vernon MS., we find *mayden* and *grom* = boy and girl:—

"Ine reche whether hit beo *mayden* other *grom*."

BACHELOR. MAID.

The derivation of *bachelor*, which comes to us from the French, is uncertain; it probably contains a Celtic root, as seen in Welsh *bachgen*, a boy (from *bach*, little); whence O.Fr. *bachelor*, a servant, apprentice in arms, a knight-bachelor.

Maid = O.E. *mægeth, mæd; maiden* (O.E. *mægd-en*, of neuter gender) is a derivative.[1]

The literal meaning of *maid* is one grown up, an adult. It is often applied to males as well as females.

---

[1] We have the same root in Goth. *mag-us*, a boy; *mag-aths*, a young girl; O.E. *mag-a*, a son (cp. Sc. *mac*), all connected with the Sansk. root *mah*, to become great, to grow.

KING.   QUEEN.

King (O.E. *cyning, cyng*) originally signified the father of a family, 'King of his own kin.'[1] *Queen* (O.E. *cwen*) at first meant wife, woman, mother.[2]

EARL.   COUNTESS.

Earl (O.E. *eorl*) is probably a contraction of O.E. *ealdor man* = elder-man, a term applied to the *heretogas* or leaders of the old English chiefs who first settled in this country.
Countess (O.Fr. *contesse, cuntesse*) is the feminine of the word *count*.

MONK.   NUN.

Monk (O.E. *munec, monc*) comes from the Greek through the Latin *monachus*. *Friar* (O.E. *frere*, O.Fr. *freire*, Lat. *frater*) signifies a *brother* of a religious order.
Nun (O.E. *nunne, nonne*) from Latin *nonna*, a grandmother. The first nuns would naturally be older women.[3]
The Old English feminine for *monk* was *munecen* = *minchen*.

WIZARD.   WITCH.

Wizard from O.Fr. *guisc-art, guisch-art*, signifies a very wise man; the French word is of Teutonic origin, *guisc* = Icelandic *visk-r*, wise. The suffix *-ard* is of the same origin as that in *drunk-ard*.
The oldest English words for *wizard* were *wigelere*, one who uses *wiles*, and *kweolere*.
Witch in old writers is a word of the common gender. The O.E. is *wicce*, to which there was probably a corresponding masculine, *wicc-a*.[4]

SLOVEN.   SLUT.

Sloven seems to be connected with O.E. *slavere*, to slobber (cp. to *slobber work* = to do work slovenly). Some etymologist connected it with slow (O.E. *slaw*).
Slut is perhaps connected with O.E. *slotere*, to defile; *slottisch*, dirty, slutty. *Slattern* (= *slatten*) probably means tattered, from the verb *slit* (pret. *slat*)[5].

The following words, though apparently different, are etymologically connected:—

NEPHEW.   NIECE.

Nephew is from the Lat. *nepos*, a grandson, through the O.Fr. *nevod* (*nief, niez*), Fr. *neveu*.[6]

---

[1] Cp. Sc. *janaka* (= genitor), father, from *jan*, to beget.
[2] Cp. Goth. *qens*, O.H.Ger. *chena*, a woman, wife; Eng. *quean*, used only in a bad sense.
[3] Cp. Gr. παπᾶς, a priest, from *papa*, a father.
[4] Cp. O.E. *webb-a*, a male weaver; *webb-e*, a female weaver.
[5] Robert of Brunne has *dowde*, a feminine term equivalent to *slattern*, for which we now write *dowd-y*.
[6] The Sansk. *naptri* shows that *nepos* (fem. *neptis*) contains the remnant of a suffix *-ter*, as in *pa-ter*. The Sansk. *naptri* = *na+pitri*, not a father, one who is not old enough to become a parent.

Niece is the Fr. *nièce* from the Lat. *neptis*, a grand-daughter.
The O.E. *nef-a* (nephew), *nef-e* (niece), are cognate with *nepos* and *neptis*, and with *nephew* and *niece*.
The O.E. forms could not, as some have suggested, given rise to *nephew* or *niece*, but both would assume a common form, *neve*, which is found in O.E. writers after the Conquest.

LORD.   LADY.

Lord (O.E. *hláford* = *hláf-weard*) is a compound containing the suffix *-weard* (*-ward*) = keeper, guardian, as in O.E. *boatward*, boat-keeper. It is generally explained as *loaf* (O.E. *hláf*), -distributor.
Lady (O.E. *hlæfdige* = *hláfweardige*[1]) is a (contracted) feminine of Lord.

LAD.   LASS.

In O.E. *ladde* is generally used in the sense of a man of an inferior station, a menial servant. It is generally considered as being connected with O.E. *leád*, *lede* (cp. Goth. jugga-*lauths*, a young man, *jugga* = young), from *leodan*, Goth. *liudan*, to grow up.
Lass does not occur in O.E. writers before the fourteenth century, and only in Northern writers. It is probably a contraction of *laddess*.

In the following pairs *one* is a compound :—

MAN.   WOMAN.

See remarks on MAN, p. 83, § 71.

BRIDEGROOM.   BRIDE.

See remarks on GROOM, p. 83, § 71.
Notice too that the masculine is formed from the feminine.
These terms are mostly applied to newly-married persons. " And is the *bride* and *bridegroom* coming home?"—SHAKESPEARE.
In O.E. (fourteenth century) *bryd* (*brud*), by metathesis, often becomes *burd* (*bird*), and is employed in the sense of *maiden*: hence *burnes and burdes* = young men and maidens.

HUSBAND.   WIFE.

Husband is not the *band*, *bond*, or support of the house, as some have ingeniously tried to make out, but signified originally the *master of the house*, *paterfamilias*.
Hus = house ; *bond* = O.E. *bonda*, a participial form of the verb *bu-an*, to inhabit, cultivate ; so that *bonda*[2] = husbandman, the possessor as well as the cultivator of the soil attached to his *house*. Bond-men came to signify (1) *peasants*, (2) *churls, slaves;* hence the compounds *bond-slave, bond-age*, which have nothing to do with the verb *bind*, or the noun *bond*.
Wife was often used in older writers in the sense of *woman;* hence it occurs in some compounds with this meaning, as *fish-wife, house-wife, hussy* = housewife ; *goody* = good-wife.

---

[1] In later writers *hlæfdige* became *lafdie, lavdi*, lady.
[2] Cp. Icel. *bóndi*, a husbandman, from *bua*, to cultivate, dwell ; Dan. *bonde*, peasant, countryman.

SIRE.   MADAM.

Sir is from O. Fr. *sires*, Fr. *sire*, Lat. *senior*.
Madam = Fr. *madame* = my lady = *mea domina*.
Spenser frequently uses *dame* in the sense of lady.
Sire and *dam* are still applied to the father and mother of animals.
Grandsire and *beldam* are sometimes found for grandfather and grandmother.

Names of Animals.

BOAR.   SOW.

Boar (O.E. *bar*), originally only one of many names for the male swine. *Eofor* (cp. Dan. *ever-swin*) and *bearh* died out very early; the latter still survives in *barrow-pig*.
The general term of this species was *Swine* (O.E. *swin*, cp. *swinstede* = pigsty; *suner*, *sounder*, a herd of swine).
Pig (O. Du. *bigge, big*) is not found in the oldest English; in later writers it is mostly applied to young swine.
Gris (*grise, grice*), from O.N. *gris,* is used by our older writers for a young pig.
Farrow = O.E. *fearh* = a little pig.

BULL.   COW.

Bull (O.E. *bulle*) is not found in the oldest English. It probably comes from the Icelandic *boli*.
Bullock (O.E. *bulluca*) is properly a little bull, a bull-calf.
Cow = O.E. *cu*.[1]
The Fr. *bœuf* also signifies *bull*. The general term of the species was *Ox* (O.E. *oxa*). There were other special designations, as *steer* (O.E. *steor, steorc,* terms applied to the *males* of other species; cp. Ger. *stier,* a bull; O.H. Ger. *stero,* ram. See note on **Stag**).
Heifer = O.E. *heah-fore, heafre* [*hecforde*], of which the first syllable signifies high, great. Cp. *heah-deor* = roe-buck.

BUCK.   DOE.

Buck = O.E. *bucca*; *doe* = O.E. *da, dama*. In O.E. *hæfer* signifies he-goat, cognate with Lat. *caper*; *rah, râ* = roe = *caprea*.
Kid (cognate with Lat. *hædus*) = O.N. *kid*; an O.E. word for *kid* was *ticcen,* Ger. *zick-lein*.

HART.   ROE.

Hart, O.E. *heorut, heort* = horned; cp. *cervus*. *Hind* = cerva.
Deer (O.E. *deor* = Gr. θήρ, Lat. *fera*) was once a general term for an animal (wild), hence Shakespeare talks of 'rats and mice, and such small *deer*.'

STAG.   HIND.

Stag = Icel. *steggr*, which was applied to the males of many species. In the English provincial dialects *stag* or *steg* = a gander or a cock.
Bailey has *stagg-ard*, a hart in its fourth year.

RAM (O.E. *ramm*).
WETHER (O.E. *wæther*).   EWE (O.E. *eowu, eow*).

---

[1] Wickliffe has *shee-oxe*.

88   ENGLISH ACCIDENCE.   [CHAP.

HOUND.   BITCH.

Hound = O.E. *hund*, cognate with Lat. *canis*.
Dog does not occur in the oldest English. It is found in the cognate dialects, O.Dan. *dogge*, Icel. *doggr*. *Tike* occurs sometimes in O.E. for a dog.
Bitch = O.E. *bicc-e*.

STALLION.   MARE.

Stallion (O.Fr. *estalon*) has supplanted the O.E. *hengest* and *steda* (steed).
Horse (O.E. *hors*) was originally of the neuter gender.
Mare (O.E. *merihe*), the feminine of an original masculine, *mearh*.

COLT. }
FOAL. }   FILLY.

Foal, O.E. *fola*, Ger. *füllen*, Lat. *pullus*.
Filly = Scotch *fillok*, Welsh *ffilog*.

COCK.   HEN.

Hen had a corresponding masculine, *hana*, in O.E. : cp. Ger. *hahn* and *henne*.

GANDER.   GOOSE.

Gander (O.E. *gan-d-ra*) and *Goose* (O.E. *gôs* = *gons, gans*) are related words.
The *d* and *r* in gander are merely euphonic; *a* is the masculine suffix and the root is *gan* = *gans*, a goose; cp. Icel. *gâs*, goose; *gasi*, gander; also Ger. *gans*, Gr. χήν, Latin *anser* (= *hanser*).

DRAKE.   DUCK.

Duck = O.E. *doke* = diver (connected with the verb to *duck*, O.Dan. *duiken*, O.H.G. *tûchan*, to dive, plunge) has no etymological connection with *Drake*.
The word *drake* can only be explained by a reference to the cognate forms: O.Norse *and-rik-a*, O.H.Ger. *ant-richo*, *ant-recho*, which suggests an O.English *end-ric-e* (which, however, does not occur in O.E. literature).
In O.E. *ened*, *end* = duck (cp. O.H.Ger. *anut*, Ger. *ente*, Lat. *anas*); *rice* = king, cp. Lat. *rex*.
So that *d-rake* is a contraction of *end-rake* = duck-king, king of the ducks.[1]

RUFF.   REEVE.

Reeve seems a true feminine of Ruff.

MILTER.   SPAWNER.
DRONE.   BEE.

73. II. **The Gender marked by difference of termination.**

The feminine is usually formed from the masculine.

A. Obsolete modes of forming the feminine :—

[1] The suffix *-rich* is found in some of the German dialects: in *taüber-rich*, a male dove; *enterich*, a drake; *ganse-rich*, a gander.

(1) By the suffix -en.

In the oldest English *-en* was a common feminine suffix, as—

M.	F.
Cas-ere (emperor)	Caser-n (empress).
Fox	Fyx-en (vixen).
God, a god	Gyden (goddess).
Manna (man-servant)	Mennen (woman-servant).
Wulf (wolf)	Wylfen (she-wolf).

In modern English we have only preserved *one* word with this suffix—vixen.

Vix-en is formed from *vox*, the Southern form of *fox*. The change of vowel is regular: compare *god* and *gyden*.

In Scotch, *carl-in* = an old woman.

In the thirteenth and fourteenth centuries we find a few more of these feminines, as—*minchen*,[1] a nun; *wolvene*, a she-wolf; *dovene*, a she-dove; *schalkene*, a female servant, from *schalk* (O.E. *scealc*), a man-servant, which exists in *marschal* and *seneschal*.

(2) By the suffix -ster.

In the oldest English we have a numerous class of words ending in *-ster* (*stre*, *stere*), corresponding to masculine forms in *-ere*.

M.		F.
bæc-ere	(baker)	bæc-estre.
fithel-ere	(fiddler)	fithel-stre.
hearp-ere	(harper)	hearp-estre.
sang-ere	(singer)	sang-estre.
seam-ere	(sewer)	seam-estre.
tæpp-er	(bar-man)	tæpp-estre.
webb-ere	(weaver)	webb-estre

Up to the end of the thirteenth century *-ster* was a characteristic sign of the feminine gender, and by its means new feminines could be always formed from the masculine.

In the twelfth and thirteenth centuries we find some curious forms, as—

bellering-estre, a female bell-ringer.
wic-then-estre, a weekly woman-servant.
hordestre, a cellaress.
wasshestre, a washerwoman.

In the fourteenth century we find the suffix **-ster** giving place to the Norman-French **-ess**, and there is consequently a want of uniformity in the employment of this termination. Thus Robert of Brunne uses *sangster*, songster, as a

---

[1] This suffix is found in several of the Aryan languages: cp. Ger. *säng-er* (singer) and *sängerinn*; *fuchs* (fox) and *füchs-inn*; Gr. ἡρωίνη, hero-*ine* (O.Fr. *héro-ine*), Latin *regina*.

Margravine and *Landgravine* contain the Romance suffix *-ine* (as in *heroine*) and not the Teutonic *-in*.

Lithuanian *gandras*, stork; *gandr-enē* (f.).

Sansk. *Indra* (name of a god); *Indrani* (the wife of Indra).

The Sanskrit shows that *n* is no mark of gender, but of *possession*; the *ī* is the sign of gender, which appears in Lithuanian *-enë*, but is lost in the English *-en*, Ger. *-inn*.

masculine.[1] In Purvey's Recension of Wickliffe's translation of the Scriptures we find *songstere* used for the masculine singer; and Wickliffe uses *webbestere* as a masculine.

Daunstere (a female dancer), *hotestre* (hostess), *tombestere* (= *daunstere*) are hybrid words, and etymologically as bad as *sleeresse*, &c.

In the "Pilgrimage of the Lyf of Manhode" (beginning of fifteenth century), we have only one word in *-ster* as the name of a female, viz. *hangestre* = the feminine of *hangman* or *hangere* (p. 144).

The following feminines in *-ess* occur in this work:—*meyeresse, enquerouresse, bigilouresse, condyeresse, constablesse, jogelouresse, forgeresse, skorcheresse, enchantouresse, bacouresse, graveresse, gold-smithesse, disporteresse*.

Still a good number of words with this suffix are to be found as feminines late in the fifteenth century, as—

kempster	= *pectrix*.	baxter	= *pistrix*.
webster	= *textrix*.	salster	= *salinaria*.
dryster	= *siccatrix*.	brawdster	= *palmaria*.
sewster	= *sutrix*.	huxter	= *auxiatrix*.

We have now only one feminine word with this suffix, viz. spinster: but *huckster* was used very late as a feminine. *Hucksterer* and *man-huckster* are new masculines formed from the feminine.

When the suffix *-ster* was felt no longer to mark the gender, some new feminines were formed by the addition of the Romance French -ess to the English -ster, as songstr-ess and seamstr-ess,[2] which hybrid forms are, etymologically speaking, *double* feminines.

The suffix *-ster* now often marks the agent with more or less a sense of contempt and depreciation, as *punster, trickster, gamester*.

In Elizabethan writers we find *drugster, hackster* (swordsman), *teamster, seedster* (sower), *throwster, rhymester, whipster*, &c.

B. Romance suffixes.

To replace the obsolete English modes of forming the feminine, several suffixes are used to mark the gender.

(1) Lat. -or (m.), and -ix (f.).

M.	F.
adjutor	adjutrix.
testator	testatrix.
&c.	&c.

---

[1] The Northern dialects of the twelfth and thirteenth centuries seldom employ this suffix, and it is often found, as in Robert of Brunne, in masculine nouns (marking the agent).

In the "Ormulum" we find *huccesterr* = *huckster*, which is probably masculine.

In Wickliffe we find signs that this suffix was going out of use to mark gender in the double forms that he employs, as *dwell-stere* and *dweller-esse, sleestere* and *sleeresse, daunstere* and *daunseresse*.

[2] Howell uses *hucksteress* and *spinstress* as feminines. Ben Jonson uses *seamster* and *songster* to express the feminine; while Shakespeare uses *spinster* sometimes as = spinner.

(2) Romance -ine.

M.	F.
hero	heroine.
landgrave	landgravine.
margrave	margravine.

(3) Romance -a.

M.	F.
sultan	sultan-a.
signor	signor-a.
infant	infant-a.

In O.E. the Romance fem. suffix -*ere* is used in *chambrere*, Fr. *chamberière* = chamberwoman; *lavendere* = laundress. "God hath maad me (Penitence) his *chaumbrere* and his *lavendere*."—*Pilgrimage*.

(4) The French -**ess** is, however, the ordinary feminine suffix, and the only living mode of forming fresh feminines; -*ess* is Med. Lat. *issa*, and occurs in the Old English *abbud-isse* = abbess.

In the twelfth and thirteenth centuries we find *contesse* = countess; *emperesse* = empress. In the fourteenth century -*ess* began to take the place of the English -*ster*, and was no doubt at first added only to Romance words; after a time it was added to Teutonic as well as to borrowed words.

In the Elizabethan period we find that it was added more frequently to distinguish the feminine than at present.

Spenser has *championess, vassaless, warriouress*, &c. Chapman uses *heroess, butteress, waggoness, rectress*, &c. (*See* Trench's "English Past and Present," p. 156.)

(1) The suffix -*ess* is added to the simple masculine, as—

M.	F.
baron	baron-ess.
giant	giant-ess.
&c.	&c.

(2) The masculine ending is dropped before the suffix, as—

M.	F.
cater-er	cater-ess.
sorcer-er	sorcer-ess.
&c.	&c.

(3) The masculine ending (-*or*, -*er*) is shortened before the addition of -*ess* :—

M.	F.
actor	actress.
conductor	conductress.
&c.	&c.

(4) Duchess is from O. Fr. *ducesse, duchesse;* marchioness, from Med. Lat. *marchio;* mistress, O.E. *maisteresse,* from *master,* O.F. *maister.*

74. III. **Gender is sometimes denoted by composition.**

In the oldest English we find traces of a qualifying word compounded with a general term, as *man-cild* = man-child, boy; *carl-catt,* tom-cat; *carl-fugol,* a male bird; *wif-man* = woman; *cwen-fugol,* a female bird. In later times we find *cnave-child* = boy.

(1) By using the words male and female.

M.	F.
male-servant	female-servant.

(2) By using man, woman, or maid.

M.	F.
man-servant	maid-servant.
men-singers	women-singers.

Sometimes we find *servant-man, servant-maid, washer-woman, milk-man milk-maid.*

(3) By the use of he and she, mostly in the names of animals.

M.	F.
he-goat	she-goat.
he-bear	she-bear.

In Shakespeare's time *he* and *she* were used as nouns; and not only did people talk of *he's* and *she's* for males and females, but even of the *fairest he* and the *fairest she;* whence *he* and *she* are also compounded with substantives, especially to convey a contemptuous or ridiculous sense, as " Howl, you *he* monks and you *she* monks."— DRANT'S *Sermons.*

Cp. he-devil   she-devil.

He and *she* were not thus used in the oldest English; it is an idiom "common to the Scandinavian and the English, which in awkwardness surpasses anything to be met with in any other speech."—MARSH. We find this idiom as early as the beginning of the fourteenth century, the earliest expressions being *he-beast* and *she-beast.*

(4) *Dog* and *bitch,* as *dog-fox, bitch-fox,* &c.
(5) *Buck* and *doe,* as *buck-rabbit, doe-rabbit,* &c.
(6) *Boar* and *sow,* as *boar-pig, sow-pig.*
(7) *Ewe* in *ewe-lamb* (Gen. xxi. 18).
(8) *Colt* and *filly,* as *colt-foal, filly-foal.*

---

[1] "The *he* hathe two pynnes . . . 'and the *she* hathe none."—LAURENCE ANDREWE, *Babys Book,* p. 231.

(9) *Cock* and *hen*, as *cock-sparrow*, *hen-sparrow*.

"Take hede of those egges that be blont on bothe endes, and thei shal be *henne chekens*, and those that be longe and sharpe on bothe endes shal be *cocke chekens*."—L. ANDREWE, *Babys Book*, p. 222.

In names of animals the class-name is frequently treated as neuter, as "In *its* natural state the hedgehog is nocturnal."
So also names of children, as, *child*, *boy*, &c.

II. NUMBER.

75. Some languages, as Sanskrit, Greek, &c., have three numbers, *singular* (marking one object), *plural* (more than one), *dual* (two).
The oldest English had the *dual* number only in the personal pronouns, which we no longer preserve.

76. In the oldest English there were several plural endings, *-as*, *-an*, *-u*, *-a*, *-o*. After the Norman Conquest these were reduced (1) to *-es*, *-en*, *-e;* (2) to *-es*, *-en;* and finally the suffix *-es* or *-s* became the ordinary plural ending.

Thus **-as** was originally only the plural sign of one declension of masculine nouns, as, *fisc*, fish, pl. *fiscas*.

When **-as** became **-es**, it still remained for the most part a distinct syllable, as in the following passage in Chaucer:—

> "And with his *stremēs* dryeth in the *grevēs*
> The silver *dropēs* hongyng on the *leevēs*."

Spenser has several instances.

> "In wine and oyle they wash his *woundēs* wide."—*F. Q.* i. 5. 17.

Hawes has many instances of the fuller form *-es*, as—

"The *knightēs* all unto their *armēs* went."—*Pastime of Pleasure*, p. 131.

77. Though we have only one plural ending, we make a very vigorous use of it. We have replaced foreign plurals by it, as *insects*, *indexes*, *choruses*, *ethics*, &c. We add it to adjectives used as substantives, as *goods*, *evils*, *blacks*, *sweets*, *vitals*, *commons*,[1] &c.; to verbal nouns, as *cuttings*, *scrapings*, &c.; and to pronouns, as *others*, *noughts*.

---

[1] There is an inconvenience attached to these plurals, *i.e.* they have more than one meaning: thus, *blacks* is used for *black eyes* (TREVISA), *black draperies* (BACON), *sooty particles*, and *black-a-moors*, *i.e.* black Moors; there were also white Moors. Cp. *familiars* = familiar friends and familiar spirits.
While we can talk of our *betters*, our *superiors*, we cannot, like Heywood, speak of our *olders* and *biggers*, nor complain, with the author of "The Booke of Nurture," of not knowing our "*breefes* from *longes*" = short and long vowels. Cp. "my *worthies* and my *valiants*."—DRANT.

78. The reduction of -es to -s causes the suffix to come into direct contact with the last letter of the substantive to which it is added, and by which it is affected.

(*a*) If the substantive ends in a flat mute, a liquid, or a vowel, *s* is pronounced flat, as *tubs, lads, stags, hills, hens, feathers, trees, days, folios*.

(*b*) If the substantive ends in a sharp mute, *s* takes the sharp sound, as *traps, pits, stacks*.

(*c*) The fuller form *-es* is retained when the substantive ends in a sibilant or palatal sound, such as *ss, sh, x, ch;* as *glasses, wishes, foxes, churches, ages, judges*.

(*d*) Words of pure English origin ending in *-f, -fe, -lf,* with a preceding long vowel (except *oo*) retain the older spelling, but only sound the *s*, as *leaf, leaves; thief, thieves; wife, wives; shelf, shelves; wolf, wolves*.

In *roof, hoof, reef, fife, strife*, the *f* is retained and *s* only added. We sometimes find *elfs, shelfs,* instead of *elves, shelves*.

(*e*) In Romance words *f* remains unchanged, and the plural is formed by *s*, as *briefs, chiefs, griefs*.

Exceptions.—In O. E. we find *prooves, kerchieves, beeves*.

(*f*) Words ending in *-ff, -rf,* form the plural by the addition of *s*, and the *f* is left unchanged, as *cliff, cliffs; dwarf, dwarfs*.

We sometimes find *staves, wharves, dwarves, scarves, mastives,* written for *staffs, dwarfs, wharfs, scarfs, mastiffs;* and in old writers, *cleeves, turves,* for *cliffs, turfs;* also *helves* = handles. In Rastall's Chronicles, 1529, we find *torves* pl. of *turf*.

(*g*) Words terminating in a single *y* keep the old orthography, and *y* is changed into *i*, as *fly, flies; city, cities*.

In Old English the singular ended in *-ie*, as *flie, citie*.

Y remains unchanged if it is diphthongal or preceded by another vowel, and *s* only is added, as *boy, boys; play, plays; valley, valley's*.

We sometimes find *vallies, monies, monkies, pullies,* &c. *Alkaii* has for its plural *alkalies*.

(*h*) Words in *-o* (not those in *-io*), mostly of foreign origin, form the plural in *-es* (sounded as *z*), as *echoes, heroes, potatoes*.

Words in *-io* add *s*, as *folios, seraglios*.

A few of later origin in *-o* and *-oo* add *s*, as *dominos, grottos, tyros, cuckoos, Hindoos*.

(*i*) Particles used as substantives take -*s* or -*es* for their plural, as *ups* and *downs;* *ayes* and *noes* (or *aye's* and *no's*); the *O's* and *Macs;* *pros* and *cons;* *et-ceteras.*

(*j*) In compounds the plural is formed by *s*, as *blackbirds*, *paymasters.*

When the adjective (after the French method) is the last part of the compound, the sign of the plural is added to the substantive, as *attorneys-general*, *courts-martial*. So in prepositional compounds, as *sons-in-law*, *fathers-in-law*, *lookers-on*, *men-of-war.*

(*k*) When *full* is compounded with a noun, *s* is added to the last element, as *handfuls*, *cupfuls;* but not if the terms are kept distinct, as "*two handfuls of marbles;*" "we have our *hands* full of work."

In Old English such forms as *handful*, *shipful* were mostly regarded as adjective compounds, and did not take the plural sign.

79. Plural formed by vowel-change—

foot,	O.E.	*fôt;*	plural	feet,	O.E.	*fét.*
tooth,	O.E.	*tôth;*	plural	teeth,	O.E.	*téth.*
mouse,	O.E.	*mûs;*	plural	mice,	O.E.	*mûs.*
louse,	O.E.	*lûs;*	plural	lice,	O.E.	*lŷs.*
goose,	O.E.	*gôs;*	plural	geese,	O.E.	*gês.*
man,	O.E.	*man;*	plural	men,	O.E.	*men.*

All these words once had a plural ending. The vowel of the plural suffix, though lost, has left its influence in the change of the root-vowel, which, philologically speaking, is no inflection; cp. O.Sax. *fôti* = feet, *bôci* = O.E. *béc* = books.

See remarks on Vowel-change, p. 58, § 47.

80. Plurals in -en (O.E. -an).

(1) There were a larger number of these words in the oldest English which formed the plural in -*an*, only *one* is now in common use, **oxen** = O.E. *ox-an.*

Shoon, O.E. *scon*, and *hosen*, O.E. *hosan*, are more or less obsolete.

Spenser frequently uses *eyen* = O.E. *eagan*, Provincial English *een;* and *foen* = O.E. *fan, fon*, foes.

(2) Some words that now form their plural in *n* originally ended in a vowel, and have therefore conformed to plurals in *n*.

Kine.—The *e* is no part of the plural, as we find in O.E. *kin* and *ken*. Cow originally made its plural by vowel-change, O.E. *cu*, a cow, plural *cy*. Cp. O.E. *mus* (mouse), *mis* (mice).

In O.E. we find *ky, kye, kine*, still preserved in the North of England.

Child-r-e-n.—In the oldest English *child* (*cild*) formed its plural by strengthening the base by means of the letter *r*, and adding *u*, as *cild-r-u*.

In the twelfth and thirteenth centuries we find *cild-r-u* converted into (1) *child-r-e* and (2) *child-r-e-n*.

In the fourteenth century we find in the Northern dialects *childer* = children, where the *-re* has become *-er* (cp. O.E. *alra* = (1) *alre*, (2) *aller*, (3) *alder*).

In O.E. of the thirteenth and fourteenth centuries we find *calvren, lambren*, and *eyren* (eggs).

O.E. *cealf* (calf) had for its plural—(1) *cealf-r-u*; (2) *cal-v-r-e*; (3) *calveren*; (4) *calves*.
O.E. *lamb*, pl. (1) *lamb-r-u*; (2) *lamb-r-e*; (3) *lambr-e-n*; (4) *lambs*.
O.E. *æg* (egg), pl. (1) *æg-r-u*; (2) *ey-r-e*; (3) *ey-r-e-n*.

Brethren.—In the oldest English the plural of *brother* was *brothru* (*brothra*). In the thirteenth century this became (1) *brothr-e*, (2) *brothr-e-n* (*brotheren*), (3) *brethr-e*, (4) *brethr-e-n*, (5) *brotheres* (*brothers*).

In the Northern dialects in the fourteenth century we find *brethre* becoming *brether*.[1]

The *e* in *brethren* seems to have arisen from the dative singular (*brether*).
In the thirteenth and fourteenth centuries, we find that the oldest English *dohtru* became *dohtren, doughtren, dehtren*, and *dehter*.
Sister and *mother* once belonged to the same declension.
TREEN = O.E. *treow-u* is used by Sackville ("Induction")[2]:—
"The wrathful Winter, 'proaching on apace,
With blustering blasts had all ybar'd the *treen*."

81. Some words, originally neuter and flexionless in the plural, have the same form for the singular and the plural.

1. Deer = O.E. *deor*, pl. *deor*.
2. Sheep = O.E. *sceâp*, pl. *sceâp*.
3. Swine = O.E. *swin*, pl. *swin*.
4. Neat = O.E. *neât* (used collectively to include *steer, heifer, calf*).[3]

This class once included the following words :—*folk, year, yoke, head, score, pound, hair, horse*,[4] &c.

---

[1] "These be my mother, *brether*, and sisters."—Bp. PILKINGTON (died 1575).
[2] *Sistren* occurs in the "Fardell of Facion" (1555).
[3] In O.E. *goat* is treated as a plural :—"Jabel departed the flokkis of *scheep* from the flokkis of *goot*."—CAPGRAVE, p. 8. Also *worm* :—"All kindes of beastes, fowle, and *wormes*."—*Fardell of Facion*.
[4] "Tame and well-ordered *horse*, but wild and unfortunate children."—ASCHAM.

82. Many substantives are treated as plurals and take no plural sign, as—

(1) Words used in a collective sense: *cavalry, infantry, harlotry, fish, fowl, cattle, poultry, fruit.*

Capgrave uses *gander* as a plural. In the "Fardell of Facion" we read that "*quail* and *mallard* are not but for the richer sort."

(2) Names expressive of quantity, mass, weight, as: *pair, brace, couple, dozen, score, gross, quire, ream, stone, tun, last, foot, fathom, mile, chaldron, bushel.*

Also *cannon, shot, shilling, mark; rod,* and *furlong* (*Fardell of Facion*).

In the phrase **horse and foot** we have either a contraction of (*a*) *horsemen* and *footmen,* or of (*b*) *men on horse* (O.E. *men an horse*) and *men on foot* (O.E. *men a foot*).

83. Some substantives have a double plural form, with different meanings, as—

Brothers (by blood), *brethren* [1] (of an order or community).

Cloths (sorts of cloth); *clothes* (garments, clothing).

Dies (a stamp for coining, &c.); *dice* (for gaming).

Peas (the pl. of pea); *pease* (collective). *Pea,* O.E *pisa,* is derived from Lat. *pisum*. In O.E. we find pl. *pesen* (and *peses*). The *s* belongs to the *root*, and is no inflexion. When the old pl. ending was lost, *pease* was looked upon as a plural, and a new singular, *pea*, was coined.[2]

Pennies (a number of separate coins); *pence* (collective). *Penny,* O.E. *penig,* pl. *penegas* (*pennyes, pans, pens*), without any distinction of meaning. When *pence* is compounded with a numeral as the name of a separate coin, we can regard it as a singular, and make it take the plural inflexion, as *two sixpences.*

84. Foreign words usually take the English plural. Some few keep their original plural, as—

	Sing.	Plural.
Latin (1)	*arcanum*	*arcana.*
	addendum	*addenda.*
	datum	*data.*
	erratum	*errata.*
	stratum	*strata.*
	magus	*magi.*

---

[1] This distinction is, of course, comparatively recent.

[2] Spenser has—

     " Not worth a *pese.*"

Surrey—
         " a *pese*
    Above a pearl in price."
   " Not worth two *peason*" = *peasen.*

	Sing.	Plural.
	radius	*radii.*
	minutia	*minutiæ.*
	species	*species.*
	&c.	&c.
Greek (2)	*axis*	*axes.*
	basis	*bases.*
	ellipsis	*ellipses.*
	&c.	&c.
Romance (3)	*monsieur*	*messieurs.*
	bandit	*banditti.*
	&c.	&c.
Hebrew (4)	*cherub*	*cherubim.*
	seraph	*seraphim.*

Some of these have the English plural, as—*appendixes, calixes, vortexes, criterions, automatons, phenomenons, memorandums, spectrums, focuses, funguses, similes, beaus, seraphs, cherubs,* as well as their original plurals, *appendices, calices, vortices, criteria, automata, phenomena, memoranda, spectra, foci, fungi, similia, beaux, seraphim, cherubim* (and *seraphin, cherubin*[1]).

85. Some have two plurals with different meanings, as—

indexes (of a book)   *indices* (signs in algebra).
geniuses (men of genius)   *genii* (spirits, supernatural beings).
parts (abilities)   *parts* (divisions).

86. Many substantives are used only in the plural, as—

(1) Substantives denoting things that consist of more than one part, and consequently always express plurality, as—

(*a*) Parts of the body: *lights, lungs, veins, kidneys, whiskers, chitterlings, intestines, bowels.*

(*b*) Clothing: *breeches, slops, trowsers, drawers, mittens, garters.*

(*c*) Tools, instruments, implements, &c; *shears, scissors, pliers, snuffers, tongs, scales,* &c. (Shakespeare uses *ballance* as a plural.) "A peyre of *ballaunce.*"—DRANT.

(2) Names of things considered in the mass or aggregate, as—*ashes, embers, cinders, lees, molasses.*

87. Many foreign words are used only in the plural, as *aborigines, fæces, literati, prolegomena,* &c.

---

[1] *Cherubims* and *seraphims* occur in Elizabethan English.

88. The English plural sign sometimes replaces the original plural, as *nomads, pleiads, hyads, rhinoceroses.*

Of a similar kind are—

    abstergents (= *abstergentia*).
    analects   (= *analecta*).
    arms   (= *arma*).
    annals   (= *annales*), &c.

89. The plurals of some substantives differ in meaning from the singulars, as *antic, antics; beef, beeves; chap, chaps; draught, draughts; checker, checkers; forfeit, forfeits; record, records; scale, scales; spectacle, spectacles; grain, grains; ground, grounds; water, waters; copper, coppers; iron, irons; compass, compasses; return, returns;* &c. &c.

So too verbal substantives, as *cutting* and *cuttings; sweeping* and *sweepings,* &c.

90. Many *adjectives* used as substantives form their plural regularly, as *good, goods; captive, captives; lunatic, lunatics;* cp. *commons, eatables, betters, superiors, odds, extras.*

To this class, with English plural substituted for foreign adjective plural, belong *acoustics, analytics, ethics, optics, politics.*

91. Some plural forms are sometimes treated as singulars, as *amends,*[1] *bellows,*[2] *gallows,*[3] *means,*[4] *news,*[5] *odds,*[6] *pains,*[7] *sessions, shambles, small-pox,*[8] *tidings,*[9] *wages.*

Most of these are comparatively late plurals, and the singular was once used where we employ the plural.

92. **Alms, eaves, riches,** though treated as plurals, are singular in form.

Alms = Gr. ἐλεημοσύνη; O.E. *ælmesse, álmesse, almes.* In O.E. we find pl. *elmessen, almesses.*[10]

---

[1] *Amends* from Fr. *amende.* Robert of Brunne has "*the amends was.*"
[2] O.E. "a gret *belygh;*" "a peyre *belyes.*"—*Pilgrimage,* pp. 111, 116.
[3] O.E. pl. = *galgan.*
[4] *Means* (Fr. *moyen,* Lat. *medium*).
[5] *News* (Fr. *nouvelles,* Lat. *nova*).
[6] *Odds* in *it is odds* = it is most probable.
[7] *Pain.* There is some confusion with the double origin of the word—(1) from O.E. *pin,* pain, torment; (2) from Lat. *pœna.*
   In the singular *pain* = suffering; in the plural = sufferings, trouble.
[8] -*Pox* = -poc-s; as in *chicken-pock, pock-mark.*
[9] *Tidings.* O.E. *tidende.* The plural is rare in O.E.
[10] Cp. "he asked *an alms.*" (Acts iii. 3.) "All a common *riches.*"—JOHN FLETCHER, *Wit without Money.*

Riches = O.Fr. *richesce;* O.E. *richeise, richesse.* In O.E. we find pl. *richesses. Alms* and *riches* are etymologically no more plurals than are *largess* and *noblesse.*

Eaves = O.E. *yfes, efese* = margin, edge.

We sometimes find *esen*-droppers = eaves-droppers; *esen* = O.E. *efesen*, eaves.

93. **Summons** is a singular form (= O.Fr. *semonse;* O.E. *somons*), and is usually treated as such, making the pl. *summonses.*

94. Proper names form the plural regularly.

(*a*) A few originally adjectives take no plural sign, as *Dutch, English, Scotch.*

(*b*) Many geographical names are frequently plural in form, as *Athens, Thebes, the Netherlands, Indies, Azores, Alps.*

(*c*) In names of persons, when a descriptive term is added, only the last adds *s* for the plural, as *master bakers, brother squires,* the *two doctor Johns.*

We, however, may say the *Miss Browns* or the *Misses Brown.*

Where two titles are united the last now usually takes the plural, as *major-generals :* a few old expressions sometimes occur in which both words, following the French idiom, take the plural, as *knights-templars, lords-lieutenants, lords-justices.*

III. CASE.

95. In some languages nouns (substantives and adjectives) take different forms (cases) in different relations in a sentence.

The moveable or variable terminations of a noun are called its *case-endings.*

"At Athens, the term *case,* or *ptōsis*, had a philosophical meaning : at Rome, *casus* was merely a literal translation : the original meaning of *fall* was lost, and the word dwindled down to a mere technical term. In the philosophical language of the Stoics, *ptōsis*, which the Romans translated by *casus*, really meant 'fall' ; that is, to say, the inclination or relation of one idea to another, the falling or resting of one word on another. Long and angry discussions were carried on as to whether the name of *ptōsis*, or fall, was applicable to the nominative ; and every true Stoic would have scouted the expression of *casus rectus,* because the subject, or the nominative, as they argued, did not fall or rest on anything else, but stood erect, the other words of a sentence leaning or depending on it. All this is lost to us when we speak of cases."—MAX MÜLLER.

96. The oldest English had six cases : Nominative, Vocative, Accusative, Genitive, Dative, Instrumental.

In the Aryan languages the case-endings are attenuated words—of all of which the origin is very obscure.

CASE.

The nominative ending *s* (as in *rex* = *reg-s*) is connected with the demonstrative pronouns, O.E. *se, seo, thæt*; Gr. ὁ, ἡ, τό; Sansk. *sa, sâ, tat*; Eng. *the*.

The dative suffix was originally a preposition, signifying *to* or *for*: cp. the pronouns—Lat. *tibi* with Sansk. *tu-bhyam*; Sansk. *abbhi*, Gr. ἀμφί, O.E. *umbe* and *be*, which we see again in the plural of Latin nouns of the third, fourth, and fifth declensions. In Sansk. this *abhi* was shortened to *ai* (*e*), and is still more disguised in Latin and Greek.

The ablative termination was *t* or *d*, as Sansk. *acvāt* = O. Lat. *equod*, from a horse; this *t* or *d* is probably connected with the demonstrative *ta*: cp. Lat. *in-de*, *unde*.

The locative had the ending *i*, denoting the relation expressed by our preposition *in*, to which it is related.

The instrumental, expressing the relation by or with, ended in *a*.

The accusative had the letter *m* for its suffix.

The genitive ended in *s* or *sya*, which is supposed to be a *demonstrative pronoun* (cp. Sansk. *syas, syâ, tyat*, this, that). In the possessive pronouns, Sansk. we find *tyas, tyâ, tyam*, as *madiyas, madiyâ, madīyam* = *meus, mea, meum*. It is therefore probable that the genitive ending was nothing more than an adjective termination.

In Sansk. adjectives are formed by the suffix -*tya* (= *sya*).

In Greek the form cognate with *tya* was σιο-ς. From δῆμος, people, came the adjective δημόσιος (belonging to the people). In Greek, an σ between two vowels of grammatical terminations is elided: thus the genitive of γένος is not γένεσος, but γένεος or γένους; hence δεμόσιο would become δεμοῖο, the Homeric genitive of δῆμος, in later Greek replaced by δήμου.—MAX MÜLLER.

We have something like it in English. Compare the force of the suffix *n* in *wooden* with that of *n* in *mine, thine*.

"The Latin *genitivus* (genitive) is a mere blunder, for the Greek word *genikē* could never mean *genitivus*. *Genitivus*, if it is meant to express the case of origin or birth, would in Greek have been called *gennētikē*, not *genikē*. Nor does the *genitive* express the relation of son to father. For though we may say 'the son of the father,' we may likewise say, 'the father of the son.' *Genikē*, in Greek, had a much wider, a much more philosophical meaning. It meant *casus generalis*, the general case, or rather the case which expresses the genus or kind. This is the real power of the *genitive*. . . . The termination of the genitive is, in most cases, identical with those derivative suffixes by which substantives are changed into adjectives."—MAX MÜLLER.

POSSESSIVE CASE.

97. In modern English we have no case-endings of substantives except *one*, the possessive, the representative of the older genitive.

The nominative and accusative have no formative particles to distinguish them, and their position in a sentence, or the sense, is the only means we have of distinguishing them from one another.

98. In the oldest English there were various declensions, as in Latin and Greek: so there were different genitive suffixes (*a*) for the singular, (*b*) for the plural.

The suffix -*es* originally belonged to the genitive sing. of some masculine and neuter substantives; it was not the genitive sign of the feminine until the thirteenth century, and then for the most part only in the Northern dialect (cp. *Lady-day* with *Lord's day*).

Late in the fourteenth century we find traces of the old plural ending *-ene*, *-en* (*-ena*), as *kingen-en* = *of kings*. (*Piers Plowman*.)

Probably before the thirteenth century *-es* began to take its place:—"Alre *louerdes* louerd, and alre *kingene* king."—*O.E. Hom.*, Second Series.

99. The suffix **-es** was a distinct syllable in Old English, as—

"Ful worthy was he in his *lordēs* werre."—CHAUCER.

Traces of this form we have in Elizabethan writers :—

"Then looking upward to the heaven's beams,
With *nightēs* stars thick powder'd everywhere."
SACKVILLE'S *Induction*.

"Of *aspēs* sting herself did stoutly kill."—SPENSER, *F. Q.* i. 5, 50.

"To show his teeth as white as *whalēs* bone."
SHAKESPEARE'S *Love's Labour's Lost*, v. 2.

100. The sign of the possessive is now **-s** for both numbers; and it is subject to the same euphonic modifications as the sign of the plural (see § 78).

The loss of the final vowel is indicated by the apostrophe ('), as *boy's*, &c.[1]

When a word in the singular of more than two syllables ends in *s*, *x*, *ge*, **s** is omitted but (') retained, as—*Lycurgus'* sons, *Socrates'* wife.

In poetry this frequently happens with respect to words of more than one syllable, especially if the following word begins with a sibilant, as—

The *Cyclops'* hammer; young *Paris'* face; your *highness'* love; for *justice* sake; for *praise* sake; the *Phœnix'* throne; a *partridge'* wing (Shakespeare); *princess'* favourite (Congreve); the Prior of *Jorvaulx'* question (W. Scott).

In O.E., fifteenth century, if the noun ended in a sibilant or was followed by a word beginning with a sibilant, the possessive sign was dropt, as a *goose* egg, the *river* side.

101. In compounds the suffix is attached to the last element, as —the *son-in-law's* house; the *heir-at-law's* will; the *Queen of England's* reign; *Henry the First's* reign.

---

[1] (') was at first probably used to distinguish the genitive from the plural suffix. Its use may have been established from a false theory of the origin of the genitive case, which was thoroughly believed in from Ben Jonson's to Addison's time—that *s* was a contraction of *his;* hence such expressions as "the *prince his* house," for "the *prince's* house."

Sometimes we find *s* added to the principal substantive instead of to the attributive or appositional word, as "It is *Othello's* pleasure, our noble and valiant general."—SHAKS. "For the *Queen's* sake, his sister."—BYRON. In O.E. this was the ordinary construction, as late as the sixteenth century. "Stephen concluded a marriage atween Eustace his sone and Constaunce the *kynges* sister of Fraunce" [= the king of France's sister].—FABYAN.

THE CASE ABSOLUTE.

102. In the oldest English the *dative* was the absolute case, just as the ablative is in Latin. About the middle of the fourteenth century the *nominative* began to replace it. Milton has a few instances of this construction (in imitation of the Latin idiom), as "*me* overthrown," "*us* dispossessed," "*him* destroyed."

"Schal no flesch upon folde by fonden onlyue,
 Out-taken yow aȝt (eight)."—*Allit. Poems*, p. 47, l. 357.

"Thei han stolen him *us slepinge*."—WICKLIFFE, *Matt.* xxviii. 21.

"*Hym* thâ gyt *sprecendum*, hig cômon fram tham heah-gesamnungum."
 Mark v. ?

"*Thinre dura belocenre*, bide thine fæder."—*Matt.* iv. 13.

CHAPTER XI.

ADJECTIVES.

103. IN modern English the adjective has lost the inflexions of *number*, *gender*, or *case* belonging to the older stages of the language.

104. In Chaucer's time, and even later, we find (*a*) an inflexional *e* to mark the plural number; (*b*) an inflexional *e* for the definite adjective—that is, when preceded by a demonstrative pronoun or a possessive pronoun, as—

> " Whan Zephirus eek with his *sweetē* breethe
> Enspired hath in every holte and heethe
> The tendrē croppes, and the *yongē* sonne
> Hath in the Ram his *halfē* cours ironne,
> And *smalē* fowles maken melodie."
> CHAUCER'S *Prol. to C. Tales.*

This *e* in the oblique cases of the definite form, in the oldest English, became *an*, of which, perhaps, we have a trace in the phrase "in the *olden* time."
We often replace an inflexional *e* or *n* by the word *one*. Cp.
"And the children ham lovie togidere and bevly the velaʒrede of the *greaten*."—*Aʒenbite*, p. 739.
" The vissere hath more blisse vor to nime ane *gratne* visse thane *ane littlene*."—*Ib.* p. 238.
" These *tweyne olde*" (= these two *old ones*).—*Pilgrimage*, p. 111.
" I sigh toward the tour an *old oon*[1] that come and neihede me."—*Ib.* p. 23.
" I sigh *an old oon* that was clumben anhy up on thy bed."—*Ib.* 205.

105. Chaucer has instances of the Norman-French plural *s* in such phrases as *cosins germains*, in other *places delitables*.

In C.E. the adjective of Romance origin frequently took a plural termination (*-es*, *-s*) when placed after its substantive,[2] as—
" *Wateres principales*."—*Early Eng. Poems*, p. 43.
" *Vertues cardinals*."—*Castele of Love*, p. 37.
" *Chanouns reguleres*," "*causes resonables*," "*parties meridionales*."
MAUNDEVILLE.

---

[1] The writer of the *Pilgrimage* only uses the *oon* when the adjective is accusative.   [2] Stow has *heyres males* = male heirs.

106. It is also found without a following substantive, as—

"Of romances that been *reales*
Of popes and cardinales."—CHAUCER'S *Sir Thopas*.

"He ous tekth to knawe the greate things vram the little, the *preciouses* vram the *viles*, the zuete vram the zoure."—*A3enbite*, p. 76.

In this last example the unborrowed adjectives *greate, little*, &c., express the plural by the final *e*.

Sometimes the plural *s* replaces the final *e* when the adjective is used substantively, as—

"They love their *yonges* very well."—LAWRENCE ANDREWE.

Ones sometimes replaces the plural sign, as "If it fortuned one of the *yonges* to dye than these *olde ones* wyll burye them."—*Ib*.

Cp. *wantons, empties, calms, shallows, worthies, orderlies, godlies*.

107. Shakespeare has preserved one remnant of the older case-endings of the plural adjective in the compound *alderliefest* = the dearest of all, the most precious of all. (2 *K. Hen. VI*. i. 1.)

Alder (sometimes written *alther*) is another form of *aller* = al-re = al-ra (= *omnium*), the genitive plural of *all*.

In Old English writers of the fourteenth and fifteenth centuries, we find *bath-er*, of both, for which we sometimes find *bothes*, as "your *bothes* paynes."—*Pilgrimage*, p. 167.

I. COMPARISON OF ADJECTIVES.

108. Comparison is a variation or change of form to denote degrees of quantity or quality. It belongs to adverbs as well as adjectives.

"The suffixes of comparison were once less definite in meaning than at present, and were used to form many numerals, pronouns, adverbs, prepositions, in which compared correlative terms are implied."—MARCH.

109. There are three degrees of comparison: the positive, *high;* the comparative, *higher;* the superlative, *highest*.

The comparative is formed by adding *-er* to the positive; the superlative by adding *-est* to the positive.

This rule applies to (1) all monosyllabic adjectives; (2) all dissyllabic adjectives with the accent upon the last syllable, as—*genteel', genteeler, genteelest;* (3) adjectives of two syllables, in which the last syllable is elided before the comparative, as—*able, abler, ablest;* (4) adjectives of two syllables ending in *y*, which is changed to *i* before the suffixes of comparison, as—*happy, happier, happiest*.

Orthographical changes:—

(1) A final consonant preceded by a short accented vowel is doubled, as *wet, wetter, wettest; red, redder, reddest; cruel, crueller, cruellest*.

(2) A single final *y* is changed to *i*, as *happy, happier, happiest;* but *y* with a preceding vowel remains unchanged, as *gay, gayer, gayest*.

(3) Adjectives ending in a silent or unaccented *e* add -*r* and -*st*, instead of -*er* and -*est*, to the positive, as *polite, politer, politest; noble, nobler, noblest.*

110. When the adjective has more than two syllables, the comparison is expressed by *more* and *most*, as—*eloquent, more eloquent, most eloquent.*

This mode of comparison is probably due to Norman-French influence, and it makes its appearance at the end of the thirteenth century, as "*mest gentyl*" (ROBERT OF GLOUCESTER), and becomes of frequent occurrence in Chaucer and Wickliffe, as *most mighty, most clear.*

In poetry we find even monosyllabic adjectives compared (for the sake of euphony) by *more* and *most*, as "Ingratitude *more strong* than traitors' arms" (SHAKESPEARE). "Upon a lowly asse *more white* than snow" (SPENSER).

Older writers on grammar make the mode of comparison depend on the ending, not the length of the adjective; if the adjectival ending is -*ing*, -*ish*, -*ed*, -*en*, -*ain*, -*al*, -*ent*, -*ive*, -*ous*, the comparison is made by *more* and *most*. The best writers, however, are not guided by this rule.

"Ascham writes *inventivest;* Bacon, *honourablest*, and *ancienter;* Fuller, *eminentest, eloquenter, learnedst, solemnest, famousest, virtuousest,* with the comparative and superlative adverbs, *wiselier, easilier, hardliest;* Sidney even uses *repiningest;* Coleridge, *safeliest.*"—MARSH.

111. Double Comparisons are not uncommon both in old and modern English, as *more hottere, most fairest* (Maundeville); *moost clennest* (Piers Plowman); *more kinder, more corrupter* (Shakespeare); *most straitest* (*Acts of Apostles*, xxvi. 5).

The comparison is sometimes strengthened by adverbs, as *still busier, far wiser,* the *lowest of the low*. So Chaucer has *fairest of faire* (*Knightes Tale*).

Adjectives with a superlative sense are not usually compared. In poetry, we find, however, *perfectest, chiefest* (Shakespeare), *extremest* (Milton), *more perfect* (Eng. Bible), *lonelier* (Longfellow).

112. The r of the comparative stands for a more original s, as seen in the allied languages of the Aryan speech.

	Sanskrit.	Greek.	Latin.	Gothic.	O.E.	Eng.
Comparative—	*máh-î-yas.*	μεῖ-ζον.	major. majus.	*ma-iz-a.*	*mâra.*	*more.*
Superlative—	*máh-ish-tha.*	μέγ-ιστον.	—	*ma-ist-s.*	*mæst.*	*most.*

The superlative was originally formed from the comparative by means of the suffix -t.

113. In numerals and pronominal words, &c. we find a relic of an old comparative, as in *other*, Lat. *al-teru-s;* Gr. ἕ-τερο-ς; Sansk. *án-tar-á; whether,* Lat. *u-teru-s;* Gr. κό-τερο-ς; Sansk. *ka-tará.* By Sanskrit grammarians the origin of -*ther*, -*teru*, -*tero*, -*tara* is said to be found in the Sanskrit root *tar* (cp. Lat. *trans*, Eng. *through*), to cross over, go beyond.

114. An old superlative ending common to many of the Aryan languages is *-ma*, as—Eng. *for-ma, fru-ma*; Lat. *pri-mu-s*; Gr. πρῶ-το(s); Sansk. *pra-tha-má*.

Ma is found in composition with *ta*, as in the numerals—Lat. *septimus*; Gr. ἔβ-δυ-μο(ς); Sansk. *sap-ta-ṃá*.

In Latin, *-ti-mu-s* (as in *septimus*) is added to the old comp. *is*, whence *-istimu-s*, and *-issimus* (by assimilation).

II. IRREGULAR COMPARISONS.

115. OLD, ELDER, ELDEST (O.E. *eald, ald; yldra, eldra; yldest, eldest*).

Elder and eldest are archaic, and can only be used with reference to living things.[1] As *than* cannot be used after *elder*, it is evident that its full comparative force is lost.

Older and oldest are the ordinary comparatives now in use.

The vowel change in *elder*, &c. is explained by the fact that there was originally an *i* before *r* and *st*, which affected the preceding *a* or *ea*, hence O.E. *eald* and *eldra, strang* and *strengra*, &c.

116. GOOD, BETTER, BEST (O.E. *gód; betera, betra; betest, betst*).

The comparative and superlative are from a root *bet* (or *bat*), good, found in O.E. *bet-lic*, goodly, excellent; *bet-an*, to make good, amend.

Best = *bet-st*, illustrates the law that a dental is assimilated to a following sibilant.

In O.E. we find a comparative adverb, *bet* (the sign of inflexion being lost).

117. Bad, Evil, Ill } worse, worst { O.E. *yfel; wyrsa, wyrs; wyrrest, wyrst*.

Wor-se, wor-st, are formed from a root, *weor*, which is cognate with Latin *vir-us*.

The *-se* is an older form of *-re* (*er*).

The Dan. *værre* (O.N. *verri*) found its way into English writers of the North of England. Gower uses it in the following lines:—

"Of thilke *werre* (war)
In whiche none wot who hath the *werre* (worse)."

Spenser uses it with reference to the etymology of the word *world*:

"The world is much *war* than it was woont."

Chaucer sometimes uses *badder* for *worse*.

---

[1] This distinction is recent: cp. the following from *Earle's Micro-cosmographie* (1628): "His very atyre is that which is the *eldest* out of fashion." (Ed. ARBER, p. 29.)

118. MUCH, MORE, MOST (O. E. *micel, mâra, mæst*).

Much is from O.E. *micel*, through the forms *michel, muchel.*

More is formed from the root *mag* (or *mah*[1]), so that *more* = *mahre* and *most* = *mah-st.*

In O.E. *micel* = great ; *mare, more* = greater ; *mast, mest, most* = greatest. A contracted form of *mare* (properly adverbial), *ma, mo,* is used by O.E. writers. It is found also in Shakespeare under the form *moe*
Alexander Gill makes *mo* the comparative of *many ; more* the comparative of *much.*

Many = O.E. *maneg,* Goth. *manegs,* contains the root *mang,* a nasalized form of *mag (mah).*

119. LITTLE, LESS, LEAST (O.E. *lytel ; læssa (læs) ; læsest, læst).*

les-s = O.E. *las-se, les-se = læs-sa = læs-ra.*
least = *les-st = læs-est.*

Lesser is a double comparative, as "the *lesser* light" (*Eng. Bible*), Shakespeare has *littlest (Hamlet,* iii. 2).

In O.E. we find *lyt* = little, which has nothing to do with the root of *less,* which is cognate with Goth. *lasivóza* (infirmior), the comp. of *lasiv-s* (infirmus); cp. *lazy.*
We also find in O.E. *min* and *mis* = O.N. *minni,* Goth. *minniza* = less, Lat. *min-or ;* Goth. *mins* = Lat. *minus.*

120. NEAR, NEARER, NEAREST (O.E. *neâh, nêh ; nŷra, neâr, nearra ; neâhst, nêhst.* Later forms of the thirteenth and fourteenth centuries were—*negh ; nerre (ner) ; next (neghest).*

By the Old English forms we see that *nigh, near, next,* are their proper representatives. Shakespeare uses *near*[2] as a comparative adverb.
Nea-r = neah-r ; next = negh-st or *neah-st.* (The guttural of course was once pronounced.)
High was once similarly compared—*heah (heh, hegh)* ; *hêhra, hêrra (herre)* ; *heâhst, hêhst (heghest, hext).*[3]

121. Near, for *negh* or *nigh,* first came into use in the phrase '*far and near,*' in which *near* is an adverb, and represents the oldest English *neorran* = near (adv.), analogous to *feorran* = *afar.*

---

[1] This root is found in Sansk. *mah* (= *magh*), to grow, become great ; also in O.E. *mæg-en* = *main.*

[2] "The *nere* to the Church the ferther from God."—HEYWOOD'S *Proverbs,* C.
"The *near* in blood the nearer bloody."—*Macbeth,* ii. 3.

[3] "When bale is *hekst* boote is *next.*"—HEYWOOD'S *Proverbs,* E. iii. back.
Hawes (*Past. of Pl.* p. 60) uses the old *ferre* :—
  "My mynde to her was so ententyfe
  That I folowed her into a temple *ferre,*
  Replete with joy, as bright as any sterre."

In this we see the positive is replaced by an *adverb*,[1] and not by the comparative adjective, as is usually supposed.

Nearer, nearest, are formed regularly from *near*.

122. FAR, FARTHER, FARTHEST (O.E. *feor, fyrra, fyrrest*. Later forms, *fer, ferre (ferrer), ferrest*).

Farther is for *far-er*;[2] the *th* seems to have crept in from false analogy with *further*. *Farthest = far-est. Further = O.E. furthor = ulterius*, the comparative of *furth = forth*. The superlative in O.E. was *forth-m-est*.

LATE, LATER, LATEST (O.E. *late, lator, latost*); late, latter, last (O.E. *læte-mest = last*).

Last = O.E. *latst:* cp. *best = betst*.[3]

Latter and *last* refer to order, as "The *latter* alternative;" "The *last* of the Romans."
Later and *latest* refer to time. This distinction is not always strictly observed by our poetical writers.

RATHER. The positive and superlative are obsolete.

Rathe was the positive, as "the *rathe* primrose" (Milton): here *rathe* means early.

Rather means sooner, and is now used where *liefer* was once employed.

The O.E. forms were *hræd* (ready), *hræthra, hrathost*.

123. Adjectives containing the superlative m.

The Old English *for-m-a* signifies *first*, the superlative of a root *fore*. *Fyrm-est = for-m-ost* also had the same meaning, but is a double superlative.

First (O.E. *fyrrest, fyrst*) is the regular superlative of *fore*.

Former is a comparative formed from the old superlative.

In O.E. we have *forme* and *foremeste* for first.
" Adam our *forme* fader."—CHAUCER.
" Adam oure *foremeste* fader."—MAUNDEVILLE.
Forme fader was afterwards changed to—(1) *forne fader*; (2) *formerfather*.

---

[1] The adverb seems to be comparative.
[2] By some, *further* is explained as *more to the fore*, as if it contained the comparative suffix *-ther*.
[3] In the "Ormulum" we have *late, lattre, lattst* = late, latter, last.

124. The suffix -most (O.E. *mest*), then, in such words as *utmost* is a double superlative ending, and not the word *most*. The analogies of the language clearly show that *most* was never suffixed to express the superlative.

after-m-ost   = O.E. *æfte-m-est, æfter-m est*.
further-m-ost = furthest   = O.E. *forth-m-est*.

  In O.E. we find *forther-m-ore* and *backer-m-ore*.

hindmost, hindermost   = O.E. *hindu-ma, hinde-ma*.

  Chaucer uses *hinderest*: cp. O.E. *innerest, overest, upperest, utterest*.

hither-m-ost is not found in the oldest English.

in-m-ost, inner-m-ost   = O.E. *inne-m-est, inne-ma*.
lower-m-ost, (nether-m-ost   = O.E. *nithe-m-a, nithe-m-est*).
mid-m-ost   = O.E. *mede-ma, mede-mest*.
out-m-ost, outer-m-ost }
ut-m-ost, utter-m-ost   }   = O.E. *ute-ma, ute-mest*.
up-m-ost, upper-m-ost, over-m-ost = O.E. *yfe-mest, ufe-meste*.

125. Over = upper (cp. *a-b-ove*) in O.E. writers:

   " Pare thy brede and kerve in two,
    The *over* crust tho *nether* fro."
          Boke of Curtasye, p. 300.

" With tho *ove-m-ast* [uppermost] lofe hit [the saltcellar] shalle be set."
               Ib. p. 322

126. In O.E. we find superlatives of south, east, west, as—

     suthemest, eastemest, and *westemest*.

Comp. endmost (O.E. *endemest*), topmost, headmost.

III. NUMERALS.[1]

127. NUMBERS may be considered under their divisions—Cardinal, Ordinal, and Indefinite Numerals.

---

[1] The origin of the numerals is involved in much obscurity.
One seems to have been another form of the pronoun *a*, he, that.
  In Gr. εἷς (= ἑνς) we have a form cognate with *some, same*; cp. Lat. *sim-plex, sim-ilis, semel, singuli*.
  Two. In Lat. this assumes the form *bi, vi* (prefixes), *bis*; Gr. δις (adverb).
  Three = that what goes beyond, from the root *tri (tar)*, to go beyond.
  Four. The original form is said to signify *and three*, i.e. 1 *and three*. Sansk. *chatur*, Lat. *quatuor; cha = qua* = and ; *tur = tuor* = three.
  Others explain *cha = ka =* one.   [*Five*

XI.] ADJECTIVES. 111

1. Cardinal.

128. One. O.E. *an;* Goth. *ains;* Gr. εἷς; Lat. *unus;* Sansk. *ê-ka*.

Out of the O.E. form *an* = one was developed the so-called indefinite article an ánd (by loss of *n*) a.

In O.E. we find *one* = *ana* = alone.

Two. O.E. *twa;* Goth. *tvai;* Gr. δύο; Lat. *duo;* Sansk. *dva;* O.Sax. *tuê*.

Twain = two, O.E. *twegen*.

We had another word for two in the Northern dialects, of Scandinavian origin, viz. *twin*, originally a distributive : cp. Goth. *tveihnai*, O.N. *tvennr*.
Thrin for three also occurs in O.E. Northern writers, O.N. *thrennr*.

Three. O.E. *thri, threo;* Goth. *threis;* Gr. τρεῖς; Lat. *tres;* Sansk. *tri*.

Four. O.E. *feower;* Goth. *fidvor;* Gr. τέτταρες, τέσσαρες; Lat. *quatuor;* Sansk. *katvar*.

This numeral has lost a letter, *th*, and there is an O.E. compound —*fether-foted, fither-foted* = quadruped—which *fether* is, of course, more original than *four*.

Five. O.E. *fîf;* Goth. *fimf;* Gr. πέντε; Lat. *quinque;* Sansk. *panchan*.

In *five* we see that a nasal has disappeared.

Six. O.E. *six;* Goth. *saíhs;* Gr. ἕξ; Lat. *sex;* Sansk. *shash*.

Seven. O.E. *seofon;* Goth. *sibun;* Gr. ἑπτά; Lat. *septem;* Sansk. *saptan*.

Eight. O.E. *eahta;* Goth. *ahtaú;* Gr. ὀκτώ; Lat. *octo;* Sansk. *ashtan*.

Nine. O.E. *nigon;* Goth. *niun;* O.Sax. *nigun;* Gr. ἐννέα; Lat. *novem;* Sansk. *navan*.

In the fourteenth century we find *neghen* for nine. The *gh* or *g* represents an original *v*.

Five = that which comes after [four].
The Sansk. *panchan* is connected with *pashcha* = coming after, as in *pashchât*, behind, after.
Six. Sansk. *shash* = Zend. *kshvas*, which is probably a compound of *two* and *four*.
Seven is connected with a root *sap*, to follow = that which follows [six].
Eight is originally a dual form. Sansk. *ashtân* = *a* + *cha* + *tan* = 1 + and + 3.
Nine = *new* = that which comes after eight and is the beginning of a new quaternion.
Ten = two and eight.

Ten. O.E. *týn, ten;* Goth. *taíhun;* Gr. δέκα; Lat. *decem;* Sansk. *dashan.*
The Gothic shows that *tyn* or *ten* = *tegen* or *týgen.*

Eleven. O.E. *end-lif (endleof);* Goth. *áin-lif;* Gr. ἕν-δεκα; Lat. *undecim;* Sansk. *êka-dasha.*
Eleven = *end* = *en* = one + *lev-en* = *lif* = ten.

Twelve. O.E. *twelf;* Goth. *twa-lif;* is a compound of *twa* = two + *lif* = ten.

The suffix *-lif* is another form of *tig* = ten, which we find in O.E. *twen-tig*, Goth. *tvai-tig-jus* = 2 × 10 = twenty. So that *-lif* corresponds to Gr. -δεκα; Lat. *-decim.* (In Lat. *l* and *d* are sometimes interchangeable, as *lacryma* and *dacryma.*) In such words as *laugh, enough, gh*, originally a guttural, has become *f.*
In Lithuanian we find *wieno-lika* = 11; *dwy-lika* = 12.
In the Fr. *onze, douze;* the Lat. *-decim* has undergone a greater change than *-tig* into *-lif.*
The Sansk. *dva-dasha* = 12 is represented in Hindûstânî by *bá-rah;* and *shô-dasha* = 16, by *sô-lah.*

129. The numbers from thirteen to nineteen are formed by adding *-teen* (O.E. *-tyne*) = ten, to the first nine numerals.

130. The numerals from twenty to ninety are formed by suffixing *-ty* (O.E. *tig*) = ten, to the first nine numerals.

131. **Hundred.** In the oldest English we find *hund* = hundred. In the Northumbrian dialect *hundrad, hundrath* occurs. *Hund* originally signified *ten* (cp. Lat. *centum,* Gr. ἑ-κατον, Sansk. *shata*); it is nothing else but a shortened form of *tegen, -tegen-d,* Goth. *taihun, taihun-d,* ten. The syllable *-red* = *-rœthr* is also a suffix used in Icelandic, with the same force as *-tig.*[1]

In the oldest English *hund* was added to the numerals from 70 to 100, as *hund-seofentig* = 70; Goth. *sibun-têhund;* Gr. ἑβδομή-κοντα; Lat *septua-ginta.*
It is probable that the original form was not *hund-seofentig,* but *hund-seofonta;* O. Sax. (*h*)*ant sibunta* (decade seventh).
Hundred could also be expressed by *hund-tentik (hund-teontig)*: cp. Goth. *taihun-têhund.*

132. **Thousand** = O.E. *thûsend;* Goth. *thûsendja;* Slavonic *tusantja;* Lithuanian *túk-stanti;* in which perhaps we have a combination of ten and hundred. The Sanskrit *sahasras,* 1,000 = a going together.

---

[1] Some suppose that *hund red* = *hund-are* (like *cent-uria*) with suffix *-d.* In O.E. of the fourteenth century we find *hunder* and *hundreth.* In O.N. *hundrath* = hundred: cp. *Áttrœtkr,* containing 80; *tírœtkr,* containing 100.

133. For expressing DISTRIBUTIVES (how many at a time) we employ—

(1) The preposition by, as *by ones, by twos, two by two.* So in O.E. *be anfealdum,* one by one; *be hundredes, be thousandes.* (Maundeville.)

(2) And, as *two and two.*

(3) With each and every, *two each, every four.*
There are also other expressions, as *two apiece, two at a time.*

134. MULTIPLICATIVES are expressed—

(1) By placing the cardinal before the greater number, as *eight hundred.*

(2) By adjectives, with suffix -fold, as *twofold,* &c.

(3) By Romance adjectives in -ple (ble), as *dou-ble, tre-ble, tri-ple,* &c.

(4) By the adverb once, as *once, twice.*

(5) By the word times; three *times* one are three.
In O.E. we used *sithe, sithes* = times; as *two sithes tpo* = 2 × 2.

135. Both. O.E. *begen* (m.), *bâ* (n.); Goth. *bai, ba*; Ger. *bei-de.*
In the thirteenth and fourteenth centuries we find *bey, ba, bo, boo* = both; gen. *beire (bother, botheres).*
Sometimes *ba* is joined to *twa* (two), as *bâtwâ, butwa, butu.*
Bo-th is a derivative of *bo* or *ba,* by means of the suffix *-th.* Cp. Goth. *baj-oths;* O.N. *bâthir.*
As we find *bathe* first in the Northern dialects, it is probably due to Scandinavian influence.
The O.E. *begen* softened to *beyne* occurs in the literature of the fourteenth century:—

"Well thou maiht, 3if thou wolt, taken ensaumple of *beyne,*
Bothe two in heor elde children heu beore."—*Vernon MS.*

2. Ordinals.

136. The ordinals, with the exception of *first* and *second,* are formed from the cardinal numbers, and were originally superlatives formed by the suffix *-ta* (*th*).

First. For the etymology of this word see § 123.

I

Second (Lat. *secundus* = following) has replaced the O.E. *other* (a comparative form).

In O.E. *other* (= on-ther = one of two) might signify the first or the second of two. It is sometimes joined with the neuter of the article, as *thæt other*, which in the fourteenth century was represented by *the tother* (= thet other); the first was sometimes expressed by *the ton* (*the toon*), *the tone* = thet one.

Third = O.E. *thridda, thridde; -de* (= *-dja*) is an adjective suffix = *tha*: cp. Lat. *ter-tiu-s*.

Fourth = O.E. *feor-tha*.

Fifth = O.E. *fíf-ta*.

Sixth = O.E. *six-ta*.

Seventh, Ninth, Tenth = O.E. *seofŏtha, nigŏtha, teotha*.

In thirteenth and fourteenth centuries these were—

sevethe, nethe, and *tethe* (in the Southern dialects).
sevende, neghende, tende (in the Northern dialects).
seventhe, ninthe, tenthe (in the Midland dialects).

The Midland forms are formed from the Northern ones, and made their appearance in the fourteenth century; and the latter are of Scandinavian origin.[1] In the Northumbrian Gospels we find *seofunda*.

Eighth stands for *eight-th*; O.E. *eaht-o-tha*.
In O.E. (thirteenth and fourteenth centuries) we find *aghtende*.

Eleventh[2] = O.E. *endlefta, ællefta* (*elleuende, endlefthe* in the thirteenth and fourteenth centuries).

Twelfth = O.E. *twelfta* (*twelfthe, twelft,* in the thirteenth and fourteenth centuries).

Thirteenth = O.E. *thretheŏtha* [*threttethe* and *threttende, thirtende,* thirteenth and fourteenth centuries].

So up to nineteen, the oldest English forms end in *-othe* (without *n*) as: fourteen, *feowerteotha;* fifteen, *fifteotha;* sixteen, *sixteotha;* seventeen, *seofonteotha;* eighteen, *eahtateotha;* nineteen, *nigonteotha*.

The corresponding forms in use in the thirteenth and fourteenth centuries were: fourteen, *fourtethe, fourtende, fourtenthe;* fifteen, *fyftethe, fiftende, fiftenthe;* sixteen, *sixtethe, sextende, sixtenthe,* &c.

Twentieth = O.E. *twentug-otha* (*twentithe*).

---

[1] Cp. O.N. 7 *siŏundi,* 9 *niundi,* 10 *tiundi,* 13 *threttandi,* 15 *fimtandi,* &c.
[2] For origin of *n* see remarks on Seventh.

IV. INDEFINITE ARTICLE.

137. The indefinite article, as we have seen, is a new development after the Conquest of the numeral *one* (*án*).
Before a word beginning with a consonant the *n* is dropped.
One + the negative *ne* give us none, O. E. *nán*.
None is only used predicatively or absolutely;[1] when used with a following substantive the *n* is dropped, whence *no*.

Before comparatives *no* is in the instrumental case, as "*no* better," &c. Cp. "*the better*," &c.

V. INDEFINITE NUMERALS.

138. **All** = O. E. *eall, eal* (see note on the old genitive plural, *aller, alder*, § 107).

139. **Many** = O. E. *manig, maneg*.[2]
In the thirteenth century we find for the first time the indefinite article used after it, as: *on moni are wisen* (Laȝamon), *mony enne thing* = *many a wise, many a thing*. Hawes has *many a fold*.

140. **Fela**, *feola, fele*, Ger. *viel* (many), were once in common use as late as the eighteenth century.

141. **Few** = O. E. *feáwa, feá*.
In O. E. we find *fa, fo*, and *fone* as well as *fewe, few*.

---

[1] By absolutely is meant without a following substantive.
[2] Many is also a noun, as in "a great *many*."
　　"A *many* of our bodies."—*Hen. V.* v. 3.
　　"O thou fond *many*."—2 *Hen. IV.* i. 3.
　　"The rank-scented *many*."
　　"In *many's* looks."—*Sonnets*, 93.
"A *meanye* of us were called together."—LATIMER'S *Sermons*.
"Than a gret *many* of old sparowes geder to-geder."—L. ANDREWE.
"And him fyligdon mycele *mænigeo* = and there followed him (a) great *many* (or multitude)."—*Matt.* iv. 25.

CHAPTER XII.

PRONOUNS.

142. ON the nature of the Pronoun see p. 80, § 62.

143. The classes of Pronouns are : (1) Personal Pronouns, (2) Demonstrative Pronouns, (3) Interrogative Pronouns, (4) Relative Pronouns, (5) Indefinite Pronouns.

I. Personal Pronouns.

(1) SUBSTANTIVE PRONOUNS.

144. The personal pronouns have no distinction of gender. There are two persons : the person who speaks, called the *first* person ; the person spoken to, the *second* person.

(*a*) *Inflexion of the Pronoun of the First Person.*[1]

			O. English.	
SING.	*Nom.*	I	*Ic*	*Ich** *Uch**
	Gen.	—	*min*	
	Dat.	me	*me*	
	Acc.	me	*mec*	*me*
PLURAL	*Nom.*	we	*we*	
	Gen.	—	*ûser*	*ure*
	Dat.	us	*ûs*	
	Acc.	us	*ûsic*	*us*

145. In I the guttural has disappeared ; it is radical and exists in the allied languages, as Sansk. *ah-am;* Gr. ἐγώ ; Lat. *ego;* Goth. *ik.*
By noticing the oblique cases we see there are two stems, *ah* (*ic*) and *ma,* of the first person.

146. In O.E. we find the pronoun agglutinated to a verb, as *Ichabbe = Ich + habbe* (I have) ; *Ichille = Ich + wille* (I will), &c.
In the provincial dialects of the South of England it still exists ; cp. *"chill"* in Shakespeare's *King Lear.*

---

[1] Those marked thus (*) are later forms.

147. Me (dative) is still in use (1) before impersonal verbs, *methinks* = it appears to me; *me seems, me lists;* (2) after interjections, as, *woe is me, well is him;* (3) to express the indirect object, *to me,* or *for me*.[1]

Me = for me. It is often a mere expletive in Elizabethan writers, and no doubt the original force of the pronoun was forgotten.

See the dialogue between Petruchio and his servant Grumio, in *Taming of Shrew*, i. 2 :—

"*Pet*. Villain, I say, knock *me* here soundly.

"*Gru*. Knock you here, sir? Why, sir, what am I, sir, that I should knock you here, sir?

"*Pet*. Villain, I say, knock *me* at this gate, and rap *me* well, or I'll knock your knave's pate.

"*Gru*. My master is grown quarrelsome. I should knock you first, and then I know after who comes by the worst. . . .

"*Hortensio*. How now, what's the matter?

"*Gru*. Look you, sir, — he bid me knock him, and rap him soundly, sir. Was it fit for a servant to use his master so?"

In O.E. we find the dative construed before the verb *to be* and an adjective, as: *me were leof* = it would be lief (preferable) *to me*. Traces of this idiom are to be found in Shakespeare, as: *Me had rather* (*Rich. II.* iii. 3) = O.E. *me were lefer* = *I had liever*.

Shakespeare has also: *you were best* = it were best *for you*.

The dative me has lost a suffix *r* (sign of dative): cp. Goth. *mi-s*, Ger. *mi-r*.

The acc. me = *mec*: cp. Goth. *mik;* Ger. *mich*.

148. We: Goth. *weis;* Ger. *wir;* Sansk. *vayam*, where *w*, like Sansk. *va*, represents an *m;* the suffix *-s* (*-r*) is a relic of an old demonstrative *sma* joined to the first pronoun: cp. Sansk. *asmê*. Gr. ἡ-μεῖς, so that (originally) we = *I* + *that* (or *he*).

149. Us (dat.): Goth. *unsis;* Ger. *uns*. The letter *n* disappears as usual before *s* in Old English.

U = an older *a* (= *ma*), as in Sanskrit *a-sma-byam:* *-s* (*ns*) represents the particle (*sma*), so that the case-ending has disappeared altogether.

Us (acc.): Goth. *u-nsi-s;* Ger. *uns;* Sansk. *a-smâ-n.* Us then = *muns* = *mans* = *masm*.

150. The O.E. had a dual number for the first and second persons, which went out of use towards the close of the thirteenth century.

---

[1] "He plucked *me* ope his doublet."—*Julius Cæsar*, i. 2.

151. *(b) The Pronoun of the Second Person.*

			Old English.	
SINGULAR.	*Nom.*	thou	*thu.*	
	Gen.	—	*thín.*	
	Dat.	thee	*the*	
	Acc.	thee	*thec,*	*the.*
PLURAL.	*Nom.*	ye, you	*ge*	—
	Gen.	—	*eower,*	*gure.* *
	Dat.	you	*eow,*	*guw.* *
	Acc.	you	*eowic,*	*eow, guw.*

152. **Thou:** Goth. *thu;* Gr. σύ, τύ; Lat. *tu;* Sansk. *tva-m.* The stem is *tva,* which is weakened to *tu* and *yu.*

153. The use of the plural for the singular was established as early as the beginning of the fourteenth century.

Thou, as in Shakespeare's time, was (1) the pronoun of affection towards friends, (2) good-humoured superiority to servants, and (3) contempt or anger to strangers. It had, however, already fallen somewhat into disuse; and, being regarded as archaic, was naturally adopted (4) in the higher poetic style and in the language of solemn prayer.—ABBOTT.

154. **Thee** (dat.): Goth. *thu-s;* Gr. σοί; Lat. *tibi;* Sansk. *tubhyam.* See remarks on *me* (dat.).

Thee (acc.): Goth. *thuk;* Ger. *dich;* Gr. τέ, σέ; Lat. *se;* Sansk. *tvâm.* See remarks on *me* (acc.).

155. **Ye:** Goth. *ju-t;* Gr. ὑμεῖς; Lat. *vos;* Sansk. *yusmê, yûyam.* The Sanskrit *yu-smê = tu + sma = thou* and *he.*[1] The dual *git* originally signified *thou + two = you two.*

The confusion between *ye* and *you* did not exist in Old English. *Ye* was always used as a nom., and *you* as a dat. or acc. In the English Bible the distinction is very carefully observed, but in the dramatists of the Elizabethan period there is a very loose use of the two forms. Not only is *you* used as nominative, but *ye* is used as an accusative.[2]

"Vain pomp and glory of the world, I hate *ye.*"—SHAKESPEARE.
"And I as one consent with *ye* in all."—SACKVILLE.

You (dat.): Goth. *izwi-s;* O. Sax. *iu;* Gr. ὑμῖν; Lat. *vo-bis;* Sansk. *yu-sma-bhyam* and *vas.*

You (acc.): Goth. *izwis;* O. Sax. *iu;* Gr. ὑμᾶς; Lat. *vos;* Sansk. *yusmân (vas).*

---

[1] That is, *sma* = he, that, this, &c.
[2] I am inclined to look upon the origin of *ye* for *you* in the rapid and careless pronunciation of the latter word, so that, after all, the *ye* in the above extracts should be written *y'* (= you); *ye* or *you* may be changed into *ee*: cp. *look ee* = *look ye.*

In English *you* has been developed out of the O.E. *eow*, which represents *yu = tu*, the stem of the second personal pronoun; the case suffix having wholly disappeared.

(c) *Demonstrative Pronoun of the Third Person.*

156. **He, She, It.** This pronoun is sometimes, but incorrectly, called a personal pronoun: it has distinction of gender, like other demonstrative pronouns in O.E., which the personal pronouns have not.¹

			Old English.
MASCULINE.	*Nom.*	he	*he.*
	Gen.	—	*his.*
	Dat.	him	*him.*
	Acc.	him	*hine, him.**
FEMININE.	*Nom.*	she	*heo, hi,* zi,* 3ho,* ho,* sco.**
	Gen.	—	*hire.*
	Dat.	her	*hire.*
	Acc.	her	*hi, heo.**
NEUTER.	*Nom.*	it	*hit.*
	Gen.	—	*his.*
	Dat.	it	*him.*
	Acc.	it	*hit.*

PLURAL.

Nom.	They	*hi, heo, hii,* þa,* þai,* þei.**
Gen.	—	*hira, heora, here, her, þar,* þair.**
Dat.	Them	*hem, heom, hem,* ham,* þam,* þaim.**
Acc.	Them	*hi, heo, hem,* þam,* þo.**

157. The Old English pronouns were formed from only one stem, *hi;* but the modern English contains the stems *hi, sa,* and *tha.*

He. For *he* we sometimes find in Old English *ha, a* (not confined always to one number or gender=*he, she, it, they*). It occurs in Shakespeare, as "'*a* must needs" (2 *Hen. VI.* iv. 2); *quoth 'a;* and is also common in other old writers, as—"has *a* eaten bull-beefe" (S. Rowlands); "see how *a* frownes" (Ib.).

Hi-m (dat.) contains a real dative suffix *m*, which is also found in the dative of adjectives and demonstrative pronouns.²

---

¹ The demonstrative character of this pronoun is seen in such expressions as, "What is *he* at the gate?" (Shakespeare); "*He* of the bottomless pit" (Milton, *Areopagitica*); "*hii* of Denemarch" (Robert of Gloucester); "*thai* of Lorne, *thai* of the Castel" (*Barbour*); "*they* in France" (Shakespeare); "*them* of Greece" (North's *Plutarch*). Those marked thus (*) are later forms.

² *Him* was also the dative of *it*, and we often find it applied to inanimate things in the later periods of the language.

Hi-m. (acc.). This was originally a dative form, which in the twelfth century (in *Laȝamon* and *Orm.*) began to replace the accusative.

Hi-ne.—The old accusative was sometimes shortened to *hin* and *in*, and still exists in the South of England under the form *en*, as—"Up I sprung, drow'd [threw] down my candle, and douted [put out] *en;* and hadn't a blunk [spark] o' fire to teen *en* again."—(*Devonshire Dialect.*)

158. **She**, in the twelfth century, in the Northern dialects, replaced the old form *heo*. The earliest instance of its use is found in the A.-Sax. Chronicle.[1] After all, it is only the substitution of one demonstrative for another, for she is the feminine of the definite article, which in O.E. was *seo* or *sia;* from the latter of these probably comes *she*.

In the Lancashire dialect the old feminine is still preserved under the form *ho*, pronounced something like *he* in *her*.

Her (dat.) contains a true dative (fem.) suffix, *-r* or *-re*.

Her (acc.) was originally dative, and, as in the case of *him*, has replaced an accusative; the old acc. was *hi, heo*.

159. **I-t** has lost an initial guttural.[2] The *t* is an old neuter suffix (cp. *tha-t*, *wha-t*) cognate with *d* in Latin—*illu-d, istu-d, quo-d, qui-d*. It is often a kind of indeterminate pronoun in O.E.; *it* was a man = there was a man; *it arn* = *there are*.

It (dat.) has replaced the true form him.
For the history of the word his see *Adjective Pronouns*.

160. **They.**—In the thirteenth century this form came into use in the North of England, and replaced *hi* or *heo;* the earliest forms of it are *þeȝȝ, thei, tha*.

The Southern dialect kept up the old form *hi* or *heo* nearly to the end of the fourteenth century.

They is the nom. plural of the definite article, O.E. *tha*, probably modified by Scandinavian influence.[3]

---

[1] 1140 (Stephen). Ðær efter *scæ* ferde ofer sæ." In the thirteenth century, the ordinary form of *she* is *sco*, found in Northern writers; *sche* (*scæ*) is a Midland modification of it.

[2] We find this *h* disappearing as early as the twelfth century (as in *Orm.*).

[3] The O. Norse forms bear a greater resemblance to *they, their*, and *them* than the O.E. ones.
 O. Norse *thei-r, theirra, theim*.
 O.E. *tha, thára, thám*.

The Midland and Southern dialects changed O.E. *tha* to *tho*, not to *thei* or *they*.

> "Or gif *thai* men, that will study
> In the craft of Astrology," &c.—BARBOUR's *Bruce*.

Them (dat.), O. E. *þām*, is the dative plural of the definite article, and replaced O. E. *heom, hem*.

The-m (acc.) is a dative form; the true accusative is *thá* or *they*. It has replaced the O. E. *hi* or *heo*.

We often find in the dramatists *em* (acc.), usually printed *'em*, as if it were a contraction of *them*, which represents the old *heom, hem*, as—

> "The sceptre and the golden wreath of royalty
> Seem hung within my reach.
> Then take *'em* to you
> And wear *'em* long and worthily."—ROWE.

161. TABLE showing the origin of she, they, &c.

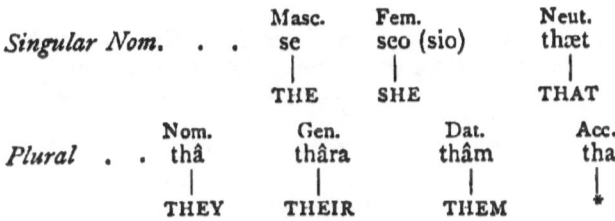

Definite Article.

	Masc.	Fem.	Neut.
Singular Nom.	se	seo (sio)	thæt
	THE	SHE	THAT

	Nom.	Gen.	Dat.	Acc.
Plural	thâ	thâra	thâm	tha
	THEY	THEIR	THEM	

We have said nothing about the genitives of the personal pronouns, because they are now expressed by the accusative with a preposition. For the origin of the pronominal genitives, see *Adjective Pronouns*.

(2) REFLEXIVE PRONOUNS.

162. Reflexives in English are supplied by the personal pronouns with or without the word **self**.

"I do repent *me*."—SHAKESPEARE's *Merchant of Venice*.
"Signor Antonio commends *him* to you."—*Ib*.
"My heart hath one poor string to stay *it* by."—*King John*.
"Come, lay *thee* down."—LODGE's *Looking Glass*.
"Ladies, go sit *you* down amidst this bower."—*Ib*.
"All (files) have hid *them* in the weeds."—JOHN FLETCHER's *Faithful Shepherdess*.

163. The addition of **self** renders the reflexive signification more emphatic, as—

(I) *myself*, (thou) *thyself*, &c.

Singular . 1st person, *myself*; 2d person, *thyself, yourself.*
Plural . . ,, *ourselves*; ,, *yourselves.*
Singular (3d person) . masc. *himself*; fem. *herself*; neut. *itself.*
Plural ,, . *themselves.*

164. Self[1] was originally an adjective = same, as "in that *selve* moment" (CHAUCER).
" A goblet of the *self* " = " A piece of the same."—*Boke of Curtasye*, l. 776.
"That *self* mould" (SHAKESPEARE, *Rich. II.* i. 2). Cp. *self-same*
In the oldest English *self* was declined as a definite or indefinite adjective; as *Ic self* and *Ic selfa* = I (my)self, and agreed with the pronouns to which it was added; as nom. *Ic selfa*; gen. *min selfes*, dat. *me silfum*, acc. *mec silfne*.

165. In O.E. sometimes the *dative* of the personal pronoun was prefixed to the *nominative* of self, as—(1) *Ic me silf*; (2) *thu the silf*; (3) *he him silf*: (1) *we us silfe*; (2) *ge eôw silfe*; (3) *hi him silfe*.

166. In the thirteenth century a new form came in, by the substitution of the *genitive* for the *dative* of the prefixed pronoun in the first and second persons, as—*mi self, thi self*, for *me self, the self*; *our self, your self*, for *us self, you self*.
No doubt *self* began to be regarded as a noun. Cp. *one's self*.

" Speak of thy fair *self*, Edith."—J. FLETCHER.
" My woeful *self*."—BEN JONSON.
" Thy crying *self*."—SHAKESPEARE.
" For at your dore *myself doth* dwell."—HEYWOOD, *The Four P.'s*.
" *Myself hath* been the whip."—CHAUCER.

Hence *self* makes its plural, *selves*, like nouns ending in *-f, -fe*; cp. "To our gross *selves*" (Shakespeare)—a formation altogether of recent origin. "To prove their *selfes*" occurs in Berner's Froissart.[2]

167. Such phrases as *Cæsar's self* (North), *Tarquin's self* (Shakespeare), are not, philologically speaking, so correct as *Attica self* (North), &c. Comp.

" And knaw kyndly what God es
And what *man self* es that es les."
HAMPOLE'S *Pricke of Consc.*, p. 4.

---

[1] Self, Goth. *silba*, Ger. *selbe*, probably contains the reflexive *si* (Lat. *se*), and *-lf* = *lb*, life, soul (as in Ger. *leib*, body). The Sansk. *âtman*, soul, is used as a reflexive.

[2] In O.E. the plural was marked by *e* or *-en*: when this disappeared it left the plurals *ourself, yourself, themself*; but as *we* and *you* were often used in the singular number, a new plural came into use, so we now say *yourself* (sing.), *yourselves* (pl.).
Cp. " We have saved *ourself* that trouble."—FIELDING.
' You, my Prince, *yourself* a soldier, will reward him."—LORD BYRON.

168. In *himself, themselves, it self* (not *its self*) the old dative remains unchanged; *his self, themselves,* are provincialisms. With own, *his* and *their* may be used.

169. In O.E. *one* was sometimes used for *self*.

> " And the body with flesshe and bane,
> Es harder than the saul by it *ane*."
> HAMPOLE, *Pricke of Consc.*, p. 85.

> " Whan they come by them *one* two"
> = " When they two came by themselves."
> *Morte d'Arthur*, p. 14.

(3) ADJECTIVE PRONOUNS.

170. The adjective pronouns, or, as they are sometimes called, the possessive pronouns, were originally formed from the genitive case of the personal pronouns, and were declined like adjectives.

In modern English, the possessive adjective pronouns are identical in form with the old genitives of the personal pronouns, and are indeclinable.

Traces of the older adjectival forms are found in the fourteenth century.

171. **Mine, my, thine, thy,** O.E. *min, thin*. The *e* in *mine* and *thine* only marks the length of the preceding vowel, and is no inflexional syllable.

-n is a true genitive suffix as far as English is concerned, but is of adjectival origin.[1]

In the twelfth century the *n* dropped off before a consonant, but was retained (*a*) in the oblique cases, (*b*) in the plural (with final *e*), (*c*) when the pronoun followed the substantive, (*d*) before a word commencing with a vowel.

The fourth or euphonic use of *mine* and *thine* is exceedingly common in poetry, as—

> " Give every man *thine* ear, but few *thy* voice."—SHAKESPEARE.

Of the third usage we have instances as late as Shakespeare's time, as brother *mine*, uncle *mine*.

172. **His**, a true genitive of the root *hi*.
In O.E. we often find a plural *hise*.

He-r, O.E. *hi-re*, contains a genitive suffix, -r (re).

---

[1] Goth. *meina, theina*; Gr. ἐμοῦ, σοῦ (τεοῖο); Lat. *mei, tui*; Sansk. *mamd, tava*. The Gothic forms correspond to Sansk. *mad-iya, tvad-iya*, the *n* in *meina, theina* representing *d* iu *mad-tya*, &c.

Its, O.E. *his*. This form is not much older than the end of the sixteenth century. It is not found in the Bible, or in Spenser, rarely in Shakespeare[1] and Bacon, more frequently in Milton, common in Dryden, who seems to have been ignorant of the fact that *his* was once the genitive of *it*, as well as of *he*.

"And the earth brought forth grass, and herb yielding seed after *his* kind."— *Gen.* i. 12.

"*It* shall bruise thy head, and thou shalt bruise *his* heel."—*Gen.* iii. 15.

"And that same eye, whose bend doth awe the world,
Did lose *his* lustre."—*Julius Cæsar*, i. 2.

173. Along with the use of *his* we find, in the fourteenth century, in the West Midland dialect, an uninflected genitive *hit*.

"Forthy the derk dede see *hit* is demed ever more
For *hit* dedeȝ of dethe duren there ȝet."[2]—*Allit. Poems*, B. l. 1021.

This curious form is found in our Elizabethan dramatists:—

"*It* knighthood shall fight all *it* friends."—*Silent Woman*, ii. 3.

"The innocent milk in *it* most innocent mouth."

"The hedge-sparrow fed the cuckoo so long,
That it's had *it* head bit off by *it* young."—*Lear*, i. 4.

"That which groweth of *it* own accord."[3]—*Levit.* xxv. 5.

174. For *its own* we have a curious form that occurs frequently in older writers, namely '*the own*,' as—"A certeine sede which groweth there of *the own* accorde."—*Fardell of Facion*, 1555.
It occurs in Hooker, but is altered in the modern reprints to *its own*. The earliest instance of this usage is found in Hampole's "Pricke of Conscience," p. 85 (A.D. 1340):—

"For the saule, als the boke bers wytnes,
May be pyned with fire bodily,
Als it may be with *the awen* body."

175. Ou-r, you-r, O.E. *u-re (us-er), eow-er (gure*[4]).
All these forms contain a genitive pl. suffix (adjectival), -r (-re). See note on *Alder*, p. 105.

Thei-r has also a genitive pl. suffix, -r, and has replaced the older *hi-re (heo-re, he-re, he-r)*. See Table, p. 121.

---

[1] Mr. Abbott notices that it is common in Florio's Montaigne.
[2] "Therefore the dark Dead Sea it is deemed evermore,
For *its* deeds of death endure (last) there yet."
[3] The modern reprint of the edition of 1611 has altered *it* to *its*.
[4] A later form.

(4) Independent or Absolute Possessives.

176. Mine, thine, his, hers, its, ours, yours, theirs, are called independent or absolute because they may be used without a following substantive, as this is *mine*, that is *yours*.

> "The tempest may break out which overwhelms thee
> And *thine*, and *mine*."—BYRON.

177. Hers, ours, yours, theirs, are double genitives containing a pl. suffix *r* + a sing. suffix *-s*. These forms were confined in the thirteenth and fourteenth centuries to the Northern dialects, and are probably due to Scandinavian influence. Sometimes we find imitations of them in the Midland dialects, as *hores*, *heres* = theirs. The more ordinary forms in the Southern dialects than these in *-s* are *hire* (*hir*), *oure* (*our*), *youre* (*your*), *here* (*her*), as—" I wol be *your* in alle that ever I may."—CHAUCER.

In Old English we sometimes find *ouren* = ours; *heren* = theirs, and in provincial English we find *hisn*, *hern*, *ourn*, *theirn*.

II. Demonstrative Pronouns.

178. The demonstratives, with the exception of *the* and *yon*, are used substantively and adjectively.

(1) **The** (usually called the *Definite Article*) was formerly declined like an adjective for number, gender, and case, but is now without any inflexion.[1]

SINGULAR.

Masc.	Nom.	se, the.*
	Gen.	thæ-s, the-s,* thi-s,* tha-s.*
	Dat.	tha-m, tha-n,* the-n.*
	Acc.	tha-ne, the-ne,* tha-ne,* the-n,* tho-ne.
	Inst.	thí, thé.
Fem.	Nom.	seo, theo,* tha,* the.*
	Gen.	thǽ-re, tha-re,* the-re.*
	Dat.	thǽ-re, tha-re,* the-re.*
	Acc.	thá, theo,* the.*
Neut.	Nom. and Acc.	thæ-t, that,* thet.*
	Gen. and Dat.	like the Masc.

---

[1] Later forms which were in partial use during the twelfth, thirteenth, and fourteenth centuries are distinguished thus (*).

PLURAL.

Nom. thâ, thaie,* tho,* the.*
Gen. tha-ra, thæ-ra, thare,* there.*
Dat. thâ-m, thæ-m, than,* thon,* then.*
Acc. thâ, thaie,* tho,* the.*

The inflexions began to drop off about the middle of the twelfth century.

The, before a comparative, is the old instrumental *thi*, as *the more* = eo magis, &c.

(2) **That.** In the O.E. Northern dialects *that* was used irrespective of gender, as *thatt* engell; *thatt* allterr (*Orm.*), and in the fourteenth century we find it as a demonstrative, as now, taking the place of the older *thilk* (*thilke*). See next page. Then it took for itself the following plurals: (*a*) *tho* (or *tha*), the old plural of the definite article; (*b*) *thos* (*thas*), the old plurals of *this*.[1]

In the Southern and some of the Midland dialects, we find *thes, these, thise, thos* = these.

(3) **Those** = O.E. *thas*, the old plural of *thes* = this.

The history of the word *that* should be borne well in mind:—(1) It was originally neuter, (cp. *i-t, wha-t*); (2) It became an indeclinable *demonstrative*, answering in meaning to *ille, illa, illud*; (3) It took the pl. (1) of *the*; (2) of *this*.

(4) **This** (=*hic, hæc, hoc*) = O.E. *thes* (m.), *theos* (f.), *this* (m.), as formerly declined like an adjective. Here again the *neuter* has replaced the masculine and feminine forms, which, however, in the south of England were to be found as late as 1357.

In Wickliffe we have *thisis fader* = the father of *this* man.

The O.E. *thes* is (as seen by the O.Sax. *thĕse*) contracted, and it contains the root *the* (or *tha*, as in *the*) and a lengthened form of *se* (the), Sansk. *sya*. This *se* (*sya*) had the force of Lat. *-c, -que*, as in *hi-c, quis-que*.

These = O.E. *thâs, thes,* these,* thise,* this.*

---

[1] The *e* is no sign of inflexion, but marks the length of the vowel *a*.

Koch supposes *those* to be a lengthened form of the old pl. *tho*. He seems to have overlooked the Northumbrian use of *thas* (which in the Midland dialects would be represented by *thos*). Koch's statement is: "Es kann nicht die fortbildung von Ags. thâs sein." Cp. the following passage from Hampole's *Pricke of Consc.* p. 30:—

"Alle *thas* men that the world mast dauntes,
Mast bisily the world here hauntes;
And *thas* that the world serves and loves,
Serves the devil, as the book proves."

This refers to the more immediate object, *that* to the remoter object.

> "What conscience dictates to be done,
> Or warns me not to do,
> *This* teach me more than hell to shun,
> *That* more than heaven pursue."—POPE.

179. We have three demonstratives containing the adjective *-lic*, like, with the instrumental case of the particles *so*, *the*, and *i* (Goth. *i-s*).

(1) Such: O.E. *swilc*[1] = *swi*, the inst. of *swa* = *so*, and *-lc* = *lic* = like.
Such then signifies *so-like* (cp. Ger. *solch* = *so-lich*); *such like* is a pleonastic expression.
In the Northern dialects we find *slyk*, *sli*, *silk*, of Scandinavian origin, whence Scotch *sic*.

In O.E. *suche ten*, &c. = ten times as much (or as many), &c.
"The lengthe is *suche ten* as the deepnesse."—*Pilgrimage*, p. 235.

(2) Thilk = the like, that, that same = O.E. *thy-lic*, *thy-lc* (*thelk*,* *thulk*,* *thike**); Provincial English *thuck*, *thucky* (*theck*, *thick*, *thicky*, *thecky*). *Thi* = the instrumental case of *the*. and *lk* = like. It corresponds exactly to Lat. *ta-lis*, Sansk. *ta-drisha*, Gr. τηλίκος.

> "I am *thilke* that thou shouldest seeche."—*Pilgrimage*, p. 5.
> "She hadde founded *thilke* hous."—*Ib.* p. 7.

Thys-lic (whence *thyllic*) = this like, is sometimes found in O.E.

(3) Ilk = same: 'of that *ilk*.'
> "This *ilk* worthe knight."—CHAUCER.
> "That *ilk*² man."—*Ib.*

Ilk = O.E. *ylc*; *i* or *y* = the instrumental case of the stem *i* = he, that, and *-lk* = *-lc* = like.

180. Same: Gothic *sama*, O.N. *samr*, Lat. *similis*, Gr. ὅμος, Sansk. *sama*. In the oldest English *same* is an adverb = together, and not a demonstrative.
As the word makes its appearance for the first time in the Northern dialects, it is no doubt due to Scandinavian influence.[3]
It is joined to the demonstratives *the*, *this*, *that*, *yon*, *yond*, *self*.

---

[1] In O.E. of the thirteenth and fourteenth centuries there are various forms of this compound, as *swulc*, *sulch*, *swulch*, *swich*, *swuch*, *soch*.
[2] *That ilk*, O.E. *that ylca*, was originally neuter. *Ilk* = same must be distinguished from O.E. *ilk*, *ilka*, each, each one.
[3] *Sam...sam* = whether...or, is found in O.E.

181. Yon, yond, yonder. Goth. *jains* (m.), *jaina* (f.), *jainata* (n.), that. In the oldest English *yond* (*geond*) is only a preposition = through, over, *beyond*, or an adverb = *yonder*. The root *ge* is a *pronominal* stem that occurs in *yea*, O.E. *gea*; *ye-s*, &c.[1]

Yond makes its appearance as a demonstrative for the first time in the "Ormulum" (twelfth century).

It is seldom used substantively, as in the following passages from Old English writers:—

> "I am the kynge of this londe & Oryens am kalled,
> And the ȝondur is my quene, Betryce she hette."
> *Chevelere Assigne*, l. 232.

> "Ys ȝone thy page?"—R. OF BRUNNE, *Spec. of E. Eng.*, p. 119.
> "The ȝond is that semly."—WILL. OF PALERNE.

182. So. O.E. = *swa*.

> "Folly (I say) that both makes friends and keeps them *so*."—BP. KENNET'S *Translation of* ERASMUS' *Praise of Folly*.

> "If there were such a way; there is none *so*."—GOWER, ii. 33.

In O.E. *so* (inst.) is used before comparatives like *the* (O.E. *thi*): "*swo leng the werse*" = *the* longer *the* worse; "*swo leng swo* more."—*O.E. Hom.* Second Series, pp. 85, 87.

III. Interrogative Pronouns.

182*. The Interrogative Pronouns are **who, which, what, whether**, with the compounds **whoever, whatever, whethersoever, whichsoever**.

183. Who. O.E. *hwa, hwo,* ho** (masc. and fem.), *hwæt, hwat,* wat** (neut.); Goth. *hva-s* (m.), *hva* (neut.); Sansk. *kás* (m.), *ká* (f.), *ka-t* (neut.); Gr. κο-s, πos; Lat. *quis, quæ, quod.*[2]

It is only used of persons, and is masculine and feminine.

Whose. O.E. *hwas, whos,* hos,* was,* wos,** gen. sing. Originally of all genders, now limited to persons, though in poetry it occasionally occurs with reference to neuter substantives. It is also used absolutely, as "*Whose* is the crime?"

Whom (dat. sing.). O.E. *hwam,* wham,* wom,** originally of all genders.

The accusative *hwone* (*hwæne*) was replaced in the twelfth and thirteenth centuries by *wham*, but instances of the older *hwone* are to be found under the forms *hwan, wan, wane*.

---

[1] We have the same root perhaps in O.E. *anent, auence*; O.H. Ger. *ennont*; Mid. H. Ger. *jen-unt* = beyond. *Geonre* = Ger. *jener*, occurs in King Alfred's translation of *St. Gregory's Pastoral*.

[2] Those marked thus (*) are later forms.

184. Wha-t, originally the neuter of *who*. In the "Ormulum" *what* is used adjectively, without respect to gender, as *"whatt* mann?" *"whatt* thing?" just as we say, *"what* man?" *"what* woman?" *"what* thing?" Without a noun it is now singular and neuter; with a noun it is singular or plural, and of all genders.

What in Old English was used in questions concerning the nature, quality, or state of a person, as *hwæt is þes = quis est hic* (Matt. iv. 41).

"*What* is this womman, quod I, so worthily atired?"—*Piers Plowman.*

What is followed by *a*, like *many, such, each,* &c.

185. What for = *what sort of a*, is an idiom that made its appearance in the sixteenth century, and is similar to the German *was für ein*, as *What is he for a vicar?* = *Was, für einen Vikar, ist er? What sort of a vicar is he?* Spenser, Palgrave, and Ben Jonson have instances of it.

186. Whether.—O. E. *hwæther, whether*,[1] *wher;* Goth. *hva-thar* = which of the two.[2] It has become archaic; but was very common in the seventeenth century.

"*Whether* is greater, the gift or the altar?"—*Matt.* xxiii. 19.

It is very rarely used adjectively, as in the following passage:—

"Thirdly (we have to consider) *whether state* (the Church or the Commonwealth) is the superior."—BP. MORTON in *Literature of the Church of England,* vol. i. p. 109.

In the thirteenth century it is rarely inflected; and the following passages are almost unique:—

(*a*) "*Hwetheres* fere wult tu beon? Mid *hwether* wult tu tholien?"[3]—*Ancren Riwle*, p. 284.

(*b*) "Now *whether his* hert was fulle of care."[4]—*Morte d'Arthur.*

Whether his = *whetheres.* I have seen *who his* = *whose*, an analogous formation.

(*c*) Bishop Hall uses the rare compound **whethersoever**.

"What matters it whether I go for a flower or a weed, here? *Whethersoever* I must wither. (Uterlibet, arescam necesse est.)"

---

[1] See *Comparatives*, § 113, for origin of -*ther*.
[2] Koch says: "Es wird im Nags. fast flexionslos."
[3] "Of which of the two wilt thou be the associate? With which of the two wilt thou suffer?"
[4] "Now of which of the two was the heart full of care?" The writer is speaking of Launcelot and Queen Guenever.

187. Which, O.E. *hwilc, hulic, while,* whulc,* whulch,* wuch,* woch,** a compound of *hwi*, the instrumental case of *hwa*, who, and *lic* = *like*. Cp. Lat. *qua-li-s*. It is used as a singular or plural, and of any gender.[1]

In O.E. it has the force sometimes of (*a*) *quis*, as *Hwylc is mín môdor?* Who is my mother? (*b*) *quantus* :—

"*Whiche* a sinne violent."—GOWER, iii. 244.
"*Allas wʒuch* serwe and deol ther wes!"—*Castel of Love*, p. 5.

IV. Relative Pronouns.

188. The relative pronouns are *who, which, that, as*.

In O.E. *who, which, what*, were not relative, but interrogative pronouns; *which, whose, whom*, occur as interrogatives as early as the end of the twelfth century, but *who* not until the fourteenth century,[2] and was not in common use before the sixteenth century. *That* and *what* originally referred only to *neuter* antecedents.

The relatives in the oldest English were :—
(1) *se* (m.), *seo* (f.), *thæt* (n.) : also the def. article. (2) *the*, indeclinable. (3) *the* in combination with *se, seo, thæt* ; as *se the, seo the, thætte*. (4) *swâ, so*. (5) *thæt thæt*, whatever. (6) *swylc . . . swylc* = such . . . such.

189. Who as a relative is not recognized by Ben Jonson, who says "one relative *which*." It is now used in both numbers, and relates to masculine or feminine antecedents (rational).

190. *Who* is very rarely employed by Hawes ; frequently by Berners ; not uncommon in Shakespeare ; used only once or twice by Sackville.

"And other sort   *   *   *
 *   *   *   *
Who, fearing to be yielded, fled before ;
Stole home by silence of the secret night:
The third unhappy and enraged sort
Of desp'rate hearts, *who*, stain'd in princes' blood,
From traitorous furour could not be withdrawn."—SACKVILLE.

191. *Who . . . he* is used like Ger. *wer*, quisquis = whoso : 3—

---

[1] Those marked thus (*) are later forms.
[2] That is to say, used freely, like Latin *qui*. Cp. the following :—
"Who of ʒou dredende the Lord, herende the vois of his servaunt. *Who* ʒide in dercnesses."—*Wickliffite Version, Isaiah* l. 10.
[3] This construction is common in Shakespeare, where we should use *whoever*:—
"O now *who* will behold
The royal captain of this ruin'd band ?
Let *him* cry, ' Praise and glory on his head.'"
Henry V. iv. Prol.
"*Whom* he did foreknow, he did predestinate."—*Rom.* viii. 29.
"*Who* seems most sure, *him* soonest whirls she (Fortune) down."
SACKVILLE'S *Henry Stafford*.

RELATIVE PRONOUNS.

> "*Who* is trewe of his tonge,
> * * * *
> *He* is a god by the Gospel."
> *Piers Pl.* (ed. Wright), p. 20.

"And *who* wylle not, *thay* shalle be slone."—TOWNLEV, *Mysteries*, p. 71.

"A hwam mai *he* luue treweliche *hwa* ne luues his brother, Thenne *hwase* the ne luues *he* is mon unwreastest." (Ah! whom may he love truly *whoso* loveth not his brother; then whoso loveth not thee is a most wicked man.)—*O.E. Hom.* First Series, p. 274.

The demonstrative may be omitted, as—

> "*Who* steals my purse steals trash."—*Othello*, iii. 3. 157.

192. The O.E. *whan, wan* is sometimes found in the fourteenth century as an objective case (representing O.E. *hwone* and *hwam*):—

> "Seint Dunstan com hom a3en . . .
> Ladde his abbey al in pees fram *wkan* he was so longe."
> *E. Eng. Poems*, p. 37.

"This(e) were ure faderes of *wan* we beth suththe ycome."—ROBERT OF GIOUCESTER.

193. In Gower we find the demonstrative *the* joined to *whose* and *whom*, so that *the whose* = whose; *the whom* = whom:—

> "*The whos* power as now is falle."—*Confessio Amant.* ii. 187.
> "*The whom* no pité might areste."—*Ib.* iii. 203.
> "Your mistress from *the whom* I see
> There's no disjunction."—*Winter's Tale*, iv. 4.

Whose that = whoso:—

> "To Venus *whos* prest *that* I am."—*Confess. Amant.* ii. 61.
> "And dame Musyke commaunded curteysly
> La Bell Pucell wyth me than to daunce
> *Whome that* I toke wyth all my plesaunce."
> HAWES, *Pastime of Pleasure*, p. 70.

194. Shakespeare uses *who* of animals and of inanimate objects regarded as persons, as—

> "A lion *who* glared."—*Jul. Cæsar*, i.
> "The winds
> *Who* take the ruffian billows by the tops."—*2 Hen. IV.* iii. 1.
> "And as the *turtle* that has lost her mate
> *Whom* griping sorrow doth so sore attaint."
> SACKVILLE's *Henry Stafford*.

195. **Which now relates only to neuter antecedents, but this is comparatively a modern restriction.** Cp. "Our Father *which* art in heaven."

> "Then Warwick disannuls great John of Gaunt,
> *Which* did subdue the greatest part of Spain."—*3 Hen. VI.* iii. 3.
> "Adrian *which* popē was."—GOWER, i. 29.
> "She *which* shall be thy norice."—*Ib.* i. 195.

196. Compounds of *which* with *the, that, as*, &c. are now archaic:—

> "'Twas a foolish guest,
> *The which* to gain and keep he sacrificed all rest."—BYRON.

"The better part of valour is discretion, in the *which* better part I have saved my life."—1 *Hen. IV.* v. 4.

"The chain
Which God he knows I saw not, for *the which*
He did arrest me."—*Comedy of Errors*, v. 1.

"The civil power, which is the very fountain and head from *the which* both these estates (Church and Commonwealth) do flow, and by *the which* it is brought to pass that there is a Church in any place."—BP. MORTON.

"His food, for most, was wild fruits of the tree,
Unless sometimes some crumbs fell to his share,
Which in his wallet long, God wot, kept he,
As on *the which* full daint'ly would he fare."
SACKVILLE'S *Induction*.

"*The which* was cleped Clemene."—GOWER, ii. 34.

"Among *the whichë* there was one."—*Ib.* ii. 375.

"The Latin worde *whyche that* is referred
Unto a thynge whych is substancyall,
For a nowne substantive is wel averred."
HAWES, *P. of P.* p. 24; see p. 14.

"Theis... yatis (gates) *which that* ye beholde."—SKELTON, i. 384.

"Man, the *which that* wit and reason can."—GOWER, i. 34.

"Thing *which that* is to lovē due."—*Ib.* ii. 18.

"Thing *which as* may nought been acheved."—*Ib.* ii. 380.

"This abbot *which that* was an holy man."
CHAUCER'S *Prioress' Tale*, l. 630.

"The sond and ek the smale stones
Whiche *as* sche ekes out for the nones."
GOWER, *Specimens of E. Eng.*, p. 373.

197. **That**, originally only the *neuter* singular relative, now agrees with singular and plural antecedents of all genders.[1]

That came in during the twelfth century to supply the place of the *indeclinable relative* the, and in the fourteenth century it is the ordinary relative. In the sixteenth century, *which* often supplies its place; in the seventeenth century, *who* replaces it. About Addison's time, *that* had again come into fashion, and had almost driven *which* and *who* out of use.

---

[1] That introduces always an adjective clause, while *who* and *which* are not always so used; as—

(1) I met a man *who* told me he had been called = I met a man *and he* told me, &c.

(2) It's no use asking John, *who* knows nothing of it = It's no use asking John, (*since, seeing that, for* &c.) he knows nothing of it.

In (1) the second clause is co-ordinate in *sense* with the preceding; in (2) it is adverbial.

"*That* is the proper restrictive explicative, limiting or defining relative."—BAIN'S *English Grammar*, p. 23.

Addison, in his "Humble Petition of *Who* and *Which*," makes the petitioners thus complain: "We are descended of ancient families, and kept up our dignity and honour many years, till the Jack Sprat *that* supplanted us."

198. There is another point in which *that* resembles the indeclinable *the;* both being followed and not preceded by a preposition, as—"*thæt* bed, se lama *on* læg" (*Mark* ii. 4) = "The bed *wherein* the sick of the palsy lay" (*English Version*), or = the bed *that* the lame man lay *on*.

So in O.E., fourteenth century:—

"The ston *that* he leonede *to*."—*Vernon MS.* fol. 4*a*.

And, as in our Version, the *relative adverb* is sometimes found :

"He eode in to the cite *ther* alle his fon *inne* were."—*Ib.*

As was used sometimes to replace *that*, as—

"For ther is a welle fair ynou3
In the stede *as* he lai *on*; as me ma3 ther iseo."
E. Eng. Poems, p. 55.

"On Englysshe tunge out of Frankys
Of a boke *as* I fonde *ynne*."
R. OF BRUNNE'S *Handlynge Synne*, p. 3.

199. **That**, in virtue of its being neuter, is sometimes used for *what*, and a preposition may precede it.

"I am possess'd of *that* is mine."—SHAKESPEARE'S *Much Ado*, i. 1.

"Throw us *that* you have about you."
Ib., *Two Gentlemen of Verona*.

"We speak *that* we do know, and testify *that* we have seen."—*St. John* iii. 11.

"What wight is that which saw *that* I did see."
Ferrex and Porrex, p. 69.

"Eschewe *that* wicked is."—GOWER'S *Confess. Amant.* i. 244.

"*That* he hath hyght, he shall *it* hold."—*Morte d'Arthur*, p. 132.

200. The O.E. *thæt thæt* = whatever, as "*thæt thæt* later bith, thæt hæfth angin" = that that later is, that hath beginning.
We still find it for *that which*—

"*That that* I did, I was set on to do't by Sir Toby."
Twelfth Night, iv. 2.

"*That that* is, is."—*Ib.* v. 1.

"*That that* that gentleman has advanced, is not *that*, that he should have proved to your Lordship."—*Spectator*, 80.

201. **What** = that which, refers to singular and neuter antecedents. It is used both substantively and adjectively.

"*What* is done cannot be undone."—*Macbeth*, v. 1.

"Look *what* I speak, my life shall prove *it* true."—*Ib.* iv. 3.

"No ill luck stirring but *what* lights upon my shoulder."
Merchant of Venice, iii. 1.
"The entertainer provides *what* fare he pleases."—FIELDING.

202. Such expressions as the following are archaic, as—

"He it was, whose guile
Stirred up with envy and revenge deceived
The mother of mankind, *what* time his pride
Had cast him out from heaven."—MILTON.

"At *what* time Joas reigned as yet in Juda."—HOLINSHED.

"For *what* tyme he to me spak,
Out of hys mouth me thoghte brak
A flamme of fyre."—R. OF BRUNNE, *Specimens*, p. 119.

203. It is a vulgarism to use *what* with an antecedent noun or pronoun, as—

"A vagrant is a man *what* wanders."

Yet we find some instances of this in older writers, as—

"I fear nothing *what* can be said against me."—*Hen. VIII.* v. 1.
"To have his pomp and all *what* state compounds."
Timon of Athens, iv. 2.
"Either the matter *what* other men wrote, or els the maner how other men wrote."—ASCHAM'S *Scholemaster*, p. 142.
"Offer them peace or *aught what* is beside."
Ed. I. in Old Plays, vol. ii. p. 37.

204. **What that, that what,** are archaic, as—

"*What* man *that* it smite
Thurghout his armur it wol kerve and byte."
CHAUCER'S *Squyer's Tale*, l. 10471.
"*That what* we have we prize not to the worth."—*Much Ado*, iv. 1.
"*That what* is extremely proper in one company, may be highly improper in another."—CHESTERFIELD.
"*What that* a king himselfe bit (= bids)."
GOWER, *Confess. Amant.* i. 4.
"But *what that* God forwot mot needes be."—CHAUCER.
"What schulde I telle . . .
And of moche other thing *what that* then was?"
R. OF BRUNNE'S *Handlynge Synne*, Prol.

205. So *what as* = what that :—

"Here I do bequeathe to thee
In full possession, half that Kendal hath,
And *what as* Bradford holds of me in chief."
DODSLEY, *Old Plays*, ii. 47.

206. As (O. E. *eall-swa, alswa, also,* * *alse,* * *ase,* * *als ;* * cp. O. E. *hwa-swa* and *hose* = whoso) possesses a relative force on account of its being a compound of *so*,[1] and is usually employed as such when preceded by the demonstratives *such, same, so much*.[2]

"All *such* reading *as* was never read."—POPE.

"Unto bad causes swear
Such creatures *as* men doubt."—*Julius Cæsar*, ii. 1.

"For all *such* authors *as* be fullest of good matter ... be likewise alwayes most proper in words."—ASCHAM'S *Scholemaster*, p. 136.

"Some *such* sores *as* greve me to touch them myself."
   Ed. 1. in Old Plays, vol. ii. p. 20.

"*Such one as* is already furnished with plentie of learning."—*Ib.* p. 113.

"These are *such as* with curst curres barke at every man but their owne friends."—GOSSON, *School of Abuse*, p. 18.

"For tho sche thoghtē to beginne
Such thing *as* semeth impossible."
   GOWER, *Specimens of E. Eng.* p. 373.

"Of *sich as* loves servauntes ben."—*Romaunt of the Rose*, l. 145.

"In *thilke* places *as* they habiten."—*Ib.* 660.

After *so, as* occurs sometimes—

"*So* many examples *as* filled xv. bookes."—ASCHAM, p. 157.

In Shakespeare it is found after *this, that*:

"*That* gentleness *as* I was wont to have."—*Julius Cæsar*, i. 2.

"Under *these* hard conditions *as* this time is like to lay upon me."—*Ib.*

But in O. E. writers we sometimes find *as* = such as :—

"Drau3tes *as* me draweth in poudre" =characters *such as* one draws in powder (dust).—*E. Eng. Poems*, p. 77.

"Talys shall thou fynde therynne,
Mervelys some *as* Y fonde wrytyn."—R. OF BRUNNE, p. 5

207. For **such** ... **as** the oldest English has *swylc* ... *sywlc* = such .. such :—

"He sece *swylcne* hlaford *swylcne* he wille."—*Æths. V.* i. 1 : = let him seek such a lord as he may choose.

At the end of the twelfth century we find *as* for *swylc* :—

"Withth all *swillc* rime *alls* her iss sett."—*Orm.* D. 101.

Cp. the following, where *alse* = as if = the older *swilc* :—

"He wes so kene, he wes swa strang
Swilc hit weore an eotand."—*La3.* A. p. 58.

---

[1] We find *so* ... *so* = for *as* ... *so* :—
"*So* the sea is moved, *so* the people are changed."—DR. DONNE'S *Sermons*.

* Those marked thus (*) are later forms.

"He wes swa kene, and so strong,
  Alse he were an eatande [= giant]."—Laȝ. B. p. 58.

(A = earlier text early thirteenth century ; B = later thirteenth.)

Sometimes *so* is found after *swylc*:—

"And *swilche* othre [scnuen] *so* the apostle her nemde."—*O.E. Homilies*, Second Series.

"*Swylcra* yrmtha *swa* thu unc ær scrife" = Of *such* miseries *as* thou previously assigned to us (two).—*Exeter Book*, 373.[1]

208. **Who-so, what-so, who-so-ever, which-so-ever** are relatives (indefinite), like the Latin *quisquis, quicunque.*

The latter parts of the compounds, used adjectively, are sometimes separated by an intervening noun, as—

"We can create, and in *what* place *soe'er*
  Thrive under evil."—MILTON, i. 260.

"Upon *what* side *as ever* it falle."—GOWER, *Confess. Amant.* i. 264.

209. *What* is used sometimes for *whatever :*—

"And, speak men *what* they can to him, he'll answer
  With some rhyme rotten sentence."
    HENRY PORTER in LAMB's *Dram. Poets*, p. 432, Bohn's Series.

"*What* thou herē yef no credence."
    GOWER'S *Confess. Amant.* i. 59.

In O.E. we find *who that ever, what that ever, who-as-ever, what-as-ever, what-als-ever.*

"Yn *what* cuntre of the worlde *so ever that* he be gone."—*Gest. Rom.* i.

"*Who that ever* cometh thedir he shalle fare well."—*Ib.*

210. **Who-ever, whatever, which-ever** are relative and interrogative. They do not occur in the oldest English, and are comparatively late forms.

V. Indefinite Pronouns.

211. The indefinite pronouns do not specify any particular object. Some are used substantively, others adjectively. Most of them may be used in both ways. The indefinites are (in addition to the indefinite relatives) *who, what, some, none, no, aught, naught, enough, any, each, every, either, neither, other, else, sundry, certain.*

---

[1] In the Sax. Chron. A.D. 1137, there is a similar displacement :—
"Hi wenden thæt he sculde ben *alsuic alse* the eom was" = they thought that he should be *all such as* the uncle was.

XII.] INDEFINITE PRONOUNS. 137

212. **Who** = any one, some one.

"Timon, surnamed Misantropos (as *who* should say Loupgarou, or the man-hater)."—NORTH'S *Plutarch*, 171.

"Suppose *who* enters now,
A king whose eyes are set in silver, one
That blusheth gold."—DECKER'S *Satiro-Mastix.*

"'Twill be my chaunce els some to kill wherever it be or *whom*."—DAVIS, *Scourge of Folly*, DODSLEY'S *Old Plays*, ii. p. 50.

": 'Is mother Chat at home ?' 'She is, syr, and she is not; but it please her to *whom*.'"—*Ib.* p. 61.

"The cloudy messenger turns me his back
And hums, as *who* should say, 'You'll rue the time
That clogs me with this answer.'"—*Macbeth*, iii. 6.

"As *who* would saye Astrologie were a thing of great primacie."—DRANT'S *Sermons.*

"Sche was as *who* seith, a goddesse."
GOWER, *Specimens of E. Eng.* p. 376.

"Thay faught[en] alle that longë day,
Who had it sene, wele myght he syghe."
Morte d'Arthur, p. 126.

"I will not live
Who wolde me all this world here give."
CHAUCER'S *Dream*, l. 618.

"If ther were not *who* to sle it," &c.—*Pilgrimage*, p. 12.

"*Alswa* (= als wha) say here, may lyf na man
Withouten drede, that witte can."—HAMPOLE, *P. of C.* p. 69.

"As *hwa* se seie he this is mare then theof."—*O E. Hom.*, First Series, p. 281.

"Thenne aȝaines kinde gath *hwa* that swuche kinsemon ne luueth."—*Ib.*, p. 275.

Who is sometimes joined to *some*. See § 217.

213. **What** is indefinite in such expressions as "I tell you *what*" (= something), "I know not *what*," "*what* not," "elles *what*" (Chaucer).

"Come down and learne the litte *what*
That Thomalin can sayne."—SPENSER'S *Shep. Cal.*, July.

"As they spek of many *what*."
ROBERT OF BRUNNE, *Handlynge Synne*, *Specimens*, p. 110.

"Which was the lothliest[e] *what*."—GOWER, i. 98.

"As he which cowthe mochel *what*."—*Ib.* i. 320.

"Love is bought for litil *what*."—*Ib.* ii. 275.

"A little *what*."—WICKLIFFE, *John* vi. 7.

"Gif thaer *hwat* to lafe si" = If there be anything remaining.—*Quoted by Sachs from Ettmüller.*

In the oldest English we find *änes hwæt* and *swilces hwæt* = somewhat.

. For other compounds, see *some*, § 217.

214. Some (O.E. *sum, som,** *aliquis, quelque*) is used both adjectively and substantively.

(1) It has the force of the indefinites *a, any, a certain*, as—

" And if *som* Smithfield ruffian take up *som* strange going ; *som* new mowing with their mouth ; wrinchyng with the shoulder ; *som* brave proverb, some fresh new othe, . . . *som* new disguised garment . . . whatsoever it cost, gotten must it be."—ASCHAM, *Scholemaster*, p. 44.

" And yet he could roundlie rap out so many uglie othes as *som* good man of fourscore yeare old hath never heard named before."—*Ib.* p. 48.

" *Some* holy angel
Fly to the court of England."—*Macbeth*, iii. 6.

"The fireplace was an old one, built by *some* Dutch merchant long ago."—DICKENS.

" *Sum* holi childe."—*Life of Becket*, p. 104.

" Ther was *sum* prest."—WICKLIFFE, *Luke* i. 5.

"*Sum* 3ong man suede him."—*Ib., Mark* xiv. 51.

" Bot len me *sum* fetel (vessel) tharto."—*Specimens of E. Eng.*, p. 156.

" The33 wisstenn thatt him wæs *summ* unncuth sihhthe shæwedd."—*Orm.* 228.

" *Sum* dema wæs on sumere ceastre."—*Luke* xviii. 2.

We find it sometimes with the genitive plural in O.E., as—

" Tha com his feonda *sum.*"—*Matt.* xiii. 25.

(2) It expresses an indefinite part or quantity, as—

" It is *some* mercy when men kill with speed."—WEBSTER'S *Duchess of Malfy.*

" The annoyance of the dust, or else *some* meat
You ate at dinner, cannot brook with you."
MIDDLETON'S *Arden of Feversham.*

" And therefore wol I make you disport
As I seyde erst, and do you *som* comfort."
CHAUCER, *Prol.* l. 770.

(3) *With plural substantives,* as " *some* years ago."

" *Some* certain of the noblest-minded Romans."—*Jul. Cæsar*, i. 3.

" And *some* I see . . .
That twofold balls and treble sceptres bear."—*Macbeth,* iv. 1.

" There be *som* serving men that do but ill service to their young masters."—ASCHAM, *Scholemaster*, p. 48.

" I write not to hurte any, but to profit *som.*"—*Ib.*

(4) *With numerals,* in the sense of *about* :—

" Surrounded by *some* fifty or sixty fathoms of iron cable."—DICKENS.

"What a prodigy was't
That from *some* two yards high, a slender man
Should break his neck."
J. WEBSTER, *The White Devil.*

"*Some* half hour to seven."
BEN JONSON, *Every Man in his Humour.*

"A prosperous youth he was, aged *some* four and ten."—GREEN, p. 66.

"*Some* dozen Romans of us."—*Cymb.* i. 7.

"*Some* day or two."—*Rich. III.* iii. 1.

"Tha wæron hi *sume* ten year on tham gewinn."—BOETH. xviii. 1.

(5) *With the genitive pl.*, O.E. "*eode eahta sum*" = he went one of eight. We find in modern Scotch a remnant of this idiom in the phrase "a *twasum* dance," a dance in which two persons are engaged.

"Bot it (boat) sa litell wes, that it
Mychte our the watter bot *thresum* flyt" (carry).—BARBOUR'S *Brus*, p. 63.

(6) In *apposition instead of the partitive genitive*, as—
"ʒef thou havest bred ant ale
      *   *   *
Thou del hit *sum* about."—BARBOUR'S *Brus*, p. 98.

"Hit nis noʒt riʒt the tapres tende, bote *hi* were her some" (*i.e.* except *some of them* were here).—*Specimens of E. Eng.* p. 41.

"*Summe* heo fleiʒen to Irelonde."—*Laʒamon*, iii. 167.

"*Sume* tha boceras."—*Matt.* ix. 3.

"Ge magon gehyran *sume* his theawas."—*Ælfric*, Dom. i. *in mense Septem.*

"Ac *sume* ge ne gelyfath."—*John* vi. 64.

Instead of this contraction the partitive genitive was used as early as the twelfth century.

"*Sum of the sede* feol an uppe the stane and *sum* among theornen."—*O. Eng. Hom.*, First Series, p. 133.

"*Summe* off ure little floce."—*Orm.* l. 6574.

"Lo here a tale of ʒow *sum.*"
R. OF BRUNNE, *Handlynge Synne*, p. 309.

"*Summe* of hem camen fro fer."—WICKLIFFE'S *Int.* viii. 3.

"The kynge and *somme* of hys defendede hem faste."—ROBT. OF GLOUCESTER, l. 1290.

215. Some ... some = *alius ... alius; alter ... alter.*

"*Some* thought Dunkirk, *some* that *Ypres* was his object."—MACAULAY.

"The work *some* praise,
And *some* the architect."—MILTON, *P. L.* i. 731.

"For books are as meats and viands are, *some* of good, *some* of evill substance."
—*Areopagitica*, ed. *Arber*, p. 43.

"*Some* say he is with the Emperor of Russia,
Other *some*, he is in Rome."—*Comedy of Errors*, iii. 2.

In O.E. we find the singular as well as the plural,[1] as—
"*Sum* man hath an 100 wyues, *sume* mo, *sum* less."—MAUNDEVILLE, p. 22.

(a) *Singular:*—
"*Som* man desireth for to have richesse,
And *som* man wolde out of his prisoun fayn."
CHAUCER'S *Knightes Tale.*

"He mot ben deed, the kyng as schal a page ;
Som in his bed, *som* in the deepe see,
Som in the large felde, as men may se."—*Ib.*
"*Sum* was king and *sum* kumeling (foreigner)."
Gen. and Ex. l. 834.
"*Anum* he sealde fif pund, *sumum* twa, *sumum* an."—*Matt.* xxv. 15.

(b) *Plural:*—
"*Somme* the hed from the body he smote,
Somme the arms, *somme* the scholders."
LONELICH'S *St. Graal*, p. 128.

"Thus may men se that at thoo dayes *summe* were richere then *summe* and redier to give elmesse."—CAPGRAVE, p. 10.
"Of *summe* sevene and sevene, of *summe* two and two."—*Ib.* p. 16.
"He bylevede ys folc *somme* aslawe and *some* ywounded."—ROBERT OF GLOUCESTER, l. 4855.

Byron ("Don Juan") uses *some's* = one's—
"Howsoe'er it shock *some's* self love."

Heywood uses *somes*—
"But of all *somes* none is displeased
To be welcome."

216. *Some* is also used indefinitely with *other, another*—

"Who ... hath ... not worshipped *some* idol or another."—THACKERAY'S *Hist. of H. Esmond.*
"By *some* device or other."
SHAKESPEARE'S *Comedy of Errors*, i. 1.
"By *some* accident or other."—HOBBES.

Some ... *many*—
"She pulleth up *some* be the rote,
And *manye* with a knyf sche schereth."
GOWER, *Specimens of Early Eng.*, p. 373.

217. COMPOUNDS OF SOME.—*Somebody, something, some-one, somewhat, othersome, some-who.*

---
[1] Abbott's *Shakespearian Grammar*, p. 6.

Somebody[1]—

> "Ere you came by ther grove I was *sombody*,
> Now I am but a noddy (*i.e.* a nobody)"
> *Damon and Pythias*, in Dodsley's *Old Plays*.

Something—

> "When as we sat and sigh'd,
> And look'd upon each other, and conceived
> Not what we ail'd, yet *something* we did ail."
> DANIEL'S *Hymen's Triumph*.

> "For't must be done to-night,
> And *something* from the palace."—*Macbeth*, iii. 1.

> "Sir, you did take me up when I was nothing,
> And only yet am *something* by being yours."
> B. and F. *Philaster*.

Some who—

> "But if *somwho* the flamme staunche."—GOWER'S *Confess.* i. 15.

> "Than preyede the rich mon Abraham
> That he wolde sende Lazare or *sum other wham*
> To hys brethryn alle fyve."
> R. OF BRUNNE'S *Handlynge Synne*, p. 209.

Somewhat—

> "From them I should learn *somewhat*, I am sure,
> I never shall know here."—WEBSTER'S *Duchess of Malfy*.

> "*Duch.* What did I say?
> *Ant.* That I should write *somewhat*."—*Ib.*

> "There is *somewhat* in the winde."
> *Damon and Pythias*, in *Old Plays*, i. 193.

"Ther nys no creature so good, that him ne wanteth *somewhat* of the perfeccionin of God."—CHAUCER (ed Wright), ii. p. 333.

"Ther where he was schotte another chappelle standes, and *somwhat* of that tre."—R. OF BRUNNE'S *Chron*.

> "He come to Pers there he stode
> And askede hym sum of hys gode,
> *Sumwhat* of hys clothing."—*Ib.*, *Handlynge Synne*.

"Thi brother hath *sumwhat* ageins thee."—WICKLIFFE, *Matt.* v. 23.

"*Sumwhatt* Icc habbe shæwedd ȝuw."—*Orm.* 958.

Some one replaced the O. E. *sum man*.

> "*Some one* comes."—LONGFELLOW.

> "*Some one* among you all,
> Shew me herself or grave."—T. HEYWOOD'S *Silver Age*.

---

[1] Before *somebody* could get into use *body* must have been used for *wight*, *person*, as—

"A doughty *body* in alle his lyf."—*Gest. Rom.*

"The servaunts yede to her chaumber and founde *nobody*."—*Ib.* 35.

Robert of Brunne has *sum oun* (*Handlynge Synne*, p. 294) = some one; Robert of Gloucester has *somewanne* = *somewhom* = something.

Somdel = somedeal, is very common for *somewhat*.

Other some—

"*Other some* [houses are made] with reede."—HAKLUYT, p. 504.
"Though some be lyes,
Yet *other some* be true."—DODSLEY's *Old Plays*, ii. p. 74.

218. All and some—

This phrase is exceedingly common in O.E. and is equivalent to *all and one* = *one and all, each and all*. It has also the force of wholly, altogether; hence it is supposed that *some* = *same*, O.E. *samen*, together. Cp. Spenser's phrase "Light and dark *sam*."

"Stop your noses, readers, *all and some*."—DRYDEN, *Abs. and Achith.*
"This other swore *alle and some*."—*Specimens of E. Eng.* p. 106.
"The tale ys wrytyn *al and sum*,
In a boke of Vitas patrum."
                R. OF BRUNNE'S *Handlynge Synne*, l. 169.
"For everi creature go schal
By that brugge, *sum* or *al*."
                Old Eng. Miscell. p. 225.

By tmesis we have "*all together and sum*."

"Whyle they were *alle together and sum*."
                Play of the Sacrament, l. 402.

"Neither fals witnesse thou noon bere
On no mannys matere, *al neither somme*."—*Baby's Boke*, p. 49.
"(I have) nother witte enough *whole and some*."
                Damon and Pythias, Old Plays, p. 232.

219. One (O.E. *an, on,* *oon**)[1] is the numeral *one* with extended applications. It is used substantively and adjectively. When used substantively, it has a plural ones and a genitive one's, and may be compounded with *self*.

"*One* can only attribute the chameleon character in which *one* seems to figure to the want of penetration of *one*'s neighbours."—*Evening Standard*, Sat. Oct. 1, 1870, p. 1, col. 3.
"Once more I am reminded that *one* ought to do a thing *oneself* if *one* wants it to be done properly."—*Ib.* p. 1, col. 3.
"It is a pretty saying of a wicked *one*."
                TOURNEUR'S *The Revenger's Tragedy.*

"Go, take it up, and carry it in. 'Tis a huge *one*; we never kill'd so large a swine; so fierce, too, I never met with yet."—BEAUMONT AND FLETCHER, *The Prophetess.*

---

[1] Those marked thus (*) are later forms.

"To yeelde *one's* heart unto commiseration is an effecte of facilitie, tendernesse, and meeknesse."—MONTAIGNE'S *Florio*, p. 2.

" Well, well, such counterfeit jewels
Make true *ones* oft suspected."—WEBSTER'S *White Devil*.

220. Sometimes *one* = *some one* :—

" But here cometh *one;* I will withdraw myself aside."—LILY'S *Sapho. and Phao.*

" I hear *one's* pace, 'tis surely Carracas."
R. TAYLOR'S *The Hog hath lost his Pearl.*

" For taking *one's* part that is out of power."—*King Lear,* i. 3.

The earliest use of a genitive of *one* in its present acceptation is found in the *Morte d'Arthur,* p. 10.

" Lady thy sleve thou shalt of shere,
I wolle it take for the love of thee ;
So did I nevyr no *ladyes* ere,
But *one*[1] that most hath lovide me."

The plural of *one* occurs as early as Chaucer's time, as—"we thre ben al *oones.*"[2]

221. Chaucer, too, uses *one* as a substantive with an adjective where it seems to be a substitution for *wight*, or *person*, as—

" I was a lusty *oon*."—CHAUCER, l. 6187.

In the thirteenth century we find *thing*, properly neuter, used in a similar manner :—

" So that this tuo *lithere thinge* : were at one rede."[3]
Early Eng. Poems, p. 50.

One is used for *thing* in *Chevelere Assigne,* p. 15 :

" But what broode *on* is this on my breste,
  *   *   *   *
And what *longe on* is this that I shall up lyfte."

But this *one* is sometimes used instead of repeating the noun, as—

" Who embrace instead of the true [religion] a false *one,*" where Hooker, Book v. ch. ii. 2, omits the indefinite *one.*
So Milton, *Areop.* p. 45 : " It is a blank vertue, not a pure."
This usage does not explain the employment of *one* when it is preceded by a demonstrative, as *the, this,* &c., as *the mighty one.* Here the older writers employed the definite adjective with a final (inflexional) *e,* as *the gode.* The loss of this ending no doubt led to the introduction of *one* to supply its place. See p. 104.

222. The indefinite **one**, as in *one says*, is sometimes, but wrongly, derived from the Fr. *on,* Lat. *homo.* It is merely the use of the numeral one for the older *man, men,* or *me.*

---

[1] One = *ones* = the sleeve of one. Perhaps the *e* marks here the gen. fem.
[2] In the oldest Eng. *one* could have a plural, as *each one* = *anra gehwylc* = each of ones.
[3] *Lithere thinges* = wicked ones. This phrase is applied to Quendride (Kenelm's sister), and Askebert (Kenelm's guardian).

In the "Morte d'Arthur" *man* is replaced by *one* when it relates to a *feminine* word.[1]

"He is *man* of such apparayle,
 Off hym I have fulle mychelle drede."—*Morte d'Arthur*, p. 69.
"Launcelot than full stylle stoode,
 As *man* that was moche[l] of myght."—*Ib.* p. 118.
"And *one* that bryghtest was of ble."—*Ib.* p. 142.

223. Sometimes *he* occurs where we use *one* [2]—
"As *he* that ay was hend and fre."—*Morte d'Arthur*, p. 23.

Gower uses *he*, *she*, instead of the old relative after *as*, as—
"As he that was of wisdom slih."—*Specimens of E. Eng.* p. 367.
"As sche which dede hir hole intent."—*Ib.* p. 374.

Cp. "——— he died
 As *one that* had been studied in his death,
 To throw away the dearest thing he own'd."—*Macbeth*, i. 4.

"As *one* who would say, come follow . . ."
 Belphegor in LAMB's *Dram. Poets*, Bohn's Series, p. 532.

224. **Man.**

"For your name,
Of . . . and murderess, they proceed from you,
As if *a man* [= one] should spit against the wind;
The filth returns in 's [= one's] face."—WEBSTER's *White Devil.*

"As though *a man* would say," &c.—DRANT's *Sermons.*

"Vor the more that *a mon* can, the more wurthe he is."—ROBT. OF GLOUC.

"Vor, bote *a man* conne Frenss, *me* telth of him lute."—*Ib.*

"So, *that man that wolde* [= siquis] him wul arise, delicacy is to despise."—GOWER, iii. 40.

"Off thys bataille were to telle
 A *man that* it wele undyrstode
 How knyhtes undyr sadels felle."—*Morte d'Arthur*, p. 89.

225. *Appositional use of* one.

This use of *one* has become archaic, having been replaced by the partitive genitive.

---

[1] The form *men* for the singular, from which *me* comes by falling away of *n*, is to be explained by the fact that in the twelfth century, a final -*an* became -*en*; but *men* is often treated as a plural form in O. E.

[2] This use of *one* after *as* deserves some notice, as it has never been thoroughly explained.
This idiom answers to the Latin *quippe qui*, and, therefore, *one* is the substitute for a relative. In the twelfth and thirteenth centuries we find a *relative* instead of *one*; in later times *he* and *man* were substituted for it.
"He com himself alast *ase the thet* was of alle men veirest."—*Ancren Riwle*, p. 388.
Ase the thet = as he that = as *one* that.
"The sunne nis boten a schadewe *ase theo thet* loseth here liht."—*O.E. Hom.* First Series, p. 185.
Ase theo thet = as *she* that = as *one* that.

"I am *oon* the fayreste."—CHAUCER'S *Troylus and Cryseide*. c. v. 1.
"He was *oon* in soothe, without excepcioun,
——— *oon* the best on lyve."—*Ib. Compl. of L. Lyfe*, xxiii.
"So fair a wight as she was *oon*."—GOWER'S *Confess. Am.* ii. 70.
"An other such as he was *one*."—*Ib.* ii. 15.
"Lawe is *one* the best."—*Ib.* iii. 189.
"Suche a lemman as thou hast *oon*."—*Morte d'Arthur*, p. 25.
"Such a dynte he gaffe hym *one*.'—*Ib.* p. 117.
"For thys is *one* the mostē *synne*."—ROBT. OF BRUNNE, p. 6.

In Shakespeare we find *one* with superlatives—

"He is *one* the truest manner'd."—*Cymb.* i. 6.
"*One* the wisest prince."—*Hen. VIII.* ii. 4.

In the fifteenth century we find the partitive form in use, as—
"*One of* the strengest pyl."—LONELICH'S *Seynt Graal*, vol. i. p. 101.

Cp. the old use of *some*. See p. 123, § 169.

226. *Use of* one *before proper names.*[1]

"You may say *one* Albert, riding by
This way, only inquired their health."—R. TAYLOR'S *Lingua*.

227. For use of *one* = own, self, alone, see p. 123, § 169.

228. *One* = the same.

"That's all *one* to me."—GREEN, p. 86.
"'Tis all *one*
To be a witch as to be counted *one*."—DECKER'S *Witch of Edmonton*.

229. **None, no** (O. E. *nân, non,** *noon, na** = *ne* + *ân* = not one).[2]

No is formed of *none* by the falling away of *n*, and stands in the same relation to *none* as *my* and *thy* to *mine* and *thine*, and *a* to *an*. *None* is used substantively and absolutely, and *no* adjectively—

"But I can finde *none* that is good and meke."
HAWES, *P. of P.* p. 136.
"For surely there's *none* lives but 3 painted comfort."
KYD'S *Spanish Tragedy*.
"Thou shalt get kings, though thou be *none*."—*Macbeth*, i. 3.
"For overlop (omission) moht I mac *non*."
Specimens of E. Eng. p. 150.

It seems to be emphatic after the substantive—

"Satisfaction can be *none* but by pangs of death."
Twelfth Night, iii. 4.

---

[1] This construction occurs in Robert of Gloucester: "The castel hild *one* Wyllam Louel," l 9352.   [2] Those marked thus (*) are later forms.
[3] But = *tha thas not* painted, &c.

"And save his good broadsword he weapon had *none*."—W. SCOTT.
"For pok (poke, bag) no sek no havd he *nan*."
Specimens of E. Eng. p. 155.

In O.E. (fourteenth century) *non* (none) and *no* are used much in the same way as *an* and *a*; *none* before a vowel, &c.

"It toucheth to *non* other se."
MAUNDEVILLE, *Specimens of E. Eng.* p. 203.
"Sche doth *non* harm to *no* man."—*Ib.*
"And for to fall it hath *none* impediment."—HAWES, *P. of P.* p. 44.

230. **No**, though equivalent to *not one*, is often united to a plural substantive; thus we find in O.E.:

"*None* monekes."—*Specimens of E. Eng.* p. 80. "*Non* houses."—MAUNDEVILLE, p. 63. I.e. *No monks; no houses.*

None is sometimes followed by *other*—

"Thou shalt have *none other* gods before me."—*Deut.* v. 7.

In O.E. it is always *non other*, not *no other*, which would have sounded as strangely as *a other*.

231. **No one** (= not *one one*) is tautological, but it evidently replaces the O.E. *no man, no wight*.[1]
Sometimes *not one* is used in its place.

232. **Nothing, pl. Nothings.**

"The other sorts of devils are called in Scripture dæmonia .... and which St. Paul calleth *nothings*: for an idol, saith he, is *nothing*."—HOBBES, v. p. 2111.

233. **Aught, naught**—
Aught, ought (O.E. *awiht, aht*). *Awiht* contains the prefix *â* (as in O.E. *â-ge-hwylc* = *æghwylc*, each; *æf-re* = ever; *âhwæther, âwther, âther, outher, æg-hwæther, ægther* = either; *â-n* = one; *æ-n-ig*, any), the original signification of which is *ever, aye* (cp. Goth. *aiw*, Gr. *αεί*; Goth. *ai-r*, O.E. *æ-r, ere*), and *wiht* (Goth. *waihts*), *wight, whit*, creature, thing, something.

"For *aught* I know, the rest are dead, my lord."
WEBSTER'S *Appius and Virginia.*

"Amongst so many taousand authors you shall scarse find one by reading of whom you shall be *anywhit* better."—BURTON'S *Mel.* p. 7.
Cp. "To luite ne to muche *wiht*."—*Castel of Love,* l. 638.
"Thereof he ete a lytelle *wight*."—*Morte d'Arthur,* p. 36.
"Syr Evwayne, knowistow *any wight*?"—*Ib.* p. 5.

---

[1] "Sche was vanyssht riht as hir liste,
That *no wyht* bot hir-self it wiste."—GOWER, in *Spec. of E. Eng.* p. 371.

234. **Naught** (O.E. *nâwiht*,[1] *naht*) and *not* (O.E. *noght*, *nat*) are negative forms of *aught*, so that *not a whit* is pleonastic; in *a whit* the *a* must not be considered as the article; *a whit* = *awhit* = *awiht* or *aught*.

Naughts is used by Green (p. 157) for *nothings*—

"We country sluts of merry Fressingfield
Come to buy needless *naughts* to make us fine."

235. **Enough** (O.E. *genóh*, *ynough*,* *ynow*,* *enow*, *anow*. Cp. Goth. *ga-nohs*, Ger. *genug*).[2]

Sometimes we find *enow* used as a plural, corresponding to O.E. *inohe*, *inowe*, in which the plural is marked by the final *e*.

"Have I not cares *enow* and pangs *enow*?"—BYRON.
"Servile letters *anow*."[3]—*Areopagitica*, p. 40.

236. **Any** (O.E. *ænig* = *ullus*) is an adjective formed from the numeral *án*, one. In O.E. we find *æni*, *æi*, *ei*, for *any*, and Laȝamon has genitives, *æies* and *æines*.

"*Ay* two had disches twelve."—*Sir Gaw.: Specimens*, p. 224.

We find a distinction in O.E. made between the singular *eny*, *any*, and the plural *anie*, *anye*.

"And ȝif that *eni* him wraththed adoun *he* was anon."
ROBT. OF GLOUC.

237. Compounds are *anyone*, *anybody*, *anything*, O.E. *any wight*, *any man*, *eny persone*.

"Unnethe *eni mon* miȝte [h]is bowe bende."—ROBT. OF GLOUC.

Any originally had a negative *nænig* = *nullus*, of which a trace exists in the twelfth century.

"Niss *nani* thing" = there is not anything.—*Orm.* i. 61, l. 1839. "*Nani man*" = not any man.—*Ib.* p. 216. We use *none* instead:—"And as I had rather have *any* do it than myself, yet surely myself rather than *none* at all."—ASCHAM's *Scholemaster*, p. 157.

238. **Each** [O.E. *æ-lc* = *â-ge-lic*; from *â* (see remarks on *aught*), and *lic* = like; later forms are *elc*, *elch*, *euch*, *uch*, *ych*, *ech*, *ilk*].

It is properly singular, but has acquired a distributive sense. It is used substantively and adjectively.

---

[1] As an adverb *no whit* is found as well as *naught* = *not*.
"I am *no whit* sorry."—DODSLEY's *Old Plays*, ii. 84.
"Ector ne liked *no wight*
The wordis that he herd there."—*Morte d'Arthur*.
[2] Those marked thus (*) are later forms.
[3] Milton (*Areopagit.*, p. 28, ed. Arber) writes *anough*, adv.

"Of the fruit
Of *each* tree in the garden we may eat."—MILTON'S *P. L.* ix. 661.
"Simeon and Levi took *each* man his sword."—*Gen.* xxxiv. 25.
"Cloven tongues sat upon *each* of them."—*Acts* ii. 3.
"At *each* his needless heavings."—*Winter's Tale*, ii. 3.
"I a beam do find in *each* of three."—*Love's Labour's Lost*, iv. 3.

Each and *every* are used alike by Spenser:—
"She *every* hill and dale, *each* wood and plaine did search."—*F. Q.* i. 2, 8.

239. *Each* is sometimes used for *both*—
"And each though enemies to *either's* reign
Do in consent shake hands to torture me."
SHAKESPEARE'S *Sonnets*, 28.

Hence it often happens that *each* is wrongly followed by pronouns and verbs as the plural number.
"*Each* in her sleep *themselves* so *beautify*."—*Rape of Lucrece*, 404.
"How pale *each* worshipful rev'rend guest
Rise from a clergy or a city feast."—POPE'S *Imit. Hor.* ii. 75.

240. In the twelfth and following centuries, we find *each* followed by *an, a, on* = one.
"*Ille an* unnclene lusst,
Annd *ille an* ifell wille."—*Orm.* 5726.
"Heo bigonne to fle *echon*."—ROBT. OF GLOUCESTER. 378.
"*Ilkon* of the knightes had a barony."—R. OF BRUNNE'S *Chronicle*.
"And *ilka* lym on *ilka* syde."—HAMPOLE'S *P. of C.*
"Thei token *ech on* by hymself a peny."—WICKLIFFE, *Matt.* xx. 10.
"For hit clam *uche a* clyffe."—*Allit. Poems.*

Each one is a remnant of this, as—
"The princes of Israel, being twelve men: *each one* was for the house of his fathers."—*Num.* i. 44.

Each other sometimes = each alternate, every other, as—
"*Each other* worde I was a knave."—*Gammer Gurton's Needle.*

241. Every is a compound of *ever* and *each*, O. E. *æver-elc, ever-ilk, ever-each*. It was unknown in the oldest stage of the language; it occurs in Laȝamon (ab. 1200).
"*Everilc* he ke te, on *ile* he gret (wept)."—*Gen. and Ex.*
"*Everich*[1] of you schul brynge an hundred knightes."
CHAUCER'S *Knightes Tale*, l. 993.

[1] Here means *each* one [of you (two)].

INDEFINITE PRONOUNS.

> "Carry hym aboute to *every* of his friendes."
> *Fardell of Facion*, 8.
> "*Every* of your wishes."—*Antony and Cleop*. ii. 2.

We also find O. E. *evrichon, evcrilkan* = everyone. *Everybody* and *everything* are later formations.

The history of *every* having been forgotten in the sixteenth century, we find *every each*, like *not a whit, no one*, &c.

> "*Every each* of them hath some vices."—BURTON'S *Mel.* p. 601.

242. **Either** [O. E. (1) *æg-hwæther, æither, aither;* (2) *â-hwæther, âwther, âther, owther, outher, other.*]¹

Ei = *æg* = *â*, see remarks on *aught; -ther* = comparative suffix. See § 113. So *either* = any one of two, and sometimes it is used for *each* and *both*, but not so frequently in modern as in O. E.

> "The king of Israel and Jehoshaphat sat *either* of them on his throne."—2 *Chron.* xviii. 9.

Either has a possessive form—

> "Where *either's* fall determines both their fates."
> ROWE, *Lucan*, vi. 13.
> "They are both in *either's* power."—*The Tempest.*

> "Confute the allegations of our adversaryes, the end being truth, which once fished out by the harde encounter of *either's* argumentes .... both partes shoulde be satisfyed."—GOSSON'S *School of Abuse*, p. 46.

243. **Neither** (O. E. *nâhwæther, nâuther, nouther*²), the negative of *either* as *naught* is of *aught*.

> "Now new, now old, now both, now *neither*,
> To serve the world's course, they care not with whether."
> ASCHAM'S *Scholemaster*, p. 84.

> "*Neither* of either, I remit both twain."
> *Love's Labour's Lost*, v. 2.

> "Truth may lie on both sides, on either side or on *neither* side."—CARLYLE'S *French Revolution*, iii. 163.

> "Ac hor *nother*³ ... in pur ri3te nas."—ROBT. OF GLOUCESTER, *Specimens of E. Eng.* p. 68.

---

[1] Cp. "For *outher* he sal the tane hate
And the tother luf after his state,
Or he sal the tane of tham mayntene
And the tother despyse."—HAMPOLE'S *P. of C.* p. 31.
"Bot with the world comes Dam Fortone,
That *eyther* hand may chaunge sone."—*Ib.* p. 36.

[2] Cp. "He ne had *nouther* strenthe ne myght,
Nouther to ga ne ghit to stand."—*Ib.* p. 13.

[3] Neither of them.

It is sometimes, but wrongly, found with a plural verb, as—
"Thersites' body is as good as Ajax',
When *neither are* alive."—*Cymb.* iv. 2.

244. Other (O.E. *ô-ther*, Goth. *an-thar* = one of two, second and other. See remarks on numerals, p. 114).

This word originally belonged to the indefinite declension, making its plural *othre*, leaving *other* as the plural when the final *e* fell away, as

"Whan *other* are glad
Than is he sad."—SKELTON, i. 79.
"Some *other* give me thanks."—*Comedy of Errors*, iv. 3.
"Some *other* . . . . do not utterlie dispraise learning, but *they* saie," &c.—ASCHAM'S *Scholemaster*, p. 54.
"Awei sche bad alle *othre* go."
GOWER, in *Specimens of E. Eng.* p. 374.
Cp. "*Other some.*"—*Acts* xvii. 18.

A new plural was afterwards formed by the ordinary plural suffix *s*.

Other's (O.E. *othres, otheres*) is a true genitive.
"Let ech of us hold up his hond to other,
And ech of us bycome *otheres* brother."
CHAUCER, *Specimens of E. Eng.* p. 353
"And eyther dranke of *otheres* bloode."—*Gest. Rom.* p. 19.

245. Another is a later form;[1] *sum other* was once used instead of it.

246. One another, each other, are sometimes called reciprocal pronouns; but they are not compounds: in such phrases as "love each other," "love one another," the construction is, *each* love the *other*, *one* love *another*; *each* and *one* being subjects, and *other* and *another* objects, of their respective predicates.

In O.E. we find *each to other* = to each other.
We sometimes find *ayther other* = either other, in this sense, as—
"Uche payre by payre to plese *ayther other*."—*Allit. Poems*, p. 46.
"*Her eyther* had killed *other*."—*Piers Plowman*, Pas. v. 1. 165.

Other what = *what else* occurs in Dodsley's *Old Plays*, ii. 67,—
"What strokes he bare away, or
Other-what was his gaines, I wot not."
"And (he) speketh of *other-hwat*."—*Ancren Riwle*, p. 96.

247. Else (O.E. *elles*, the genitive of the demonstrative root, *ele, el*, as in Lat. *alius*[2]).

---

[1] *Another* is used in the *Ormulum*.
[2] In the oldest English we find a comparative *elra*.

We find it in O.E. after *ought*, *nought*, as in modern English. It has acquired an adverbial sense = *aliter*. Cp. O.E. *owiht elles* = aught of other = aught else.

> "A pouder * * * *
> I-maad, outher of chalk, outher of glas,
> Or *som what elles*."—CHAUCER, l. 13078.

> "Bischopes and bachelers, bote maistres and doctours,
> Liggen in London in lenten and *elles*."
> *Piers Plowman*, Prol. l. 91.

> "So, what for drede and *ellis*, they were both ensuryd."
> *Tale of Beryn*, l. 1122.

In the oldest English we had *elles hwæt* = aught else.[1] Sometimes we find *not else* = nought else.

> "In Moses' hard law we had
> *Not else* but darkness.
> All was *not else* but night."—DODSLEY's *Old Plays*, p. 39.

24 . Sundry (O.E. *synderig* = singularis, *sundrie*, *sondry* = separate) is now used in the plural—

> "For *sundry* weighty reasons."—*Macbeth*, iii. 1, iv. 3.

It occurs, however, sometimes as a singular in older writers in the sense of separate.

> "Alc hefde *sindri* moder."—*Laȝ.* i. 114.

> "Thor was in helle a *sundri* sted."—*Gen. and Ex.* 1984, p. 57.

So in Shakespeare—

> "The *sundry* contemplation
> Of my travels is a most humorous sadness."
> *As You Like It*, iv. 1.

249. Several is used for *sundry*—

> "To every *several* man."—*Julius Cæsar*, iii. 2.

> "Two *several* times."—*Ib.* v. 5.

> "Truth lies open to all, it's no man's *several*."—BEN JONSON.

> "By some *severals*."—*Winter's Tale*, i. 2.

250. Divers (O.E. *diverse*, O.Fr. *divers*), and different (Fr. *différent*), and O.E. sere, ser (O.Fr. *sevre*, separated ; *sevrée*, separation), are sometimes employed for *sundry*.

251. Certain (from Lat. *certus*) is singular and plural, and is used substantively and adjectively.

---

[1] *els what* in Chaucer.

" A *certain* man planted a vineyard."—*Mark* xii. 1.

" There came from the ruler of the synagogue's house *certain* which said."—*Ib.* v. 35.

" To hunt the boar with *certain* of his friends."—*Venus and Adonis.*

Cp. its use as a substantive in the following passages :—

" A *certayn* of varlettes and boyes."—Berner's *Froissart.*

" A *certain* of grain."—*Fardell of Facion.*

" Beseeching him to lene him a *certeyn*
Of gold, and he wold quyt it him ageyn."—Chaucer, l. 12952.

" ȝit I wolle have another *certayne.*"—*Gesta Rom.* p. 23.

CHAPTER XIII.

VERBS.

252. VERBS may be classified into (*a*) transitive, requiring an object, as "he *learns* his lessons;" (*b*) intransitive, requiring no object, as "the sun *shines*."

253. Transitive verbs only have a passive voice.
Transitive verbs include (1) *reflexive verbs*, in which the agent and object are identical, as "he *hurt himself*," " I'll *lay me* down ;" and *reciprocal verbs*, as "*to love one another*." These verbs admit of no passive voice.

254. Intransitive verbs include a large number that might be classed as frequentative, diminutive, inceptive, desiderative, &c.
Some intransitive verbs, by means of a preposition, become transitive, and may be used passively, as "the man *laughs at* the boy," "the boy was *laughed at* by the man."
Some intransitive verbs have a causative meaning, and take an object, as "he ran," "he *ran* a thorn through his finger." See Causative Verbs, under the head of VERBAL SUFFIXES.

255. Some transitive verbs are *reflexive* in meaning, though not in form, and appear at first sight as if used intransitively, as "he *keeps* aloof from danger," *i.e.* he *keeps himself*, &c. Cp. "he *stole* away to England."
Sometimes a transitive verb has a *passive sense*, with an active form, as "the cakes *ate* short and crisp" = the cakes *were eaten* short and crisp.

256. Intransitive verbs may take a noun of kindred meaning or object, called the cognate object, as to *die* a *death*, to *sleep* a *sleep*, to *run* a *race*.

257. Verbs used with the third person only are called impersonal verbs, as me *thinks*, me *seems*, it *rains*, it *snows*.

258. The verb affirms action or existence of a subject, under certain conditions or relations, called **voice, mood, tense.**

In some languages verbs undergo a change of form for voice, mood, and tense; the root being modified by certain suffixes before the person-endings are added.

Thus in Latin the root *reg* is modified by the suffix *s*,[1] to express *time* or *tense;* so the root *reg* becomes by this addition a *stem* to which the person-ending -*i* is suffixed; whence *rexi*, the perfect of *reg-ere*.

Voice.—There are two voices—(*a*) the *active*, in which the subject of the verb is represented as acting, as "I *love* John;" (*b*) the *passive*, in which the subject of the verb is represented as affected by the action, as "I am loved by John."

The passive voice has grown out of reflexive verbs; but our language has never developed, by change of the verb, a reflexive form, so that the passive voice in English is expressed by the passive participle combined with auxiliary verbs. The Scandinavian dialects have a special form for reflexive verbs. See p. 6.

259. There are five moods—(1) the *indicative* makes a simple assertion, states or asks about a fact; (2) the *subjunctive* expresses a possibility: it is sometimes called the conditional or conjunctive mood; (3) the *imperative* denotes that an action is commanded, desired, or entreated; (4) the *infinitive* states the action without the limitations peculiar to *voice, tense*, &c., and is merely an abstract *substantive;* (5) *participles* are adjectives.

260. The tenses are three—(*a*) *present*, (*b*) *past*, (*c*) *future*.

An action may be stated with reference to time, present, past, and future, as (*a*) indefinite, (*b*) continuous and imperfect, (*c*) perfect, (*d*) perfect and continuous.

Hence we may arrange the *tenses* according to the following scheme:—

TENSE.	INDEFINITE.	IMPERFECT CONTINUOUS.	PERFECT.	PERFECT CONTINUOUS.
Present ..	I praise.	I am praising.	I have praised	I have been praising.
Past[2] ...	I praised.	I was praising.	I had praised.	I had been praising.
Future ..	I shall praise.	I shall be praising.	I shall have praised.	I shall have been praising.

[1] This *s* was originally a part of the root *as*, to be.
[2] Sometimes called *imperfect*.

STRONG VERBS.

261. For *I praise, I praised*, we sometimes use *I do praise, I did praise*, which are by some called emphatic present and past tenses.

I am going to praise	is called *intentional present.*	
I was going to praise	,, ,,	*past.*
I shall be going to praise	,, ,,	*future.*

In English we have only *change of form* for the *present* and *past;* the other tenses are expressed by the use of auxiliary verbs.

262. There are two **numbers**, singular and plural; three **persons**, first, second, and third.

263. **Conjugation.**—Verbs are classified according to the mode of expressing the past indefinite tense, into (*a*) strong verbs, (*b*) weak verbs.

Strong Verbs.—The past tense of strong verbs is expressed by a change of vowel only; nothing is added to the root.

Weak Verbs.—The past tense indefinite of weak verbs is expressed by adding to the verbal root the syllable *d* or its euphonic substitute *t*. The *e* before *d* unites the suffix to the root.

The distinction between strong and weak verbs must be clearly borne in mind.

(1) *Strong verbs* have vowel change only; their past tense is *not* formed by adding -*d* or -*t*.

(2) The passive participles of strong verbs do *not* end in -*d* or -*t*, as do those of weak verbs.

(3) All p. participles of strong verbs once ended in -*en* (-*n*);[1] but in very many p. participles this suffix has dropt off. The history of a word is sometimes necessary to be known before its conjugation can be decided.

Weak verbs sometimes have a change of vowel, and the addition of -*d* or -*t*, as *bough-t;* but this change is no result of reduplication.

STRONG VERBS.

264. All strong verbs in the Aryan languages originally formed their perfect tense by reduplication, that is by the repetition of the root: thus from the root *bhug* = bend was originally formed (1) *bhug-bhug;* (2) *bhu-bhug* (by shortening the first root); then by adding the personal ending (3) *bhu-bhôga*, which is the Sanskrit verb = I bowed or bent, and this is found in Gr. πέ-φευγα, Lat. *fŭgi* (= *fufugi*), Goth. *baug*, O.E. *beáh*, English *bowed*.

In the Latin, Gothic, and O.E. forms, the vowel change shows that the initial letter of the root has gone, and the first consonant is

---

[1] The passive participle in -*n* is only an adjective like *wooden*. Cp. Lat. *plenus* original form = (1) *na*, whence (2) *an* = (3) *en*.

the initial of the reduplicated syllable. Thus, Latin, *fugi* = *fu* + *fug-i* = *fu* + *ug-i*.[1]

Thus, we see, the perfect of *facio* was probably formed: (1) *fa-fac-i*, (2) *fe-fic-i*, (3) *fcici*, (4) *feci*.

In languages belonging to the Teutonic group, we have even clearer examples of reduplication, as well as of the loss of it.

The verb *held* (past definite of *hold*, O.E. *heald-an*) was originally *heold;* but Gothic preserves the fuller form, *hai-hald;* O.H.Ger. *hialt* (i.e. *heihalt*); Ger. *hielt*.[2]

In our verb *held* the first *h* is the reduplicated letter. The vowel *e* is the result of the union of the vowel of the reduplicated syllable with that of the root.

265. The several stages would be (1) *ha-hald*, (2) *ha-hild*, (3) *haild*, (4) *held*.[3]

```
Cp. Goth. haitan  = to call    . .  perf. haihait.
   O.E.  hâtan        ,,      . . .   ,,   hêht, hêt.
   Goth. rêdan   = to rede (advise)   ,,   rairôth.
   O.E.  râedan       ,,      . . .   ,,   reórd.
   Goth. lêtan   = to let .   . . .   ,,   lailôt.
   O.E.  lætan        ,,      . . .   ,,   leórt (= leolt ; r for l).
   Goth. laikan  = to leap .  . . .   ,,   lailaik.
   O.E.  lâcan        ,,      . . .   ,,   leólc.
   O.E.  on-drædan = to dread .       ,,   on-dreord.
```

266. In Old English we have two verbs that preserve the reduplicated syllable and the initial root letter—

(1) **Did**, the past tense of *do*, O.E. *dide*, O. Sax. *dë-da*. It belongs, therefore, to the class of *strong* verbs.

We have a cognate root in τίθημι, and Lat. *do;* Sansk. *dha*. The Sans. perf. is *dadhâu* = Lat. *dedi*.

(2) **Hight**—

" An ancient fabric rais'd t' inform the sight,
There stood of yore, and Barbican it *hight*."—DRYDEN.

" That wretched wight
The Duke of Gloucester, that Richard *hight*."
SACKVILLE, *Duke of Buckingham*.

" Johan *hight* that oon, and Alayn *hight* that other."
CHAUCER, *The Reeve's Tale*.

Behight = promised. So little was this form understood in the sixteenth century that we actually find *behighteth* = promiseth, used by Sackville, as if from a present *behight:* cp. *ought* and *must*, originally past tenses which have acquired a present meaning.

Hight = *was called* is the past indefinite of the O.E. *hâtan*, *hate*, *hote*, to call, corresponding to Goth. *haihait*. See § 265.

---
[1] I lent my steps, fled.
[2] The change of vowel in the perfect is due to the coalescence of the vowel of the reduplicated syllable with the root vowel.
[3] For *ai* = ê, see § 47, p. 58.

267. DIVISION I. *Class I.*

The **first division** of strong verbs includes those whose past tenses clearly point to an original reduplication; the vowel of passive participles undergoes no change.[1]

	PRES.	PAST.	P.P.		PRES.	PERFECT.	P.P.
(1)	fall	fell	fallen	O.E.	fealle	feoll	feallen
	hold	held	held	,,	healde	heold	healden
	behold	beheld	beholden*				
	hang	hung	hung hangen*	,,	hange	hêng	hangen
	gang, go	—	gone	,,	gange	geong	gangen
(2)	sweep	swep*	swepen*	,,	swâpe	sweop	swâpen
	hate*	hight	hoten*	,,	hâte	hêht hêt	hâten
	blow	blew	blown	,,	blâwe	bleow	blâwen
	know	knew	known	,,	cnâwe	cneow	cnâwen
	crow	crew	crown	,,	crâwe	creow	crâwen
	sow	sew*	sown	,,	sâwe	seow	sâwen
	mow	mew*	mown	,,	mâwe	meow	mâwen
	throw	threw	thrown	,,	thrâwe	threow	thrâwen
(3)	let	let*[2] leet*	leten*	,,	lǽte	leort, leot, lêt	lǽten
(4)	sleep	slep* sleep*	slepen*	,,	slǽpe	slêp	slǽpen
	leap	lep* leep*	lopen*	,,	hleâpe	hleop	hleâpen
	beat	bet* beet* beat	beaten	,,	beâte	beot	beâten
	hew	hew*	hewn	,,	heâwe	heow	heâwen
(5)	row	rew*	rowen*	,,	rôwe	reow	rôwen
	grow	grew	grown	,,	grôwe	grew	grôwen
	flow	flew	flown	,,	flowe	fleow	flôwen
(6)	weep	wep*	wepen*	,,	wêpe	weop	wêpen

(1) Many verbs once belonging to this division have either become obsolete or have adopted a weak form for the past tense and p. participle, as—

Well (O.E. *weallan*, to well up), fold, walk, low, row, span, leap, sweep, weep.

In the provincial dialects we find strong forms of some of these verbs still in use, as *to row*, past *rew*, p.p. *rowen*; *to leap*, past *lop*,

---

[1] Forms marked * are obsolete, and *weak* forms have taken their places, as *slept, hewed, wept, leapt, rowed*. Some of these weak forms came in early—*slepte, dredde* = dreaded, as in the *Ormulum*.

[2] *Let* in twelfth century has a weak form, *let-te, lætte*.

loup, p. p. *loupen ; to weep*, past *wep ;* to *sleep*, past *slep ; to beat*, past *bett* (Scotch). Cp. :—
"Some to the ground were *lopen* from above."—SURREY, *Æn.* ii.
"She brouhte the greyn from hevene to erthe and *seew* it. The erthe ther it was *sowe* was never ered."—*Pilgrimage*, p. 43.
" For while they be *folden* together as thorns."—*Nahum* x. 10.
" And sighing sore, her hands she wrung and *fold.*"
SACKVILLE'S *Induction.*

(2) **Let** (past), though strong in form, is weak as regards its pronunciation ; it is weak in the p. p. : **beat** is weak in pret., but strong in p. p.

(3) **Hew, sow, mow,** have now weak past tenses, but strong passive participles, as well as weak ones.
In the Bible we have p. p. *hewn* and *hewed.*
The provincial dialects have strong forms, as *hew* = hewed, *sew* = sowed, *mew* = mowed, *snew* = snowed.

(4) **Hung** (past) = O. E. *heng ;* it has also a weak past, *hanged,* and a weak p. p. *hanged.* In O. E. we find *hangian,* a derivative, and weak verb, making its past tense *hangode.*

(5) Some passive participles have sprung from the past tense, as hung = *hangen ;* held = *holden ;* fell = *fallen* (Shakespeare, *Lear,* iv. 6).
Others have contracted forms of p. p., as *sown* = *sowen,* &c.

268. The second division of strong verbs includes those that have vowel change in the past tense and in the passive participle.

These verbs were of course originally reduplicate, but the evidence is not so clear as in the first class of verbs. Cp. *set* (= did sit), Goth. *sat,* with Sansk. *sa-sad-a* (pl. *sēd-ima*), Lat. *sed-i ; bound* (O. E. *band*), Goth. *band,* Sansk. *ba-bandh-a.*[1]
Here the *past tense* contains the *original vowel,* while the vowel *a* of the present tense has been weakened to *i :* so such verbs as *give, help* stand for more ancient roots, as *gaf, halp,* which in the preterite preserve the original root vowel.
Sometimes the root of the present is strengthened by an infixed letter, as *ga-n-g,* go, *sta-n-d, bri-n-g, thi-n-k.* Cp. Lat. *fu-n-do, tu-n-do,* &c.

269. DIVISION II. *Class I.*[2]

				O.E.		
PRES.	PAST.	P.P.	PRES.	PERF. *sing.*	PERF. *pl.*	P.P.
(1) help	halp* holp*	holpen	helpe	healp	hulpon	holpen
delve	dalf* dolve*	dolven*	delfe	dealf	dulfon	dolfen

[1] This is seen by the Sansk. root *bandh* compared with perfect *babandha.*
[2] Forms marked thus (*) are obsolete.

XIII.] STRONG VERBS. 159

	Pres.	Past.	P.P.	Pres.	O.E. Perf. sing.	Perf. pl.	P.P.
	melt	malt* molt*	molten	melte	mealt	multon	molten
	yield	yold* yald*	yolden*	gilde	geald	guldon	golden
	swell	swoll* swall*	swollen	swelle	sweal	swullen	swollen
(2)	swim	swam	swum	swimme	swamm	swummon	swummen
	climb	clamb* clomb*	clomben*	climbe	clamb	clumbon	clumben
	be-gan	began	begun	on-ginne	ongann	ongunnon	ongunnen
	spin	spun span*	spun	spinne	spann	spunnon	spunnen
	win	wan	won	winne	wan	wunnon	wunnen
	run	ran	run	rinne yrne	ran arn	runnon urnon	runnen urnen
	bind	bound	bound	binde	band	bundon	bunden
	find	found	found	find	fand	fundon	funden
	grind	ground	ground	grinde	grand	grundon	grunden
	wind	wound	wound	winde	wand	wundon	wunden
	slink	slunk	slunk	—	—	—	—
	drink	drank	drunk	drince	dranc	druncon	druncen
	shrink	shrank	shrunk	for-scrince	-scranc	scruncon	scruncen
	sink	sank	sunk	since	sanc	suncon	suncen
	stink	stank	stunk	stince	stanc	stuncon	stuncen
	sing	sang	sung	singe	sang	sungon	sungen
	spring	sprang	sprung	springe	sprang	sprungon	sprungen
	sting	stang	stung	stinge	stang	stungon	stungen
	swing	swung	swung	swinge	swang	swingon	swungen
	wring	wrung	wrung	wringe	wrang	wrungon	wrungen
	ring	rang	rung	hringe	hrang	hrungon	hrungen
	cling	clang	clung	clinge	clang	clungon	clungen
	ding	dang* dung*	dungen*	—	—	—	—
(3)	carve	carf*	corven*	ceorfe	cearf	curfon	corfen
	starve	starf*	storven*	steorfe	stearf	sturfon	storfen
	worth	warth* worth*	worthen*	weorthe	wearth	wurthon	worthen
	burst	burst barst* brast*	burst borsten* bursten*	berste	bearst	burston	borsten
	thrash	throsh*	throshen*	thersce	thearsc	thurscon	thorscen
(4)	fight	fought	fought foughten*	feohte	feaht	fuhton	fohten

Here the root vowel was originally *a*, weakened to *i* in the present and to *u* in the past pl. and p.p.

(1) To this division once belonged milk, yield, swallow, bellow, stint, burn, mourn, spurn, ding, carve, starve, burst.

Cp. " Forth from her eyen the crystal tears out *brast*."
SACKVILLE'S Induction.

" When Adam *dalve*, and Eve span,
Who was then the gentleman?
Up start the carle and gathered good,
And thereof came the gentle blood."
BP. PILKINGTON (Parker Soc. p. 125).

"I waked : herewith to the house-top I *clamb*."—SURREY, *Æn. II.*
"Who willingly had *yielden* prisoner."—*Ib.*
"The *yolden* ghost his mercy doth require."—SURREY'S *Ecclesiastes.*
"Many founden it (*greyn*) and *throsshen* it."—*Pilgrimage,* p. 43.
"Which hath *dung* me down to the infernal bottom of desolation."—NASH'S *Lenten Stuff.*

(2) We have many verbs with mixed strong and weak forms; the past tense may be weak and the p.p. strong, as, past, *clomb,* and p.p. *climbed;* or the past may be strong and the p.p. weak, as, past, *delved,* p.p. *dolven.* *Clemde* occurs in fourteenth century English.

Swollen has almost given way to *swelled.*

Helped has replaced the old past, *holp;*[1] *holpen* as a p.p. is archaic, *helped* being now the regular form.[2]

(3) Sometimes a strong participle is used simply as an adjective, as drunken, molten—"a *drunken* man," "*molten* lead;" in *Micah* i. 4, *molten* is used as p.p.; so in Elizabethan writers, *sunken, shrunken.*

"And the metalle be the hete of the fire *malt*"—CAPGRAVE, p. 9.
"My heart is *molt* to see his grief so great."
SACKVILLE'S *Induction.*
"As gold is tried in the oven, wherein it is *molten.*"—COVERDALE.

(4) The verbs swim, begin, run, drink, shrink, sink, ring, sing, spring, have for their proper past tenses *swam, began, ran,* &c., preserving the original **a**; but in older writers (sixteenth and seventeenth centuries) and in colloquial English we find forms with u, which have come from the passive participles.[3]

Sometimes we actually find the past tense doing duty for the passive participle; thus Shakespeare has **swam** = *swum* (*As You Like It,* iv. 1), drank = *drunk.*

(5) Many of those forms that originally had **a** in the past now have u, as spun, slunk, stunk, stung, flung, swung, wrung, clung, and strung (a modern form). "Sche *flang* from me" (Heywood's *Proverbs,* C. 4). *Slang* (1 Sam. xvii. 49).

---

[1] *Holp* is a preterite in Shakespeare. See *King John,* i. 1; *Rich. II.* v. 5.
[2] *Holpen:* "He hath *holpen* his people Israel"—Eng. Bible; "he *halp* his brother"—CAPGRAVE, p. 30; *holp* for *holpen* is found in Shakespeare, *Tempest,* i. 2.
[3] Some grammarians have ascribed these past tenses to the pret. pl.; but this is hardly probable, for we do not find these forms in use in the thirteenth and fourteenth centuries, i.e. *swum* for *swam* in past sing.; what we do meet with is a change of *a* into *o*, as *swom, begon, song* (*soong*). Ben Jonson has *to fling,* past. *flang, flong,* p.p. *flong,* &c.

A few verbs have *ou*, which has arisen out of an *o* or *oo*, as bound = O.E. *bond* = *band;* found = *fond* (*foond*) = *fand;* ground = *grond* (*groond*) = *grand.*

(6) Wound = past of *to wind* (up), but *winded* = past tense of *to wind* a horn; but Walter Scott has "his horn he *wound*" (*Lady of the Lake*).

(7) *Foughten* occurs in *Henry V.* iv. 6: cp. "a hard-*foughten* feeld" (Heywood's *Proverbs*, E. 111). *Starven* p.p. is used by Sackville: "her *starven* corpse" (*Induction*); "hunger-*starven*" (Hall's *Satires*); but "hunger-*storved*" (*Gam. Gurton's Needle*).

270. DIVISION II. Class II.

	PRES.	PAST.	P.P.	PRES.	O.E. PERF.	P.P.
(1)	steal	stole	stolen	stele	stæl[1]	stolen
(2)	come	came	come	cume	com	cumen
(3)	bear	bore bare	born borne*	bere	bær	boren
	shear	shore*	shorn	scere	scær	scoren
	tear	tore	torn	tere	tær	toren
(4)	speak	spoke spake	spoken spoke*	sprece brece	spræc bræc	sprecen brocen

(1) The old verbs quell (*kill*) and nim (to take, rob) once belonged to this class.

(2) In O.E. (fourteenth century, especially in the Northern dialects) we find the old *æ* represented often by *a*:—*stal, bar, schar, tar, spac, brac; bare, brake, spake*, are archaic; in the Southern dialect we find *æ* often changed to *e*, as *ber* (*beer*), *spec, brek.*

(3) Born and Borne, though the same words, have different meanings: *borne* = carried; *born* = brought forth.

(4) In older writers, and sometimes in modern poetry, we find the *n* falling away (as in Old English): hence *broke*[2] = *broken; spoke* = *spoken; stole*[4] = *stolen.* Shakespeare has "I have *spake*" (*Henry VIII.* ii. 4).

(5) Shakespeare, *Cymbeline*, v. 5, has *becomed.*

(6) The *e* in *stole*, &c., is no inflexion; it merely marks the length of the preceding vowel.

---

[1] The pret. pl. has a long vowel, as *stâlon, cwâmon, bâron*, &c.
[2] *Measure for Measure*, v. 1.   [3] Walter Scott, *Kenilworth.*
[4] Milton.

271. DIVISION II. *Class III.*

	PRES.	PAST.	P.P.	PRES.	O.E. PERF.	P.P.
(1)	give	gave	given	gife	geaf	gifen
	weave	wove	woven	wefe	wæf	wefen
(2)	eat	ate eat	eaten eat	ete	æt	eten
	get	got gat*	gotten got	ongite¹	ongeat	ongeten
	sit	sat	sat seten*	sitte	sæt	seten
	tread	trod	trodden trod	trede	træd	treden
	bid	bade bid	bidden bid	bidde	bæd	beden
	—	quoth	—	cwethe	cwæth	cweden
(3)	—	was	—	wese	wæs	wesen
(4)	wreak	—	wroken*			
	lie	lay	lain lien*	licge	læg	legen
	see	saw	seen	sco (seohe)	seah PRET. *pl.* sâwon	ge-sên

(1) **Quoth**, originally perfect, is now used as a present tense; the root of the present is seen in *bequeathe.* The present of **was** is lost; we have parts of the verb in *wast, were, wert.*

(2) **Mete** (measure), **wreak**,² **weigh, fret, knead**, once strong, have become weak. Cp.

"We shall not all *unwroken* die this day."—SURREY, *Æn.* ii.

(3) In O.E. (thirteenth and fourteenth centuries) we find *gaf* and *gef, et* and *eet, quath* and *quod.*

(4) **Bid** = bade, arises out of the passive participle; *beden* = *bidden* occurs in the fifteenth century; so *seten* for *sat.*

Boden = *bidden,* invited. "It happed hym that was *boden,* in lokyng on the walle to espye this ymage," &c. (Caxton's *Golden Legend,* fol. cclxix. col. 1). This verb properly belongs to Class VI. (Div. II.).³

Heywood uses the phrase "a *geven* horse" (*Proverbs,* B. ii.).

(5) Walter Scott has **eat** = *ate.*

(6) **Gat** is used by Shakespeare for *got* (past).

(7) The ending of the passive participle has sometimes fallen away, as in **bid** = *bidden; sat,* the past indef., is used instead of the old participle *seten.*

---

¹ *Ongite* = perceive, understand.
² Spenser has a strong p.p. *wroken (Shep. Cal.).*
³ Cp. O.E. *beode, beâd, boden,* to bid, order.

Double forms of the p. p. are *eaten* and *eat;*[1] *bidden* and *bid;*[2] *gotten* and *got;*[3] *trodden* and *trod;*[4] *woven* and *wove;*[5] *lien*[6] (= O. E. *i-leye* = *ilsien* = *ge-legen*) and *lain*.

272. DIVISION II. *Class IV.*

PRES.	PAST.	P.P.	PRES.	O.E. PERF.	P.P.
stand	stood	stood	stande	stôd	standen
swear	swore	sworn	swerige	swôr	sworen
shape	shope*	shapen*	scape	scôp	scapen
heave	hove*	hoven*	hebbe	ahôf	hafen
grave	grove*	graven*	grafe	grôf	grafen
shave	shove*	shaven*	scafe	scôf	scafen
lade	—	laden	hlade	hlôd	hladen
wash	wesh*	washen*	wasce	wôsc	wæscen
bake	book*	baken*	bace	bôc	bacen
shake	shook	shaken	scace	scôc	scocen
forsake	forsook	forsaken	—	—	—
take	took	taken	tace	tôc	tacen
awake	awoke	awoke	wace	wôc	wacen
ache	ok*	oken*	ace	ôc	acen
draw	drew	drawn	drage	drôh	dragen
gnaw	gnew*	gnawn*	gnage	gnôh	gnagen
laugh	lough*	laughed	hleahhe	hlôh	hleahhen
slay	slew	slain	sleahhe	slôh	sleahhen
wax	wex* wox*	waxen*	weaxe	weôx	weaxen

(1) Fare, wade, ache, gnaw, wash, step, laugh,[7] yell, wax,[8] bake,[9] have at present weak past tenses and passive participles.

Cp. " Sapience this bred turnede and *book* it."—*Pilgrimage*, p. 44.
Beuk = book occurs in Ramsay's *Gentle Shepherd*, ii. 1.
Gnew = gnawed occurs in *Mirrour for Magistrates*, vol. ii. p. 74.
" *Gnew* and fretted his conscience."—TYNDALL'S *Prol. to Jonas*, Parker Soc. p. 456. Shakespeare has *begnawn*, *Tam. of Shrew*, iii. 2.
" He *flay* a lion."—CAPGRAVE.
" Both *flayn* and hedid " (= beheaded).—*Ib. Chron.* p. 61.
" Zoroaster *low* as no child did but he."—*Ib.* p. 26.
" There he *wesh* me, there he bathed me."—*Pilgrimage*, p. 8.
" And in here owen blood han *washen* hem."—*Ib.*
" She . . . *heff* up hire axe to me."—*Ib.* p. 111.
" She said her hede *oke*."—*La Tour Landry*.

---

[1] Shakespeare, *King John*, i. 1. [2] Milton, *Paradise Lost*, vii. 304.
[3] English Bible. [4] Shakespeare, *K. Richard II.* ii. 2.
[5] Milton, *Par. Lost*, ix. 839. [6] Eng. Bible and Shakespeare, now archaic.
[7] Scotch has *leugh* = laughed (past). [8] Spenser has *woxe*, past, *woxen*, p.p.
[9] *Baken* = baked, p.p. in *Leviticus* ii. 4. " My spirit is *waxen* weak and feeble."—*Ps. lxxvii.* COVERDALE.

(2). (*a*) Strong forms have been replaced by weak ones in the past tense of **shape, grave, shave, lade,** &c. Strong participles of these are occasionally met with, as **shapen** (*Ps.* li. 5), **graven** (p.p. in Byron, *Childe Harold*, i. ; as an adjective, in English Bible, *Ex.* xx. 4; p.p. *Ps.* xcvii. 7), **loaden**=laden (Milton, *P. Lost*, iv. 14; Bacon, *Essays*). "The heavier the ship is *loaden*, the slower it goes" (Bp. Pilkington, p. 208). Cp.

"And masts *unshave* for haste."—SURREY, *Æn.* iv.

"With such weapons they *shope* them to defend."—*Ib. Æn.* ii.

(*b*) We have also double forms, a strong and a weak one, in the past tense, as **woke** and **waked**; **hove** and **heaved**.

(*c*) We sometimes in Shakespeare find forms of the past tense employed for the p. participle, as **arose** (*Comedy of Errors*, v. 1) = *arisen;* **shook** (*King John*, iv. 2; *Othello*, ii. 1; Milton, vi. 219) = *shaken;* **forsook** (*Othello*, iv. 2) = *forsaken;* **took** (*Twelfth Night*, iv. 2; *Julius Cæsar*, ii. 1) = *taken;* **mistook** (*Julius Cæsar*, i. 2; Milton, *Arcades*) = *mistaken;* **shaked**, too, occurs for *shaken* (*Ps.* cix. 25; *Troilus and Cressida*, i. 3; *Henry V.* ii. 1; *Tempest*, ii. 1).

(3) **Stood**, p.p. is properly a past tense; the old p.p. = *standen*. Cp. the p.p. *understanden* and *understand*.

"Have I *understand* thy mind?"—COVERDALE, p. 457.

(4) **Sware** occurs in *Mark* vi. 23, *Titus Andronicus*, iv. 1; but the *a* is not original, but probably has come in through false analogy with *spake, bare,* &c.

273. DIVISION II. *Class V.*

O. E.

PRES.	PAST.	P.P.	PRES.	PERF. *sing.*	PERF. *pl.*	P.P.
(1) shine	shone	shone	scíne	scân	scinon	scinen
(2) drive	drove	driven	drífe	drâf	drifon	drifen
shrive	shrove	shriven	scrífe	gescraf	gescrifon	gescrifen
thrive	throve	thriven	—	—	—	—
rive	rove*	riven	—	—	—	—
(3) bite	bot*	bitten	bíte	bât	biton	biten
smite	smote	smitten	smíte	smât	smiton	smiten
write	wrote	written	wríte	wrât	writon	writen
a-bide	abode	abiden*	bíde	bâd	bidon	biden
chide	chode* chid	chidden	cíde	câd	cidon	ciden
ride	rode	ridden	ríde	râd	ridon	riden
slide	slode* slid	slidden slid }	âslíde	âslâd	âslidon	âsliden

STRONG VERBS.

Pres.	Past.	P.P.	Pres.	O.E. Perf. sing.	Perf. pl.	P.P.
stride	strode	stridden	strithe	strâth	strithon	strithen
writhe / wreathe	writhed	writhen*	writhe	wrâth	writhon	writhen
rise	rose	risen	â-rise	ârâs	ârison	ârisen
arise	arose	arisen				
strike[1]	struck	struck stricken	strice	strâc	stricon	stricen

(1) Gripe (= grasp), spew, slit, wreathe (writhe), sigh, rive, once belonged to this class, but have become weak: riven is used as an adjective.

(2) Most of these verbs have changed the *â* of the past into *o*, as shone, drove, &c.

The older forms sometimes occur, as drave (in English Bible and Shakespeare), smate, &c. "Absalom *drave* him out of his kingdom" (Coverdale); "*strake* me with thunder" (Surrey, *Æn.* ii.); "he with his hands *strave* to unloose the knots" (*Ib.*).

(3) Just as we found *sung* = *sang*, *swum* = *swam*, properly participial forms, so we find, in the sixteenth and seventeenth centuries, driv = *drove*, smit = *smote*, rid = *rode*, ris = *rose*, writ = *wrote*. Cp. bit for O.E. *bot*, *boot*.

(4) Shortened forms of the participles occur, as writ = *written* (*Twelfth Night*, v. 1; *Richard II.* ii. 1), smit = *smitten*, chid = *chidden*, slid = *slidden*.

Chid, O.E. *cídde*, *chidde*, is a weak form: "the eldest *chidde* with the knight" (*La Tour Landry*, p. 19).[2]

(5) Past tenses are also used for the participles, as drove = *driven* (2 *Henry VI.* iii. 2), rode = *ridden* (*Henry IV.* v. 3; *Henry V.* iv. 3), smote = *smitten* (*Coriolanus*, iii. 1), wrote = *written* (*Lear*, i. 2; *Cymbeline*, iii. 5), arose = *arisen* (*Comedy of Errors*, v. 1).

(6) Weak forms of the passive participle are rived (*Julius Cæsar*, i. 3), strived (*Rom.* xv. 20), shrived (*King John*, ii. 4).

(7) In shone for *shinen*, abode for *abiden*, struck for *stricken*, we have the substitute of the past tense for the p. participle.

(8) For stricken and driven we sometimes find *strucken* (Milton, ix. 1064; *Julius Cæsar*, iii. 1); "the clock hath *strooken* four"

---

[1] *Orm.* has *strike*, *strac*, as in modern English; in the oldest English *strice* = I go.
[2] *Chode* occurs in the Bible (*Gen.* xxxi. 36, *Numbers* xx. 3). *Chide*, p.p. in Shakespeare.

(Lodge's *A Looking-glass for London*); *droven* = *driven* (*Antony and Cleopatra*, iv. 7).

(9) **Shined** = *shone* (*Ezek.* xliii. 2). *Shinde* occurs in the fourteenth century.

(10) **Wreathen**, as adjective, occurs in *Timon of Athens*, iii. 2, "that sorrow-*wreathen* root;" "*wreathen* cables" (Surrey, *Æn.* iv.). It occurs in *The Newfounde World* as a p.p. : " out of which may be *wrong* or *writhen* water." *Abiden* occurs in the English Bible. " He had *bid*" = *abiden* = endured (Sidney's *Arcadia*).

274. Division II. *Class IV.*

				O.E.		
Pres.	Past.	P.P.	Pres.	Perf. *sing.*	Perf. *pl.*	P.P.
creep	crop*	cropen*	creope	creâp	crupon	cropen
shove	shof*	shoven*	sceofe	sceâf	scufon	scoien
cleave	clave*	cloven	cleofe	cleâf	clufon	clofen
	clove					
shoot	shot	shotten*	sceote	sceât	scuton	scoten
seethe		sodden	seothe	seâth	sudon	soden
		sod				
choose	chase*	chosen	ceose	ceâs	curon	coren
	chose					
freeze	froze	frozen	freose	freâs	fruron	froren
lose	lost	losen*	forleose	forleâs	forluron	forloren
suck	sook*	soken*	sûce	seâc	sucon	socen
fly	flew	flown	fleoge }	fleâh	flugon	flogen
flee	flew*	—	fleohe }			

(1) Many verbs belonging to this class have become weak, as creep,[1] cleave, seethe, lose, chew, rue, brew, dive, shove, slip, lot, fleet, reek, smoke, bow, suck, lock. Cp.

> "She *shof* me with hire knyf."—*Pilgrimage*, p. 132.
> "*Shoven* on thilke spere."—*Ib.* p. 130.
> "Ther *sook* never noon suich milk."—*Ib.* p. 205.

(2) Creep, cleave, bereave, flee, lose, shoot, shorten the long vowel of the present in the weak form of their past tenses.

(3) **Clave** and **cloven** occur in the English Bible (*Genesis* xx. 3, *Ps.* lxxviii. 15, *Acts* ii. 3); *cleft*, p.p., in *Micah* i. 4 (cp., too, a "*cleft* palate," but a "*cloven* foot"); *chase* in Surrey's poems;[2] *shotten*

---

[1] Cp. Scotch *crap* (*Gentle Shepherd*, v. 1).
[2] "Shelton for love, Surrey for lord thou *chase*."—P. 92 (Bell's edition).

occurs in *shotten herring* (1 *Henry IV.*) = a herring that has deposited its roe ; *forlorn* (Milton, *Paradise Lost*, ii. 6—15) = *forlosen*.[1] Milton has *frore*, Spenser *frorne* = *frozen ; froze* = *frozen* occurs in Shakespeare, 2 *Henry IV.* i. 1. *Sodden* occurs in English Bible ; cp.

> " Twice *sod* simplicity."—*Love's Labour's Lost*, iv. 2.
> " *Sodden* water."—S. ROWLANDS.
> " Beer he protests is *sodded* and refined."—*Ib*.
> " With rost or *sod*."—*Ib*.

(4) **Cleave**, O.E. *clifian*, to cling to, adhere to. This is properly a weak verb, and its past tense is *cleaved ;* yet *clave* is sometimes found (*Ruth* i. 14 ; *Acts* xvii. 34).

(5) **Flee** has a weak past tense and p.p., *fled*.

275. Some verbs that have now a strong past tense, or p.p., were once weak, as—

	PRES.	PAST.	P.P.
(1)	wear	wore ware*	worn
(2)	stick	stuck stack*	stuck
(3)	betide	betid[2]	betid
(4)	dig	dug digged*	dug digged*
(5)	hide	hid	hidden hid
(6)	spit	spit* spat[2]	spitten* spitted* spat
(7)	show	—	shown shewed showed

Stack = *stuck* is used by Surrey :

"Which he refused and *stack* to his intent."—*Virgil*, ii. (ed. Bell), p 170.

---

[1] " With gastly lookes as one in manner *lorne*."—SACKVILLE, *Induction*, st. 78. *Forlore* (cp. *frore*) : " Thou hadst not spent thy travail thus, nor all thy pain *forlore*."—SURREY (ed. Bell), p. 80.

[2] *Betid* and *spat* are only apparently weak ; in O.E. we find *be-tid-de, spatte*.

WEAK VERBS.

276. The verbs of the strong conjugation we have seen form the past tense by a change of the root-vowel; weak verbs by means of a suffix *-d* or *-t*.

This suffix is a mutilated form of the auxiliary verb *do*.[1]

In O.E. the perfect of *do* was di-*de*, in O.Sax. *deda*. In O.E. the suffix of the perfect of weak verbs was *-de;* in Goth. and O. Sax. *-da*. In the plural (Gothic) it has a longer form—*dedum:* thus from Goth. *nasian*, O.E. *nerian*, to save, was formed. Goth. *nasi-da*,[2] I saved; *nasi-dedum*, we saved. O.E. *nere-de*, I saved; *nere-don*, we saved.

277. The suffix *-de* was originally united to the root by means of a vowel *e* or *o*,[3] as O.E. *ner-e-de* = saved; *luf-o-de* = loved.

In Gothic and Old High German there were *three* conjugations of weak verbs, according to the vowel that was between the root and suffix of the perfect:—

(1) The first conjug. had *i*, as Goth. *nas-i-da*, O.H.Ger. *ner-ita*, O.E. *ner-e-de* = preserved.

(2) The second conjug. had *ô*, as Goth. *salb-o-da*, O.H.Ger. *salp-ô-ta*, O.E *sealf-o-de* = anointed.

(3) The third conjug. had *ai* Goth., *ê* O.H.Ger. Goth. *hab-ai-da*, O.H.Ger *hap-ê-ta*, wanting in O.E.

278. The oldest English had *two* conjugations of weak verbs—

(1) With vowel *e* between root and suffix.
(2) ,, ,, *o* ,, ,, ,,

279. Modern English has in reality only one class with vowel *e* between root and suffix.

In *thank-e-d*, past indef., *thank* = root; *e* = connecting vowel; and *-d* = contracted form of *did*.

In *thank-e-d*, p.p. *thank* = root; *e* = connecting vowel; *d* = participle suffix cognate with Gothic *-da(s)*, Lat. *-tu(s)* (= *to-s*), Gr. *-to(s)*, Sansk. *-tâ(s)*.[4]

(1) This *e*, however, is only preserved when the suffix *d* is to be united to a root ending in a dental, as *wett-e-d*, *head-e-d*, *waft-e-d*.

---

[1] Cp. Gr. pass. first aorist ἐτύφ-θ-ην, where the tense suffix is the θη (= O.E. *de*) of τί-θη-μι.

[2] Represents a more original *nasi-dêda*.

[3] This *e* or *o* is represented in Sanskrit by the suffix *-aya*, which appears in Gothic *hab-ai-da* = O.E. *hæf-de* = ha-d.

[4] This termination is evidently an old demonstrative, like *-en* (= *na*) of strong verbs; hence the passive participle denotes possession, having properties of, as *shoulder'd*, having shoulders.

In all other cases, though we write *ed*, we drop the *e* in pronunciation, and *loved, praised*, &c., are pronounced as *lov'd, prais'd*, &c.

If the verb ends in a flat consonant or a vowel, *ed* has the sound of *d*; if in a sharp consonant, it has the sound of *t*.

(*a*) There are some orthographical variations—(1) the change of *y* (not preceded by another vowel) into *i* before the addition of *ed*, as *carry, carried;* (2) doubling of a simple consonant after a short vowel before *ed* is added, as *beg, begg-ed, wet, wett-ed*.

T is sometimes written for *d*, especially in older writers, after combination of consonants, as *smell, smelt; pass, past; burn, burnt*. We also meet with it after *p* and *k*, as *whipt, dropt, knockt*.

(*b*) The loss of the final *e* (of O.E. *-ed-e*) no longer enables us to distinguish the past tense from the passive participle.

(2) Before the addition of the suffix *d* the radical vowel is shortened, as *hear, heard; flee, fled*.[1]

(3) If a root ends in *d*, the suffix *d* is dropped and the radical vowel, if long, is shortened, as—

Pres.	Past.	P.P.
lead	led	led[2]
feed	fed	fed
read	read	read
spread	spread	spread

(4) *t* has replaced *d* in some verbs ending—

(*a*) In *-l* (to indicate more clearly that the radical vowel is shortened), as

feel	felt	felt
deal	dealt	dealt

(*b*) In a combination of liquids, as—

smell	smelt	smelt
burn	burnt	burnt

(5) Sometimes *d* and *t* are found side by side, as—

mean	meant	meant
	meaned	meaned
dream	dreamt	dreamt
	dreamed	dreamed

---

[1] In O.E. these verbs retain the fuller form, as—
    herde (perfect), *herd* (p.p.).
    fledde   ,,   *fled* ,,

[2] O.E. *læde; læd-de; læd-ed*: later forms, *lede; ledde (ladde); iled, ilad*.

(5) *t* replaces *d* after *p, f, v, ch, s,* and the radical vowel, if long, is shortened, as—

Pres.	Past.	P.P.
creep	crept	crept
sleep	slept	slept
weep	wept	wept
cleave	cleft	cleft
pitch	pitched	pitched
	pight*	pight*
lose	lost	lost

Elizabethan writers have the following old forms :—

blench	blent	blent
drench	dreynt	dreynt
ming (mingle)	meynt	meynt

Chaucer and other writers of his time have—

singe	seynde	seynd
sprenge (sprinkle)	spreynte	spreynd, spreynt
quenche	queynt	queynt
clenche (clinch)	cleynte	cleynt

(7) Verbs ending in *ld, nd, rd,* change the *d* into *t* in the past tense and passive participle, and the suffix disappears, as—

build	built (builded)	built[1] (builded)
gild	gilt (gilded)	gilt (gilded)
bend	bent	bent (bended)[2]
rend	rent	rent
gird	girt	girt

(8) The suffix *d* is dropped after *d, t,* the combination *st, rt, ft,* and the present, past, and passive participles have the same form, as—

rid	rid	rid
shred	shred	shred
cut	cut	cut
light	light	light
put	put	put
shut	shut	shut
cast	cast	cast
left	left	left
hurt	hurt	hurt

[1] We meet with this change in the fourteenth century. In the earlier periods we find *bulde* = built, in which the *d* has dropt or become assimilated to the root.

[2] These forms have different meanings, as " He was *bent* upon mischief," " On *bended* knees."

Some of these verbs have the regular form, as *lighted, quitted*, &c., and in O.E. of the fourteenth century we find *cutted, putted*.

(9) Vowel change with the addition of (*a*) d, (*b*) t—[1]

	Pres.	Past.	P.P.	Pres.	O.E. Perf.	P.P.
(*a*)	tell	told	told	telle	tealde	teald*
	sell	sold	sold	selle	sealde	seald
(*b*)	reck	rought*	rought*	rece	rōhte	rōht
	reach	raught*	raught*[2]			
	seek	sought	sought	sêce	sôhte	sôht
	teach	taught	taught	tæce	tæhte	tæht
	stretch	stretched	stretched straught*	strecce	streahte	streaht

The *t* for *d* in *sought*, &c., is due to the fact that the *c* is a sharp guttural, so was the *ch* in *teach, reach*, &c.; the guttural afterwards passed into a *continuous* mute on account of the following *t*.

280. Catch, caught, caught, does not occur in the oldest English; in Laʒamon we find *cacche, cahte, caht*. This verb has conformed to the past tense of *teach*, &c.

Analogous to the above forms we find *fraught* (adj.), as well as *freighted; distraught* and *distracted*.

> "His head dismember'd from his mangled corpse,
> Herself she cast into a vessel *fraught*
> With clotter'd blood."—SACKVILLE's *Duke of Buckingham*.

> "And forth we launch full *fraughted* to the brink."—*Induction*.

281. The following verbs are peculiarly formed—

	Pres.	Past.	P.P.
(1)	clothe	clothed, clad	clothed, clad

In the oldest English *clâthian* = to clothe; perf. *clâthode*, p.p. *clâthod*.

In the thirteenth and following centuries we find *clothien, clethen*, to clothe; perf. *clethed, clothed*, and *clad, cled*; p.p. *clothed, clad*.

Clad seems to have arisen out of analogy with such O.E. forms as *ladde* = led, *radde* = read.[3]

---

[1] The change of vowels in these verbs is explained by the fact that they have all lost a suffix *i* (= *ya* = *aya*), which influenced the original sounds *a* and *o* of the stems; and in the perfects and p. participles we have a return to the original *a* or *o* sound: thus O.E. *sellan*, to sell, represents a primitive *selian* Goth. *saljan*; loss of *i* causes the doubling of the consonant in *sellan*.

[2] "Into his arms a hie he *raught*."—SURREY.

[3] *Cleth-d* = *cledde* = *cladde* = *clad*.

	PRES.	PAST.	P.P.
(2)	make	made	made
O.E.	*mace*	*macode*	*macod*

The loss of *k* occurs as early as the thirteenth century.

(3) **Have, had, had**; O.E. *habbe, hæfde, hæfed*.
In later periods we have, in the past tense, *hæfde, hedde, hadde;* in p.p. *ihaved, ihafd, yhad*.

(4) **Say, said, said**; O.E. *secge, sægde (sæde), sægd (sæd)*.
Lay, laid, laid; O.E. *lecge, legede (lêde), leged, led*.
In *say, lay* (= O.E. *seye, leye*), *y* is a softening of *cg*.

(5) **Bring, brought, brought**; O.E. *bringe, brohte, broht*.
In the oldest English we also find *bring, brang, brungen*, from which we see that the root is *brang = brag*.

(6) **Buy, bought, bought**; O.E. *bycge, bohte, boht*.
In the thirteenth and fourteenth centuries, to buy = *buggen;* so *y* represents *g*, which appears again in the past tense.

(7) **Think, thought, thought**; O.E. *thence, thôhte, thôht*.
The root of this verb is *thak:* cp. Goth. *tagkja*, I think (= *tha-n-kia*); cp. *ga-n-ge, sta-n-d*, &c.

(8) **Methinks,**[1] **methought, methought**; O.E. *thyncth, thûhte, gethuht*.

(9) **Work, wrought, wrought**; O.E. *wyrce, worhte, worht*.
The *i* in O.E. *wyrke* has been changed under the influence of the *w* to (1) *u*, (2) *o;* cp. O.E. *wurchen* and *worchen*, to work.

Wrought is archaic, but in poetical composition is common; worked is quite a modern form.

Went was originally the past tense of *wend*, O.E. *wendan*, to turn, go; it replaced O.E. *eo-de, ʒede, yode*.

VERBAL INFLEXIONS.

282. The elements in the verb are (1) the root; (2) mood suffixes; (3) tense suffixes; (4) the person-endings (the mood and tense suffixes come before the person-endings); (5) connecting vowel between root and suffixes.

---

[1] Cp. German *denken* = to think; *dünken* = to seem.

In the Aryan dialects the original person-endings were pronouns, which in their full form were for (*a*) the singular:—(1) *Ma*, (2) *tva*, (3) *ta* : these were weakened to (1) *mi*, (2) *ti*, (3) *ti*; and *ti* of the second person became further weakened to *si*.

(*b*) The plural suffixes are compounds: (1) *mas* (= ma-si), (2) *tas* (= ta-si), (3) *an-ti*; *ma-si* = I + thou = we; *ta-si* = thou + thou = ye; *an-ti*[1] = he + he = they.

The subjunctive (or conjunctive) in the Teutonic dialects was originally an optative mood, the original suffix of which was *ya* = go. In Gothic this suffix was weakened to *i* in present subj. and became *ja* in perfect subj.

The Sansk. subj. of root, *as*, to be (Eng. *a-m*), *s-ya-m* (= *as-ya-m*), Gr. εἴην (= ἔσ-γη-μ), Lat. *sim* (= *es-iĕ-m*), O.E. *sy* (= *as-y* = *as-ya-m*).

Of the mode of forming tense we have already spoken. See §§ 264, 267.

283. (1) PRESENT INDICATIVE.

In some verbs the person-endings were added at once to the root without any connective vowel, as in the verbs **go** and **do** :—

Go, O.E., sing., *gá, gǽst, gǽ-th* = go, goest (=go-st), goeth, goes (=gos).
       pl.   *gá-th, gáth, gá-th* = go, go, go.
Do, O.E., sing., *dó-m, dĕ-st, dĕ-th* = do, do-st, do-th (*does*).
       pl.   *dó-th, dó-th, dó-th* = do, do, do.

In other verbs a connecting vowel came in between the root and the suffixes; this often disappears in modern English:—

	Goth.	O.E.	
Singular. 1	*bair-a,*	*ber-e*	= *bear.*
2	*bair-i-s,*	{*ber-e-st* / *bir-st*}	= *bear-e-st.*
3	*bair-i-th*	{*ber-e-th* / (*bir-th*)}	= *bear-e-th* (*bear-s*).
Plural. 1	*bair-a-m,*	*ber-a-th*	= *bear.*
2	*bair-i-th,*	*ber-a-th*	= *bear.*
3	*bair-a-nd,*	*ber-a-th*	= *bear.*

In the Old English dialects (thirteenth and fourteenth centuries) we find in the plural—

	Southern.	Midland.	Northern.
1	*ber-eth,*	*ber-en,*	*bere* (*ber*)
2	*ber-eth,*	*ber-en,*	*beres* (*bers*)
3	*ber-eth,*	*ber-en,*	*beres* (*bers*)

---

[1] *An* = *ana-s*, this, that, he (Sansk.).

[2] In O.H.Ger. we have older forms :—

Sing.	1 gâ-m	*Plur.*	gâ-mes
	2 gâ-s		gâ-t
	3 gâ-t		gâ-nt

The Gothic *bair-a*, O.E. *ber-e*, stand for more primitive forms, *bair-a-m, ber-e-m*; but the *m* having disappeared in the oldest forms of these languages, the connecting vowel represents the person-ending.

In Chaucer this *e* was a distinct syllable, as "I *dredĕ* nought that eyther thou shalt die," &c. In modern English it has wholly disappeared; in the plural the connecting vowel and suffixes are lost.

In O.E. (as in Laʒamon) we find *i* (= *ye* = *ya* = *aya*) the connecting vowel in the infinitive, as *lov-i-en*, *lov-i-e*, &c. and in the present indic. as *Ich lov-i-e*, &c. It is still heard in infinitives in the South of England, as to *milky*, to *mowy*, &c.

Many strong verbs lost this suffix *i* and doubled the final consonant, as O.E. (1) *sitte*, (2) *sit-est*, (3) *sit-eth* = (1) sit, (2) sittest, (3) sitteth.

The silent *e* in some few verbs like *hav-e*, *liv-e*, which adds nothing now to the length of the preceding vowel, was once sounded.

284. (2) PRESENT SUBJUNCTIVE.

This mood originally had a tense suffix which came between the connecting vowel and the personal ending.[1]

		Goth.	O.E.		Eng.
Singular.	1	*bair-a-u*,	*ber-e*	=	bear.
	2	*bair-a-i-s*,	*ber-e*	=	bear.
	3	*bair-a-i*,	*ber-e*	=	bear.
Plural.	1	*bair-a-i-ma*,	*ber-en*	=	bear.
Singular.	1	*sôk-ja-u*,	*sêc-e*	=	seek.
		&c.	&c.		&c.

285. (3) PAST INDICATIVE.

Strong verbs in O.E. lost their connecting vowel, as :—

		Goth.	O.E.	
Singular.	1	*hai-hald*	= *heold*	= held.
	2	*hai-hals-t*	= *heold-e*	= heldest.
	3	*hai-hald*	= *heold*	= held.
Plural.	1	*hai-ha-aum*	= *heold-on*	= held.

286. Weak verbs added the syllable *-de* (*-te*) to the root; in O.E. the connecting vowel was lost in some verbs (see §§ 277—279).

		Goth.	O.E.	
Singular.	1	*sôk-i-da*	= *soh-te*	= sough-t.
	2	*sôk-i-dês*[2]	= *soh-test*	= sough-t.
	3	*sôk-i-da*	= *soh-te*	= sough-t.
Plural.	1	*sok-i-dêdu-m*	= *soh-to-n*	= sough-t.
		&c.	&c.	&c.

[1] The O.E. *e* = *a* + *i*.
[2] This *-des* may be for *-ded-t*; in the Teutonic languages when a dental is added to another dental the first becomes *s*, as *wit-te* = wist, *mot-te* = *moste* = must.

287. In the fourteenth century we find the second person-ending *-e* of strong verbs sometimes changed to *est*, as *thou gave* and *thou gavest* (in Wickliffe we find *holpedist*). The old plural *-un, -on*, became *-en*, and the *n* frequently falls away, so we have *held-en* and *helde*, &c. In modern English the older endings have all disappeared.

288. (4) PAST SUBJUNCTIVE.

In strong verbs the connecting vowel was $e = ya$, as:—

	Goth.	O.E.	Eng.
Singular. 1	bĕr-ja-u	= bær-e	= bore.
2	bĕr-ei-s	= bær-e	= bore.
3	bĕr-i	= bær-e	= bore.
Plural. 1	bĕr-ei-ma	= bær-e-n	= bore.
	&c.	&c.	&c.

In some weak verbs it is lost:—

Singular. 1	sôk-i-dĕd-ja-u	= sôh-te	= sough-t.
2	sôk-i-dĕd-ei-s	= sôh-te	= sough-t.
3	sôk-i-dĕd-i	= sôh-te	= sough-t.
Plural. 1	sôk-i-dĕd-ei-ma	= sôh-ton	= sough-t.

In Gothic pl. we see, (1) *sok* root, (2) *i* connecting vowel, (3) *ded* tense suffix, (4) *ja* mood suffix, (5) *u = um = mi* (*ma*) personal suffix.

288*. The IMPERATIVE is properly no mood, but is merely the root + a personal pronoun in the vocative.

In O.E. the imperative plural ended in *-th*, as *go-eth* (⇒ *gâ-th*), go ye; *ber-eth* (= *ber-ath*), bear ye.

PERSONAL ENDINGS.

289. (1) The suffix of the first person was originally m, as in *a-m*. In O.E. we have, *gedo-m*, I do; *beom*, I be; *geseam*, I see.

In the Northern dialect of the oldest period we find *m* weakened to *n* in perfect as *Ic giherdun*, I heard.

(2) The suffix of the second person was originally s (= *si = ti = ta = tva*). In O.E. we sometimes find *s* for *st*, as *thou hæfes* = thou hast, which is the regular inflexion of the Northern dialects in the fourteenth century; but the ordinary person-ending is st.

This termination is subject to certain orthographical modifications:—

(*a*) After a final *e* -st is added, as *love-st*.

(*b*) *Y* (not diphthongal) is changed to *i* before st, as *criest*.

(*c*) In verbs of one syllable with a short vowel, the final consonant is doubled, as *beggest, puttest*.

(*d*) After a sibilant, palatal (*s, ch*), *est* is added, as *bless-est, teach-est*, &c.

In the strong perfects in O.E. the pronoun *si* (= *tva*) becomes *e*[1] (O.Sax. *-i*; Goth. *-t*). We have replaced this by *est*. (See § 282.)
In weak verbs the ending is -st; but we often find *s* in O.E. as *thu brohtes, thu sealdes*, &c.
The subjunctive mood has lost the personal suffix *-st*.

(3) The suffix of the third person is -th (= *ta* = *that, he*). This as early as the eleventh century was softened to s. We have two forms; s in common use, th archaic and still used in poetry.

The verbal suffix **s** is subject to the same euphonic changes as the plural **s** of substantives.

The plural suffixes (1) *-ma-si*, (2) *-ta-si*, (3) *-an-ti* are in O.E. reduced to one for all three persons. (See § 283.)
Spenser and Shakespeare have a few examples of the plural *-en*,[2] as "they *marchen*" (Spenser, i. 4, 37). Cp.

" And then the whole quire hold their hips and laugh,
And *waxen* in their mirth."—*Midsummer Night's Dream*, ii. 1.
" For either they [women] be full of jealousy,
Or masterfull, or *loven* novelty."
BURTON'S *Anatomy of Mel.* p. 604.

It was archaic in Spenser's time, and is seldom used by Hawes or Sackville.

In O.E. when the pronoun followed the verb the inflexion was dropped, as *ga ge*, ye go.

INFINITIVE MOOD.

290. (1) The infinitive is simply an abstract noun. In O.E. the sign of the infinitive was the suffix *-an*, corresponding to Sanskrit nouns in *ana*, as *gam-ana-m*, from *gam*,[3] to go.

(2) In Sanskrit the dative and locative singular of these abstract nouns (as *gam-an-âya*, dat.; *gamanê*, loc., were used as infinitives. In Greek we have this suffix in -εναι, -ναι, -ειν (λελοιπ-έναι, διδό-ναι, τύπτ-ειν).
In Gothic the infinitive (*-ana*) lost its case sign and the suffix *a*, and therefore always ends in *-an*; in Frisian and Old Norse it is shortened to *-a*; in Dutch and German it is *-en*.

(3) In the twelfth and following centuries the *an* was represented by *en* or *e*, as *breken* and *brekë* = to break.

---

[1] It is omitted in the Northern dialects of the thirteenth and fourteenth centuries.
[2] " In former times, till about the reign of Henry the Eighth, they (the persons of the plural) were wont to be formed by adding *-en*, but now, whatsoever the cause, it hath quite grown out of use."—BEN JONSON.
[3] In *gam-ana-m* the *m* is merely a neuter suffix.

In Wickliffe the suffix is for the most part *e;* in Chaucer and *Piers Plowman* we find *-en* and *-e*. When this *e* became silent the infinitive was only distinguished by the preposition *to*,[1] which is not found before the simple infinitive until about the end of the twelfth century.

"No devel shall 3ow *dere.*"—*Pass.* vii. l. 34.
"Shall no devel at his ded-day *deren* hym a my3te."—*Ib.* vii. l. 50.
"To *bakbite* and to *bosten* and *bere* fals witnesse."—*Ib.* ii. l. 80.

Spenser and Shakespeare have an archaic use of it, as "*to killen*" (*Pericles*).
"Henceforth his ghost . . .
In peace may *passen* over Lethe lake."—*F. Q.* i. iii. 36.

In Hall's Satires we find "to *delven* low," p. 51.

(4) The infinitive had a dative form expressed by the suffix *e*,[2] and governed by the preposition *to*.

This is sometimes called the *gerundial* infinitive: it is also equivalent to Lat. *supines;* as, *etanne*, to eat; *faranne*, to fare, go.

(5) In the twelfth century we find this ending *-enne* (*anne*), confounded with the participial ending *-ende* (*inde*),[3] as:—
"The synfulle [man fasteth] *for to clensen* him, the rihtwise for to *witiende* his rihtwisnesse."—*O. E. Hom.*, Second Series, p. 57.
In the fourteenth century, we find "to *witinge*" = to wit; "to *seethinge*" = to be sodden (WICKLIFFE, *Text* A.),[4] the participle *-ende* (*-inde*) having taken also the form *-inge*. Cp. "This ny3te that is to *comyng*" (*Tale of Beryn*, l. 347).
In the fifteenth and following centuries these forms dropt out of use.

(6) The extract given above shows that the dative infinitive assumed the form of the simple infinitive as early as the twelfth century.

In the *Ormulum* there is only one suffix *-en* for both infinitives.

We find a trace of this dative infinitive in Sackville—
"The soil, that erst so seemly was *to seen*,
Was all despoiled of her beauty's hue."—*Induction*.
"And with a sigh, he ceased
To tellen forth the treachery and the trains."—*Duke of Buckingham*.

291. Because the suffix *-ing* represents (1) *-ung* in verbal substantives, as *showing* (O.E. *sceawung*); (2) *-ende* or *-inde* in present participles, as "he is *coming*," "he was *coming*" (O. E. he is *cumende*, he wæs *cumende*), and sometimes represented the dative infinitive *-enne* (rarely the simple infinitive *-en*): English grammarians have of late years put forth a theory concerning the infinitive, which is neither supported by O.E. usage nor is in accordance with the general direction of changes that have taken place in regard to these suffixes.

---

[1] Cp. *for to;* the *for* is, of course, pleonastic, but, no doubt, was used to distinguish it from the simple infin. with *to* before it.
[2] The *n* is always doubled before the addition of this *e* in the oldest English. In later times *-enne*, *-anne* became *-ene*, then *-en* or *-e*.
We have traces of *-ene* as late as the middle of the fourteenth century.
[3] So in the oldest English occasionally.
[4] Cp. "And the dragoun stood before the womman that was to *beringe* chiild . . . And she childede a sone male, that was *to reulinge* alle folkes."—WICKLIFFE.

(1) It is said that the infinitive in *-en* has become *-ing* in such phrases as, "*seeing* is *believing*"¹ = to see is to believe. We know, however, (*a*) that the suffix *-en* disappeared in the sixteenth and following centuries, and (*b*) that it rarely in O.E. writers became *-inge* or *-ing*.²

It is quite evident that although, in sense, *seeing* and *believing* are equivalent to infinitives, they are not so in form, but merely represent old English substantives in *-ung*.

Cp. "The *giving* a bookseller his price for his book has this advantage."—SELDEN's *Table Talk*. "*Quoting* of authors is most for matter of fact."—*Ib*.

Such a phrase as "it is hard *to heal* an old sore" may be converted into "it is *hard healing* an old sore;" but tracing phrases of this kind only as far back as the sixteenth century, we find that a preposition has disappeared after the verbal substantive, as:—"it is yll *healyng* of an olde sore" (HEYWOOD's *Proverbs*), and "it is evill *waking* of a sleeping hog" (*Ib*.).

(2) It is asserted that the O.E. infinitive in *-enne* actually exists under the form *-ing* in such expressions as "fit *for teaching*," "fond of *learning*," &c.

In these cases we have merely the verbal nouns governed by a preposition doing duty for the old dative infinitive, and altogether replacing it.

We have seen, too, that the old infinitive in *-ing*, as *to witinge*, &c. died out about the end of the fourteenth or the beginning of the fifteenth century.

(3) These forms in *-ing* are no doubt very perplexing, and we find even Max Müller thrown off his guard by them. He says, "The vulgar or dialectic expression '*he is a going*' is far more correct than '*he is going*.'" If so, "*he was a going*," &c. must be more correct than "*he was going*;" but on turning to similar expressions in O.E. writers we find "*he is gangende*" and "*he wæs gangende*" used to translate Latin present and imperfect tenses; but never "he is *on gangung*," he is *a* going.³ Compare

"The thyef is *comynde*."—A3*enbite*, p. 264.
"That Israelisshe folc was *walkende*."

O.E. *Hom*., Second Series, p. 51.

---

¹ Mr. Abbott quotes "*Returning* were as tedious as (to) go o'er."—*Prov*. iii. 4. This form is also used as object. :—

"If all fear'd *drowning* that spy waves ashore,
Gold would grow rich, and all the merchants poor."
TOURNEUR, *The Revenger's Tragedy*.

² In the *Romance of Partenay*, written about the beginning of the sixteenth century, or the latter part of the fifteenth, we find instances of infinitives in *-ing* for *-en* after an auxiliary verb (which we never get in modern English), but we can draw no conclusions from the exceptional usage of so late a work:—

"Our lorde will receyve hym of hys grace,
And off all hys syn *yeuyng* hym pardon"—(l. 1528).
"And [they] shall
Enlesing [= lesen] the Rewme and also the land"—(l. 5625).

We also find in this work passive participles of strong verbs in *-ing*, *-yng*, instead of *-en*, as *taking* = *taken*. In Elizabethan writers we find *loading* = *loden* = *laden*, and *beholding* = *beholden*. Shakespeare (1 *Hen. IV*.) has *moulten* = *moulting*!

3 In the dramatists of a much later period we find it, as—

"Your father is *a going*, good old man."—SHIRLEY's *Brothers*.

The *a* in these expressions was used before verbal substantives beginning with a consonant, and is a shortened form of *an* which was used before vowels; *an* is merely a dialectical form of *on*. (Cp. "Now off, now *an*."—WYATT'S *Poems*, ed. Bell, p. 136.)

292. In O.E. writers after the Conquest we find the verbal noun with *on, an, in*,[1] *a*, employed (1) after verbs of motion, as "he wente *on hunting*," "he fell *on sleeping*," &c.

(2) After the verbs *is, was*, to form present and imperfect tenses, with *passive* signification, as "*the churche* was *in byldynge*" (ROBT. OF BRUNNE'S *Chronicles*, i. cxcvii.), "as this was *a doyng*" (*Morte d'Arthur*, lib. II. c. viii.), "he rode *in huntinge*" (*Gest. Rom.*). Ben Jonson retains these expressions, and states that they have the force of gerunds.[2]

Cp. "I saw great peeces of ordinance *makyng*."—CORYAT'S *Crudities*.

"Women are angels, *wooing* (= in wooing)."—*Tr. and Cr.* i. 2.

(3) The verbal substantive with *a* could be used after the verb *be* where no time was indicated, as "he is long *a rising*" = "he is long *in rising*."
In O.E. we could substitute an abstract noun with a different suffix, as "he wente forth *an hunteth*"[3] = he went forth *on hunting* (or *a hunting*).
About the beginning of the eighteenth century we find the *a* frequently omitted, and it is now only allowed as a colloquialism.

(4) After verbs of motion the verbal subst. is not only preceded by *on, an, a*, but by *to*[3] and *of*.

"If two fall *to scuffling*, one tears the other's band."—SELDEN'S *Table Talk*.

"A dog had been at market to buy a shoulder of mutton; coming home he met two dogs by the way that quarrell'd with him; he laid down his shoulder of mutton, and fell *to fighting* (= *a fighting*) with one of them; in the meantime the other dog fell *to eating* (*an eating*) his mutton; he seeing that, left the dog he was fighting with, and fell upon him that was eating; then the other dog fell *to eat*[4] (= *an eating*); when he perceived there was no remedy, but which of them soever he fought withal, his mutton was in danger; he thought he would have as much of it as he could, and, therefore, gave over fighting, and fell *to eating* himself."—*Ib.*

(5) We usually abridge sentences containing the verbal substantive, so that it looks like a gerund, as "*For the repealing of my banished brother*,"[5] can now be expressed by "*For repealing my banished brother*."

Cp. "*Up peyn of losing of a finger*" = upon pain of losing a finger.—CAPGRAVE'S *Chron.* p. 195.

---

[1] The infinitive sometimes replaces it in Shakespeare, as—

"Eleven hours I spent *to write* it o'er."—*Rich. III.* iii. 6.

Here, "*to write*" is equivalent to "*in writing*."

[2] See Marsh's *Lectures on the English Language* (ed. Smith), pp. 462, 472. In all the instances quoted by Marsh, the subject of the sentence preceding the verbal noun represents an inanimate object.

[3] Old and New Test. in Vernon MS.

[4] Nash (*Peter Penniless*) has "*fall a retayling*." In *Gammer Gurton's Needle* we have "Hodge fell *of swearing*."

[5] Quoted by Mr. Abbott, from *Jul. Cæsar*, iii. 1, who says that the expressions common in O.E. began to be regarded as colloquial in Shakespeare's time. Cp. Touchstone's words in *As You Like It*, ii. 4 :—

"I remember *the kissing of* her battes,
.. and *the wooing of* a peas-cod instead of her."

PRESENT (OR ACTIVE) PARTICIPLE.

293. The present participle is formed by the suffix -ing, which has replaced the O.E. *-ende* (*end*); *-inde, -ande* (*and*),[1] as O.E. *gâ-nd, dô-nd* = going, doing; *comende, wepinde, rydande*, &c.

The suffix -ing arises out of -inde, and took place first in the Southern dialect during the twelfth century, though the older form did not die out until after 1340.

Laʒamon has "*goinde ne ridinge.*"

The Northern dialects carefully distinguished (as did the Lowland Scotch dialect up to a very late period) the participle in *-and* from the noun in *-ing* (O.E. *-ung*):

" Than es our birthe here *bygynnyng*
Of the dede that es our *endyng*;
For ay the mare that we wax alde
The mare our lif may be ded talde.
Tharfor whylles we er here *lyffand*
Ilk day er we thos *dyhand*."—HAMPOLE, *P. of C.* p. 58.

Ben Jonson's *Sad Shepherd* contains some passages written in imitation of the Northern dialect, and in it he makes use of the participle in *and*. " Twa *trilland* brooks " (act ii. 2), " a *stinkand* brock," "*pleasand* things," " while I sat *whyrland* of my brazen spindle," " *barkand* parish tykes," &c.—*Ib.*

Chaucer rarely uses the participle in *and;* he has several instances of Norman-French participles, as *sufficant, consentant,* &c.

Spenser has *glitterand, trenchand,* but his use of them is archaic.

For Passive Participles, see p. 155, § 263, p. 168, § 279.

ANOMALOUS VERBS.

294. Be.—The conjugation of this verb contains three distinct roots—(1) *as*, (2) *be* (*bu*), (3) *was*.

		1	2	3		1	2	3
Present Indicative ...	Sing.	am	art	is	Pl.		are	
Subjunctive	Sing.	be	be	be	Pl.		be	
Past Indicative ...	Sing.	was	wast (wert)	was	Pl.		were	
Subjunctive	Sing.	were	were	were	Pl.		were	

Infinitive.	Imperative.	Pres. Part.	Passive Part.
be	be	being	been

---

[1] The *-nd* is the real participial suffix, and *e* is the connecting vowel.

In O.E. of the thirteenth and fourteenth centuries *-inde* is found only in the South, and *-end* in the Midland, and *-and* in the Northumbrian dialects (and in dialects influenced by the Northumbrian). In the oldest periods of the language *-ende* is W. Saxon, *-and* Northumbrian.

ANOMALOUS VERBS.

			Goth.	O.E.	
Pres. Indic. ...	Sing.	1	i-m	eo-m (eam)*	beo-m, beo
		2	i-s	ear-t	bi-st, beost
		3	is-t	is	bi-th, beth, beoth, bes
	Pl.	1	sij-u-m	ar-on arn*	beo-th, sind, sinden,* sunden* beth* (syndon)
		2	sij-u-th	ar-on arn*	beo-th, sind (syndon)
		3	si-nd	ar-on arn*	beo-th, sind (syndon)
Pres. Subj. ...	Sing.	1	si-ja-u	wes-e	beo, sí
		2	sij-ai-s	wes-e	beo, sí
		3	sij-ai	wes-e	beo, sí, seo*
	Pl.	1	sij-ai-ma	wes-e-n	beo-n, ben,* si-n, séon*
		2	sij-ai-th	wes-e-n	beo-n, si-n
		3	sij-ai-na	wes-e-n	beo-n, sin
Past Indic. ...	Sing.	1	was	wæs	wes*
		2	was-t	wǽr-e	were*
		3	was	wǽs	wes*
	Pl.	1	wês-um	wǽr-on	weren*
		2	wês-uth	wǽr-on	weren*
		3	wês-un	wǽr-on	weren*
Past Subj. ...	Sing.	1	wês-ja-u	wǽr-e	were*
		2	wês-ei-s	wǽr-e	were*
		3	wes-i	wǽr-e	were*
	Pl.	1	wês-ei-ma	wǽr-e-n	weren*
		2	wês-ei-th	wǽr-e-n	weren*
		3	wês-ei-na	wǽr-e-n	weren*
Imperative ...	Sing.	2	wis	wes	beo, seo,* sí*
	Pl.	2	wis-i-th	wesath	beoth, beth*
Infinitive	...	...	wis-a-n	wesan	beon, ben*
Pres. Part.	...	...	wisands	wesende	
Passive Part.	...	...	wisans	gewesen	yben* [1]

295. Am = *ar-m*, that is *as-m*;[2] *as* is the root, *m* the first personal pronoun.

---

[1] Those marked thus (*) are later forms.
[2] Cp. Sansk. Present Indic. (1) *as-mi*, (2) *a-si*, (3) *as-ti*, Pl. (1) *smas*, (2) *stha*, (3) *santi*.
Pres. Subj. *s-yâ-m, syâs, syât; syâ-mas, s-yâ-ta, s-yâ-nt*.
The root *be* exists in Lat. *fu-i*; Sansk. *bhav-ami*, I be, first person of root *bhu*.

Ar-t = *as-t; t* = the second personal pronoun.

Is.—The root *as* is here weakened to *is*, and the suffix *th* or *t* is dropped (cp. Goth. *is-t*).

Are = *ase*, represents the old northern English *aron*,[1] *arn*, *er*. It is of Scandinavian origin. Cp. O.N. *em*, I am; *ert*, thou art; *er*, he is; *er-um*, we are; *eruth*, ye are; *eru*, they are.

The O.E. *s-ind* = Sansk. *santi* (= *as-santi*); *sindon* is a double plural; *sunden* occurs as late as 1250; *sinden* is in the *Ormulum*.

The root **be** was conjugated in the present tense, singular and plural, indicative, as late as Milton's time,

I be.	We be, O.E. *ben*.
Thou beest.	Ye be, ,, ,,
O.E. (He beth or bes.)	They be, ,, ,,

The first person is found in the English Bible. Compare

" If thou *beest* Stephano, touch me."—*Tempest*, ii. 2.
" If thou *beest* he."—MILTON, *Paradise Lost*, i. 84.

The third person *beth* and *bes* were in use in the fourteenth century; the latter with a future signification.

The pl. is very common, as :—

" *We be* twelve brethren."—*Gen.* xlii. 32.
" There *be* more marvels yet."—BYRON, *Childe Harold*.
" As fresh as *bin* the flowers in May."—PEELE.

Bin = *be* with *n* as plural suffix.

In the present subjunctive, only the root *be* is employed, and all the inflexions are lost.

296. Was.—The O.E. *wesan*, to be, is cognate with Goth. *wisan;* O.N. *vera*, to be, abide; Sansk. *vas*, to dwell.

It is a strong verb, the old past tense being *wæs;* the suffix of the first personal pronoun is gone, as in the preterites of all strong verbs.

Was-t.—We have seen that all strong verbs in the oldest English had the suffix *e* for the second person singular. In the Gothic *was-t* we have an older suffix, *t* (suffix of second person, as in *ar-t*), altogether lost in O.E.

But *wast* is not found in the oldest English; it is quite a late form, not older than the fourteenth century.[2] The O.E. form was *were* (that is, *wese*),[3] from which we have formed, after the analogy of *shall* and *will*, wer-t,[4] which is sometimes, but wrongly, used for

---

[1] *Ar-on* is not found in the old English West-Saxon dialect.
[2] It occurs in Wickliffe (*Mark* xiv. 67).
[3] " Litel thou *were* tempted, or litel thou *were* stired."—*Pilgrimage*, p. 33.
[4] The O. Norse = *var-t*.

the subjunctive *were* (second person singular), as "thou *wert* grim." (*King John*, ii. 3).

Were = O.E. *wer-e-n;* that is, *wes-e-n.*

297. In O.E. we have negative forms, as *nam*, I am not; *nart*, thou art not; *nis*, he is not; *nere*, were not, &c.

298. Can.

		1	2	3		1	2	3
Present Indicative	...	Sing.	can	canst	can	Pl.		can
Subjunctive	...	Sing.	—	—	—	Pl.		—
Past Indicative	...	Sing.	could	couldst	could	Pl.		could
Subjunctive	...	Sing.	—	—	--	Pl.		—

					O.E.	Goth
Present Indicative	...	...	...	Sing. 1	can, con	kann
				2	canst	kant
				3	can, con	kann
				Pl. 1	cunnon	kunnum
Present Subjunctive	...	...	...	Sing.	cunne	kunjau
				Pl.	cunnon	kuneima
Past Indicative	...	...	...	Sing. 1	cu-the	kun-tha
				2	cuthest	kun-thes
				3	cuthe	kun-tha
				Pl. 1	cuthon	kun-thêdum
Past Subjunctive	...	...	...	Sing.	cuthe	kunthêdjau
				Pl.	cuthon	kun-thêdeima
Past Passive	...	...	...		cuth	kunths
Infinitive	...	...	...		cunnan	kunnan

Many verbs in Teutonic and other languages, having lost their present tense, express the meaning of the lost tense by means of the preterite, as Lat. *odi, cœpi, memini,* Gr. οἶδα.

Can is one of these, being equivalent to *novi*. It was originally the preterite of a verb cognate with Goth. *cennan,* to bring forth, so that *can* originally was equivalent to *genui*.

Can (first and third persons).—No personal suffixes, as in the past tense of all verbs originally strong.

Can-st stands for *can-t*.

The plural inflexions (cp. O.E. *cunnon, cunnen*) have disappeared.

Could.—The O.E. forms *couthe, coude,* show that a non-radical *l* has crept in, probably from false analogy with *shall* and *will*.

O. E. *Coude* = Goth. *cun-tha* (= *cun-da*), has the tense suffix *d* of weak verbs.

We have the old past participle of the verb in *un-couth* (O.E. *un-cuth* = unknown).

In Chaucer we find infinitive *conne*, to be able, as "I shal not *conne* answere." Shakespeare has, "to *con* thanks." "He shulde *can* us no thank."—BERNER'S *Froissart*.

Con = learn, study (as *con* a lesson), makes past tense and passive participle *conned*.

Cunning = knowing, is really a present participle of *can* (con).

299. Dare.

		Sing. 1	2	3		Pl. 1	2	3
Present Indicative	...	Sing. dare	darest	dares	Pl.	dare		
Subjunctive	...	Sing. dare	dare	dare	Pl.	dare		
Past Indicative	...	Sing. durst	durst	durst	Pl.	durst		
Subjunctive	...	Sing. durst	durst	durst	Pl.	durst		

Infinitive.	Imperative.	Pres. Part.	Passive Part.
dare	dare	daring	dared

			O.E.		Goth.
Present Indicative ...	Sing.	1	dear	(dar)[1]	dars
		2	dearst	(darst)	dart
		3	dear	(dar)	dars
	Pl.		durron	(durren, durre)	daurs-um
Present Subjunctive..	Sing.	1	durre	—	—
Past Indicative	...	Sing. 1	dors-te	(durste)	daursta
		2	dors-test	(durstest)	daurstes
		3	dorste	(durste)	daursta
	Pl.	1	dorsten	(dursten)	daurstêdum
Subjunctive ...	...	Sing.	dorste	(durste)	
		Pl.	dorsten	(dursten, durste)	
Infinitive	...	...	durran	(dore)	dauran

Dare.—The root is *dars* (cp. Gr. θαρρεῖν, θαρσεῖν).

The third person dare (O.E. *dar*) is strictly correct. Cp.

"A bard to sing of deeds he *dare* not imitate."
WALTER SCOTT, *Waverley*.

In the *Pilgrimage of the Lyf of Man* we find p.p. *dorre*:—

"Whi art thou swich and swich that thou *darst* passe the lawe ... whens cometh it thee and how hast thou *dorre* be so harde."—P. 78.

---

[1] Forms in parentheses are later ones.

Wickliffe has infinitive *dore*:—

"The which thing that I shulde *dore* don, me styride the studie of Orygen."

Dare makes a new preterite, *dared*, when it signifies to challenge, as "he *dared* me to do it."

300. Shall.

		1	2	3		1	2	3
Present Indicative	... Sing.	shall	shalt	shall	Pl.	shall		
Subjunctive ...	... Sing.	—	—	—	Pl.	—		
Past Indicative	... Sing.	should	shouldst	should	Pl.	should		
Subjunctive ...	... Sing.	—	—	—	Pl.	—		

				O.E.		Goth.
Pres. Indic.	... Sing.	1	sceal	scal[1]	schal	skal
		2	scealt	scalt	schalt	skal-t
		3	sceal	scal	schal	skal
	Pl.	1	scul-on	sculon	schulen	skulum
Pres. Subj.	... Sing.		scyle	scule	schule	skuljau
	Pl.		scylen	sculen	schulen	skuleima
Past Indic.	... Sing.	1	sceolde	scolde	schulde	skulda
		2	sceoldest	scoldest	schuldest	skuldes
		3	sceolde	scolde	schulde	skulda
	Pl.		sceoldon	scolden	schulen	skuldêdum
Past Subj.	... Sing.		sceolde	scolde	schulde	skuldêdjau
	Pl.		sceoldon	scolden	schulen	skuldêdeima
Infinitive	...	...	sculan			skulan
Pres. Part.	...	...				skulds

Shall often occurs in O.E. in the sense of *to owe*, as—

"Frend, as I am trewe knyght,
And by that feith I *shal* to God and yow,
I hadde it nevere half so hoote as now."
— CHAUCER, *Tr. and Cr.* l. 1600

"Thise dette ssel (owes) ech to othren."—*Aȝenbite*, p. 145.

"Hû micel *sceal* thu?" = How much owest thou?—*Luke* xvi. 5.

Shall is historically a preterite of a present *skila*, which signifies *I kill*, and so *shall* = I have killed, I must pay the fine or *wer geld*; hence I am under an obligation, I must.

---

[1] The second and third columns of O.E. are later forms.

301. May.

		1	2	3		1	2	3
Present Indicative ...	Sing.	may	mayst	may	Pl.		may	
Past Indicative ...	Sing.	might	mightst mightest	might	Pl.		might	

				O.E.		Goth.
Pres. Indic.	Sing.	1	mæg	mæi	mow	mag
		2	meaht	miht	maist	mag-t
		3	mæg	mæi	—	mag
	Plural.	1	mâgon	magen	mughen mawen mowen	mâgum
Pres. Subj.	Sing.	1	mâge	mæi	mughe mowe	magjau
	Plural	1	mâgen	mægen	mughen mowe	mageima
Past Indic.	Sing.	1	meahte	mihte	moughte	mahta
	Plural.	1	meahton	mihten	mighten	mahtêdum
Past Subj.	Sing.	1	meahte	mihte	mighte	mahtêdjau
	Plural.	1	meahten	mihten	mighten	mahtêdeima
Infinitive	...	...	magan	mowen	mowe	magan
Pres. Part.	...	...	mægende	mowend mi3tand	mowing	—
Pass. Part.	...	...	meaht	might*	—	mahts

May (first person).—The *y* here represents an older *g*.

Might.—The second person singular, we see, had originally the suffix *t*, like *shalt, wilt*, &c.

"Amende thee while thow *myght*."—*Piers Plowman.*

In the fourteenth century we find this suffix dropping off, as "No thing thou *may* take from us" (Maundeville, p. 29). Skelton, too, uses this uninflected form, as "thou *may* see thyself" (i. 145).

May = possession, is the preterite of a primitive *mig-an* (crescere, gignere), and signified originally, I have begotten, produced; hence, I am able.
  In O.E. fourteenth century we find inf. *mowe*, pres. part. *mowende, mowinge* (WICKLIFFE, *Jer.* xlvi. 10), p.p. *might, mogt:*—

"Who shall *mowe* fi3te."—WICKLIFFE, *Apoc.* xiii. 4.

"This con I wot wel, me not to have *mo3t* remene."—*Job*, Prol. p. 871.

"If goodly had he *might*."—CHAUCER.

302. Will.

			1	2	3		1	2	3
Present Indicative	...	Sing.	will	wilt	will	Pl.		will	
Subjunctive	...	...	Sing.	—	—	—	Pl.	—		
Past Indicative	...		Sing.	would	wouldst	would	Pl.		would	
Subjunctive	...	...	Sing.	—	—	—	Pl.	—		

O.E.

Pres. Indic. ...	Sing.	1	wile	wille	wolle, wole, wol
		2	wilt	wult	wolt
		3	wile	wille	wulle, wole, wol
	Pl.	1	willath	wulleth	wolleth, wolen, wilen
Pres Subj. ...	Sing.	1	wille	wolle	wulle
Past Indic. ...	Sing.	1	wolde	wolde	
	Pl.	1	wolden	wolden	
Past Subj. ...	Sing.		wolde		
Infinitive	...	...	willan	wilen	wolen
Pres. Part. ...	...		willende		

(1) In O.E. won't we have a trace of the O.E. *wol* (*wole*).

(2) In O.E. we find infinitive *wolen*, as "he shall *wolen*" (Wickliffe, *Apoc.* xi. 6); p.p. *wold*—

"And in the same maner oure Lord Crist hath *wolde* and suffred."
    CHAUCER, *Melibeus*, p. 159 (Wright).

(3) Negative forms occur in O.E., as *nille* = will not; *nolde* = would not; *willy nilly* = *will* ye, *nill* ye, *will* he, *nill* he, "*Will* you, *nill* you" (*Taming of the Shrew*, ii. 1).

"To *will* or *nill*."—BEN JONSON, *Catiline*.

Cp. O.E. "For *wolny, nulni,* hi sul fle," &c.—*Early Eng. Poems*, p. 12.
Wolny = *wolen hi,* will they; *nulni* = *nolen hi,* nill they.

(4) In O.E. we find two weak verbs, *willian* and *wilnian*, to desire; the former of these exists in *will* = to desire.

"And Venus in her message Hermes sped
    To blody Mars *to will* him not to rise."—SACKVILLE, *Induction*.

"For what wot I the after weal that fortune *wills* to me."
    SURREY, *Faithful Lover*

"Which mass he *willed* to be reared high."—*Ib.*, *Æneid*.

303. Owe.

		1	2	3		1	2	3
Present Indicative	... Sing.	owe	owest	oweth	Pl.	owe		
Subjunctive ...	... Sing.	—	—	—	Pl.	—		
Past Indicative	... Sing.	ought	oughtest	ought	Pl.	ought		
Subjunctive ...	... Sing.	—	—	—	Pl.	—		

Infinitive.	Present Participle.	Perfect.
owe	owing	—

			O. E.			Goth.
Pres. Indic.	Sing.	1	âh	og*	ow*		áih
		2	âge	agest*	ouh*	owest*	áih-t
		3	âh	ouh*	oweth*		áih
	Plural	1	âgon	agen*	owen*		áigum
Past Indic.	Sing.	1	âhte	aȝte*	owȝte*		áihta
	Plural	1	âhton	aȝten*	owȝten*		áihtêdum
Infinitive		...	âgan	aȝen*	ogen*	owen*	áigan
Pres. Part.		...	âgende				
Pass. Part.		...	âgen	aȝt	ought	owed	aihts[1]

(1) **Owe** (O.E. *âh*, Goth. *aih*, I have) no longer exists in the sense of *have*, possess. It is the past of an infinitive *eigan*, to labour, work; whence *owe* originally signified I have worked, I have earned, hence (*a*) I possess, have, (*b*) I have it as a duty, I ought.

(2) **Owe** *as an independent verb*:—

Cp. *Hwæt dô ic thæt ic êce lîf âge?* = what must I do that I may have eternal life?—*Mark* x. 17.

"And all thatt iss, and beoth,
He shop and *ah*."—*Orm.* 6777.

"God *ah* (= owes) the littell mede."—*Ib.*

"By the treuthe ich *ou* to the."—ROBT. OF GLOUCESTER, 6524.

"He *owȝte* to him 10,000 talentes."—WICKLIFFE, *Matt.* xviii. 24.

"Ȝeld that thou *owist.*"—*Ib.* xviii. 28.

"You *ought* him a thousand pounds."—SHAKESPEARE.

"The knight, the which that castle *aught.*"
SPENSER, *F. Queene*, VI. iii. 2.

(3) As an auxiliary, it first appears in Laȝamon's *Brut*, "he *ah to* don" = he has to do, he must do.

"I *owe* for to be cristned."—WICKLIFFE, *Matt.* iii. 14.

---

[1] Those marked thus (*) are later forms.

> "And gladder *oughte* his freend ben of his deth
> Whan with honour up yolden is his breth."
> CHAUCER, *Knightes Tale*.

(4) It occurs impersonally with datives, as—
> "Wel *ought* us werche."—CHAUCER.

(5) **Owe** as a weak verb, signifying to be in debt, is conjugated regularly: present (1) *owe*, (2) *owest*, (3) *owes* (*oweth*); past (1) *owed*, (2) *owedst*, (3) *owed*.

(6) **Ought**, properly a past tense, is now used as a present, to signify moral obligation.

(7) **Own**, to possess, has probably arisen out of the derivative O. E. verb, *áhnian* (= *ág-nian*), to possess; or from the old participle passive of *owe—ágen* (*awen*, *owen*). Shakespeare uses *owe* for *own*.

304. Must.

		1	2	3		1	2	3
Present Indicative ...	Sing.	—	—	—	Pl.	—	—	
Subjunctive ...	Sing.	—	—	—	Pl.	—		
Past Indicative ...	Sing.	must	must	must	Pl.	must		
Subjunctive ...	Sing.	—	—	—	Pl.	—		

			O.E.		Goth.
Present Indic.... Sing.	1	môt	mote*	môt
	2	môs-t	mote*	môst
	3	mô-t	mote*	môt
Pl.	1	môton	moten*	môtum
Past Indic. ... Sing.	1	môste	moste*	môsta
Pl.	1	môston	mosten*	môstêdum

(1) The verb *mot* in Old English denoted permission, possibility, and obligation (= *may*, *can*, &c.).

Spenser uses the old verb *mote*, as—
> "Fraelissa was as faire, as faire *mote* bee."

(2) **Must** has now the force of a present as well as of a past tense, and denotes necessity and obligation. Chaucer uses *moste* as a present tense.

305. Wit.

		1	2	3		1	2	3
Present Indicative ...	Sing.	wot	—	wot	Pl.	wot	—	
Subjunctive ...	Sing.	—	—	—	Pl	—		
Past Indicative ...	Sing.	wist	—	wist	Pl.	wist		
Subjunctive ...	Sing.	—	—	—	Pl.	—		

	Infinitive. wit		Present Participle. witting		Past Participle. wist
			O. E.		Goth.
Present Indic.	Sing.	1	wât	wot	wait
		2	wâst	wost	waist
		3	wât	wot	wait
	Pl.	1	witon	witen	witum
Past Indic.	Sing.	...	wiste	wuste	wissa
	Pl.	...	wiston	wusten	wissêdum
Infinitive	...	...	witan		witan
Present Part.	...	...	witende		
Pass. Part.	...	...	witen	iwist, wist	

The original signification of O.E. *wat*, Goth. *wit*, is "I have seen" (cp. Gr. οἶδα), hence *I know*, from the root *wit* or *vid*, to see.

(1) Shakespeare has I wot, he wot, you wot, they wot.

(2) The old second person singular has given way to *wottest;* and *wotteth* or *wots* is sometimes found for *wot*.

(3) Wist, the true past tense of *wit*, occurs frequently in the English Bible; but Sackville uses *wotted*, as—

"I, which *wotted* best
His wretched drifts."—*Duke of Buckingham*.

(4) Unwist = unknown, undiscovered:

"Couldst thou hope, *unwist*, to leave my land?"
SURREY, *Æneid* iv.

(5) Wotting = O.E. *witende* (*witing*), occurs in the *Winter's Tale* (ed. Collier), iii. 2. Cp. *unwitting, unwittingly*.

(6) To wit, a gerundial infinitive, is used as an adverb = namely.

To *weet*, a causative of *wit* = to learn, as—

"Then we in doubt to Phœbus' temple sent
Euripilus to *weet* the prophesy."—SURREY, *Æneid* ii.

(7) *Must* and *wist* have an *s*, which is not found in the roots *mot* and *wit*.

The past tenses are formed by adding to the root *t*, as *mot-te*, *wit-te;* but, by a common law in the Teutonic dialects, the first *t* is changed to *s:* hence *mos-te, wis-te*.

306. *Mind*, in the sense of to remember, as "*mind* what you are about," has a non-radical *d*.

	Pres.	Perf.	Inf.	
O.E.	geman	gemunde	gemunan	(meminisse)
Goth.	man	munda	munan	,,
O.N.	man	munna / munda	muna	(recordari)
O.N.	—	—	munu	(μέλλειν)

The O.E. (ge)-*man* is the past of an old form *mina*, cogito. In the Northern dialects of the fourteenth century, we find the O.N. *mon, mone, mun* = must, shall, used as an auxiliary verb.

307. **Own.** I *own* I have done wrong = I grant or confess I have done wrong. This verb seems to have arisen out of O.E. *an, on*, the first person singular of *unnan*, to grant, concede (cp. Ger. *gönnen*) :—

"Miche gode ye wold him *an*."—*Trist.* l. 66.

"Y take that me gode *an*."—*Ib*. iii. 7.

308. **Do,** in "How do you *do* ?"
In the first verb we have the ordinary do = *facere*; the second *do* = *valere*, = O.E. *dugan*, to avail, prevail (Ger. *taugen*), Scotch *dow*.

		O.E.
Present Indicative	1	deâh
	2	duge
	3	deâh, degh,* dowes*
Pl.	1	dugon
Past Indicative, Sing.	1	dohte, dowed* [1]

309. Tenses formed by Composition.

(1) Tenses are formed, not only by suffixes added to the verbal root, but by using auxiliary verbs along with the participles or infinitive mood. This is called the analytical mode of expressing time. The perfect tense is denoted by *have* and *is*; the future by *shall* and *will*.

"The primary meaning of the word *have* is 'possession.' It is easy to see how 'I *have* my arms stretched out' might pass into 'I *have* stretched out my arms,' or how, in such phrases as 'he *has* put on his coat,' 'we *have* eaten our breakfast,' 'they *have* finished their work,' a declaration of possession of the object in the condition denoted by the participle should come to be accepted as sufficiently expressing the completed act of putting it into that condition; the present possessive, in fact, implies the past action, and, if our use of *have* were limited to the cases in which such an implication was apparent, the expressions in which we used it, would be phrases only. When, however, we extend the implication of past action to every variety of cases, as in 'I *have* discharged my servant,' 'he *has* lost his breakfast,' 'we *have* exposed their errors;' when there is no idea of possession for it to grow out of; or with neuter verbs, 'You *have been* in error,' 'he *has* come from London,' 'they *have* gone away;' where there is even no object for the *have* to govern; where condition and not action is expressed; and 'you *are* been,' 'he *is* come,' 'they *are* gone,' would be theoretically more correct (as they are alone proper in German):—then we have converted *have* from an independent part of speech into a fairly formative element."—WHITNEY.

---

[1] Those marked thus (*) are later forms.

(2) In O.E. writers of the fourteenth and fifteenth centuries *have* was weakened to *ha*, and in the sixteenth century we find it coalescing with the passive participle.

"The Jewes wolden *ha broken* his bones."
Legends of Holy Rood, p. 139, l. 237.
"Therefore ech man *ha* this in memorye."
LYDGATE, *Arund. MS.* fol. 376.
"I *ha* thereto plesaunce."—*Ib.* fol. 27.
"I knowlech to a *felid*."—WICKLIFFE, *Apol. for the Lollards*, p. 1.[1]
"It shuld *a fallen* on a bassenet or a helme."—FROISSART, I. ch. ii. 25.
"Richard might . . . *asaued* hymself if he would *afled* awaie."—*Life of Richard III.* in Hardyng, p. 547, reprint of 1812.[2]

(3) *Do* and *did* are used for forming emphatic tenses, as "I *do* love," "I *did* love."

This idiom did not make its appearance till about the thirteenth century, and did not come into general use before the fifteenth century.

Do (not causative) seems to have been used first as an auxiliary before imperatives, as—

"*Do* gyf glory to thy Godde."—*Allit. Poems*, C. l. 204.

Lydgate is the earliest writer I know of that uses the modern construction of *do* and *did* as tense auxiliaries.

In O.E. *do* = to make, cause, as—

"And if I do that lak,
Doth strepe me, and put me in a sak
And in the next ryver *do* me drenche."
CHAUCER, *C. Tales*, ll. 10074-5.

It was also used as at present, to save the repetition of the principal verb, as—

"I love you more than you *do* me."
SHAKESPEARE, *King John*, iv. 1.
"He slep no more than *doth* the nightingale."
CHAUCER, c. vii. l. 98.

(4) In O.E. *gan, can*, was used as a tense auxiliary = *did*.
But the details of this usage must be sought in the syntax of auxiliary verbs.

---

[1] Quoted by Marsh.   [2] Ibid.

CHAPTER XIV.

ADVERBS.

310. ADVERBS are mostly either abbreviations of words (or phrases, as *likewise = in like wise*) belonging to other parts of speech, or particular cases of nouns and pronouns.

They modify the meaning of verbs, adjectives, and adverbs, and may be classified according to their meaning into adverbs of—

(1) PLACE, answering to the question (*a*) WHERE? (*b*) WHITHER? (*c*) WHENCE? as (*a*) *here, there, anywhere, elsewhere, somewhere, nowhere, yonder, below, before, behind, within, without;* (*b*) *hither, thither, hitherwards, backwards, from below, from above;* (*c*) *hence, thence.*

(2) TIME, answering to the question WHEN? (*a*) PRESENT, as *now, to-day, at present, forthwith,* &c.; (*b*) PAST, as *yesterday, lately, forwards, of yore;* (*c*) FUTURE, as *to-morrow, soon, by and by;* (*d*) DURATION OF TIME (how long), as *long time, still, ever,* &c.; (*e*) REPETITION (how often), as *again, once, seldom, oft, daily;* (*f*) RELATIVE TO SOME OTHER TIME (how soon), as, *then, after, forthwith, first, last.*

(3) MANNER or QUALITY, as (*a*) *well, wisely, slowly, quickly*—some of these are interrogative, demonstrative, or indefinite, as *how, so, thus, nohow,* &c.; (*b*) affirmation, as *yes, yea, truly, indeed,* &c.; (*c*) negation, as *not, nay;* (*d*) doubt, uncertainty, as *likely, perhaps.*

(4) MEASURE, QUANTITY, DEGREE, as *much, little, enough, half, much, scarce, far, very, exceedingly.*

(5) CAUSE, INSTRUMENTALITY, as *why, wherefore, whence.*

311. According to their origin, or form, adverbs are divided into the following classes:—

I. Substantive Adverbs.

I. With case-endings:

(1) GENITIVE SINGULAR, *need-s,* O.E. *needes,* "he must *needs* (of necessity) die."

In O.E. we find the genitive used adverbially, as

"Fure, the never ne atheostrede, *winteres* ne *sumeres.*"—*La3.* 2861.
"Heo wolden feden thone king, *dæies* and *nihtes.*"—*Ib.* 3255.

" Ich not to hwan thu bredst thi brod
Lives ne *deaths* ne deth hit god."—*Owl & Nightingale*, l. 1634.

Cp. O.E. *willes*, willingly ; *sothes*, of a truth ; his *thonkes* = of his own accord, &c.

The termination has disappeared in many of the older words, as *day and night, summer and winter*. Cp.

"We shul be redy to stonde with you, *lyfe and dethe*."—*Gest. Rom.* p. 37.

The preposition *of* has taken the place of the genitive suffix, as *of necessity, of course, of force, of purpose, of right, of a truth, of a day*. We actually find in the sixteenth century "*of a late dayes*," as well as "*of late days.*"

Sometimes we have *of* (or *in, at, a, on*) with the old genitive, as *anights, of mornings, a mornings, on Sundays, now-a-days* = O.E. *now-on-dayes, in-a-doors*, &c.

There were some adverbs in O.E., originally dative feminine singular, ending in -*inga*, -*unga*, -*linga*, -*lunga*. A few of these, without the dative suffix, exist under the form -*ling* or -*long*, as *head-long* (O.E. *heedlinge*), *sideling, sidelong, dark-ling* (*darklong*), *flatling* and *flatlong*.

In the fourteenth century we find these with the genitive form, as *allynges* (wholly), *heedlynges, flatlynges, noselynges*.

The Scotch dialect has preserved the old suffix -*linges* under the form *lins*, as *darklins* (in the dark).

The word *grovelling* was originally an adverb ; cp. Scotch *groflins*, O.E. *gruflynges, groflinges*.

We find -*gates* = -*ways* in O.E., as *thus-gate* = thus-wise, *allegates* = always.

(2) DATIVE AND INSTRUMENTAL, *ever* (O.E. *æfre*), *never* (O.E. *næfre*), *whilom* (O.E. *hwil-unt*), *limb-meal* (O.E. *lim-mæl-um*), *piece-meal*.

(3) ACCUSATIVE, *ay* (O.E. *â*, Goth. *aiw*), *the while* (O.E. *thâ hwîle*), *somewhile* (*sumehwîle*), *some deal* (*sumne dæl*), *alway* (O.E. *ealne weg*), *otherwise* (*ôthre wîsen*), O.E. *the morn*[1] = to-morn ; cp. *nowise, noway, sometime*.

In such phrases as "He went *home*," "They wandered *north* and *south*," "I saw him *yesterday*," "They cry *day and night* unto him," "Can ye *aught* tell?" the words *home, north, south, yesterday*, &c. are adverbial accusatives.

(*a*) Many of the old accusatives now have a genitive form, as *other-way-s, always, longways, straightways, anothergates* (cp. O.E. *algates* = always, *thusgates*, &c.), *sideways, sometimes, otherwhiles, somewhiles, the whilst*. In the *Ayenbite* and in *Piers Plowman* we find *therhuile, therhuyl, therhuyls*.

(*b*) In most English Grammars that I have seen *a* in *a-year, a-day* = yearly, daily, is treated as the indefinite article used distributively.

---

[1] *The* was originally instrumental = O.E. *thŷ*.

A reference to older writers at once shows that this treatment is wholly incorrect.

"Thrywa *on geare*" = thrice a year.—*Exod.* xxiii. 17.
"An halpenny *on day*" = a halfpenny a day.—*Boke of Curtasye*, l. 616.

In some few words of French origin we have substituted *a* or *on* for Fr. *en* or *a*, especially in older writers; *around*, O.E. *on rounde*, O.F. *en rond*. Cp. *a fine* and *in fine*, *a stray*, *on stray*, &c.

In O.E. we find *in* for *a* before words of French origin, as—

"Thet corn *a gerse*, the vines *in* flouring" = the corn in grass, the vine in flowering.—*Ayenbite*, p. 36.[1]

In *a-feared*, *a-feard*, *an hungered*, *an hungry*, O.E. *a fingered*, *a dread*, the prefix *a* is a corruption of the O.E. *of*, an intensitive prefix, sometimes equivalent to *for* in *forswear*. In O.E. we find *a thirst*, *on thirst*, and *of thirst*.

A is also a weakened form of the preposition *of* or *o*. "A dozen *a* beer" (S. ROWLAND'S *Diogenes*), "God *a* mercy," "man-*a*-war."[2] Cp. "Body *o* me," "two *a* clock," and "two *o* clock."

In the compound *Jack-an-apes*, the *a* or *o* becomes *an* before a vowel, just as we find in O.E. *an* before vowels and the letter *h*, and *a* before consonants, as *an erthe* = in earth, *an hand* = in hand, &c.

II. PREPOSITIONAL: *a-way*[1] (O.E. *on-wæg*), *a-back* (O.E. *on-bæc*), *a-gain* (O.E. *on-geán*), *a-day* (*on-dæge*), *to-day* (O.E. *tó-dæge*), *to-night* (O.E. *tó-nihte*), *a niht* (*on niht*), *to-morn*, *to-morrow* (O.E. *tó-mergen*), O.E. *to-yere* (this year), *to-eve* (yesterday evening), *to-whiles* = meanwhile, *adown* (O.E. *â-dune*).

Cp. *abed*, *afoot*, *asleep* (*on sleep*), *alive* (*on life*), *ahead*, *on head*, *on-brood*, *a-broach*, *ashore*, *arow*, *aloft*, *apart*, *among*, *across*, *aside*, *a height*, *an end*, *a-front*, *a-door*, *besides* (O.E. *besides*, *besiden*), *of kin* (akin), *of kind* (naturally), *of purpose*, *because*, *by chance*, *perhaps*, *perchance*, *perforce*.

In O.E. we find *asidis*, *on sidis hand* = aside, apart; *by northe*, *by southe*, *by pecemeale*, *by cas* (by chance).

Other but more recent adverbial forms of this nature are—*by no means*, *by any means*, *beforehand*, *at hand*, *in front*, *at night*, *at times*, *at length*,[3] *at-gaze* (*agaze*), *by degrees*, *up-stairs*, *indoors*, *in fact*, *in deed*.

The preposition is sometimes omitted, as "they went *back*" (= aback), "this stick was broke *cross*" (= across).

---

[1] Cp. "Innes *a* Court men" (Earle's *Cosmog.* ed. Arber, p. 41).

[2] The *a* = *an* has the same meaning as *on*: but *an* was used before consonants, *a* before vowels. Cp. *anon*, *anende*.
It occurs as an independent word, as—,
"Thin holy blod thet thou ssedest *ane* the rod."—*Ayenbite*, p. 1.
"The robe of scarlet erthan thet the kuen his do *an*."—*Ib.* p. 167.

[3] In Earle's *Cosmog.* (ed. Arber) we find *at the length*, *at bedsides* (p. 24), *in summe* (p. 33).

II. Adjectival Adverbs.

(1) In O.E. many adverbs are formed from adjectives by means of the suffix -*e*.[1] Thus an adjective in -*lic* = like was converted into an adverb by this means, as *biterlic* (adjective), *biterlíce* (adverb), *bitterly*.

The loss of the adverbial *e* reduced the adverb to the same form as the adjective : hence O.E. *fæste, faste*, became *fast; faire, fair*, &c. ; *he smot him hardĕ* = he smote him *hard*.

Cp. to work *hard*, to sleep *sound*, to speak *fair*.

In Elizabethan writers we find the adverbial -*ly* often omitted, as "*grievous* sick," "*miserable* poor."

(2) Many adjective forms, especially those of irregular comparison, as *well, much, little*, &c., are used as adverbs.

(3) GENITIVE FORMS, as *else* (O.E. *elles*), *backwards, forwards, upwards, eftsoons, uneathes, unawares*.

(4) ACCUSATIVE, *ere* (O.E. *ær*), *enough* (O.E. *genóh*), *backward, homeward*.

(5) DATIVE, *seldom :* cp. O.E. *on-ferrum* = afar ; O.E. *miclum*, greatly ; *litlum* and *lytlum* = paulatim.[2]

"Lere hem *litlum* and *lytlum*."—*Piers Plowman*, B. p. 286.

In later times the inflexion dropped, and we often find the prepositional construction instead, as *by little and little*.[3] Cp.

" So did the waxen image (lo) *by smale and smale* decrease."
"They love the mullet greate, And yet do mynce her *smale and smale*."—*Ib*.
" My rentes come to me *thicke and thicke*."—*Ib*. ii. 3.

DRANT'S *Horace*, Sat. ii. 2.

(6) INSTRUMENTAL, *yore* (O.E. *geâra*), *yet* (O.E. *geta*), *soon* (O.E. *sona*).

(7) PREPOSITIONAL FORMS, *amidst*[4] (O.E. *on-middum, amidde, a-middes*), *towards* (O.E. *to-weardes*), *together* (O.E. *tô-gæder*), *afar, anew, alate, aright, abroad, afar, aloud, along, agood, a-cold, ala.i, anon, at large, a-high, on high, in vain* (O.E. *on ídel*), *in general, in short*,[5] *at the full, to right, on a sudden, at unawares* (*at unaware* occurs in DRANT'S *Horace*), *at all* (O.E. *alles*), *withal, of yore, of new, of late, of right* [O.E. *of fresh, of neere, in open* (= openly), *in playne* (= plainly)].

Prepositions sometimes accompany the comparative and superlative, as *for the worse*, &c.; *at last*, O.E. *atte laste* = at the last ; *atte wyrst, at the worst*, &c. : cp. O.E. *atte beste*, at the best ; *at least*, &c.

---

[1] Probably the old dative ending.
[2] Sometimes in O.E. we find -*en* for -*um*, as *whilen, selden*.
[3] The genitive form is sometimes met with, " by *littles* and *littles*."
[4] The *t* in such words as *amidst, amongst*, is merely euphonic ; cp. O.E. *alongst* (= along), *onest* (= once).
[5] *In few* also occurs in Elizabethan literature ; cp. *in brief*, &c.

III. Numeral Adverbs.

Once, O.E. *æne, ene, anes, enes, ans;* **Twice**, O.E. *twi-wa*,[1] *twiwe, twien, twie, twies, twis;* **Thrice**, O.E. *thri-wa, thriwe, thrie, thries, thrys.*

The *-ce = -s = -es.* In *betwixt* (= O.E. *betweohs*) the last letter is not radical: cp. *amidst.*

An on (= *in one instant*), *at one, at once, atwain, atwo, in twain,* O.E. *a twinne, a thre,* &c. *for the nonce.*[2]

312. IV. Adverbs formed from Particles.

A.—Prepositional Adverbs.

(1) **Aft** (O.E. *æft, eft*), *after* (O.E. *æft-er*), *afterwards,* &c.; *abaft = a + be + aft* (O.E. *be-æftan*).

(2) **By** (O.E. *bî, big*), *for-by, by and by.*

(3) **For**, as in *be-fore* (O.E. *beforan*), *for-th, forthwith, afore, afore-hand, beforehand.*

(4) **Hind**, as in *behind* (O.E. *behindan*), *behindhand;* O.E. *hindan, hindweard.*

(5) **In**, as in *within* [O.E. *innan, binnan* (= *be-innan*), *withinnan, withinnen*], O.E. *inwith.*

(6) **Neath**, as in *be-neath, underneath* (O.E. *neothan, be-nythan, underneothan, nithor, nither,* down).

(7) **On**, *onward.*

(8) **Of** (O.E. *of* = from, *off*), off.

(9) **To**, too.

(10) **Through** (O.E. *thurh;* later forms, *thurf, thurch, thuruh, thorgh*), *thorough, throughly, thoroughly.*

(11) **Under**, *underfoot, underhand.*

(12) **Up**, *upper, uppermost, upward.*

(13) **From** the old form *ufan* (*ufon*) we get *above* (= O.E. *â-bufan, abuven*), *over* (= O.E. *ofer*); cp. O.E. *be-ufan, bufan, with-ufan, onufan* = above; *ufanweard,* upwards; *ufanan,* from above.[3]

---

[1] The *-wa* in *twi-wa,* &c. = *war* (O.N. *-var,* Sansk. *vara*), originally signified *time:* we have cognate suffix in Septem-*ber,* &c.
[2] Cp. O.E. *for then anes* or *for than anes,* where the *n* originally belonged to the demonstrative; cp. the oldest English *for tham anum.*
[3] Later forms are *buven, ouenan, bibufen.*

(14) **Out**, *about* (O.E. *ût, ûte, utan, b-utan, ymb-utan*), *without* (O.E. *withutan, withouten*), *abouts, thereabouts.*

In O.E. we have *inwith, outwith.*

B.—Pronominal Adverbs.

Table of Adverbs connected with the Stems **he, the, who.**

PRONOMINAL STEMS.	PLACE WHERE.	MOTION TO.	MOTION FROM.	TIME WHEN.	MANNER.	CAUSE.
who	where	whither	whence	when	how	why
the	there	thither	thence	then	thus	the
he	here	hither	hence	—	—	—

(1) Adverbs connected with the demonstrative **the**:—

There (O.E. *thâr, thær*), originally *locative; re* is probably a shortened form of *der* (Sansk. *ta-tra* = *there*).

Thither (O.E. *thider*) contains the locative suffix *-ther*,[1] corresponding to O.N. *thathra*, Sansk. *ta-tra; thitherward* (O.E. *thiderweard, thiderweardes*).

Then (O.E. *thanne, thonne, thenne*), accusative singular.[2] It is the same word as the conjunction *than*.

We find in O.E. *tha, tho* = then, thence; *nouthe* = now then.

Thence (O.E. *than-an, than-on, thonon, thananne;* later forms, *thanene, thannene, thenne-s, then-s*) has two suffixes: (1) *n*, originally perhaps the locative of the demonstrative stem *na* (existing in adjectives in *-en*, and in passive participles); and (2) the genitive *-ce* = *-es*, which came in about the thirteenth century.

---

[1] It is of the same origin as the comparative suffix from *tar*, to go beyond.
[2] Cp. Latin *tu-m, tun-c, ta-m, tandem, ta-men, tantus, tot*, &c., all containing the demonstrative stem *ta*, cognate with English *the*.

In O.E. northern writers we find *thethen* = O.N. *thathan* = thence; old Scotch writers have *thyne*.

<small>In Latin we find suffix -*n* in *superne*, from above. In O.E. we have *eást-an*, from the east; *west-an*, from the west, &c.; *hind-an*, from behind.</small>

The (O.E. *thî*) before comparatives is an adverb, and is the instrumental case of the definite article the: *the more*, O.E. *thî mare = eò magis*.

In O.E. we have *for-thi* or *for-thy* = therefore, as—

"*Forthy* appease your griefe and heavie plight."
SPENSER, *F. Q.* II. i. 14.

Thus (O.E. *thus*), probably an instrumental case of this; in O. Saxon *thius* = inst. case of *thit*, the neuter of *thèse* (this).

Lest = O.E. *thŷ lǽs* (or *the lǽs*) + *the* (indeclinable relative), which, by omission of *thy*, became weakened to *leoste, leste*.

(2) Adverbs connected with the demonstrative stem he (hi):—

Here (O.E. *her*). On the origin of the suffix -*r*, see remarks on *there*, p. 198.

Hither (O.E. *hider*). See remarks on *whither*.

Hence (O.E. *hinan, heonan, heonane, heona*; later forms, *hennene, henne, hennes, hens*).

In O.E. northern writers we find *hethen* = O.N. *hethan*.

<small>In Gothic we have an accusative *hina*, corresponding to *then* or *than*. We have the same root perhaps in *hin-d-er, be-hind*.</small>

(3) Adverbs from the interrogative stem who:—

Where (O.E. *hwær, hwar*). See remarks on *there*.

Whither (O.E. *hwæ-der, hwider*), *witherward*. See remarks on *thither*.

When (O.E. *hwanan, hwana, hwanon*; later forms, *whenene, whenne, hwanne, whennes, whens*), *whence*.

In O.E. northern writers we find *whethan* = O.N. *hvethan*. See remarks on *thence*.

How (O.E. *hu, hwu*[1]), why (O.E. *hwî*), are instrumental cases of *who*.

In O.E. we have *for-why* = wherefore, because. In the English Bible the mark of interrogation is *wrongly* printed after it.

---

[1] Capgrave actually writes *who* for *how*.

(4) From the reflexive stem **si** :—

So (O. E. *swâ*), an instrumental case of *swa* = so.

Also and **as** are compounds of *so* with the adjective *all*.

(5) From the demonstrative stem **ya**, *yon, yond, yonder, beyond*. See Demonstrative Pronouns, § 181, p. 128.

(6) From the relative stem **ya** :—

In Sansk. *ya-s, yâ, ya-t* = qui, quæ, quod.

Yea (O. E. *gea, gia*; later forms, *yha, ya, ye*; Goth. *ja*)

Ye-s (O. E. *ge-se*; later forms, ʒ*is, yhis*).

The suffix *s* (*-se*) in yes is the present subjunctive of the root *as*, to be; O. E. *sî*, Ger. *sei* = let it be. In O.E. there was a negative *ne-se*; O. E. *næs* = not = *ne wæs* = was not.

Ye-t (O.E. *gyta, geta, gyt*) contains the same root.[1] The Latin *ja-m* contains a cognate stem.

(7) From an interrogative stem **ye** :—

Yesterday (O. E. *gystran-dæg*). This adverb is cognate with Goth. *gi-s-tra*, Lat. *heri* (*he-s-ternu-s*), Gr. χθές, Sansk. *hy-as* (= *ha-dyas*). The suffix *-tra* (*-ter*) is comparative.

(8) From the demonstrative **sam** :—

Sam, together, used by Spenser = O.E. *saman, samen*; cp. O. E. *sam-od, sam-ad*; Goth. *sam-ath*, together; Gr. ἅμα ; Lat. *simul*.

(9) From **Sun-dor** :—

Asunder (= O.E. *on sundron, on sundrum*) and *sun-der* (O.E. *sundor*, Goth. *sun-dro*, separately, apart).

(10) From the demonstrative **na** :—

(*a*) **Now** (O. E. *nu*[2]),—cp. Lat. *nu-n-c, num, nam, ne*, Gr. νῦν ; (*b*) **ne** = not, as in Chaucer; (*c*) **no** (O.E. *na*); and (*d*) **nay**.

 " His hors was good, but he *ne* was nought gay."—Prol. l. 74.

In O. E. *ne* = neither, nor. Spenser uses it—
 " *Ne* let him then admire,
 But yield his sence to bee too blunt and bace."—*F. Q.* ii. Intr. 4.

---

[1] **If** (O.E. *gif, yif*) is by some philologists connected with Goth. *iba, ibai,* perhaps, lest; which is probably the dative case of *iba* = doubt : cp. Icel. *ef* doubt, if.

[2] Cp. O. E. *nutha, nouthe* = now then.

This particle enters into the following words :—none, nought, nor, neither, never.

(11) Not = nought.   See *aught*, § 233, p. 146.

For *not, not a whit*, we sometimes find *not a jot, not a bit*; cp. O.E. *nevər a del, never a whit.*
The Latin *nihil* = not a bean.[1]   In vulgar language we hear such expressions as I *don't* care *a straw*, or *a button*, &c. So in O.E. writers we get " noght a *bene* (bean)," " not a *kers* (cress)."[2]

Ay, sometimes used for *yes*, is identical with adv. *aye* = ever ; O.E. *â* as in *ever* (O.E. *æfer*).

For aye = *for ever*—
   " With endless vengeance on his stock *for aye*."
                              SACKVILLE, *Ferrex and Porrex.*

What = *why* is an adverb, as—

   " *What* should I more now seek to say in this,
   Or one jot farther linger forth my tale?"
                              SACKVILLE, *Duke of Buckingham.*
   " *What* need we any spur but our own cause?"—*Jul. Cæsar*, ii. 1.

§ 313. V. Compound Adverbs.

(1) *There, here, where*, are combined (*a*) with prepositions, as *therein, thereinto, thereabout, thereabouts, thereafter, thereat, thereon, thereof, thereout, thereunto, thereunder, thereupon, thereby, therefore, therefrom* (and O.E. *therefro*), *therewith, therewithal, thereto, thitherto; herein, hereinto, hereabout, hereafter, hereat, hereof, hereout, hereinto, hereupon, hereby, herewith, heretofore, hitherto; wherein, whereinto, whereabout, whereat, whereof, whereunto, whereupon, whereby, wherefore, wherewith, wherewithal, wherethrough.*

The pronominal adverbs have a relative force. We have seen that the O.E. indeclinable relative *the* and English *that* are *followed* by prepositions; hence *here, there, where*, are mostly *followed* by prepositions. We have a few compounds with prepositions preceding, as *from thence, from whence.*

The preposition is sometimes separated from the adverb, as " On Italiʒe, *thar* Rome nu *on* stondeth " (Laʒ. 107). See quotations under *as*, § 198, p. 133.

---

[1] Max Müller says *not a thread*. In O.E. we find the word *nifel* = trifle, nething.
[2] This is the origin of the slang expression " I don't care a *curse*."

(*b*) With *so* and *soever*, as *whereso, wheresoever, wherever, whithersoever, whencesoever, whereas*.

(*c*) With *else, some, other, every, no, each, any*, as *elsewhere, somewhere, otherwhere, everywhere, nowhere, eachwhere* (O.E. *ay-where* = everywhere), *anywhere*.

(2) How is combined with *so*, as *howso, howsoever*.

(3) Other compounds have already been noticed, see § 311, pp. 195, 196. To these may be added *erelong, erewhile, while-ere, erenow, withal, after-all, forthwith, at random*. Fr. *à randon*.

(4) Some elliptical expressions are used as adverbs, as *maybe, mayhap, howbeit, as it were, to wit, to be sure*.

CHAPTER XV.

PREPOSITIONS.

314. PREPOSITIONS are so named because they were originally prefixed to the verb, in order to modify its meaning. They express (1) the relations of space, (2) other relations derived from those of space, and marked in some languages by case-endings.

Prepositions are either simple or compound.

I. Simple Prepositions.

In (O.E. *in*) is connected with *on, an, a*, from a demonstrative stem $a + na$.

Before a dental *n* shows a tendency to disappear, as *tooth = touth*. So in our dramatists and O.E. writers we find *i'the* = in the.

At (O.E. *æt*) also contains the stem *a* (cp. Sanskrit *á-dhi*, Lat. *ad; -dhi* = Gr. -θι).

Of (O.E. *of, af, æf;* Goth. *af*, from; Lat. *ab*, Gr. ἀπό, Sansk. *apa*).

By, O.F. *bi* (cp. Sansk. *a-bhi*, of which the suffix *-bhi* = Gr. -φι, Lat. *-bi;* a nasalized form of *a-bhi* is found in Gr. ἀμφί, Lat. *amb-*, O.Sax. *umbi*, O.E. *umbe, embe, ymbe, um-*, Ger. *um-*).

For (O.E. *for*, Goth. *faúr*, O.N. *fyr, fyrir*); *a-fore* (O.E. *on-foran*).

From (O.E. *fram, from;* *fra, fro;* O.N. *frá*).

The *m* is a superlative suffix (cp. Sanskrit *para-ma-s*, from *pará*, cognate with Eng. *fore* (O.E. *fore*).

The same root is seen in **for-th,** *fur-ther, far.* Cp. Sansk. *pra*, Gr. πρo, Lat. *pro*.

On (O.Sax. *an;* O.Fris. *an, á;* O.N. *á;* Goth. *ana*), up-ON.

Up (O.E. *up*), formed from a stem $u + pa$. Cp. Sansk. *upa*, near; Gr. ἀπό, near, under; Lat. *s-ub;* Goth. *iup;* O.H.Ger. *úf*.

Out (O.E. *út*); the older form is seen in *utter, utmost.*

With (O.E. *with, wither*, from, against). We have a more original form in O.E., viz. *mid*, with ; Goth. *mith*, Sansk. *mithas*, Gr. μετά,* from a demonstrative stem *ma*. *Wither* (or *with*) is a comparative form, in which *m* is replaced by *w* (cp. Goth. *withra*).

To (O.E. *tó*). It is often used in the sense of "for," as *to frend* = "for friend" (Spenser), *to wife*, &c.

Too (adv.) is another form of the same word.

II. Compound Prepositions.

(1) Comparatives :—

After (O.E. *æf-ter*), a comparative formed from *of;* see Comparison of Adjectives. We have the same root in *aft, eft, abaft*, &c.

Over (O.E. *ofer*) is a comparative connected with *up*, and with the compound *above* (O.E. *a-b-ufan*) ; cp. Sansk. *upari*, Gr. ὑπέρ, Lat. *super;* O.E. *ufera*, higher.

Under (O.E. *un-der*, Goth. *un-dar*, Sansk. *an-tar*, Lat. *in-ter*) contains the root *in* (see p. 203), with the comparative suffix *-ther* (*-der*).

Through (O.E. *thur-h*, O.Sax. *thur-ah*, Goth. *thair-h*, Ger. *dur-ch;* from root *tár*, to go beyond ; cp. Lat. *tra-ns*, Sansk. *tíras*, across).

Thorough is merely another form of *through*.

(2) Prepositions compounded with prepositions : *into* (O.E. *intill*), *upon, beneath, underneath, afar, before, behind, beyond, within, without, throughout* [O.E. *foreby, at-fore, on-foran* (= *afore*), *tofore*].

But (= O.E. *butan* = *be-utan*) originally signified *be out*. In provincial English it signifies *without*.

Above = *a* (on) + *be* + *ove* (O.E. *bufan* = *be-ufan*). See *up* and *over*, § 312, p. 197.

About = *á* + *be* + *out* (O.E. *ábutan* = *á-be-utan*).

Among, amongst (O.E. *ge-mang, on gemong;* later forms, *amouges, amang*).

Unto in O.E. often – *until;* *unt* = Goth. *unde*, to; O.Fris. *ont*, ; O.Sax. *unt, unte;* O.E. *óth* = until.

Until = *unt* + *till*.

(3) Prepositions formed from substantives :—

Again, against, *over against* (O.E. *on-geán, agean ; to-gegness,* against; later forms, *on3ænes, a3enes, ayens* ; cp. Ger. *ent-gegen*).
Other prepositions of this class are, *instead of, in behalf of, by dint of, by way of, for the sake of ; abroad, abreast, atop, ahead, astride, adown, across.*

(4) Adjective prepositions :—

Ere (O.E. *æ-r*), before, is a comparative of the root *á*. See § 233, p. 146.
Or (O.E. *ar*) is another form of the same word.

Till (O.E. *til*, good ; Goth. *gatils*, useful ; O.N. *til*, to).
Till first makes its appearance as a preposition in the northern dialect. It occurs in the Durham Gospels (eleventh century).
In O.E. we find *intil* = into.

To-ward, towards (O.E. *tô-weard, tô-weardes*).

In O.E. we find these elements separated. Cp.

"Thy thoughts which are *to* us *ward.*"—*Psalm* xl. 5.

Other adverbs of this kind are *afterward, afterwards, upward, froward* = away from.

"Give ear to my suit, Lord ; *fromward* hide not thy face."—*Paraphrase of Psalm* lv. by Earl of Surrey.

Along, alongst (O.E. *andlang, ondlang, endelong, endlonges, an long, on longe, alonges,* through, along).
It is often used for *lengthwise*, and is opposed to *athwart* or *across.*

"The dores were alle of ademauntz eterne
Iclenched *overthwart* and *endelong.*"—CHAUCER, *Knightes Tale.*

"Muche lond he him 3ef *an long* thare sea."—*La*3. 138.

There is another **along** (O.E. *ge-lang*) altogether different from this, in the sense of "on account (of)."

"All this is '*long* of you."—*Coriol.* v. 4.

"All *along* of the accursed gold."—*Fortunes of Nigel.*

"On me is nought *alonge* thin yvel fare."
CHAUCER, *Tr. and Cr.* ii. 1. 1000.

"Vor oðe is al mi lif *ilong.*"—*O.E. Hom.*, First Series, p. 197.

Amid, amidst (O.E. *on-middan, on-middum ;* later forms, *amidde, amiddes ;* from the adjective *midd,* as in *middle, mid-most*).
In the midst is a compound like O.E. *in the myddes of ;* cp. O.E. *tô-middes* = amidst.

Other prepositions of this kind are, *around, a-slant, a-skaunt, be-low, be-twixt* (O.E. *betweoh-s, be-tweox*, from *twi*, two), *between* (O.E. *be-twconum, betwynan*), *atween, atwixt*.

An-ent is O.E. *on-efn, on-emn*, near, toward (later forms, *on-efen-t, anent, anentes, anens, anence*).

Athwart, *over-thwart, thwart* (O.E. *thwar, on thweorh;* O.N. *thwert*).

Fast by (O.E. *on fæst*, near) ; cp. *hardby, forby*.

Since (O.E. *siththan;* later forms, *siththe, sithe, sin, sen; sithens, sithence, sinnes, sins*[1]).

O.E. *no but, not but* = only.

(5) Verbal prepositions :—

The following prepositions arise out of a participial construction : *notwithstanding, owing to, outtaken* (now replaced by *except*), &c.

" Ther is non, *outtaken hem* (= iis exceptis)."—WICKLIFFE, *Mark* xii. 32.

315. III. Prepositions of Romance Origin.

(1) *Uncompounded:—per, versus, sans* (= Lat. *sine*).

(2) *Compounded:*—(*a*) Substantive — *across, vià, because, apropos of, by means of, by reason of, by virtue of, in accordance with, in addition to, in case of, in comparison to, in compliance with, in consequence of, in defiance of, in spite of, in favour of, in front of, in lieu of, in opposition to, in the point of, in quest of, with regard to, in reply to, with reference to, in respect of, in search of, on account of, on the plea of, with a view to.*

(*b*) Adjective — *agreeably to, exclusive of, inclusive of, maugre, minus, previous to, relatively to, around, round, round about.*

(*c*) Verbal, active :—*during, pending, according to, barring, bating, concerning, considering, excepting, facing, including, passing, regarding, respecting, aiding, tending, touching;* (2) passive :—*except, excepted, past, save.*[2]

---

[1] *Sith* is an adjective = O.E. *sith*, late ; *siththan* = later than, afterwards. The root is *sinth;* cp. Goth. *sinth*, a way.
[2] Many of these have arisen out of the old dative (*absolute*) construction.

CHAPTER XVI.

CONJUNCTIONS.

316. CONJUNCTIONS join sentences and co-ordinate terms. According to meaning, they are divided into—

Co-ordinate, joining independent prepositions: (*a*) *copulative*, as *and, also*, &c.; (*b*) *disjunctive*, as *or, else*, &c.; (*c*) *adversative*, as *but, yet*, &c.; (*d*) *illative*, as *for, therefore, hence*.

Sub-ordinate, joining a dependent clause to a principal sentence: (*a*) those used in joining *substantive* clauses to the principal sentence, as *that, whether;* (*b*) those introducing an *adverbial* clause, marking (1) time—*when, while, until;* (2) reason, cause—*because, for, since;* (3) condition—*if, unless, except;* (4) purpose, end—*that, so, lest*.

317. According to their origin, conjunctions may be divided into—pronominal, numeral, adverbial, substantive, prepositional, verbal, compound.

(1) **Pronominal**:—

And (O.Sax. *endi*, O.H.Ger. *anti*, from the stem *ana*).

An = if (Goth. *an*, O.E. *ono*). It is sometimes written *an,* and frequently joined to *if*.

Eke = also (O.E. *ec*), hence, *how, so, also, as, just as, as far as, in so far as, whereas, lest, then, than*,[1] *thence, no sooner than, though*,[2] *although, therefore, that, yea, nay, what . . . and* (O.E. *what . . . what*), *whereupon, whence, whether, either, neither, or, nor*.[3]

(2) **Numeral**:—*both, first, secondly*, &c.

---

[1] We occasionally find, as in Scotch, *or* and *nor* instead of *than*.
[2] O.E. *theáh*, Goth. *thau-h*, from the demonstrative stem *the*.
[3] *Or* and *nor* are contractions of *other, nother* = *either, neither*.

(3) **Substantive** :—*sometimes . . . sometimes, while, in case, upon condition, in order that, otherwise, likewise* (= *in like wise*), *on the one hand . . . on the other hand, on the contrary, because, besides, on purpose that, at times, if* (see footnote on p. 200).

(4) **Adjective (Adverbial)** : — *even, alike, accordingly, consequently, directly, finally, lastly, namely, partly . . . partly, only, furthermore, moreover, now . . . now, anon . . . anon, lest, unless* (O.E. *onlesse*), &c.

(5) **Prepositional** :—

(*a*) Originally used before the demonstratives *that* or *this*:—*ere, after, before, but, for, in* (*that*), *since* (*sith, sithence*[1]), *till, until, with* (*that*); (*b*) participial :—*notwithstanding, except, excepting, save, saving*, &c.

(6) **Verbal** :—*to wit, videlicet* (*viz.*), *say, suppose, considering, providing.*

(7) **Compounds**, being abbreviated forms of expression: *not only*,[2] *nathless, nevertheless, nathemore* (Spenser), O. E. *nathemo*, O. E. *never the later, that is, that is to say, may be, were it not, were it so, be it so, be so, how be it, albeit*, O. E. *al if*, &c.

So in O. E. we have *warne, warn* = were it not, unless (cp. O. H. Ger. *nur* = *ni wâri* = were it not), equivalent to the O. E. *nǣre thæt*, were it not. Cp. O. E. *quin* (= *qui ne* = why not), O that.

---

[1] The O. E. *sîþ-þan* = *sîþ-þam*, after that.
[2] *Not only . . . but also* = O. E. *nâ læs thæt an . . . ac eac* ; *nathless* = O. E. *nô thŷ læs* ; *lest* = O.E. *læs the* for *thŷ læs the*.

CHAPTER XVII.

INTERJECTIONS.[1]

318. INTERJECTIONS, having no grammatical connection with other words in a sentence, are not, strictly speaking, "parts of speech." They are either imitations of cries expressing a sudden outburst of feeling, as *oh, ah*, or are mere sound gestures, as *st, sh*.

Many words, phrases, and sentences have come to be used interjectionally, as *alas, zounds*, &c.

Interjections may express feelings of—

(1) **Pain, weariness**—*ah, oh, O* (O. Fr. *a, ah, ahi, O, oh, ohi*), *ay*. O.E. interjections of pain are, *a, ou, ow*.

Welaway, welladay (O.E. *wâ lâ wâ ; lâ = lo, wâ = woe ; wâ lâ*, Scotch *waly*, O.E. *awey* (alas).

Alas (O.F. *hailas, halas*), *alack, lackadaisy, alackaday, boohoo, out alas, O dear me* (? *dio mio*, my God), *heigh ho, heigh, heyday*, O.E. *hig*.

(2) **Joy**—*hey, heigh* (Fr. *hé*), *hey-day, hurrah, huzza, hilliho*.

(3) **Surprise, &c.**—*eh* (O.E. *ey*), *ha, ha, ha! what, why, how, lo, la, lawk, aha* (Lat. *ha*), *ho, hi*.

(4) **Aversion, disgust, disapproval**—*fy, fie, foh, fugh, faugh, fudge, poh, pooh, pugh* (Fr. *pouah*), *baw, bah, pah*,[2] *pish, pshah, pshaw, tut, whew, ugh* (O.E. *weu*), *out, out on, hence, avaunt, aroynt, begone, for shame, fiddle-faddle*.

---

[1] "Voces quæ cujuscunque passionis animi pulsu per exclamationem interjiciuntur."—PRISCIAN, *Inst. Gram.* l. 15, c. 7.

[2] Selden uses *pah* as adj.: "It (child) all bedawbs it (coat) with its *pah* hands." —*Table Talk*.
Shakespeare has it as an interj.: "*Fie, fie, fie! pah! pah!* Give me an ounce of civet, good apothecary, to sweeten my imagination."—*Lear*, iv. 6.

P

(5) **Protestation**—*indeed, in faith, perdy, gad,*[1] *egad, ecod, ods, odd, odd's bob, odd's pettikins, udsfoot, ods bodkins, od zooks, zooks, odso, gadso, 'sdeath, 'slife, zounds, 'sbud, 'sblood, lord, marry, lady, bi'rlady, by'rlakin, jingo,*[2] *by jingo, deuce, dyce, devil, gemminy (O gemini).*

(6) **Calling and exclaiming**—*hilloa, holla, ho, so ho, hoy, hey, hem, harow* (O. Fr. *haro*, a cry for help), *help, hoa, bravo, well done, hark, look, see, oyes, mum, hist, whist, tut, tush, silence, peace, away, bo, shoo, shoohoo, whoa.*

(7) **Doubt, consideration**—*why, hum, hem* (Lat. *hem*), *humph, what.*

(8) Many interjections are what are called "imitative words," or *onomatopœias*:—

Sounds produced (*a*) **by inanimate objects**—*ding-dong, bim-bom, ting-tang, tick-tack, thwack, whack, twang, bang, whiz, thud, whop, slap, dash, splash, clank, puff.*

(*b*) **By animate objects**—*bow-wow, mew, caw, purr, croak, cock-a-doodle-do, cuckoo, tu-whit, to-whoo, tu-whu, weke-weke, ha ha.*[3]

---

[1] In *gad, egad, od,* the name of the Deity is profanely used. In the Middle Ages people swore by parts of Christ's *body,* by His sides, face, feet, bones; hair (cp. *sfacks,* God's hair), blood, wounds (*zounds, 'od's nouns* = God's wounds), life; also by the Virgin Mary (by the *mackins* = by the maiden), by the mass: also, by the pity and mercy of God, as "by *Goddes ore;*" "*Odd's pittikens;*" by God's sanctities (God's *sonties*).

[2] *Jingo, jinkers* = St. *Gingoulph.*

[3] Used to imitate the sound of a horse's neigh, as *Job* xxxix. 25. Luther uses *hut.*

CHAPTER XVIII.

DERIVATION AND WORD FORMATION.

319. ROOTS, as we have seen, are either *predicative* or *demonstrative*, and constitute the primary elements of words. See § 58.

The root is the significative part of a word, as *bair-n*, O.E. *ber-n*, contains the root *bar*, to bear. Suffixes serve to modify the root meaning, as the *n* in *bair-n*, which is identical with the *en* in the passive participle of strong verbs: hence *bairn* = one bor-n or brought forth. Thus from the verb *spin*, by adding the suffix *-der*, denoting the instrument or agent, we get *spi-der*,[1] the spinner.

Suffixes were once independent words, which, by being added to principal roots to modify their meaning, gradually lost their independence and became mere signs of relation, and were employed as *formative* elements. Cp. the origin of the adverbial suffix *-ly*, which originally signified *like*.

To get at the root of a word we must remove all the formative elements, and such changes of vowel as have been produced by the addition of relational syllables.

A *theme* or *stem* is that modification that the root assumes before the terminations of declension and conjugation are added, as *love-d*; *lov* (= *luf*) is the root; *love* (= *lufo*) is the *theme* or *stem*; *-d* is the suffix of the past tense.

320. *Themes* are formed from roots (1) by the addition of a demonstrative root, (2) by a change of the root vowel, (3) by combining other stems, (4) by reduplication.

In English very many formative elements have been lost, especially those of demonstrative origin. Gothic has retained more of these suffixes, once common to all the Aryan languages: thus from the root *gaf* = give, the O.E. formed *gif-u* a gift, *gif-ol*, generous, liberal; *gif-ta*, marriage dowry; *gif-te-lic*, belonging to a wedding; *gif-an*, to give; *giv-en-de*, giving, a giver. Here the root-vowel *a* is weakened to *i*.

Gothic has *gab-ei*, gain, gift; *gab-ei-gs*, rich; *gab-i-g-aba*, richly; *gib-a*, gift; *gib-a-n*, to give; *gib-and-s*, a giver, giving; other derivations might be found, as *gab-ig-jan*, to enrich; *gab-ig-nan*, to be rich.

---

[1] In English a radical *n* often disappears before *d*, *th*, as tooth, O.E. *toth*, i.e. *tonth*; cp. O.H.Ger. *tand*, Ger. *zahn*, Lat. *dens*.

In O.E. *gifu*, Goth. *gib-a*, *a* or *u* is a demonstrative particle forming a feminine noun ; *gif-ta* contains the demonstrative *th* (as in *the*). In the Gothic *gab-ei* (for *gabi*) the suffix forms an abstract substantive feminine ; by adding the adjective suffix *g* (same as English *y* in *dirt-y*) we get *gabei-g*; then with the further addition of the nominative sign we have *gabei-gs*.

From *gibig* (= *gabig* or *gabeig*) we form a causative verb *gab-ig-j-an*, to enrich, and by means of the demonstrative *n* (the sign of the passive participle) we get a verb with a passive signification *gibig-n-an*, to be rich.

SUFFIXES (OF TEUTONIC ORIGIN).

321. I. Nouns (Substantives and Adjectives).

(A) Vowel Suffixes.

Many words have lost a vowel suffix in English from the earliest time. Cp. O.E. *wulf*, a *wolf*, with Lat. *lupu-s*,[1] Sansk. *vark-a-s ;* O.E. *hund*, a hound, Goth. *hund-s*, Gr. κύων, Lat. *cani-s*, Sansk. *shunas* (= *kunas*) ; O.E. *deor*, Goth. *diu-s*, Gr. θήρ, Lat. *fera*.

Modern English has thrown off, or reduced to silent letters, many older vowel endings, as—

O.E. *duru*, *dore*, a door, Goth. *daura*, Sansk. *dvar-a*, Gr. θύρα ; O.E. *cneow*, the knee, Goth. *kniu*, Gr. γόνυ, Lat. *genu*.[2]

The suffix *-ow* represents in some few substantives an older suffix, (1) *u*, (2) *wa*.

(1) *shad-ow* = O.E. *sceadu*, Goth. *skathu-s.*
meadow = O.E. *meodu*, *medu*.[3]

(2) *callow* = O.E. *cal-u*, Lat. *calvus*.
fallow = O.E. *feal-u*, *fealwe*, Lat. *fulvus*.
mallow = O.E. *mal-u*, Lat. *malva*.
narrow = O.E. *nearu*.
sallow = O.E. *salu*, O.H.Ger. *salaw*.
yellow = O.E. *geolu*, Lat. *gilvus*.
swallow = O.E. *swal-ewe*, O.H.Ger. *swal-awa*, Ger. *schwalbe*.
sinew = O.E. *sinewe*, *seonu*, O.H.Ger. *senawa*.

---

[1] *S* = sign of nominative.
[2] Eng. *bond* or *band* corresponds to Gothic *bandi*. Cp. Lat. nouns in *-ia*, as in *-ed-ia*, hunger, from root *ed*, eat ; Gr. noun in ιa, as πενία, poverty, from πενέω; Sansk. *vid-ya*, knowledge.
[3] In many others it is lost, even in the oldest English, *tôth*, tooth ; Goth. *tunthus*, &c.

The same suffix exists in HUE, O.E. *hi-w*, *heo-w;* HIVE, O.E. *hiwa*, a family : ALE, O.E. *ealu;* YARE, O.E. *gearu*, O.H. Ger. *garaw;* TRUE, O.E. *treow*, *triws*, Goth. *triggv-s*, Sansk. *dhru-va-s*.

It has fallen off in many words, as *bale, meal, nigh, nesh*, &c. Other words with this ending belong to the suffix *y*.

Cp. Lat. *eq-uu-s*, with Goth. *aih-wu-s*, O. Sax. *ehu*, Sansk. *ashva*.

Y.—In O.E. we find this suffix under the form *ig*,[1] used to form adjectives from substantives — *busy* = O.E. *bys-ig;* *dizzy*, O.E. *dys-ig*.

So, *bloody, crafty, dusty, foamy, holy, hungry, heavy, mighty, moody, many, silly, thirsty, weary*.

It can be added to almost any substantive, as *briery, fiery, earthy, woody*, &c.

It is added also to Romance roots, as *savoury, flowery*.

In the following words we find a suffix *-ig* or *h*, which has been softened down in some cases to *ow* or *y :—body*, O.E. *bod-ig*, O.H. Ger. *potah;* *honey*, O.E. *hunig*, O.H.Ger. *hon-ang;* *sallow*, O.E. *salig*, *sal-h*, O.H.Ger. *sal-aha*, Lat. *salix*, Gr. ἡλίκη ; *hollow*, Swed. *holig*.

(B) CONSONANT SUFFIXES.

K[2] (-ock, -kin, -ing, -ish, -ling).

(1) Ock (O.E. *uca*) adds a diminutive sense to *bullock* (O.E. *bull-uca*, the root), *buttock, hummock, hillock, jaddock, pinnock, mullock, ruddock*.

Haw-k, milk, silk, yolk, smack (boat, O.E. *naca*) contain this suffix.

In Lowland Scotch dialect we find *mannock, laddock, lassock, wifock*.
Proper names too, as *Davock, Bessock*.
It is sometimes reduced to *-ick*, as *lassick*, cp. *wif-ukie*, little wife ; *drappukie*, little drop.

In proper names the suffix appears, as *Pollock* (from *Paul*), *Baldock* (from *Baldwin*), *Wilcock, Wilcox* (from *William*).

(2) Kin (diminutival).—*Bumpkin, buskin, firkin, kilderkin, ladkin, lambkin, nap-kin*.

---

[1] This *g* represents an Aryan *ka*, which is represented by *-ha, -ga*, in Gothic, as *steina-ha*, stony ; *mahtei-ga*, mighty. In Latin and Greek it appears in numerous words, as *hosticus, urbicus;* πολεμικός, ἀστυκός.

[2] Originally *ka*. It is of pronominal origin ; with a connecting vowel it would assume also the forms of *aka, ika, uka*, &c.

It must be recollected that *ng* is the corresponding nasal to *k, g*, &c. Hence, we find the original forms *ika, uka*, becoming *ing, ung*. *Ka* could be weakened to *ki*, and this with an additional *n* would produce *kin ;* with a preceding *l* we get *ling ;* with *s*, we have *aska* weakened to *isk* or *ish*.

In proper names, as *Dawkin* (*David*), *Simkin* (*Simon*), *Jenkins* (*John*), *Perkins* (*Peter*).

(3) Ing (patronymic).—O.E. *Scilf-ing*, the son of *Skilf*; *Elising*, the son of *Elisa* (Elisha). Cp. names of towns in -ing-*ton*.

(4) Ing (ending in substantives which originally had an adjectival meaning). — *Atheling*, *king* (O.E. *cyn-ing*[1]), *lord-ing* (*lordling*), *penny* (O.E. *pend-ing*, *pen-ing*), *shilling*, *herring*, *whiting*, *gelding*, *sweeting*.

(5) Ing (diminutive). — *Farthing*, *riding* (= *trithing*), O.E. *tithing* (*tenth*).

These forms are properly fractional. Cp. O.N. *thrithjungr*, ⅓, *fjórthungr*, ¼.

(6) Ling = l + ing (diminutive).

(*a*) *Darling, duckling, foundling, gosling, starling, sapling, seedling, suckling, yearling, youngling*.

(*b*) It has a depreciative sense in *groundling, hireling, worldling*, &c.

(7) The diminutival -*ing* seems to have weakened to *y* (*ie*), in *Billy, Betty*; cp. Scotch *lassie, laddie*.[2]

(8) Ing (suffix of verbal nouns = O.E. *ung*[3]).—*Being, clothing, cheaping* (O.E. *ceapung*), *learning* (O.E. *leornung*).

(9) Ish (O.E. -*isc*).—(1) *English, Irish, Welsh, Scotch*; (2) *outlandish, heathenish, womanish, bookish, hoggish*; (3) *reddish, greenish, sweetish*.

L, R[4] (el, er).

(*a*) Substantives in -le, -l, O.E. -*el* (-*ol*, -*ul*, -*l*), as *angle* (= O.E. *ang-el*), *apple, beadle, bramble, bridle, devil, bundle, fiddle, ic-icle, kettle, nettle, navel, runnel, saddle, sladdle, shambles, sickle, settle*,

---

[1] Cp. Sansk. *jan-aka*, a father, producer; from *jan*, to produce. Sansk. *putraka*, a little son; from *putra*, a son.
[2] In the province of Mecklenburg we find -*ing* so used. *Jehanning* = Johnny; *kindting*, laddy. But *ie* may be a softening of -*ick* = *ock*.
[3] -*Ing* in O.E. (fourteenth century) represented (1) -*ung*, (2) -*ende*, -*inde*, (3) -*enne*; it now represents (1) -*ung*, (2) -*ende*, -*inde*.
[4] These two suffixes represent an Aryan *ar* (*al*). They are not, as is usually affirmed in English Grammars, diminutive suffixes, but denote the agent, instrument, &c. Cp. Lat. *sel-la* (= sed-la), seat; *agilis*, active. Gr. βη-λό-ς, threshold. καμπ-ύλο-ς, bent. Lat. *ca-ru-s*, dear. Gr. νεκ-ρό-ς, corpse.

steeple, thistle, tile, throstle, whistle, fowl, hail, heel, nail, sail, tail, soul, wheel.

In the Scotch dialect *el* has become *rel*, as *betherel* = beadle ; *gangrel*, a beggar, cp. *mong-rel.*

(*b*) Adjectives in **-le, -l** (O.E. *-el, -ol*), as *little* = O.E. *lytel; fickle* = O.E. *fic-ol* ; *brittle, evil, ill, idle, mickle, tickle* (unsteady).
O.E. *drunk-el-ew, cost-l-ew, chok l-ew, sic-l-ew.*

(*c*) Substantives in **r** (O.E. *-or, -er, -r*), as *hammer* (O.E. *hamor*), *wat-er* (O.E. *wæter*), *tear* (O.E. *teag-or, tear, tær*).
Adder, bee-r, beaver, bower, calver, chafer, finger, hunger, liver, lair, summer, silver, stair, timber, tear, thunder, wonder, water, winter.

(*d*) Adjectives in **-r** (O.E. *-or, -er, -r*), *bitter, fair, lither, slipper-y* (O.E. *sliper*, and *slider*), *meagre.*

M.[1]

(1) *Blossom, bloo-m* (O.E. *blo-ma*), *besom* (O.E. *bes-ma*), *groom* (O.E. *gu-ma*), *helm* of ship (O.E. *heal-ma*), *thumb* (O.E. *thû-ma*), *team* (O.E. *teo-ma*).

(2) A shortened form of this suffix[2] is found in *arm, barm, beam, bottom, bosom, doom, dream, fathom, gleam, halm, helm, holm, home, palm, qualm, seam, stream, slim, team, worm.*
Adjectives : *war-m* (cp. Lat. *for-mu-s*, warming ; Gr. θερ-μό-s ; Sansk. *ghar-ma-s*, warm) ; O.E. *ar-m*, poor.

(3) A suffix *ma* appears in superlatives with *m*, as *for-m-ost, ut-m-ost*, &c.

N.

Participles : *broken, beaten, hew-n*,[3] &c.
Substantives : *bai-rn, beacon, burden, churn, chin, corn, heaven, iron*(O.E. *iren*), *kitchen, maiden, main, morn, oven, rain, raven, thane,*

---

[1] Originally *man*. Cp. O.E. *na-ma;* Lat. *no-men;* Sansk. *nâ-man;* Gr. γνω-μή (opinion).
We find this suffix in the participles of the present, perfect, and future tenses in Greek and Sanskrit, as Gr. διδό-μενο-ς, τετυμ-μένος ; Sansk. *dâ-sya-mânas* = Gr. δω-σό-μενος.

[2] *m* for *ma* (or *mi*), as *dim*, O.H.Ger. *tou-m*, smoke, Lat. *fu-mus*, Sansk. *dhu-ma;* halm, Lat. *cala-mu-s*, Sansk. *kala-ma-s.*

[3] Originally *na*. We find this suffix in Sanskrit passive participles, as *bhug-na-s*, bent ; *bhag-na-s*, broken ; in Gr. nouns of participial origin, as τέκ-νο-ν, child, = brought forth ; in Lat. adj., as *ple-nu-s*, full (*i.e.* filled).
It is no doubt of demonstrative origin = *this, that, here;* hence, like the *ed* of the passive participles of weak verbs, it denotes possession.

swine, token, thorn, yarn, weapon, wain; vixen,[1] O.E. *wolvene, dovene,* &c.

Adjectives: (1) *aspen, ashen, buchen, brazen, flaxen, birchen, glassen, golden, heathen, leaden, linen, oaken, oaten, silken, wheaten, wooden;* (2) *brown, even, fain, green, lean, heathen, stern;* (3) *eastern, northern, southern, western.*

These last contain suffix *r* + *n*.

In *chick-en, kitten,* the suffix *-en* has a diminutival force.

N, ND.[2]

Eve, even, evening (O.E. *æfen,* O.S. *abant,* O. Fris. *avend*), *elephant* (O.E. *olfend,* Goth. *ulbandus,* Lat. *elephantus*), *errand*[3] (O.E. *ær-end*), *fiend*[4] (O.E. *fiond, feond*), *friend*[5] (O.E. *freond, friond*), *youth*[6] (O.E. *geogoth,* O.H. Ger. *jungu-nd*), *tiding* (O.E. *tidende*), *wi-nd.*[7]

All present participles in the oldest English ended in *-nd* (*-ende, -ande;* later, *-inde, -end, -and, -inge*).

S.[8]

I. *Addice, adze* (O.E. *adesa*); *axe* (O.E. *eax;* Goth. *aqw-izi*); *bliss* (from *blithe:* cp. O.E. *milse,* from *mild*); *eaves* (O.E. *efese*).

Sel.

II. *Axle* (O.E. *eaxle;* Gr. *achsel*); *housel* (O.E. *hû-sel, hu-sl;* Goth. *hun-sl,* a sacrifice), *ousel, ouzel* (O.E. *ôsle;* O.H.Ger. *am-isala*).

L (= ls).

From the combination *-ls,* the *s* has dropt off in modern English. *Burial* (O.E. *byrgels,* a burying-place); *bridle* (O.E. *bridels*);

---

[1] The original meaning is of or pertaining to the *fox;* the feminine suffix (*e*) is lost. See remarks on *vixen* under GENDER.
[2] Originally a participial suffix, cp. O.E. *berende;* Goth. *baira-nd-s;* Lat. *ferens;* Gr. φέρων (φέροντος).
[3] From root *as,* to be quick.
[4] From *fian,* to hate.
[5] From *freon,* to love.
[6] We find *youngth* in the sixteenth-century writers, as if it were formed from *young.*
[7] From a root *vâ,* to blow.
[8] I. In the allied languages we find a suffix *-as* (*us, is*) in abstract substantives. Lat. *corpus,* a body ; Gr. φλέγ-ος, a flame (burning); Sansk. *mâhas,* greatness; O.E. *ége-sa,* fear, awe; Goth. *agis;* O.S. *egiso,* fright.
 II. This suffix in the Teutonic dialects is added (*a*) to *al, el,* whence *-sal* (*sel*), and by metathesis *-els,* as O.E. *rædels;* Ger. *räthsel;* (*b*) to the suffix *tu* (or *ta*), whence (1) *-assu* (Gothic), and (2) by addition of *n, nassu;* O.E. *niss, ness;* O.H.Ger. *nessi, nissi, niss, nass;* (3) *est,* (4) by addition of *r, ester* (*estre*).

girdle (O.E. *gyrdels*); *riddle* (O.E. *rædels*); *skittles* (O.E. *scyttels* = that which is shot forward, a bolt, bar).

N-ess.

This suffix is added to (*a*) adjectives, as *greatness, goodness, sickness, sweetness;* (*b*) substantives, as *witness, wilderness* (O.E. *wildeorness*).

It enters into combination with Romance words ending in *-able, -al, -ant, -ar, -ary, -ate, -able, -ible, -ic, -ous,* &c.

Est. *Earnest, harv-est.*

Ster. *Bolster, holster.*

Ster (O.E. *istre*), originally a sign of the feminine gender, as *spinster, huckster,* &c. See Gender, § 73, p. 89.

Upholsterer was originally (1) *upholder,* (2) *upholster.*

D, originally th.[1]

(1) It occurs in (*a*) participles, as *praised, loved;* (*b*) in adjectives with a possessive sense (cp. *-en* in *broken* and *wood-en*), as *horned, feathered, hilted, booted, an hungered, good-hearted, thick-lipped.*

(*c*) Substantives—*blood, blade, deed, flood, gleed, gold, head, seed, speed, shield, thread.*

(*d*) Adjectives—*bold, cold, dead, loud, naked, wicked* (O.E. *wicce, wikke*).

(2) Under the form th it is found in abstract substantives derived from adjectives and verbs.

Preceded by a sharp mute, &c. th is changed to t.

Substantives—*craft, dart, drought, flight, gift, height, knight, loft, night, might, slaught-er, sight, theft, draught, weight, new-t, ef-t, gannet, hornet, hart, len-ten* (O.E. *lenc-t-en, leng-t-en,* from *lang,* long). *Dearth, death, depth, health, length, mirth, strength, sloth, tilth, truth, warmth, birth, earth, kith.*

Adjectives—*bright, light, right, salt, swift, left.*

Sometimes a euphonic *s* strengthens the dental, as *be-hest, bla-s-t, du-s-t, fi-s-t, mixen* (and *muck*) = O.E. *meox, meohx;* Goth. *maihs-tu-s.*

---

[1] *Th* is a pronominal stem, as in *the, that.* Under the form *ta* (*tu*) this suffix appears in Sanskrit and Latin p. participles, as Sansk. *jna-ta-s* = Lat. *no-tu-s.* It occurs in Gr. adjectives that have a passive meaning, as πο-τό-ς, drink, φιλ-η-τό-ς, beloved. In English p. participles it appears as *d,* in *love-d,* or *t,* as in *brought.* In *uncou-th* we have the original form of the suffix.

Ther.¹

(1) This suffix, marking the agent, occurs in terms of relationship common to all the Aryan languages—*brother, daughter, father, mother, sister.*

(2) It is found in other substantives, under the forms *-ther, -der, -ter, -dle* (marking the instrument):—

Fother, feather, weather, bladder, fodder, foster, ladder, murder, rudder, laughter, needle (O.E. *nædl*; Goth. *nê-thla* (= *ne-thra*), cp. Gr. -τρε, -δρο, -δρα; -τλο, -τλη, -δλο, -δλη; Lat. nouns in *tru-m*, &c. as *ara-tru-m*, *fulgetra*, lightning).

(3) See comparatives in *-ther*, § 113, p. 106.

Er (O.E. *ere* = *er* + a demonstrative *ya*; Goth. *ei-s*; O.H.Ger. *-ari*),² as *baker*, O.E. *bæcere*.

(1) This suffix forms nouns from (*a*) strong verbs, as *grinder, rider, speaker, singer*; (*b*) weak verbs, as *leader. lover, lender*; (*c*) from substantives, as *miller, gardener, changer, treasurer.*

(2) Some few words have *i* inserted before *er*, probably under the influence of Norman French: *collier, clothier, glazier, lawyer.*

II. Noun Suffixes from Predicative Roots.

322. The following formations might really be treated under the head of *Composition*:—

I. SUBSTANTIVES.

Craft (O.E. *cræft*), *priest-craft, book-craft, leech-craft, star-craft, wood-craft.*

Cp. O.E. *stæf-cræft* (= letter-craft), grammar.

Kind (O.E. *cyn*), *mankind.*

Cp. O.E. *treow-cyn* (tree-kind), wood.

The suffix *kin* in the thirteenth and fourteenth centuries became less frequently used than in the earlier periods, and the word *kin* was employed instead, as " *alles kinnes bokes*" = books of every kind; hence arose the following compounds:—*alleskyns, noskynnes, nakin, whatkin.* Cp.

" Saga me *hwæt bôc-kinna* and hu fela syndon."—*Sol. and Sat.*

" *Quatkin* (= *whatkin*) man mai this be?"—*Cursor Mundi.*

---

[1] In Sansk. Gr. and Lat. *-tar, -ter*, is the suffix employed to form *nomina agentis*: cp. Sansk. *patar*; πατήρ; Lat. *pater*; O.E. *fader*, father, &c. from the root *pa, fa*, to feed.

[2] *Eis* (= *y-as*) in Gothic (*-a, -e*, in O.E.) denotes the agent. *Haird-ei* = O.E. *herde*; Ger. *hirt-e*. Cp. O.E. *hunta*, hunt-er; *webba*, weaver.

XVIII.]   SUFFIXES.   219

Dom[1] (O.E. *dôm*, judgment, authority, dominion; Ger. *-thum*), *thraldom, halidom, wisdom, kingdom* (O.E. *kine-dom*), *dukedom*.

Ern (O.E. *ern*; O.N. *rann*, house), *bar-n*, from *bere*, barley.
Cp. O.E. *slæpern*, a sleeping place; *horsern*, a stable.

Fare (way, course). *Thorough-fare, chaffer, welfare*.

Ard (O.E. *heard, hard*, cp. *mægen-heard*, might-hard, *iren-heard*, iron-hard; O.H.Ger. *-hart*; O.Fr. *-ard*); *bast-ard, bayard, braggart, buzzard, coward, dullard, laggard, haggard, niggard, sluggard, staggard, standard, sweetheart*. But *dastard* = O.E. *dastrod*, frightened.

Hood, head (O.E. *hâd*, state, rank, person, character; later forms *-hed, hod*; O.Fris. *hêd*; O.H.Ger. *-heit*).

(1) *Manhood, childhood, brotherhood, godhead, maidenhead*.

(2) *Hardihood, likelihood; livelihood*, which originally meant liveliness, but it now stands for the O.E. *lif-lode* (= *life-leading*) sustenance.

Lock (O.E. *lâc*, gift, sport), *wed-lock, knowledge* (O.E. *cnowlach, cnowlech* = *cnawlac*).

Lock, -lick (O.E. *-leac, -lic*) in the names of plants = *leek* (O.E. *leac*); *barley* (O.E. *berlic* = bere plant); *garlick* (spear plant); *hem-lock, char-lock*.

Meal (O.E. *mæl*, time division), *under-meal* = noontide, cp. *piece-meal*. See adverbs, § 311, p. 194.

Red (O.E. *-rêden* = mode, fashion); *hat-red, kin-d-red* (O.E. *kyn-red*).

Rick (O.E. *rîce* = power, dominion); *bishoprick*, cp. O.E. *heveneriche, kinerick* (= *kine-riche*; *kine* = royal).

Ship (O.E. *scipe, scepe* = shape, manner, form); *friendship, lordship, worship, hardship, land-skip, land-scape* (cp. O.N. *landskapr*; O.E. *landscipe*).

Wright (O.E. *wyrhta, wrihte*, a workman), *wheel-wright, playwright*.

Tree (wood), *axle-tree*, O.E. *dore-tre* (door-post, bar of a door).
Beam (tree), *horn-beam*.
Monger (dealer), *coster-monger, news-monger*.

2. ADJECTIVES.

Fast (O.E. *fæst*, fast, firm), *steadfast, shamefaced* (= O.E. *shame-fast*), *root fast, soothfast*.

Fold (O.E. *feald*, fold), *two-fold, manifold*.

Ful (O.E. *ful*, full), *hateful, wilful* (= O.E. *willesful*).

---

[1] *Dom* (or *doo-m*) is formed from the verb *do*, just as θέμις from τίθημι.

Less (O.E. *leás;* Goth. *laus*), loose from; it has no connection with *less*, the comp. of *little; fearless, joyless, guiltless.*

Ly, like (O.E. *líc;* Goth. *-leiks;* O.N. *-líkr, -légr;* Lat. *-lis;* Gr. -λικος), *godly, manly, goodly, sickly;* cp. *warlike, dovelike.*

Some (O.E. *sum;* O.N. *-samr;* O.H.Ger. *sam = same*, like), *blithesome, buxom* (= *bugh-som*), *fulsome, irksome, gamesome.*

Teen, ty = ten. See Numerals, § 129, p. 112.

Ward (O.E. *weard;* Goth. *-wairths*, becoming, leading to: connected with *weorthan*, to be, Sansk. *vrit*, Lat. *vert-ere*, to turn), *forward, toward, untoward.*

Wise (O.E. *wís*, mode, way, manner); *righteous* (O.E. *riht-wís*, rightwise); *boisterous* (O.E. *bostwys*).

Worth (O.E. *weorth*, worth), *dear-worth* (precious), *stalworth*.

III. Adverbial Suffixes.

For the suffixes *-es, -s, -um*, &c. see Adverbs, § 311, pp. 193—196.

Ly (O.E. *líce*, the dative of *líc*, like), *only, utterly, wickedly, willingly*.

Ling, long (O.E. *-lunga, -linga*, nasalized forms of *-líce, -lúce*), *darkling, headlong, sideling, sidelong.* See Adverbs, § 311; O.E. *noseling, backling*, &c.

Meal, *piece-meal, flock-meal* (used by Chapman), *limb-meal* (*Cymbeline*, ii. 4). See p. 219.

Ward, wards, *hitherward, backwards, downwards*, &c.

Wise (manner, mode), *otherwise, nowise, likewise.*

Way-s. See Adverbs, p. 194.

IV. Verbal Suffixes.

The verbal suffixes, which we find in Gothic and Old English, have nearly all disappeared.

The oldest Teutonic verbal suffixes were, as in Gothic, (1) *ja (ei)*, (2) *ô* (= *â*), (3) *ai*, all of which can be traced to a more primitive suffix *aya* (from the root *i* = go).

Thus the suffix *ô* was used to form verbs from nominal themes, as from Gothic *fisk-s*, a fish, came *fiskon*, O.E. *fisc-ia·n*, to fish.

A few *causative verbs* in modern English are expressed by vowel change, but the suffix that caused it has been lost.[1]

---

[1] Cp. *faran*, to go *fare*, and *fer-ian*, carry, *ferry*.

		O.E.	
INTR.	CAUS.	INTR.	CAUS.
to fall	to fell	feallan	fellan
to drink	to drench	drincan	drencan
to lie	to lay	licgan	lecgan
to sit	to set	sittan	settan
to rise	to raise	risan	ræran, ræsan
to wind	to wend	windan	wendan

The suffix used for causative verbs was originally *aya*, an extension of root *i*, to go; cp. Sansk. *kâr-ayâ-mi*, I cause to make. This *aya* appears in Gothic as *ja*, as *sat-ja*, I set (Sansk. *sâd-ayâ-mi*), from *sita*, I sit ; *lag-ja*, I lay, from *lig-a*, I lie.
In Sanskrit we find a causative suffix *p*, in Lat. *p* and *c*, as Sansk. *yâ-p-ayâ-mi*, I cause to go ; Lat. *ja-c-io*, cp. *rap-io*. This *p* becomes *f* in English, as *wea-v-e*; cp. O.E. *bif-ian*, to tremble, from a root *bi* (Sansk. *bhi*), to fear.

S occurs in verbs formed from nominal stems, as *clean-se*,[1] *curse*, *wanze* (to wane), tru-*st* (O.E. *treowsian*), cp. *clasp* (root *clap*), *grasp* (root *grap*, *grip*), *lisp* (root *lip*).

N originally added a reflexive or passive sense to the verb, as *learn*, from *lere;* but it has now a causative meaning, as *fatten*, *sweeten*, *lengthen*, *strengthen*.

L,[2] which adds to the root the sense of frequency, repetition, diminution, &c.—*bustle*, *crankle*, *crimple*, *dribble*, *drizzle*, *grapple*, *dangle*, *dazzle*, *kneel*, *nestle*, *prowl*, *settle*, *sparkle*, *startle*, &c.

R adds a frequentative or intensive signification—*bluster*, *flitter*, *flutter*, *glitter*, *hanker*.

K (frequentative)—*hark*, from *hear*, *lurk*, *stalk*, *skulk*, *walk*, *talk*.

323. COMPOSITION.

Two or more words are joined together to make a single term expressing a new notion, as *orchard*, *nightingale*, *handiwork*.

In Gothic we find a *vowel*[3] between the roots, as *aurti-gards*, O.E. *ort-geard* = orchard, *handu-waurhts*, O.E. *hand-ge-weorc*, handiwork.
Nightingale = O.E. *nihte-gale*, Ger. *nachtegall*, O.H.Ger. *nahtigala* = nightsinger.
In O.E. we find *nighter-tale* (= *nihte-tale*), night-time.

---

[1] This *s* was used to form substantives from adjectives, as *bliss* from *blithe*, and properly belongs to the nominal stem.
[2] This *l* seems to have come into use through verbs from nouns in -*l*, as *whistle*, *saddle*, &c.
[3] This vowel belongs to the nominal stem, as Goth. *handu-s*, hand, *aurti* = *aurtis* = wort (herb).

I. Substantive Compounds.

(1) Substantive and Substantive.

(*a*) Descriptive, as *gar-lick*, *spear-plant*, *even-tide*, *noon-tide*, *church-yard*, *head-man*.

(*b*) Appositional, as *oak-tree*, *beech-tree*.

(*c*) Genitive, as *kinsman*, *Tuesday*, *doomsday*.

Loadsman and *guardsman* had no *s* in the oldest English.

(*d*) Accusative, as *man-killer*, *blood-shedding*.

Compounds like *Lord-lieutenant*, *earl-marshal* are of French origin.

In many compound terms the elements have become changed or obsolete, and are not easily recognized.

	O.E.	
hang-nail	= *ang-nægele*[1]	= a sore under the nail
ban-dog	= *bond-doge*	= a dog chained up
bar-n	= *bere-ærn*	= barley-house
brim-stone	= *bren-ston*	= burn-stone
bridal	= *brȳd-ealu*	= { bride-ale, *i.e.* bride-feast
gospel	= *god-spell*	= God's word [2]
grunsel	= *grund-syl*	= ground-sil
heifer	= *heâ-fore*[3]	= stall-cow
huzzy	= *hûs-wīf*	= housewife
icicle	= *īs-gicel*	= ice-jag
Lammas	= *hlâf-mæsse*	= loaf-mass
mole	= *mold-weorp*	= mould-thrower
auger	= *nafo-ger, navegar*	= naveborer
nostril	= *nose-thyrel*	= nose-hole
orchard	= *ort-geard, ort-yard*	= herb garden
stirrup	= *stig-râp*	= climbing-rope
steward	= *stige-weard*	= { guardian of cattle, domestic offices, &c. *stige* = sty, stall
shelter	= *scild-truma*	= troop-shield
tadpole	= { *tâd* = toad, frog, and *pol* = pool }	= toad in the pool
titmouse	= *tīte* = little, and *mâse* = hedge-sparrow
world	= { *werold* (*wer* = man + *eld* = age).	

[1] *ang* = sore, pain.   [2] Some say *gospel* = *good tidings*.
[3] *Hea* = pen, stall ; *fore* = cow, connected with O.E. *fear*, bull, ox.

(2) Substantive and Adjective—*free-man, mid-day, mid-night, mid-summer, black-bird, alder-man.*
Cp. *neighbour* = O.E. *neáh-bur* = one who dwells near
mid-riff = O.E. *mid-hrif: mid* = middle ; *hrif* = body, uterus.

(3) Substantive and Numeral—*twi-light, sen-night, fort-night.*

(4) Substantive and Pronoun—*self-will, self-esteem.*

(5) Substantive and Verb—*grind-stone, whet-stone, pin-fold, wag-tail, rear-mouse, bake-house, wash-house, wash-tub, pick-pocket, spend-thrift,* &c.

Distaff = O.E. *distæf, dyse-stafe,* Prov. E. *dise* = to supply the staff with *flax* (*dise* = flax, hence to supply flax).

A substantive is often qualified by another substantive, to which it is joined by a preposition, as *man-of-war, will-o'-the-wisp, Jack-a-lantern,*[1] *brother-in-law,* &c.

II. Adjective Compounds.

1. Substantive and Adjective, in which the substantive has the force of an adverb, as *blood-red* = red as blood, *snow-white* = white as snow, *sea-sick* = sick through the sea, *fire-proof* = proof against fire, *cone-shaped, eagle-eyed, coal-eyed, lion-hearted.*

2. Adjective and Substantive, denoting possession, as *barefoot.*
Cp. O.E. *clǽn-heort* = having a clean heart, *án-eage* = having one eye.
In the corresponding modern forms the substantive has taken the participial suffix (perfect) of weak verbs, as *bare-footed, bare-headed, one-eyed, three-cornered, four-footed.*[2]

3. Participial combinations, in which the participle is the last element.

(*a*) Substantive and present participle, in which the first element is the object of the second, as *earth-shaking, heart-rending.*

(*b*) Adjective and present participle, in which the first element is equivalent to an adverb, as *deep-musing, fresh-looking, ill-looking.*

---

[1] *a* = *o* = *of.* We sometimes find *man-a-war, two-a-clock,* &c.: cp. " He is exceedingly censur'd by the *Innes-a-Court* men."—EARLE'S *Micro-Cosmographie,* p. 41.
[2] Just as the suffix *-en* denotes possession in *golden,* &c., so does *-ed* in such words as *booted, shouldered,* forms to which Spenser and other Elizabethan writers are very partial.

(c) Substantive and perfect participle, as *ale-fed, book-learned, death-doomed, earth-born, moth-eaten, sea-torn, wind-fallen.* (Cp. *chap-fallen, brawn-fallen.*)

(d) Adjective and perfect participle, as *dear-bought, full-fed, high-finished, new-made, well-bred, fresh-blown, high-born, dead-drunk, hard-gotten.*

III. Verbal Compounds.

1. Substantive and verb.—*Back-bite, blood-let, brow-beat, hood-wink, kiln-dry, ham-string.*

2. Adjective and verb.—*Dry-nurse, dumb-found, white-wash.*

3. Adverb and verb.—*Cross-question, doff* (= do-off), *don* (= do-on), *dout* (= do-out), *dup* (= do-up).

324. COMPOSITION WITH TEUTONIC PARTICLES.

(A) Inseparable Particles.

I. A.

(1) *A* (O.E. *â*; Goth. *us*; O.H.Ger. *-ur, -ar, -â*; Ger. *-er*), added to verbs, originally signified *from, out, away, back.* (a) From the meaning of *from, away,* arises a privative, or opposite signification, as O.E. *wendan,* to turn ; *a-wendan,* turn away, subvert. (b) It does not always alter the root-meaning, but merely intensifies it, as O.E. *abidan,* to abide.

(i.) *Ago, alight, arise, arouse* (cp. O.E. *aby,*[1] *awreke, aslake, arere, ahange*); (ii.) *abide, awake.*

(2) *A* (O.E. *â*; Goth. *âiw*; O.H.Ger. *ëo*: cp. Gr. *άεί*), ever, always. See *aught* (p. 146), *either* (p. 149).

(3) *A* = on (O.E. *an*) : *a-way, a-gain,* &c. See p. 201.

(4) *A* (O.E. *æt, at*) = back, like Latin *re*; O.E. *at-wite* = *at-witan* = reproach ; Eng. *twit.*

(5) *A* = of : *adown* = O.E. *of-dûne.*

(6) *A* (= O.E. *ge, y*), as *a-like* (O.E. *gelíc*),[2] *among* (O.E. *ge-mang*), *a-ware* (O.E. *ge-wære, i-ware*).

---

[1] *aby* = abuy = pay for, atone for ; corrupted into *abide* by Milton.
[2] This is the usual view taken of the origin of *alike,* but it would be more correct to regard it as another form of O.E. *on-lic, an-lich* = alike.

In the seventeenth century we find *anough* = enough (O.E. *genoh, ino3*); *along* (of) = on account of (O.E. *gelang, ilong*). Ready = O.E. *iredy* = *ge-ræd*.

(7) *A* (O.E. *-and*; Goth. *-anda*), back.

A-long (O.E. *and-lang, end-long, an-long*); *a-cknowledge* (O.E. *acknow* = *oncnâwan*; O.Sax. *ant-kennjan*): cp. to *an-swer* = O.E. *andswarian*; ambassador = O.E. *ambeht*, Goth. *and-bahts*.

(8) *A* (= O.E. *of*), like Lat. *per*, is an intensive:—*a*-shamed (= O.E. *of-ashamed*), *a-thirst* (= O.E. *of thirst*).

II. **Be** (O.E. *be, bi, big*) is identical with the preposition *by*.

(1) It adds an intensitive force to transitive verbs, as *bedaub, besmear*, &c.

(2) It renders intransitive verbs transitive, as *bespeak, bethink*.

(3) It has a *privative* meaning in *be-head*.

(4) It enters into combination with substantives to form verbs, as *be-friend, be-knave, be-night, be-troth*.

(5) It is added to Romance roots, as *be-charm, be-flatter, be-siege, be-tray*.
Be-lieve = O.E. *gelyfan*, Ger. *glauben*; *be-reave* = O.E. *reafian*; *be-gin* = O.E. *on-ginnan*.

(6) It is also added to nouns, as *be-half, be-hest, be-hoof, be-quest, by-blow, by-name, by-path, by-stander, by-way, by-word*.

(7) It forms part of adverbs, as *be-fore, be-sides, be-cause*.

III. **For** (O.E. *for*; Goth. *faur, fair, fra*; Lat. *per*) = through, throughly, adds an intensitive meaning, as *for-bid, for-do, for-give, for-get, for-swear*,[1] *for-lorn*.
In some words it is equivalent to *amiss, badly*, as *fore-deem, fore-spent, fore-speak, fore-shamed*: cp. O.E. *for-shapen*, transformed very much, *mis-shapen, for-wounded* = very much wounded, and hence badly wounded.[2]
It enters into combination with a few Romance roots, as *for-barred, for-judge, for-fend* (= forbid), *for-guess*.

---

[1] Cp. Lat. *per-jurare* = to swear out and out, and hence, to swear falsely; *per-eo* = *perish* = O.E. *for-fare* = to go through to the death.
[2] Cp. O.E. *for-dry*, very dry; *for-wel*, very well.

IV. **Fore** (O.E. *fore*) = before.

(1) With verbs—*fore-bode, fore-cast, fore-tell*.
(2) With participles—*fore-said, fore-told, fore-dated*.
(3) With substantives—*fore-father, fore-castle, fore-sight*.

V. **Gain** (O.E. *gægn, on-gægn, â-gain*, back, again), against.
Gain-say, gain-stand, gain-strive: cp. O.E. *ayen-bite* = remorse · *aȝen-byggen* = to redeem.

VI. **I** or **Y** (O.E. *ge*).
I-wiss (O.E. *gewiss*), truly. See *alike, among* (p. 224), *enough* (O.E. *genoh, inoh*).

VII. **Mis-** (O.E. *mis;* Goth. *missa;* O.N. *mis*), defect, error, evil.[1]
Mis-behave, mis-call, mis-trust, mis-deed.
In French compounds *mis-* = French *mes-*, from Lat. *minus;* as *mis-chief, mis-chance;* O.E. *mes-chef, mes-chaunce.*

VIII. **Nether** (O.E. *nither*), down, downward, below.
Nether-stocks (used by Shakespeare, as opposed to *upper-stocks*, or breeches), *Nether-lands.*

IX. **Sand** (O.E. *sâm*), half.
Sand-blind = sam-blind (Shakespeare) : cp. O.E. *sâm-cwic* (half-alive).

X. **To** (Goth. *dis;* O.N. *tor;* O.H.Ger. *zar, zer;* Lat. *dis-;* Gr. δι-).
This particle is of very frequent occurrence in Old English, signifying *asunder, in pieces;* it is sometimes intensive, as *to-bite, to-cleave, to-rend, to-tear;* it is often strengthened by the word *all* (= quite): "And a certain woman cast a piece of a millstone upon Abimelech's head, and *all to brake* his skull" (*Judges* ix. 53). *All-to-brake* = broke quite in pieces. See All, p. 227.

---

[1] In O.E. *mys* = wrong :—
"Als Innocentes that never dyd *mys*."
HAMPOLE, *P. of C.*, l. 3289.
It is sometimes used for *less*, as—
"Sixtene more ne *mis*."—LONELICH, *San Graal*, p. 92.

To is sometimes the ordinary preposition, as in O.E. *to-name*, an additional name ; *to-neȝen*, to approach. In adverbs it is found in *to-day, to-morrow, to-night ;* O.E. *to-year* = this year, *to-whils* = whilst.

XI. **Un** (O.E. *on;* Goth. *and;* Ger. *ent*), back. See (7) *A*, p. 225.
Un-bind, un-do, un-lock, un-wind.[1]

XII. **Un** (O.E. *un*), not, as *un-true, un-wise, un-ready, un-told, un-truth.*

XIII. **Wan** (O.E. *wan :* cp. O.E. *wana ;* Goth. *wans,* wanting), denoting deficiency, *wan-*ting in, is equivalent to *un-* or *dis-*.

Wanhope, despair ; *wan-trust, wanton* (= *wan-towen* = untrained, uneducated, wild, from O.E. *teon* [p.p. *togen, towen*], to lead).

XIV. **With** (O.E. *with*, a shortened form of *wiðer*, back, against), back, against.
With-draw, with-hold, with-say, with-stand.

(B) Separable Particles.

I. **After** (O.E. *æfter*), *after-growth, after-math, after-dinner.*
Eft (O.E. *æft, eft*), *eft-soons.*

II. **All** (O.E. *al, eal*), all-mighty, all-wise, &c.
In O.E. *al* = quite. It is added (1) to participles, as *al-brent* = quite burnt, *al-heled* = quite concealed, &c. ; (2) to verbs, as *al-breken*, to break entirely. It also comes before verbs compounded with the particle *to*.
Wickliffe has many of these forms, as *al-to-brenne* = to burn up entirely ; the particle *to-* probably becoming weakened.
In Elizabethan and later writers *all-to* = altogether, quite ; the original meaning of *to* having been lost sight of.
All to topple (*Pericles*, iii. 2, 17) = topple altogether ; *all to nought* (*Venus and Adonis*, 993) ; *all-to ruffled* (Milton).

III. **Forth** (O.E. *forth*).
Forth-coming, forth-going.

IV. **Fro, from** (O.E. *fram ;* O.N. *fra*).
From-ward, fro-ward.

---

[1] In the Durham Gospels we find *unbinda, undóa;* Laȝamon has *unbinden vndon ;* Orm. has *unn sperren,* unbar, open.

V. In (O.E. *in, inn*).

In-come, in-wit, in-land, in-sight, in-born, in-bred, in-step, in-ward, in-lay, in-fold.

In many verbs it has been replaced by a Romance form (*en, em*), as *en-dear, en-lighten, en-twine, em-bitter, em-bolden.*

VI. Of, off (O.E. *of;* Goth. *af;* O.H.Ger. *aba*), from, off.

Of-fal, off-set, off-scum, off-spring.
A-thirst (= O.E. *of-thyrst*); *an-hungred* (= O.E. *of-hyngred*): cp. O.E. *adreden* and *of-dreden; aferen* and *of-færen*. See (8) *A*, p. 225.

VII. On (O.E. *on*) = upon, forward.

On-set, on-slaught, on-ward.

VIII. Out, Ut (O.E. *ût*).

Out-bud, out-pour, out-root, out-breathe, out-break, out-cast, out-side, out-post, out-law, ut-ter, ut-most.

It has sometimes the sense of *beyond, over,* as *out-bred, out-do, out-flank.*

IX. Over (O.E. *ofer*), above, beyond, exceedingly, too much.

(1) With substantives and adjectives.—*Over-coat, over-flow, over-joy, over-poise, over-big, over-cold, over-curious:* cp. O.E. *over-hand·* = upper hand.

(2) With verbs. — (1) *over-flow, over-fly, over-gild, over-hang, over-spread, over-throw.* (2) *over-burden, over-build, over-dry, over-drunk, over-carry, over-fatigued.* (3) *over-hear, over-look, over-see.*

X. Thorough, through[1] (O.E. *thurh, thuruh;* Goth. *thairh*).

Thorough-fare, thorough-bred, through-train.

XI. Under (O.E. *under*).

(1) With verbs. — (1) *Under-go, under-stand, under-take.* (2) *under-let, under-sell, under-prize.*

(2) With substantives.—*Under-growth, under-wood.*

XII. Up (O.E. *up*).

(1) With verbs.—*Up-bear, up-braid* (O.E. *obraide*), *up-hold, up-set.*

(2) With substantives.—*Up-land, up-start, up-shot.*

(3) With adjectives.—*Up-right, up-ward.*

---

[1] *Through* is connected with a root *thar,* cognate with Sansk. *tar (tri),* to go beyond : cp. Lat. *tra-ns.*

325. SUFFIXES OF ROMANCE ORIGIN.

I. Vowel Endings.

Many words of French origin have lost an original vowel, as—
Beast: O.E. *beste*; O.Fr. *beste*; Lat. *bestia*.
Vein: O.E. *veyne*; Fr. *veine*; Lat. *vena*.
Fig: O.E. *fyge*; O.Fr. *fige*; Lat. *ficus*.

Y.

(1) In substantives this suffix frequently represents Fr. *ie*; Lat. *ia*, condition, faculty, &c. :—
Barony, company, copy, courtesy, fallacy, folly, family, fury, harmony, history, lobby, memory, modesty, many, ribald-r-y (O.E. *ribaudie*), *victory*, &c.
It is added occasionally to stems in *er*, as *baker-y, fisher-y, lecher-y, prior-y, robber-y*.
In names of countries we have *ia* as well as *y*, as *Italy, Sicily*, &c.; *Armen-ia, Assyr-ia*.
Many words in *y* have come through Lat. nouns in *-ia* (Fr. *-ie*) from Gr. -ι, -ια, -εια :—
Analogy, apology, apostasy, blasphemy, geometry, melancholy, melody, fancy (O.E. *phantasy*), *philosophy, frenzy, abbey, litany, necromancy*.

(2) It sometimes stands for Lat. *iu-m* :—
Augury, horology, larceny, obloquy, remedy, study, subsidy, O.E. *obsequy*.

(3) Y represents also Lat. *-atus*, as *attorney, deputy, ally, quarry*.

(4) Many words ending in *cy, sy*, are formed on the model of French words in *-cie*; Lat. *-t-ia* :—
Bankruptcy, chaplaincy, conspiracy, curacy, minstrelsy.
It is equivalent to the suffix *-ness* in *degeneracy, intimacy, intricacy, obstinacy*, &c.—all formed from adjectives in *-ate*.

(5) There are other words in *cy, sy*, that have arisen from Latin *-sis*, Gr. σις, as *catalepsy, epilepsy, idiosyncrasy*, &c.: see p. 239.

(6) Some words in ee arise from Lat. *-æu-s, -æu-m* :—
Pharisee, pigmy, Sadducee.

(7) **Spongy** = Lat. *spongiosus*.

(8) For *hasty, testy, jolly*, see **Ive**, p. 230.

Ancy, ency: see p. 241.
Mony: see p. 235.
Ary, ory: see p. 232.
Ee, ey: see pp. 238, 242.

II. Consonant Endings.

V.

Ve. *Octa-ve* (Lat. *octa-vu-s*), *olive* (Lat. *oliva*), *sa-fe* (Lat. *sal-vu-s;* O.Fr. *salv, sauf*).

The *v* is vocalized in the following words:—*assiduous* (Lat. *assid-uu-s;* Fr. *assidu*), *continuous, exiguous, ingenuous, perspicuous, promiscuous, residue* (Lat. *residuum*).

The common suffix *-ous* = Lat. *-osu-s:* see S.

Ive (Fr. *if;* Lat. *-ivus;* a shortened form of Lat. *-tivus*),[1] able to, inclined to.

Bailiff (Mid.Lat. *ballivus*), *captive* (*caitiff*), *motive, native, plaintiff, active, adoptive, alternative, attentive, contemplative, fugitive, laxative, furtive, pensive, restive,* &c.

In some few words *f* has dropped off, as *hasty* (O.Fr. *hastif*), *jolly* (O.E. *jolif;* O.Fr. *joli,* fem. *jolive*), *testy* (O.E. *testif*), *guilty* (O.E. *giltif*).

S.

Ous, ose (Lat. *-osu-s;*[2] O.Fr. *-os, -ous;* Fr. *-eux, -oux, -ose*), full, like.

Copious, curious, delicious, famous, glorious, &c.; *bellicose, jocose, verbose,* &c.

(1) **Ous** sometimes represents Lat. *-us,* as *anxious, arboreous, arduous, omnivorous, superfluous,* &c.

(2) It is also added to adjectival stems, as *asper-ous* (O.E. *asper*), *audacious, precipitous,* together with many others ending in *-ferous, -gerous.*

---

[1] Cognate with Sansk. *-tavya,* the suffix of the future passive participle.
[2] *Osus* is cognate with Sansk. *vâns,* the suffix of the perfect participle active; *-us* (*eris*), *-us* (*-oris*), *-ur* (*-oris*), *-ur* (*-uris*), *-or* (*-oris*), are other forms of the same suffix.

(3) It is also used in modern formations, as *contradictious, felicitous, joyous, murderous, wondrous.*

Ese (Fr. *-is, -ois, -ais;* It. *-ese;* Lat. *-ensis*), of or belonging to. *Chinese, Japanese, Maltese, Portuguese; burgess* (Mid. Lat. *burgensis;* O. Fr. *burgeis;* Fr. *bourgeois;* It. *borghese;* O. E. *bourgeis*), *courteous* (Mid. Lat. *curtis;* O. Fr. *curteis, courtois;* It. *cortese;* O. E. *curteis*), *marquis* (Mid. Lat. *marchensis;* It. *marchese;* O. F. *marcis;* O. E. *marcheis, markis*), *morass*[1] (It. *marese;* O. F. *mareis;* O. E. *mareys*).

Ess (Lat. *-issa;* Gr. -ισσα;[2] It. *-essa;* Sp. *-esa, -isa;* Fr. *-esse*): the ordinary feminine suffix of substantives, as *countess, duchess, hostess,* &c.: see GENDER OF SUBSTANTIVES.

R.

(1) **R, re,** &c. (Lat. *-ru-s*). See p. 214.

Adjectives.—*Clea-r* (Lat. *cla-ru-s;* O. Fr. *cle-r*), *pu-re* (Lat. *pu-ru-s;* O. Fr. *pu-re*), *asper, ten-d-er* (Lat. *tener;* Fr. *tendre*), *meagre* (Lat. *macer;* O. Fr. *maigre*).

Substantives.—*Figure* (O. F. *figure*), *letter* (O. Fr. *letre*).

(2) **R, er, re,** &c. (Lat. *-ri-s*).

Adjectives.—*Eager* (Lat. *acer;* O. F. *aigre;* O. E. *egre*), *vinegar* (Fr. *vin-aigre* = *vinum acre*), *familiar* (Lat. *familiaris;* O. Fr. *familier*), *regular, singular.*

Substantives.—*Air* (Gr. ἀήρ; Lat. *acr;* O. Fr. *air*), *cinder* (Lat. *cinis* (*-eris*); O. Fr. *cendre*), *cucumber* (Lat. *cucumis;* Fr. *concombre;* It. *cocomero;* O. E. *cucumere*), *flower, flour* (Lat. *flos;* O. Fr. *flor*), *gender* (Lat. *genus;* O. Fr. *genre*), *powder* (Lat. *pulvis;* O. Fr. *poldre*), *secular* (Lat. *sæcularis;* O. Fr. *seculier*), *scholar* (Lat. *scholaris;* O. Fr. *escolier*), *altar* (Lat. *altaria;* O. Fr. *alter, auter*), *collar* (Lat. *collare;* Fr. *collier*), *pillar* (Mid. Lat. *pilare;* Sp. *pilar*), *scapular* (Lat. *scapulare;* Fr. *scapulaire*).

(3) **Our** (Lat. *-or;* Fr. *-eur*), quality, state.
Ardour, colour, errour, favour, honour, labour, &c.

Devoir (O. Fr. *devoir;* Lat. *debe-re*), *leisure* (O. Fr. *loisir, leisir;*

---

[1] *Marsh* is not of Fr. origin, being another form of O. E. *mer-sc.*
[2] According to Bopp, -ισσα = -ιτ or ιδ + -ya. Thus βασίλισσα has arisen from a more original form, βασιλιδ-ya.

Lat. *licere*), *livery* (O.Fr. *livier*; Lat. *liberare*), *power* (O.F. *poer*; It. *potere*; Lat. *posse*), *recovery* (O.E. *recovere*; O.Fr. *recovrer*; Lat. *recuperare*).
It is sometimes added to a Teutonic stem, as *behav-iour*.

(4) **Ary, ier, eer, er** (Lat. *-arius, -erius*; Fr. *-aire, -ier*; It. *-ario, -orio*), relating to.

Adjectives.—*Contrary, necessary, secondary*, &c.

Substantives.—*Adversary, commissary, notary, secretary, January*, &c.; *brigadier, chandelier, engineer, mountainer* (*mountaineer*), *harpooner*, &c.

Arbalister (Lat. *arcubalistarius*; O.Fr. *arbalestier*), *archer* (Mid. Lat. *arcarius*; O.Fr. *archier*), *bachelor* (Mid. Lat. *baccalareus*; O.Fr. *bachelier*), *banner* (Mid. Lat. *banderarius, banderensis, banderetus*; Fr. *banderet*), *butler* (Lat. *buticularius*; O.Fr. *bouteillier*), *carpenter* (Lat. *carpentarius*; O.Fr. *carpentier*), *chancellor* (Lat. *cancellarius*; O.Fr. *chancelier*, O.E. *chaunceler*), *almoner* (Mid. Lat. *eleemosynarius*; O.Fr. *almosnier*; Fr. *aumônier*), *barber* (Mid. Lat. *barberius*; Fr. *barbier*), *butcher* (Lat. *buccerius*; Fr. *boucher*), *calendar* (Fr. *calendrier*), *cellarer* (Lat. *cellarius*; Fr. *cellérier*), *counsellor* (Lat. *conciliarius*; O.Fr. *conseillere*; O.E. *conseilere*), *cutler* (Fr. *coutelier*), *draper* (Mid.Lat. *draperius*; Fr. *drapier*), *falconer* (Mid.Lat. *falconarius*; Fr. *fauconier*), *farrier* (Lat. *ferrarius*; Fr. *ferreur*), *hostler* (Lat. *hospitilarius*), *mariner* (Mid.Lat. *marinarius*; Fr. *marinier*), *messenger* (Mid.Lat. *messagarius*; O.Fr. *messagier*; O.E. *messager*), *officer* (Mid.Lat. *officiarius*; Fr. *officier*), *notary* (Lat. *notarius*), *palmer* (Mid.Lat. *palmarius*; O.Fr. *palmier*), *partner* (Mid.Lat. *partionarius*; O.Fr. *partinaire*), *plover* (Fr. *pluvier*; Lat. *pluviarius*), *juniper* (Fr. *genévrier*), *laurel* (Fr. *laurier*), *poplar* (Fr. *peuplier*), *prisoner* (Mid.Lat. *prisonarius*; Fr. *prisonnier*), *quarter* (Lat. *quartarius*; O.F. *quarter*), *squire, esquire* (Lat. *scutarius*; O.Fr. *escuier, esquier*), *sorcerer* (Mid.Lat. *sortarius*), *treasure* (Mid.Lat. *thesaurarius*; O.Fr. *tresorier*), *vicar* (Lat. *vicarius*; O.Fr. *vicaire*), *vintner* (Mid.Lat. *vinetarius*), *usher* (Mid.Lat. *ætarius*; O.Fr. *uissier*).

(5) Many words in **-ory, -ary, -ry, -er** (= person or place or thing adapted for some purpose, &c.) come from Latin substantives in *-arium*.

Electuary, granary, salary, sanctuary, armory, dowry, vivary, treasury, vestry; cellar, charter, danger, exemplar (*sampler*), *hamper, larder, manor, mortar, saucer*.

(6) Lat. *-aria, -eria,* has become -ery, -ry, -er in the following :—
Buttery, chivalry (cavalry), carpentry, laundry, pantry, vintry, dowager, gutter, garter, litter, matter, forager, river.

Ry (Fr. *-rie*), collective, an art.
Cookery, fairy, jewry, nunnery, napery, poultry, poetry, spicery, surgery, &c.

L.[1]

(1) **El, le, 1.**—(*a*), [Lat. *l-u-m*].
Example, sample, file, temple.

(*b*), [Lat. *-ulus, -olus, -ilus, -elus*].
Angle, oriole, cable, carol, disciple, people, squirrel, title, veal, umbles, numbles [cp. (*h*)*umble pie*].

(*c*), [Lat. *-ula*].
Buckle, canal, table, eagle, trellis.

(*d*), [Lat. *-ela;* Fr. *-èle, -elle*].
Candle, cautel, clientele, quarrel, tutel-age.

(*e*), [Lat. *-allus, -allum; -ellus, -ella, -ellum; -illus, -illum*].
Metal, bowel, bushel, chancel, morsel, libel, mangonel, mangle, measels, quarrel (arrow), *kernel, candle, castle, gruel, mantle, panel, pommel, chapel; pestle; seal, tassel.*
To this class belong *bateau, chateau, bureau,* &c.

(*f*), [Lat. *-b-ulus, -c-ulus, -c-ulum*].[2]
Bu-g-le, chesi-b-le (chasu-b-le), fa-b-le, sta-b-le; arti-c-le, un-c-le, carbun-c-le, mira-c-le, pinna-c-le, obsta-c-le, recepta-c-le, specta-c-le, taberna-c-le, par-c-el, pen-c-il, dam-s-el, ves-s-el.
In *bottle, fennel, peril, travel,* the *c* has disappeared.

(2) **Rel, erel,** is supposed to be a combination of *er* + *el* (Fr. *er-eau, er-elle*), diminutive.
Cockerel, dotterel, hogrel, mackerel, mongrel, pickerel.

(3) (*a*) **Al, el, il, ile** (Lat. *a-li-s, e-li-s, i-li-s;* Fr. *-al, -el, -il, -ile,* forming adjectives from substantive stems), of or belonging to, capable of.

---
[1] It is connected with suffix *r*. See p. 214.
[2] The suffix *-acle* sometimes marks *instrument, place,* as *oracle, receptacle,* &c.; sometimes it seems dim., as *corpuscule.*

Equal, annual, casual, legal, loyal, mortal, &c. ; *cruel, civil, gentile, servile, subtle, gentle, genteel, hostile, fragile, able* (Fr. *habile*).

The following substantives also contain the same suffix :—*Canal, channel, charnel, carnal, cattle, chattel, coronal, fuel, hospital* (*hotel, spittal*), *jewel, minstrel, madrigal, official.*

Modern formations are numerous, as *acquittal, disposal, avowal, denial,* &c.

(*b*) Many adjectives in -al are now treated as substantives, as *cardinal, criminal, general, material,* &c.

(*c*) In many words it has taken the place of Lat. *-us, -is*:—*festival, prodigal, celestial.*

It is also added to the adjectival suffix *-ic*, as *angelical, comical, whimsical,* &c.

The following substantives are from words in *-alia, -ilia, -bilia* :—*Funerals, entrails, movables, rascal, spousals, victuals, battle* and *marvel*.

(4) **B-le, a-ble, i-ble** (Lat. *a-b-ili-s*), able to, likely to, full of.

Abominable, acceptable, culpable, reasonable, feeble, foible (O.Fr. *floible, foible ;* Lat. *flebilis*), *movable, stable.*

M.

(1) **M, me** (Lat. *mu-s, -a, -m*), that which. See p. 215.

Fir-m, fu-me, fa-me, fla-me, for-m, raisin (Lat. *racemus ;* Sp. *racimo ;* Fr. *raisin*).

(2) **M, men, mon** (Lat. *-men, -mo*), that which.

Char-m, cri-me, legu-me, real-m, volu-me.

M has become *n* in *leaven* (Lat. *leva-men ;* O.Fr. *levain*), *noun* (Lat. *no-men ;* O.Fr. *noom, non*), *renown.*

The following words contain the Greek suffix -μα :—*Apophthegm, emblem, phantom, paradigm, phlegm, problem, scheme, theme.*

(3) **Ism** (Gr. ισ-μος ; Lat. *-ismus ;* Fr. *-isme ;* a combination of μο and ις), condition, act, &c.

Baptism, barbarism, despotism, egotism (Fr. *égoïsme*), *latinism, provincialism, vulgarism,* &c.

In some words it adds a depreciative sense, as *deism, mannerism, papism.*

(4) **Mn**[1] (Lat. *-umnus, -minus*, &c.).
Autu-mn, colu-mn, ter-m, da-m-age.

(5) **Mony** (Lat. *-mon-ia, -mon-ium;* Fr. *-moin, -moine*). See M, p. 234.
Acrimony, ceremony, matrimony, sanctimony, testimony, &c.

(6) **Ment** (Lat. *-men-tu-m;* Fr. *-ment*), instrument, &c.
Experiment, firmament, garment, instrument, pavement, vestment, &c.
It is also added to Teutonic roots, as *acknowledgment, fulfilment,* &c.

N.

(1) **N, ne** (Lat. *nu-s, -a, -m*), passive suffix, like *-ed* (*en*) in English. See p. 215.
Fa-ne, plain, reign, pen, plane.

(2) **An, ain** (Lat. *a-nu-s, -a, -m;* Fr. *an, ain, aine*), of or belonging to.
Artisan, courtezan, german (O.E. *germain*), *mean, pagan, partisan, publican, pelican, sexton* (= *sacristan*), *peasan-t, Roman, Tuscan,* &c.; *captain, certain, chieftain, chaplain, fountain, porcelain, villain, sovereign* (O.Fr. *soverain;* Lat. *superanus*), *warden* and *guardian* (O.Fr. *gardian*).
Other forms of *an, ain*, are found in *citizen, denizen, mizzen, surgeon, parishioner, scrivener.*
In modern English the suffix *an* is employed without reference to its original use in forming nouns and adjectives, as *civilian, grammarian,* &c.; *censorian, diluvian, plebeian,* &c.
An becomes *ane* in *humane, extramundane, transmontane,* &c.

(3) **En, in** (Lat. *e-nu-s, -a, -m*). See An.
Alien, dozen, damson, damascene, warren, chain, florin, vermin, venom (O.Fr. *venin;* O.E. *venym*).

(4) **In, ine** (Lat. *i-nu-s, -a, -m*). See An.
Bas-in, coffin, cousin, citrine, goblin, matins, cummin, ravine, canteen (Fr. *cantine*), *patten* (Fr. *patin*), *baboon* (O.E. *babuyn, babion;* Fr. *babou-in*), *cushion* (O.E. *coschyn*), *lectern* (O.E. *letyrn;* Fr. *lutrin*), *curtain* (O.E. *cortyn*), *pilgrim* (*peregrine*), *discipline, doctrine,*

---
[1] The suffix *-umnus* is cognate with the Sansk. participial suffix *-mana;* *-monis* is the same suffix in combination with *-ia;* with the suffix *-tu-m* it becomes *-mentu-m.*

eglantine, famine, medicine, rapine; with numerous adjectives, as *aquiline, canine,* &c.

(5) **On, ion, eon, oon, in** (Lat. *o, io* [acc. *on-em*]; It. *-one;* Sp. *-on, -ona;* Fr. *-on*), act of, state of.

Apron (*napron*), *bacon, capon, dragon, falcon, fawn* (O.E. *faon, fanon*), *felon, glutton, flagon, griffon* (*griffin*), *mutton, gallon, pennon, salmon, sturgeon, simpleton, talon, champion, clarion, companion, marchioness, onion, pavilion, stallion, scorpion, pigeon, scutcheon, truncheon, mason* (Mid. Lat. *macio*).

Buffoon, dragon, balloon, batoon, carroon, harpoon, macaroon, musketoon, poltroon, saloon; origin, ruin, virgin, &c. *Custom* (= Lat. *consuetudinem*). In all other words from Lat. *-tudo*, the *in* has fallen off, as *multitude,* &c.

Lagoon (Lat. *lacuna;* Fr. *lagune*).

Many words in *-oon* are augmentative, as *balloon,* &c.; some in *-on* are diminutive, as *flagon, habergeon,* &c.

Numerous abstract substantives, as *dominion, oblivion, opinion, rebellion,* &c.

(6) **An, ean, eign, ain** (Lat. *-an-eu-s, -a, -m*).

Mediterranean, campaign, champaign, foreign (O. Fr. *forain;* Lat. *foraneus*), *mountain, strange* (O. Fr. *estrange;* Lat. *extraneus*), *sudden*.

The Latin *-aneus* appears under the forms *-ineus, -oneus,* &c., as in *sanguine, carrion* (It. *carogna,* O. Fr. *caroigne*).

(7) **Ern, urn** (Lat. *-er-na, -ur-nus*). See **An**.

Cavern, cistern, tavern, diuturn, nocturn, diurn-al, nocturn-al, &c.

C (see p. 213).

(1) **Ac, ic, oc** (Lat. *-ax, -ix, -ox*), pertaining to, possessing.

Words containing this suffix are mostly found in adjectives in combination with *-ious*, as *audacious, capacious, atrocious,* &c.

The following substantives also contain suffixes *ax* and *ix* much altered :—

Chalice, furnace, mortise, pentise (*penthouse*), *matrice* (*matrix*), *partridge, phœnix, pumice.*

(2) **Ac** (Lat. *a-cu-s, -a, -m*), having, pertaining to.

Demoniac, maniac, Syriac, barracks, carrock (*carrack*), *cassock.*

(3) **Ic** (*-ĭ-cu-s, -a, -m*), occurs as a suffix in (*a*) substantives, = art, science; (*b*) adjectives, = of or belonging to.

XVIII.]   SUFFIXES OF ROMANCE ORIGIN.   237

(a) *Arithmetic, cynic, heretic, logic, magic, music, physic, cleric, clerk, fabric, perch, park, porch.*

(b) *Aromatic, barbaric, frantic, gigantic, laconic, metallic, public, rustic, schismatic.*
It is also found in combination with *-al*, as *canonical, heretical, magical*, &c.
Indigo = the Spanish form of *Indicus* (colour), *Indian* (colour).

(4) **Ic** (Lat. *-icu-s*), of or belonging to.
Amic-able, in-im-ic-al.
In *enemy* (Lat. *inimicus*), the guttural has disappeared.

(5) **Uc** (Lat. *-uca*).   See Ac.
Festuc-ous, lettuce, periwig (wig), = O.E. *perwiche* (Fr. *perruque*; It. *perrucca*).

(6) **Ass, ace** (Lat. *-ac-eus, -a, -m; -ac-ius, -ic-ius, -oc-ius;* It. *-accio, -accia;* Fr. *-as, -asse*, &c.).
Cutlass (Fr. *coutelas*, as if from Lat. *cultellaceus*), *canvas* (It. *canavaccio*), *cuirass* (Mid.Lat. *coracium, coratium*), *moustache* (It. *mostaccio*), *cartridge* (Fr. *cartouche;* It. *cartoccio*), *menace* (Lat. *minaciæ*), *populace, pinnace* (It. *pinaccia*), *terrace* (It. *terracia;* Fr. *terrasse*), *apprentice* (Mid.Lat. *apprenticius*), *pilche* (Mid.Lat. *pellicea;* Fr. *pelisse;* It. *pelliccia*), *surplice* (= *super-pellicium*).

(7) **Esque** (Fr. *-esque;* It. *-esco;* Lat. *-is-cu-s*, a euphonic form of *-icus*), like.
Burlesque, grotesque, picturesque.
It occurs in some proper nouns :—*Danish* (O.Fr. *Danesche*); *French; morrice* (dance) = *moresque*, or *morisco.*

(8) **Atic** (Lat. *-aticus*), of or belonging to.
Aquatic, fanatic, lunatic.

(9) **Age** (Lat. *-aticum ;* Fr. *-age*) gives a collective sense.
Age (O.Fr. *edage;* Mid. Lat. *ætaticum*), *advantage, beverage, carriage, courage, carnage, herbage, heritage, homage, language, passage, marriage, outrage, personage, potage, stage, vassalage, village, voyage, vintage.*
It is sometimes added to Teutonic roots, as *cottage, fraughtage, tillage.*

T.[1]

A-te (Lat. *a-tu-s, a-su-s*), quality of, like, subject of an action.

Substantives.—*Advocate, curate, legate, private, renegade* and *runagate.*

Adjectives.—*Delicate, desolate, ordinate, inordinate.*

The suffix *atus* through French *é* has become ed, as *armed, disinherited, deformed, renowned, troubled.*

Ee (Fr. *ée*), object of an action, is another form of Lat. *-atus*, as in *appellee, legatee, grantee, vendee; army* = Fr. *armée.*

In *devotee, grandee*, the passive signification is not preserved.

E-te (Lat. *-e-tus*) :—*Complete, replete*, also *discreet, secret.*

I-te (Lat. *-i-tus*) :—*Contrite, definite, favourite, prest* (ready) = Lat. *præstitus.*

T (Lat. *-tu-s*).

Adjectives.—*Chaste, honest, modest, distinct, elect, perfect, robust, mute, strict, strait, straight, subject, sain-t.*

In *diverse, scarce* (Mid. Lat. *scarpsus* = *ex-carpsus*) we have s for t.

Substantives.—*Appetite, circuit, conduct, convent, delight, fruit, habit, market, plaint, profit, state, magistrate, course, decrease, excess, process, press.*

This suffix has become y in *clergy, county, duchy, treaty;* cy in *magistracy, papacy, primacy.*

Id (Lat. *i-du-s, -du-s*) :—*Ac-id, frig-id*, &c.

T (Lat. *-tu-m*).

Biscuit, conquest, covert (*cover*), *date, deceit, desert, fact, feat, jest, intent, infinite, interdict, verdict, joint, merit, precept, pulpit, point, script, statute, tribute, quest, request.*

With s for t, *mass, poise, response, sauce, advice, device.*

The t is lost in *decree, purpose, vow.*

T (*-ta*).

Aunt, debt, quilt, minute, plummet, rent, route, ambassade (*embassy*).

S for t occurs in *foss, noise, spouse, assize.*

Ta has become y in *assembly, causey* (causeway), *chimney, couch, country, covey, destiny, entry, jelly, journey, jury, meiny, party, pastry, valley, volley, value.*

---

[1] Connected with Sanskrit participial *-ta*, English *-ed*. See p. 217.

XVIII.] SUFFIXES OF ROMANCE ORIGIN. 239

Ade (= Lat. *-a-ta*; Fr. *-a-de*; Sp. *-ado, -ada*).
Brigade, balustrade, brocade, cavalcade, cascade, lemonade, parade, salad, &c.; *desperado, pintado, armada.*

Et (Lat. *ē-tum*), a place for or with, &c.
Arboret, budget, banquet, fagot, junket, pallet.

Et diminutive (Fr. *-et, -ette*).

Substantives.—*Aigret, aglet, amoret, bassinet, billet, basket, buffet, castlet, chaplet, casket, circlet, clicket, corbet, coronet, corset, cruet, freshet, ganet, goblet, gibbet, gullet, hatchet, lappet, lancet, leveret, locket, mallet, musket, pocket, pullet, puppet, signet, trumpet, turret, ticket, ballot, chariot, faggot, galiot, parrot (parroquet).*

Adjectives.—*Brunette, dulcet, russet, violet, watchet.*

L-et (diminutive).
Bracelet, hamlet, leaflet, ringlet, streamlet.

Ty (Lat. *-tas* [*tat*]; Fr. *té*, added to substantive and adjective stems) has the force of the suffix *-ness.*

Authority, beauty, bounty, charity, captivity, cruelty, frailty, honesty, &c.

Tude: see suffix -on, p. 236.

T (Lat. *-ti*, as *ar-s, ar-ti-s*).
Ar-t, font, front, mount, port, part, sort.
Connected with Lat. *ti* is Gr. σι-s, as in (1) *analy-sis, diagno-sis, hypothe-sis,* &c.; (2) *apocalyp-se, ba-se, ellip-se, paraphra-se,* &c.; (3) *catalep-sy, drop-sy, epilep-sy, hypocri-sy, pal-sy.*

S-ti (Lat. *-stis*), of or belonging to.
Agrestic, celestial, campestral, equestrian, terrestrial.

Ce, ise, ss (= Lat. *-ti-a*; Fr. *-esse*), condition, quality of.
Avarice, justice, cowardice, distress, duress, franchise, largess, merchandise, noblesse, prowess, riches.

Ter (Lat. *-ter*), one who is.
Master, minister.

Tor (Lat. *-tor*), agent.
Auditor, author (O.E. *auctor*), *doctor, factor.*

Dor, door, dore = Sp. *-dor*, Lat. *-tor.*
Corridor, matador, battledoor, stevedore.

Sor, another form of tor, occurs in *antecessor, confessor, successor*, &c.

Many words, originally ending in tor, have in French and English lost t; and many words in or, our, have become er.

Ambler, compiler, courier, diviner, emperor, former, founder, governor, interpreter, juror, juggler, labourer, lever, preacher, saviour, taxer.

Many words in our (Fr. *eur*) have become er under the influence of the Eng. er (O.E. *ere*).

Robber, receiver, &c.

Ter (Lat. *-trum*), instrument.
Cloister, spectre.

Ite (Lat. *-ita*, Fr. *-ite*), belonging to.
Carmelite, Canaanite, Jesuit, &c.

T (Gr. -της), he who, that which.
Apostate, comet, hermit, planet, prophet, idiot, patriot.

Id (Gr. -ιδης, Lat. *ĭdes*), relating to.
Æneid, Nereid, &c.

Ist (Gr. -ισ-της; Lat. *-ista*; Fr. *-iste*), agent.
Antagonist, baptist, evangelist, &c.; *artist, dentist, deist, florist, latinist*, &c.; *enthusiast, encomiast*, &c.

Ist-er, one who is engaged in.
Chorister, sophister (O.E. *canonistre, legistre*).

Trix (Lat. *-trix*), female agent.
Administratrix, negotiatrix.
Empress = *imperatrix* (Fr. *impératrice*), *nurse* = *nutrix* (Fr. *nourrice*).

Ture, sure (Lat. *-tura, -sura*), has an abstract signification in feminine substantives.

Concrete substantives.—*Aperture, creature, nature, picture*, &c.
Armour (Mid. Lat. *armatura*).

Abstract substantives.—*Adventure, capture, gesture, nurture, measure*, &c.

Tor-y, sor-y (Lat. *-tor-iu-s, -a, -m; -sorium, -soria;* Fr. *-oire, -oir, -toir, -soir*), (1) place, (2) of a nature to, relating to.

Substantives.—*Auditory, dormitory, monitory, oratory, purgatory, refectory, repository,* &c.

Adjectives.—*Amatory, rotatory,* &c.
The following contain (1) Lat. *-torium;* Fr. *-oire, -oir:*—*Coverture, counter, laver, mortar, mirror, parlour, escritoire.* (2) Lat. *-sorium;* Fr. *-soir:*—*censer, razor, scissors.*

Tery (Lat. *-terium;* Fr. *-trie*). Y = *iu-m* = condition: see Y, p. 229, and Ter, p. 239.
Mastery, ministry, mystery.

Nt (Lat. *-a-ns, -e-ns;* Fr. *-ent, -ant*: a participial suffix).

Adjectives.—*Abundant, discordant, distant, elegant,* &c.; *adjacent, latent, obedient, patient, prudent,* &c.

Substantives.—*Defendant, dependant, inhabitant, servant, serjeant, warrant, agent, adherent, client,* &c.
The following words contain other forms of this suffix:—*Brigand, diamond.*

Und, bund (Lat. *-undus, -bundus,* a gerundial suffix).
Facund, jocund, second, round, vagabond.

Nd (Lat. *-ndus, -nda, -ndum*), something to be done.
Garland, legend, prebend, provender, viand; deodand, memorandum.

L-ent (Lat. *-lentus, -a, -m; -lens*), full of.
Corpulent, esculent, feculent, violent, &c.

Lence (Lat. *-lentia*), fulness of.
Corpulence, opulence, succulence, &c.

Nce (Lat. *-nt-ia*), quality of, act of, result of, &c.
Abundance, chance, distance, instance, penance, indulgence, licence, presence, &c.

Ncy (Lat. *-antia, -entia;* Fr. *-ance, -ence;* It. *-anza, -enza*), quality of, result of, act of, &c.
Brilliancy, consonancy, decency, excellency, exigency, infancy, &c.

Tion, sion (Lat. *ti-o [tionis], si-o [sionis]*), act of, state of, &c.
Absolution, action, caution, citation, confirmation, &c.; *confusion, profession, benison, malison, poison, ransom, reason, treason, venison, fashion.*

Verbal.

Ise, Ize (Lat. *-ire;* Fr. *-iser;* Gr. *-ιζω*), make, give, &c. *Apologize, sermonize, tantalize,* &c.

Ish (Lat. *-ire;* Fr. *-ir;* cp. Fr. participles in *-issant: -iss* = Lat. inchoative suffix *-esc*), make, give.
Admonish, establish, finish, &c.

Ey (Lat. *-are;* Fr. *-er*), parley : cp. verbs in **-fy** ; Lat. *-ficare*, Fr. *-fier*.

326. COMPOSITION OF ROMANCE ROOTS.

We have many compounds of Romance origin (French, &c., Latin and Greek) in English, the elements of which can only be explained by a reference to those languages, as :—

(1) *Aqueduct, solstice* (cp. *bridegroom, sunrise,* &c.), *artifice, geography, homicide* (cp. *manslaughter, bloodshed,* &c.), *aëronaut* (cp. *seafarer*), *somnambulist* (cp. *night-brawler*).

(2) *Verjuice* = Fr. *verjus, vert-jus* (cp. *greyhound,* &c.).
Many Romance words have the adjective for the last element, as *vinegar* = Fr. *vinaigre* = *vinum acer,* &c.

(3) *Kerchief,* O.Fr. *cuevre chief* (cp. *catch-penny, breakwater*).

(4) *Omnipotent, grandiloquent* (cp. *almighty, deep-musing*).

(5) *Longimanous, magnanimous, quadruped* (cp. *long-handed, high-minded, four-footed*).

(6) *Carnivorous, pacific,* &c. (cp. *heart-rending, peace-making,* &c.).

(7) *Armipotent* (cp. *arm-strong, heart-sick,* &c.).

(8) *Edify, mortify* (cp. *backbite, kilndry*).

(9) *Fortify, magnify* (cp. *fine-draw, hot-press, whitewash,* &c.).

The etymology of many words is disguised through the changes they have undergone, as :—

(1) megrim (hemicranium, Gr. ἡμικρανία = pain affecting one-half the skull, from ἡμι and κρανίον).[1]
parsley = Fr. *persil,* Lat. *petro-selinum* (Gr. πέτρα σέλινον).

---

[1] "*Emigraneus,* vermis capitis, Angl. the *mygryne,* or the head-worm '*Ortus in Promp. Parv.*). Pains in the head (and capricious fancies) were supposed to arise from the biting of a worm."—WEDGWOOD.

(2) grandam = Fr. *grande dame*.
gramercy = Fr. *grand merci*.
maugre = O.Fr. *malgre* = Lat. *male-gratum*.
verdict = Lat. *vere-dictum*.
viscount = Lat. *vice-comte* from *vice* and *comes*.

(3) chanticleer = Fr. *chante*, imper. of *chanter*, and *clair*, O.F. *cler*.
curfew = Fr. *couvre-feu*.
wardrobe = Fr. *garde-robe*.

(4) dandelion = Fr. *dent-de-lion*.
debonair = O.Fr. *de bon aire*.
legerdemain = Fr. *léger de la main*.
paramour = Fr. *par amour*.
pardy = Fr. *par Dieu*, &c.

327. COMPOSITION WITH ROMANCE PARTICLES.

(1) **A, ab, abs** (Lat. *ab*, Sansk. *apa*), away from:—
Avert, abdicate, abjure, abscond, absent, &c.
Advance, advantage = Fr. *avancer, avantage*, from Lat. *ao, ante*.
B is lost in *abridge* = *abbreviare*, and *assoil* = *absolvere*.

(2) **Ad,[1] A** (Lat. *ad*, Fr. *ad*), to—
Adapt, adore, adhere, adjoin, accept, accumulate, affirm, affix, affront, aggravate, alleviate, allege, appear, apply, arrive, assail, assent, assets, attain.
Achieve, agree, amerce, amount, a-cquit (O.Fr. *a-quiter*), *acquaint* (O.Fr. *acointer* = *ad-cognitare*), *averse, avow.*

(3) **Ante, anti** (Lat. *ante*, O.Fr. *ans, ains, eins*), before:—
Ante-cede, ante-chamber.
Anticipate, &c.
Ancestor = O.Fr. *ancessor* (= *antecessor*).

(4) **Amb, am** (Lat. *ambi*), about.
Amb-i-ent, am-putate.

(5) **Circum, circu** (Lat. *circum*), round about:—
Circumstance, circumscribe, circuit, &c.

(6) **Com, con** (Lat. *cum*, O.Fr. *com, cum, con, cun*). *Com* remains unchanged before *m* and *p*; it becomes **col** and **cor** before *l* and *r*; **co** before vowels:—

---

[1] The *d* in *ad* is assimilated to the initial letters of the words to which it is prefixed, and becomes **ac, af, ag, al, ap, ar, as, at.**

Command, comprehend, collect, col-lingual, collocate, collate, &c.
Coeval, coheir, co-operate, &c.
Conceive, condemn, conduct, confirm, conjure, conqueror, consent, contain, convey.
Counsel, council, countenance.
Count (Lat. *computare,* O.Fr. *conter*), *custom* (Lat. *consuetudinem*).
Cost (Lat. *constare,* O.Fr. *co-ster*), *curry* (O.F. *conroyer*).
Couch (= Lat. *collocare,* O.Fr. *colcher*).
Accoutre (O.Fr. *accoustrer,* from Lat. *ad custodem*).
Scourge = Lat. *cor-rigia,* whence It. *corregiare,* to scourge.
Quash (O.Fr. *esquachier,* to crush, from Lat. *co-actus*).

Co occurs as a prefix with some Teutonic roots, as *co-worker, co-understanding.*

(7) **Contra, contro, counter** (Lat. *contra,* O.F. *contre*), against:—
Contra-dict, contro-vert, &c.
Counter-balance, counter-feit, &c.
Counter-weigh, counter-work.

(8) **De** (Lat. *de,* Fr. *dé*), down, from, away :—
Decline, descend, depart, &c.
It is negative and oppositive in *destroy, desuetude, deform,* &c.
It is intensitive in *declare, desolate, desiccate,* &c.

(9) **Dis, di** (Lat. *dis, di,* O.Fr. *des,* Fr. *dis, dés, di, de*), and by assimilation dif, asunder, apart, in two ; difference, negation :—
Disarm, discern, dismember, disturb, discord, distance, &c.
Differ, difficulty, disease, &c.
Dilate, dilute, diminish, divorce, diverse.
Descry, descant, despatch.

It became de in *defy, defer, delay, deluge, depart.*
Dis is joined to Teutonic roots, as *disown, dislike,* &c.

(10) **Ex, e, es** (Lat. *ex,* O.Fr. *ex, es, e*), by assimilation ef, out of, from :—
Exalt, exempt, exhale, expatriate, &c.
Elect, evade, &c.
Efface, effect, &c.

It has a privative sense in *ex-emperor, ex-mayor,* &c.

Amend = *emend ; award* (O.Fr. *esward*), *afraid* (Fr. *effrayer,* to frighten).
Escape, escheat, essay, astonish, issue (O.Fr. *issir,* Lat. *exire*).
S-ample (O.Fr. *ex-ample*), *s-carce* = *excerpt* (O.Fr. *es-cars*), *s-corch* (O.Fr. *es-corcer*), **special.**

(11) **Extra** (Lat. *extra*), beyond :—

Extraneous, extraordinary, extravagant, extra-regular, extra-work, &c. *Stray* for *estray,* from *extra* and *vago.*

(12) **In, en, em** (Lat. *in,* Fr. *en, em*), in, into, on, within ; by assimilation, il, im, ir :—

Inaugurate, innovate, invade, innate.
Illustrate, illusion, &c.
Imbibe, impart, immigrate, &c.
Irritate, irrigate.
Enchant, encounter, encumber, endure, engage, enhance, ensign, environ, envy, entice, envoy.
Embellish, embrace, embalm.
Anoint (O.Fr. *enoindre*), *ambush.*
Impair.

Em and en are found prefixed to Teutonic roots, as—

Embillow, embolden, endear, enlighten, &c.

(13) **In** (Lat. *in,* cp. Gr. ἀν, Eng. *un*), not; by assimilation, il, im, ir ; like the Eng. *un,* it is prefixed to substantives and adjectives:—

(1) *Inconvenience, impiety, illiberality,* &c.

(2) *Incautious, impolitic, illegal, irregular,* &c.

It occurs in some few parasynthetic verbs, as *incapacitate, indispose, illegalize, immortalize,* &c.

The prefix *un* sometimes takes its place, as in *unable, unapt, uncomfortable, uncertain,* &c.

(14) **Inter, intro** (Lat. *inter, intro,* O.Fr. *inter, entre*), between, within, among :—

Interpose, intercede, interdict, intercept, interfere, interlace, intermix, intermarry.
Introduce, intromit, &c.
Introduction, introgression, introit.
Entertain, enterprise, entrails.

(15) **Mis** (O.Fr. *mes, més, mé,* Lat. *minus,* O.E. *mes, mis*). This suffix enters into composition with Romance roots ; it must not be confounded with the Teutonic suffix *mis, mistake,* &c.

Misadventure, mischance (O.E. *meschaunce*), *mischief* (O.E. *meschef*[1]).

---

[1] The O.E. *bonchef* is the opposite of mischief.

(16) **Ob** (Lat. *ob*, before *c, f, p,* becomes by assimilation **oc, of, op**), in front of, against :—
VERBS : *Obey, oblige, obviate, occupy, occur, offer, offend, oppose*
SUBS. : *Obeisance, obedience, occasion, offence, office.*

(17) **Per** (Lat. *per*, Fr. *per, par*, O.E. *par*), through :—
Perceive, perfect, perform, perish, perjure, pierce, percolate, perennial, persecute, pursue, pardon, appurtenance, pertinence.
Per becomes *pel* in *pellucid*, and *pil* in *pilgrim*.
It is intensitive in *persuade, peracute*, &c.

(18) **Post** (Lat. *post*), after :—
Postpone, post-date, post-diluvian, postscript, &c.

(19) **Pre** (Lat. *præ*, Fr. *pre*), before :—
Precede, presume, pretence, &c.
Precinct, preface, prefect, prelate.
Provost (O.E. *prepost*, O.Fr. *prevost*).

(20) **Preter** (Lat. *præter*, Fr. *préter*), past :—
Preterite, preternatural, &c.

(21) **Pro** (Lat. *pro*, O.Fr. *pro, por, pur, pour*), forth, forward, before :—
Proceed, procure, progress, profess, proffer, progeny.
Purchase, purvey (= provide), *purpose, pursue, portray, portrait, portend.*

Pro = instead of, in *pronoun, proconsul*.

(22) **Re, Red** (Lat. *re, red*), back, again :—
Rebel, receive, reclaim, recreant, recover, re-adopt, re-admit, &c.
Red-eem, red-ound, redolent, render (Lat. *reddere,* O.Fr. *rendre*), *rally* (= Lat. *re* + *alligare*, Fr. *relier*).

Re is compounded with Teutonic roots, as *rebuild, remind, reopen,* &c.

(23) **Retro** (Lat. *retro*), backwards :—
Retrocede, retrograde, retrospect.
Rereward = O.E. *rereward* (It. *retro-gardia,* Fr. *arrière-garde*), *rear-guard, rear, arrear.*

(24) **Se, sed** (Lat. *se*, Fr. *sé*), apart, away :—
Secede, seclude, seduce, sedition.

(25) **Sub** (Lat. *sub*), under, up from below ; by assimilation (before *c, f, g, m, p, r, s*), **suc, suf, sug, sum, sup, sur, sus** :—
   Subject, succour, suffer, suffix, suggest, summoner, suppress, surprise, suspend, sustain, supple, sojourn (O.Fr. *so-jorner*, Lat. *sub-diurno*).

Sub sometimes enters into composition with Teutonic roots, as *sublet, sub-worker, sub-kingdom*.

(26) **Subter** (Lat. *subter*), under :—
   Subterfuge, subterraneous, &c.

(27) **Super** (Lat. *super*, O.Fr. *sovre, sore, sor, sur*), above, beyond :—
   Superpose, superscription, supernatural, superfine, superfluous, &c.
   Surface (= superficies), *surcoat, surfeit, surplice, surname, surcharge, surpass, surprise, survey,* &c.
   The Ital. *sopra* occurs in *sovereign* (It. *sovrano*, Lat. *supernus*).

(28) **Trans** (Fr. *tres*, Lat. *trans, tra*), across :—
   Transfigure, transform, translate, transitive, transmontane (tramontane).
   Be-tray (O.Fr. *trahir*, Lat. *tradere*), *treason* (= tradition), *travel, traverse, trespass.*

(29) **Ultra** (Lat. *ultra*), beyond :—
   Ultra-liberal.
   To *outrage* = O.Fr. *oultrager.*

(30) **Un, uni** (Lat. *unus*), one :—
   Unanimous, uniform.

(31) **Vice** (Lat. *vice*, Fr. *vis*), instead of :—
   Vicar, vice-agent, vice-chancellor, viceroy, viscount.

Some few *Adverbial* particles are used as prefixes :—

(32) **Bis, bi** (Lat. *bi*), twice ; bini, two by two.
   Biscuit, bissextile, biennial, binocular, &c.

(a) **Demi** (Fr. *demi*, Lat. *dimidium*) :—
   Demigod, demiquaver.
   Semi (Lat. *semi*), half :—
   Semi-column, semi-circle, semi-annual, &c.

(*b*) **Male,** *mal* (Lat. *male, mal,* Fr. *malé, mal, mau*), ill :—
Maltreat, malediction, malevolent, malcontent, maugre.

(*c*) **Non** (Lat. *non*), not :—
Nonage, nonsense.

(*d*) **Pen** (Fr. *pén-,* Lat. *pæne*), almost :—
Peninsula, penumbra, penultimate.

(*e*) **Sine** (Lat. *sine*) :—
Sinecure, sincere.

The Fr. *sans* = Lat. *sine* in *sansculotte, sansculottism,*[1] *sans-souci.*

---

[1] Fr. *culotte,* breeches ; *sansculotte* = a ragged fellow, a radical republican.

APPENDICES.

APPENDIX I.

I. KELTIC ELEMENT IN MODERN ENGLISH.

1. KELTIC words existing in the oldest English: [1]—

    Brock (badger), *breeches, clout, cradle, crock, crook, glen, kiln, mattock.*

2. Keltic words still found in English:—

    Ballast, boast, bod(-kin), *bog, bother, bribe, cam* (crooked), *crag, dainty, dandriff, darn, daub, dirk, gyve, havoc, kibe, log, loop, maggot, mop, motley, mug, noggin, nod, pillow, scrag, spigot, squeal, squall.*

3. Keltic words of recent origin:—

    Bannock, bard, brogue, clan, claymore (great sword), *clog, log, Druid, fillibeg, gag, garran,*[2] *pibroch, piggin, plaid, pony, shamrock, slab, whisky.*

4. Keltic words introduced by Norman-French:—

    Bag, barren, barter, barrator, barrel, basin, basket, bassenet, bonnet, bucket, boots, bran, brisket, button, chemise, car, cart, clapper, dagger, dungeon, gravel, gown, harness, marl, mitten, motley, osier, pot, posnet, rogue, ribbon, skain (skein), *tike.*

---

[1] These have no cognates in the other Teutonic dialects.
[2] Used by Spenser.

II. LATIN ELEMENT IN THE OLDEST ENGLISH.

Of words borrowed from the Latin in the oldest period of the language—

(1) Some kept their full forms, as :—
Cometa, corona, culter, &c.

(2) Others dropped the Latin endings, as :—
Candel, apostol, castel, &c.

(3) Some take an English suffix, as :—
Draca (Lat. *draco*), *mynetere* (Lat. *monetarius*).

(4) A few acquired the Teutonic accent, as :—
Biscop (Lat. *episcopus*), *munec* (Lat. *monachus*).

(5) Some simulated an English form, as :—
Marman-stán (Lat. *marmor*), *mere-greot* (Lat. *margarita*).

(6) A few hybrids made their appearance, as :—
Martyrdom, regollice (regularly).

abbod, abbud,	Lat.	*abbas,* abbot
albe,	,,	*alba,* aube
ancor, ancer,	,,	*ancora,* anchor
ancra,	,,	*anchoreta,* nun
antiphone, antefn	,,	*antiphonia* (ἀντιφώνεια), anthem
apostol,	,,	*apostolus* (ἀπόστολος)
bæpstere,	,,	*baptista* (βαπτιστής)
balsam,	,,	*balsamum* (βάλσαμον)
basilisca,	,,	*basilicus* (βασιλίσκος)
biscop,	,,	*episcopus* (ἐπίσκοπος)
buttor, butor,	,,	*butyrum* (βούτυρον), butter
Calend,	,,	*Calendæ,* calends
calic, calc,	,,	*calix,* chalice
camel,	,,	*camelus,* camel
canon,	,,	*canonicus,* canon
canon,	,,	*canon,* cannon
candel, condel,	,,	*candela,* candle
capitola,	,,	*capitulum,* chapter
carited,	,,	*caritas,* charity
cærfille,	,,	*cerefolium,* chervil

Caser,	Lat.	*Cæsar,* emperor
ceastre,	,,	*castrum,* chester
cedar,	,,	*cedrus* (κέδρος), cedar
cêse, cŷse,	,,	*caseus,* cheese
chor,	,,	*chorus,* choir
cisten (beâm),	,,	*castaneus,* chesnut tree
circul,	,,	*circulus,* circle
cyrs (treow),	,,	*cerasus,* cherry
cyria,	Gr.	κυριακή, church
culpian,	Lat.	*culpare,* to blame
culter,	,,	*culter,* a coulter
cipresse,	,,	*cupressus* (κυπάρισσος), cypress
cleric, clerc,	,,	*clericus* (κληρικός), cleric
cluster, clauster,	,,	*claustrum,* cloister
clûse,	,,	*clausa,* close
corona,	,,	*corona,* crown
creda (creed),	,,	*credo,* I believe
Cristen,	,,	*Christianus,* Christian
cristalla,	,,	*crystallus* (κρύσταλλος), crystal
cytere,	,,	*cithara* (κιθάρα), guitar
demon,	,,	*dæmon* (δαίμων), demon
diacon, deacon,	,,	*diaconus* (διάκονος), deacon
disc,	,,	*discus* (δίσκος), dish
diabul, deofol,	,,	*diabolus* (διάβολος), devil
discipul,	,,	*discipulus,* disciple
draca,	,,	*draco,* dragon
earce,	,,	*arca,* ark
ele,	,,	*oleum* (ἔλαιον), oil
ælmæsse, ælmesse,	,,	*eleemosyna* (ἐλεημοσύνη), alms
færs, fers,	,,	*versus,* verse
fîc,	,,	*ficus,* fig
fefer,	,,	*febris,* fever
feferfuge,	,,	*febrifuger,* feverfew
gigant,	,,	*gigans,* giant
gimm,	,,	*gemma,* gem
lilige, lilie,	,,	*lilium,* lily
leo,	,,	*leo,* lion
leon,	,,	*leæna,* lioness
lactuce,	,,	*lactuca,* lettuce
lufuste,	,,	*ligusticum,* lovage
mægester,	,,	*magister,* master
messe, mæsse,	,,	*missa* (*est concio*), mass
monec, munuc, munec, monc	,,	*monachus* (μοναχός), monk
mynster,	,,	*monasterium* (μοναστήριον), minster

mynet,	Lat. *moneta*, mint	
mynetian,	M. Lat. *monetare*, to mint	
marman-stán,	Lat. *marmor*, marble	
mere-greot,	,, *margarita* (μαργαρίτης), margarite (pearl)	
munt,	,, *mons*, mount	
nunna, nunne,	,, *nonna*, nun	
nón,	,, *nona*, noon	
offrian,	,, *offerre*, to offer	
ostre,	,, *ostrea, ostreum*, oyster	
organ,	,, *organum*, organ	
pæl, pel,	,, *pallium*, pall	
palm,	,, *palma*, palm	
palant,	,, *palatium*, palace	
papa,	,, *papa*, pope	
pard,	,, *pardus* (πάρδος), leopard	
pâwa,	,, *pavo*, peacock	
pinsian,	,, *pensare*, to weigh	
pinn (treów),	,, *pinus, pinum*, pine	
peru,	,, *pirum*, pear	
persuc, persoc (treów)	,, *persica (malus), persicum*, peach	
pipor, pepor,	,, *piper* (πέπερι), pepper	
pisa,	,, *pisum* (πίσον), pea, pease	
pistol,	,, *epistola*, epistle	
plant,	,, *planta*, plant	
plaster,	,, *emplastrum* (ἔμπλαστρον), plaster	
plum (treów),	,, *prunus, prunum*, plum	
porr, por-leác,	,, *porrus, porrum*, leek	
pople,	,, *populus*, people	
port,	,, *portus*, port	
port,	,, *porta*, gate	
post,	,, *postis*, post	
portic,	,, *porticus*, porch	
preost,	,, *presbyter* (πρεσβύτερος), elder, priest	
prâfort,	,, *præpositus*, provost	
predician,	,, *prædicare*, to preach	
prim,	,, *prima*, prime	
profian,	,, *probare*, to prove	
peterselige,	,, *petroselinum*, parsley	
pervince,	,, *vinca*, periwinkle	
psalm, salm,	,, *psalmus* (ψαλμός)	
pund,	,, *pondus*, pound	
psaltere,	,, *psalterium*, psalter	
purpur,	,, *purpura*, purple	

pytt,	Lat. *puteus*, spit
regul, regel,	,, *regula*, rule
reliquie,	,, *reliquiæ*, relics
rute,	,, *ruta*, rue
rædíce,	,, *radix*, radish
sanct,	,, *sanctus*, saint
scôlu,	,, *schola* (σχολή), school
sacerd,	,, *sacerdos*, priest
senepe,	,, *sinapi* (σίνηπι), senvy
sigel,	,, *sigillum*, seal
solere,	M.Lat. *solarium*, sollar
stræt,	Lat. *strata (via)*, street
synod,	,, *synodus* (σίνοδος), synod
tæfl, tæfel,	,, *tabula*, table
tempel,	,, *templum*, temple
titul,	,, *titulus*, title
tor,	,, *turris*, tower
truht,	,, *tructa*, trout
tunic,	,, *tunica*, tunic
turtle,	,, *turtur*, turtle
timpan,	,, *tympanum* (τύμπανον), tambour
ynce,	,, *uncia*, ounce, inch

III. SCANDINAVIAN ELEMENT IN ENGLISH.

Abroad, agate, askew, aslant, athwart, bang, bellow, bask, bole (of a tree), *blunt, bore* (tidal wave), *booty, bound* (for a journey), *brag, brink, bull, busk, buckle-to* (= *buskle*[1]), *butt*(ock), *cake, call, cast, clip, clumsy, cross, crook, cripple, cuff, curl, cut, dairy, dash, daze, dazzle, die, droop, dub, dull, earl, fell* (hill), *fellow, fleer, flit, fond, fool, fro, froth, gable, gaby* (cp. O.E. *gabbe*, to lie, deceive), *gait, grovel, glow, hale* (drag), *hit, hug, hustings, irk, keg, kid, kindle, leap* (year), *low, loft* (aloft), *lurk, neve, neaf* (fist), *niggle, niggard, mump, mumble, muck, odd, puck* (goblin), *ransack, rump, ruck, root, scald* (poet), *scare, scold, skull, scull, scant, skill, scrub, skulk, skid, sky, shaw* (wood), *sly, screw, sleeve, sledge, sled, sleek, screech, shriek, sleight, snug, sog, soggy, sprout, stagger, stag, stack, stifle, tarn* (lake), *trust, thrive, thrum, un-ru-ly* (O.E. *ro*, rest), *ugly, uproar, wafentake, window, windlass.*

[1] Bishop Pilkington.

IV. FRENCH WORDS IN ENGLISH OF TEUTONIC ORIGIN.

"The French or Frankish language is now a Romanic dialect, and its grammar is but a blurred copy of the grammar of Cicero. But its dictionary is full of Teutonic words, more or less Romanized to suit the pronunciation of the Roman inhabitants of Gaul."—MAX MÜLLER.

a-ghast (O.E. agaste), Goth. *us-gaisjan*, to make aghast, O.Fr. *agacer*.
ambassador,   Goth. *and-bahts*, O.E. *ambeht*, O.H.Ger. *ampaht*, Lat. *ambactus*, a servant, O.Fr. *ambassadeur*.
arquebuss,   Ger. *hakenbüchse*, Dutch *haak-bus*, O.Fr. *harquebuse*, Fr. *arquebuse*.
attack,   O.N. *taka*, O.E. *tacan*, take, O.Fr. *taicher, techer*, Fr. *tacher, attacher, attaquer*.
attire,   O.E. *tír*, O.H.Ger. *ziari*, Ger. *zier*, O.Fr. *tire*.
baldric,   O.H.Ger. *balderich*, girdle, belt, O.F. *baldre, baldret, baudre*.
balcony,   O.H.Ger. *palcho*, O.N. *balkr*, M.Lat. *balco*, Fr. *balcon*, Eng. *balk*.
barrier, embarrass,   O.H.Ger. *para*, Sp. *barras*, Eng. *bar*.
belfry,   Mid.H.Ger. *bërc-vrit, bër-vrit*, M.Lat. *berfredus, belfredus*, O.Fr. *berfroit, belefroi*, a watchtower.
bivouac,   O.H.Ger. *bî-wacha*, O.Fr. *bivouac, biouac*.
bush (busk),   O.N. *buskr*, O.H.Ger. *busc*, O.Fr. *bois*.
butt,   Fr. *bouter*, O.H.Ger. *bôzen*.
brand, brandish,   O.N. *brandr*, O.E. *brand*, sword, O.Fr. *brant*.
bruise,   O.E. *brŷsan*, O.Fr. *brisier, bruisier*.
carcanet,   O.H.Ger. *querca*, O.N. *kverk*, neck, O.Fr. *charchant*, Fr. *carcan*.
chamberlain,   O.H.Ger. *kamarling*, O.Fr. *chambrelenc, chambrelain*.
champion,   O.H.Ger. *campio*, O.E. *cempa*, O.Fr. *campion, champion*.
choice,   Goth. *kiusan*, O.E. *ceosan*, Ger. *kiesen*, Fr. *choisir*, to choose.
cry, descry,   O.H.Ger. *scrîan*, Ger. *schrien*, O.Fr. *escrier*, crier.
dance,   Ger. *tanz*, O.N. *dans*, O.Fr. *danse, dance*.
defile,   O.E. *fýlan*, O.Fr. *defoler*.

enamel,	O.N. *smelta*, Ger. *schmelzen*, to melt, whence M.Lat. *smaltum*, It. *smalto*, O.Fr. *esmal*, *esmail*.
eschew,	O.H.Ger. *sciuhan*, Ger. *scheuen*, *scheuchen*, O.Fr. *eschiver*, *eskiver*.
fee, fief, feoff,	O.Fr. *fiu*, *fieu*, *fied*, Goth. *faihu*, O.H.Ger. *fihu*, O.E. *feoh*, cattle.
flatter,	O.N. *fladra*, O.Fr. *flater*.
gallop (O.E. wallop),	Goth. *ga-hláupan*, O.E. *ge-hleápan*, O.Fr. *galoper*.
garnish,	O.H.Ger. *warnôn*, O.E. *wearnian*, to warn; O.Fr. *warnir*, *guarnir*, O.E. *warnisen*, provide, supply.
grate,	O.H.Ger. *chrazôn*, Ger. *kratzen*, O.Fr. *gratter*.
guide,[1]	O.E. *witian*, *betwitian*, to guard, protect; O.Fr. *guier*, to guide.
guile,	O.E. *wíle*, O.F. *guile*, *guille*.
guise,	O.E. *wíse*, O.H.Ger. *wísa*; modern Eng. *wise* (as in like*wise*), O.Fr. *guise*; cp. O.Fr. *desguiser* = to disguise.
hamlet,	Goth. *háims*, O.E. *hám*, *hom*, Fr. *hamel*, *hameau*.
haste,	O.N. *hastr*, O.Fr. *haste*.
hauberk,	O.H.Ger. *hals-berc*, O.E. *heals-beorg*, O.Fr. *halberc*, *hauberc*, *haubert*, O.E. *habergeon*.
haunt (to),	O.N. *heimta*, O.Fr. *honter*, *hanter*.
herald,	O.H.Ger. *heri-walt*, *heriolt*, O.Fr. *heralt*, *heraut*.
lansquenet,	Ger. *landsknecht*.
lecher,	O.H.Ger. *lecchôn*, O.E. *liccian*, to lick, O.Fr. *lichier*, *lecher*, whence O.Fr. *lecheor*, a lecher.[2]
march, marches,	O.H.Ger. *marcha*, O.E. *meare* (boundary, border), O.Fr. *marce*, *marche*.
marshal,	O.H.Ger. *marah-scalh* (*marah*, horse, *scalh*, servant), O.Fr. *marescal*, *mareschal*.
massacre,	O.H.Ger. *mezzalôn*, Ger. *metzeln*, to cut down, Fr. *massacre*.
pouch, poke, pocket, poach,	O.E. *pocca*, *poha*, bag, Fr. *poche*.

---

[1] Fr. words with initial *gu*, and Italian words commencing with *gua*, *gue*, *gui*, are almost invariably of Teutonic origin.
[2] *Relish* is from the same source.

quiver,	O.E. *cocer*, O.H.Ger. *kohhar*, Ger. *köcher*, O.Fr. *couire*, *cuivre*.
reward, guerdon,	O.H.Ger. *widar-lôn*, M.Lat. *wider-donum*, O.F. *werdon, guerredon*.
ribald,	O.H.Ger. *hrîba*, *hrîpa* (prostitūta), O.Fr. *ribald*, a ribald person.
rifle,	O.N. *hrîfa*, O.Fr. *riffer*, *riffler*.
ring, harangue, range, arrange,	O.H.Ger. *hring, ring*.
roast,	O.E. *rôstan*, Ger. *rösten*, O.Fr. *rostir*.
rob,	O.H.Ger. *raubôn*, O.E. *reáfian*, O.Fr. *rober*.
robe,	O.H.Ger. *roub*, O.E. *reáf*, Fr. *robe*.
seize,	O.H.Ger. *bi-sazian*, Ger. *besetzen*, O.Fr. *saisir, seisir*.
seneschal,	O.H.Ger. *sene-scalh* (old servant), O.Fr. *senescal*, seneschal.
shallop,	Du. *sloep*, Fr. *chaloupe*.
skiff,	O.E. *scip*, Ger. *schiff*, Fr. *esquif*, whence equip, O.Fr. *esquiper*.
slate,	connected with Eng. *slit*; O.Fr. *esclat*, O.E. *sklat*, slate.
spy (to),	O.H.Ger. *sprehôn*, O.Fr. *espier*.
target,	O.H.Ger. *targa*, O.E. *targe*, O.Fr. *targe*.
tire (out),	O.E. *teran*, Goth. *tairan*, Ger. *herren*, O.Fr. *tirer*.
towel,	O.H.Ger. *dwahila*, *twahila*, O.E. *þwál*, O.Fr. *toialle, touialle*.
tumble,	O.N. *tumba* (to fall forward), *tumbian* (to dance), O.Fr. *tumber*.
turn,	O.N. *turnan*, O.E. *tyrnan*, O.H.Ger. *turnian*, O.Fr. *turner, torner*.
wage, gage,	O.E. *wed*, Goth. *vadi*, O.H.Ger. *wetti*, M.Lat. *vadium*.
wait (await),	O.H.Ger. *wahta*, Ger. *waht*, O.Fr. *waite, gaite*, *guaite*, watch; O.H.Ger. *wahten*, O.Fr. *gaiter, guiater*, to wait.
war,	O.E. *wyrre*, O.H.Ger. *werra* (scandalum), O.Fr. *werre, guerre*.
ward, guard,	Goth. *wardja*, O.E. *weard*, O.H.Ger. *wart*, O.Fr. *guarde, warde*; cp. *guardian, warden*.
wicket,	O.E. *wíc*, O.N. *vík*, bight, haven, O.Fr. *wiket*, *guischet*.
wimple,	O.H.Ger. *wompal*, O.Fr. *guimple, gimple, guimpe*.

O.E. warish, guarish, O.E., O.H.Ger. *warian*, *werien*, Ger. *wahren*, O.Fr. *warir*, *guarir*, *garir*.
O.E. warnish, garnish, O.E. *wearnian*, O.H.Ger. *warnôn*, to warn, O.Fr. *warnir*, *guarnir*, provide, prepare, secure.

Some foreign words have simulated, wholly or partly, an English form :—

arblast,   O.E. *arow-blaste*, O.Fr. *arbaleste*, Lat. *arcubalista*.
beef-eaters,   Fr. *buffetiers*.
causeway,   Fr. *chaussé*, O.F. *cauchie*, M.Lat. *calceata* (*via*), Lat. *calciata* (*via*).
cray-fish (crawfish), O.H.Ger. *krebiz*, Ger. *krebs*, crab, O.Fr. *escrevisse*, Fr. *écrevisse*, O.E. *krevys*, *crevish*.
gridiron,   O.Fr. *graile*, Lat. *craticula*.
pil-crow,   O.E. *pyl-craft*, Lat. *paragraphus*, Fr. *parafe*.
runagate   = *renegate*, *renegado*.

Cp. :—
furbelow,   Fr. *falbala*, Sp. *farfala*.
lanthorn,   O.Fr. *lanterne*, Lat. *lanterna*.
pickaxe,   O.E. *pikois*.
rosemary,   O.E. *rosemaryne*, Lat. *rosmarinus*.
sparrow-grass   = Lat. *asparagus*.
somerset,   Fr. *soubresaut*, Lat. *supra saltus*.

APPENDIX II.

OUTLINES OF O.E. ACCIDENCE.

DECLENSION OF SUBSTANTIVES, &c.

FIRST PERIOD OF THE LANGUAGE.

(A.) Vowel Stems.[1]

1. MASCULINE.

dæg, day ; *hirde*, shepherd ; *gæst*, guest ; *sunu*, son ; *wudu*, wood.

		a STEM.		*i* STEM.	*u* STEM.	
Sing. ...	N.	dæg	hirde	gæst	sunu	wudu
	G.	dæges	hirdes	gæstes	suna	wudu, wudes
	D.	dæge	hirde	gæste	suna	wudu, wude
	A.	dæg	hirde	gæst	sunu	wudu
	I.	dæg-ê	hirdê	gæstê		
Pl. ...	N.	daga	hirdas	gastas (gistas)	suna	wudas
	G.	daga	hirda	gasta (gista)	suna	wuda
	D.	dagum	hirdum	gastum (gistum)	sunum	wudum
	A.	dagas	hirdas	gastas (gistas)	suna	wudas

GOTHIC.

Sing. ...	N.	dags	hairdeis	gasts	sunus
	G.	dagis	hairdeis	gastis	sunaus
	D.	daga	hairdja	gasta	sunau
	A.	dag	hairdi	gast	sunu
Pl. ...	N.	dagôs	hairdjôs	gasteis	sunjus
	G.	dagê	hairdjê	gastê	suniwê
	D.	dagam	hairdjam	gastim	sunum
	A.	dagans	hairdjans	gastins	sununs

[1] These are arranged according to their *original* stem-endings, in -*a*, -*i*, -*u*; *dæg* (orig. stem, *daga*), *gast* (orig. stem, *gasti*), *sunu*, &c.

2. Feminine.

gifu, gift ; *dǣd*, deed ; *hand* ; *duru*, door.

		a Stem.	*i* Stem.	*u* Stem.
Sing.	...	N. gifu	dǣd	hand	duru
		G. gife	dǣde	handa	(dure)
		D. gife	dǣde	handa	dura, duru
		A. gife	dǣd(e)	hand	duru
		I. gife	dǣde		
Pl.	...	N. gifa	dǣda	handa	
		G. gifa, gifena	dǣda	handa	
		D. gifum	dǣdum	handum	
		A. gifa	dǣda	handa	

GOTHIC.

Sing.	...	N. giba	dêds	handus
		G. gibôs	dêdais	handaus
		D. gibai	dêdai	handau
		A. giba	dêd	handu
Pl.	...	N. gibôs	dêdeis	handjus
		G. gibô	dêde	handiwe
		D. gibôm	dêdim	handum
		A. gibôs	dêdins	handuns

3. Neuter.

word ; *fæt*, vat ; *cynn*, kin ; no *-u* stems.

		a Stem.	*i* Stem.	
Sing.	...	N. word	fæt	cynn
		G. wordes	fætes	cynnes
		D. worde	fæte	cynne
		A. worde	fæt	cynn
		I. wordê	fætê	
Pl.	...	N. word	fatu	cynn
		G. worda	fata	cynna
		D. wordam	fatum	cynnum
		A. word	fatu	cynn

GOTHIC.

Sing	...	N. waurd	kuni
		G. waurdis	kunjis
		D. waurda	kunja
		A. waurd	kuni
Pl.	...	N. waurda	kunja
		G. waurdê	kunjê
		D. waurdam	kunjam
		A. waurda	kunja

(B.) Consonant Stems.

(1) -N Stems.

		Masc.	Fem.	Neut.
Sing	...	N. hana	tunge	eáge
		G. hanan	tungan	eágan
		D. hanan	tungan	eágan
		A. hanan	tungan	eáge
Pl.	...	N. hanan	tungan	eágan
		G. hanena	tungena	eágena
		D. hanum	tungum	eágum
		A. hanan	tungan	eágan

GOTHIC.

Sing	...	N. hana	tuggô	hairtô (= heart)
		G. hanins	tuggôns	hairtins
		D. hanin	tuggôn	hairtin
		A. hanan	tuggôn	hairtô
Pl.	...	N. hanans	tuggôns	hairtôna
		G. hananê	tuggônô	hairtanê
		D. hanam	tuggôm	hairtam
		A. hanans	tuggôns	hairtôna

(2) -R Stems.

Sing.		Pl.	
N. fæder	brôðor	fæderas	brôðru
G. fæder, fæderes	brêðer	fædera	brôðra
D. fæder, fædere	brôðer	fæderum	brôðrum
A. fæder	brôðor	fæderas	brôðru

GOTHIC.

Sing.	Pl.
N. fadar	fadrjus
G. fadrs	fadrê
D. fardr	fadrum
A. fadar	fadruns

Plurals formed by Vowel Change.

(1) *-i* stems, fem. :—

Béc, books, *byrig*, boroughs, *lýs*, lice, *mýs*, mice, *tyrf*, turfs, *gês*, geese.

(2) *-u* stems, masc. :—

Fêt, feet, *têð*, teeth, *men*.

This vowel change occurs also in the dative singular and acc. plural.

SECOND PERIOD.

I. Vowel Declension.

In the Second period of the language traces of the original vowel-stems disappear, and substantives once belonging to this class are declined according to gender. In the following table the case-suffixes are given for comparison with the older forms:—

		Masc.	Fem.	Neut.
Sing.	N.	—	—	—
	G.	-es	-e	-es
	D.	-e	-e	-e
	A.	—	-e (-en)	—
Pl.	N.	-es	-e, -en (-es)	-es
	G.	-e, -en, -ene (-es)	-e, en, -ene (-es)	-e, -en, -ene (-es)
	D.	-en, -e (-es)	-en, -e (-es)	-en, -e (-es)
	A.	-es	-e, -en (-es)	-es

(1) *Gen. sing. fem.*—Some few feminine substantives form their genitives (like masc. and neuters) in *-es* instead of *-e*.

(2) *Nom. plural fem.*—The suffix *-es* begins to replace *-e*, *-en*, as *dedes, mihtes, sinnes*, &c.

(3) *Nom. plural neuter.*—Many neuters, originally having no suffix in the plural, now take *-es*, as *londes, huses, wordes, workes, thinges*, though the original uninflected forms are frequently met with as late as the middle of the fourteenth century.

Deer, sheep, horse, &c., as in modern English, remain without inflexion.

Many substantives originally forming the plural in *-u*, have *-e* or *-en* (and sometimes *-es*), as *richen, riche* (kingdoms), *trewe, trewen* (trees), &c.

(4) *Gen. plural.*—The old suffix *-a* is now represented by *-e*, *-en*; and also by *-ene* (the gen. plural of *n* declension).

(5) *Dat. plural.*—The old suffix *-um* has become *-en* and *-e*, and occasionally *-es*.

(6) *Plurals formed by vowel change:*—*fēt* (*fæt*), *men*, &c.; *bēc* (*bæc*) is occasionally found side by side with *bokes*.

II. -N Declension.

		Masc.	Fem.	Neut.
Sing.	N.	-e	-e	-e
	G.	-en, -e (-es)	-en, -e (-es)	-en, -e (-es)
	D.	-en, -e	-en, -e	-en, -e
	A.	-en, -e	-en, -e	-e
Pl.	N.	-en, -e (-es)	-en, -e (-es)	-en, -e (-es)
	G.	-ene (-en)	-ene (-en)	-ene (-en)
	D.	-en, -e	-en, -e	-en, -e
	A.	-en, -e (-es)	-en, -e (-es)	-en, -e (-es)

In the gen. plural *-enen* sometimes occurs for *-ene*.

III. -R Declension.

(1) *Brother, moder, dohter, suster*, have no inflexion in the genitive singular. *Fader* and *faderes* (gen. sing.) are found in writers of this period.

(2) The *nom. plurals* are in *-e*, *-en*, or *-es*, as *brethre, brothre, sustre, dohtre*, &c.; *brethren, brothren, dohtren, dehtren, sustren*, &c.; *faderes, brothres, dohtres, sostres*, &c.

(3) The *gen. plural -ene* (*-enne*) sometimes disappears altogether. "*His dohter namen*" = the names of his daughters (Laʒamon).

(4) The *dat. plural* ends in *-en*, *-e* (and sometimes *-es*).

In the *Ormulum -es* occurs as the genitive singular of substantives of all genders.

The *nom. plural* is ordinarily *-es*, and even *deor* (deer) makes plural *deoress*.

The *gen. plural* ends mostly in *-es;* rarely in *-e*, as "*aller kinge king*" = king of all kings.

THIRD PERIOD.

1. Formation of the Plural.

(1) *-es* (*-is*, *-ys*), without distinction of gender.

(2) Very many plurals in *-en*, *-n*, are still preserved, representing (*a*) old plurals in *-an* of the *n* declension, (*b*) plurals originally ending in *-a*, *-u* :—(*a*) *chirchen* (churches); *eʒen, eien* (eyes); *ben* (bees);

FORMATION OF THE PLURAL.

fon (foes); *oxen*, &c.; (*b*) *honden* (hands), *sinnen* (sins), *develen* (devils), *heveden* (heads), *modren* (mothers), *sostren* (sisters), *broþren*, *ken* (kin), &c.

Plurals in *e* are not rare, as *blostme* (blossoms), *dede* (deeds), *mile* (miles), *childre* (and *childer*), *breþre* (*breþer*), &c.

(3) Many words have no plural inflexion, as *hus, hous, hors, schep, deer, pound, her* (hair); but *horses, pouudes,* and *haires* occur in this period.

(4) *Plurals formed by vowel change:*—*fet, teþ, ges, ky, hend* (hands).

2. CASE ENDINGS.

(1) Case-endings are reduced to two, genitive and dative.

(2) The *gen. sing.* for the most part ends in -*es* (-*is*, -*ys*); it is not always added to feminine substantives, as "the *quene* fader" (Robt. of Gloucester, l. 610); "the *empresse* sone" (Ib. l. 9708).

(3) The *gen. plural* ends in -*es*, and sometimes in -*ene* (-*en*),[1] as *clerkene*, of clerks, *monkene*, of monks (Robt. of Gloucester).

(4) The *dative sing.* is often denoted by a final -*e*: nom. *god*, dat. *gode*.

There are frequent traces of it, however, in the Kentish *Ayenbite* (1340).

(5) The *dative plural* is mostly like the nom. plural.

FOURTH PERIOD.

1. FORMATION OF THE PLURAL.

(1) The plural suffix is -*es* (-*is*, -*ys*, -*us*).
In Romance words -*s*, -*z*, occurs for -*es*, &c.

(2) Plurals in -*en* are (*a*) *ashen, been* (bees), *eyen, hosen, oxen,*[2] *pesen*,[3] *shoon, ton* (toes), belonging to *n* declension; (*b*) *sustren, daughtren, brethren* (*r* declension); (*c*) *children, calveren, eyren* (eggs), *lambren*[4] (with *r* inserted before *en*), originally forming plural in -*u;* *kin, ken, kien* for *cy, ky, deȝter* (daughters).

---

[1] This suffix is unknown in the Northern dialect.
[2] *Oxis* occurs in Wickliffe, Luc. xvii. 7.
[3] *Peses* occurs in Piers Plowman.
[4] *Calues, egges,* and *lambes* are also met with.

(3) Some neuter plurals have no *s*, as ʒeer, hęer (hair), *hors, hous, scheep, pownde, swyn, thing.*

(4) After numerals the plural inflexion is often dropped.

(5) *Plurals with vowel change:—fet, gees, lys, mys, mees, men,* &c.

2. Case Endings.

(1) The *gen. sing.* ends in *-es* (*-is, -ys*), *-s.*

(2) The *gen. plural* terminates in *-es.*

(3) The old *genitive plural* suffix *-ene* is still met with, as *childrene, clerkene, kyngene* (Piers Plowman).[1]

ADJECTIVES.

FIRST PERIOD.

1. Strong (or Indefinite) Declension.

		Masc.	Fem.	Neut.
Sing.	...	N. blind	blind [2]	blind
		G. blindes	blindre	blindes
		D. blindum	blindre	blindum
		A. blindne	blinde	blind
		I. blind-ê	—	blindê
Pl.	...	N. blind-e	blinde	blindu
		G. blind-ra	blindra	blindra
		D. blind-um	blindum	blindum
		A. blind-e	blinde	blindu

GOTHIC.

		Masc.	Fem.	Neut.
Sing.	...	N. blinds	blinda	blind(ata)
		G. blindis	blindaizôs	blindis
		D. blindamma	blindai	blindamma
		A. blindana	blinda	blind(ata)
Pl.	...	N. blindai	blindôs	blinda
		G. blindaizê	blindaizô	blindaizê
		D. blindaim	blindaim	blindaim
		A. blindans	blindôs	blinda

---

[1] Very rarely used by Chaucer. [2] Original form, *blindu.*

2. WEAK (or DEFINITE) DECLENSION.

		MASC.	FEM.	NEUT.
Sing.	...	N. blinda	blinde	blinde
		G. blindan	blindan	blindan
		D. blindan	blindan	blindan
		A. blindan	blindan	blinde

MASC., FEM., and NEUT.

Pl.	...	N. blindan
		G. blindena
		D. blindum
		A. blindan

GOTHIC.

		MASC.	FEM.	NEUT.
Sing.	...	N. blinda	blindô	blindô
		G. blindins	blindôns	blindins
		D. blindin	blindôn	blindin
		A. blindan	blindôn	blindô
Pl.	...	N. blindans	blindôns	blindôna
		G. blindanê	blindôno	blindanê
		D. blindam	blindôm	blindam
		A. blindans	blindôns	blindôna

SECOND PERIOD.

1. STRONG DECLENSION.

		MASC.	FEM.	NEUT.
Sing.	...	N. blind	blind	blind
		G. blindes	blindre (blinde)	blindes
		D. blinde	blindre (blinde)	blinde
		A. blindne	blinde	blind

Pl. of all gend.	N. blinde
	G. blindere (blinde)
	D. blinden (blinde)
	A. blinde

2. In the *weak* or *definite declension -an* becomes (1) *-en*, (2) *-e*. All cases of the sing. are often denoted by the final *e*.
The plural ends in *-en* or *-e*.
In the *Ormulum* all the older inflexions of both declensions are represented by *e*.

THIRD PERIOD.

In the Third period the older adjectival inflexions are represented by a final -*e*, and even this sometimes is dropped.

In Robert of Gloucester and the *Ayenbite* we sometimes find the accusative in -*ne* of the strong declension. In the *Ayenbite* we find dative plural in -*en*, in indefinites like *one*, *other*.

The plural of adjectives (mostly of Romance origin) sometimes terminates in -*es*, especially when the adjective follows the noun, as *wateres principales*. Robert of Gloucester has "foure *godes* sones," "the *godes* kny3tes."

FOURTH PERIOD.

A final *e* marks (*a*) the plural, (*b*) the definite form, of the adjective.

Plurals in *s* are common, as in the previous period.

PRONOUNS.

I. Personal Pronouns.

FIRST PERIOD.

		FIRST PERSON.	SECOND PERSON.
Sing.	...	N. Ic	þu
		G. min	þin
		D. me	þe
		A. mec, me	þec, þe
Pl.	...	N. we	ge
		G. ûser, ûre	eower
		D. ûs	eow
		A. ûs, ûsic	eow, eowic
Dual	...	N. wit	git
		G. uncer	incer
		D. unc	incer
		A. uncit, unc	incit, inc

GOTHIC.

		FIRST PERSON.	SECOND PERSON.
Sing.	...	N. ik	jut
		G. meina	theina
		D. mis	thus
		A. mik	thuk

PERSONAL PRONOUNS.

Pl.	N.	weis	jus
	G.	unsara	izwara
	D.	unsis	izwis
	A.	unsis	iswis
Dual	N.	wit	jut
	G.	ugkara (= unkara)	igkwara
	D.	ugkis	igkwis
	A.	ugkis	igkwis

		SECOND PERIOD.	THIRD PERIOD.	FOURTH PERIOD.
Sing.	N.	Ich, ic, ihc	ich, ik, I	ich, ik, I
	G.	min	—	—
	D.	me	me	me
	A.	me	me	me
Pl.	N.	we	we	we
	G.	ure	ure	—
	D.	us, ous	us, ous	us
	A.	us, ous	us, ous	us
Dual	N.	wit	—	
	G.	unker	—	
	D.	unc, unk	—	
	A.	unc	—	

		SECOND PERIOD.	THIRD PERIOD.	FOURTH PERIOD.
Sing.	N.	þu, þou	þu, þou	þou
	G.	þin	—	—
	D./A.	þe	þe	þe
Pl.	N.	ȝe	ȝe, yhe, ye	ȝe, ye
	G.	eoure, eur, ewr, ȝure	—	—
	D.	eow, ew	ȝou, yhou, ou	you, ȝow, yow
	A.	ow, ȝuw, ȝeow		
Dual	N.	ȝit	—	
	G.	inker, ȝunker	unker	
	D./A.	inc, gunc		

The dual is found as late as 1280, as in *Havelok the Dane*.

The older genitives *min*, *thin*, as early as Laȝamon's time began to be employed only as possessive adjectives; *ure, eowre, eouer, ȝure*, are mostly formed with indefinite pronouns, as *ure ech* = each of us, *ȝure nan* = none of us; but the partitive form *ech of us* is also in use at this period.

For other changes see Pronouns (Personal).

II. Pronouns of the Third Person.

First Period.

		Masc.	Fem.	Neut.
Sing.	...	N. he	heo	hit
		G. his	hire	his
		D. him	hire	him
		A. hine	hi	hit
Pl. (of all genders)		N. hi (hig)		
		G. hira (heora)		
		D. him (heom)		
		A. hi (hig)		

Gothic has no *hi* stem.

			Second Period.	Third Period.	Fourth Period.
Masc.	...	N.	He, ha	He, ha, a	He, a
		G.	His	His	His
		D.	Him	Him	Him
		A.	Hine, hin, him	Him (hine)	Him
Fem.	...	N.	Hi, heo, hie, he, ȝe, 3eo, 3ho, scæⁱ	Heo, hi, sco,¹ sche, zy, sge	Hue, heo, ho, sche, scho
		G.	Hire, heore, here	Hire	Hire (hir)
		D.	Hire, heore, here	Hire	Hire (hir)
		A.	Hi, heo, hie, hire (his, hes, es)	Hi (his, is), hire	Hire
Neut.	...	N.	Hit (it)	Hit (it)	Hit (it)
		G.	His	His²	His, hit
		D.	Him	Him	Him (it)
		A.	Hit (it)	Hit (it)	Hit (it)
Pl	...	N.	Hi, heo, hie, he,³ ha, þeȝȝ, þei, þai	Hi, hii, heo, hue, he, thei, thai	hii,⁴ þei, þai, tha (hii), a
		G.	Hire, heore, here, theȝȝre	Heore, here, her, hir, hare, þair	here, her, hir, thair, thar
		D.	Heom, hem, ham, þeȝȝm	Heom, hem, ham, þam, hom	hem, tham, hom
		A.	Hi, heo, hie, heom, ȝam (his, hes)	Hi, hii, hem (hise, is), þam, hom	hem, tham, þem

(1) In the Third period the gen. plural is used with indefinite pronouns, as *here non* (none of them), *here eyther* (each of them), &c.

---

¹ *Scæ* occurs in Saxon Chronicle (Stephen); *sco, scha* is a Northern form; *sch* a Midland variety of it; and *ho* is West Midland.
² Mostly used adjectively.
³ *Hie* and *he* are East Midland forms; *hue*, Southern (used by Trevisa).
⁴ Rare.

(2) The accusatives (singular and plural) begin in the Second period to be replaced by dative forms, but the old accusative (*hine*) is found in the *Ayenbite* (1340), and is still in use in the South of England under the form *-en*.

(3) The Northern dialect (and those with Northern peculiarities) replace the plural of the stem *hi* by the plural of the definite article.

(4) In the South of England *a = he* is still preserved. In Lancashire *ho* is used for *she*.

III. Reflexive Pronouns.

(1) In the First period *silf* (self) was declined as an adjective along with personal pronouns, as—
N. *Ic silfa;* G. *min silfes;* D. *me silfum;* A. *mec* (*me*) *silfne*, &c.

(2) Sometimes the *dative* of the personal pronoun was added to the *nom.* of *silf*, as *ic me silf; thu the silf; he him silf; we us silfe; ge eów silfe; hi him silfe*.

(3) *Silf* also stands with a substantive, as *God silf* = God himself.

(4) With a demonstrative, *silf* was declined according to the weak or definite declension, as *se silfa* = the same.

(5) In the Second period (as in La3.) the genitive shows a tendency to replace the dative, as *mi silf* for *me silf*, but it is not common; and in all other cases the old form is preserved.

In the Third and Fourth periods *mi self, thi self, our self*, &c. become more frequently used : Wickliffe has instances of the older forms, as *we us silf, 3e 3ou self*, as well as of *we our self, 3e 3oure self. His self* occurs in Northern English of the Third period.

(6) *Self* is sometimes lengthened to *selven* in the thirteenth and fourteenth centuries, as *I miselven, he him selven* (Chaucer).

IV. Adjective Pronouns.

(1) The possessives in the First period are—*min* (my), *thin* (thy), *his* (his, its), *hire* (her), *ûre* (our), *eower* (your), *hira, heora* (their), *uncer* (our two), *incer* (your two).

Sin is found in poetry as a reflective possessive of the third person.

(2) In the Second period the possessives are—First person, *min* (sing.), *unker* (dual), *ure* (plural). Second person, *thin* (sing.), *inker*, *ȝunker* (dual), *eowre*, *eoure*, *ȝure* (plural). Third person, *his*, *hire* (sing.), *hire*, *here*, *heore*, *theȝȝre* (plural).

Min is thus declined :—

		FIRST PERIOD.		SECOND PERIOD.	
		MASC.	FEM.	MASC.	FEM.
Sing.	N.	min	min	min, mi	mine, min, mi
	G.	mines	minra	mines, min	mire, mine, min, mi
	D.	minum	minre	mine, min, mi	mire, mine, min, mi
	A.	minne	mine	minne, mine, min, ini	mine, min, mi
Pl.	N.	mine		mine, min, mi	
	G.	minra		mire, mine	
	D.	minum		minnen, mine, min	
	A.	mine		mine	

Thin is similarly declined.

Ure is declined as follows in the First period :—

		MASC.	FEM.	NEUT.
Sing.	N.	ûser, ûre	ûser, ûre	ûser, ûre
	G.	ûseres, ûsses, ûres	ûserre, ûsse, ûrre	same as masc.
	D.	ûserum, ûssum, ûrum	ûserre, ûsse, ûrre	,,
	A.	ûserne, ûrne	ûsere, ûsse, ûre	ûser, ûre
Pl.	N.	ûsere, ûsse, ûre	—	ûser, ûre, &c.
	G.	ûsera, ûssa, ûre	—	same as masc.
	D.	ûserum, ûssum, ûrum	—	,,
	A.	ûsere, ûsse, ûre	—	ûser, ûre

In the Second period we sometimes find *ure* and *eower* (*ȝure*) inflected like adjectives of the strong declension, as " *Ures formes faderes* gult" = the guilt of our first father (Moral Ode).

(*a*) As *mine* and *thine* are the plurals of *min* and *thin*, so in the Second and Third periods *hise* is the plural of *his*.

(*b*) *Hire* (her) is generally uninflected. Laȝamon has plural *hires*, as " *hires* leores " = her cheeks.

(*c*) In the *Ormulum* we find genitive *theȝȝres*, as " till eȝȝþerr þeȝȝres herrte " = to the hearts of them both.

(3) In the Third period the dual forms disappear, and the possessives are—*min*, *thin*, *his*, *hire*, *our*, *oure*, *ȝoure*, *here*, *thair*; absolute

possessives—*oures, urs; ʒoures, yhoures; thaires, thairs*, as well as *oure, ure; ʒoure, here*.

The plurals *mine, thine, hise*, &c. are in use.

(4) In the Fourth period we find plural *hise;* and *oures, youres, heres, hores* (theirs), are more commonly used than in the Third period.

V. Demonstrative Pronouns.

First Period.

		Masc.	Fem.	Neut.
Sing.	... N.	se (þe¹)	seo (þeo, thiu¹)	þæt
	G.	þæs	þǽre	same as masc.
	D.	þam, þæm	þǽre	,,
	A.	þane, þone	þâ	þæt ,,
	I.	þŷ, þê	þâ	same as masc.
Pl. (of all genders)	N.	þâ		
	G.	þâra, þǽra		
	D.	þâm, þǽm		
	A.	þâ		

GOTHIC.

		Masc.	Fem.	Neut.
Sing.	... N.	sa	sô	thata
	G.	this	thizôs	as masc.
	D.	thamma	thizai	,,
	A.	thana	thô	thata
	I.	thê		
Pl.	... N.	thai	thôs	thô
	G.	thizê	thizô	as masc.
	D.	thaim	thaim	,,
	A.	thans	thôs	thô

In the SECOND PERIOD we find *se* replaced by *the;* and often all inflexions are dropped, so that we get an uninflected *the* as in modern English.

MASCULINE.

Singular.	N.	þe, þa
	G.	þæs, þas, þes, þeos, þis, þe
	D.	þan, þon, þane, þone, þonne, þeonne, þen, þa, þe
	A.	þene, þane, þæne, þene, þanne, þone, þon, þe
	I.	þe

---

¹ Old Northern forms.

The old Kentish dialect of the thirteenth century is more archaic than other Southern dialects, and has *se* (m.), *si* (fem.), *thet, that* (n.).

"Nu lordinges þis is þe miracle þet þet godspel of te dai us telþ. ac great is þe tokningge. *Se* leprus signefieþ þo senuulle men. *si* lepre þo sennen. þet scab bitokned þo litle sennen, *si* lepre betokned þo grete sennen þet biedh diadliche."

"This is *si* glorius miracle."
"This is *si* significance of the miracle."
"þo seide þe lord to his sergant."
"Of þo holi gost; in þa time."[1]

FEMININE.

Singular.	N.	þeo, þa, þie, þe, þo
	G.	þare, þære, þere, þer, þe
	D.	þare, þære, þere, þe
	A.	þa, þeo, þe, þo

NEUTER.

Singular.	N. and A.	þat, þæt, þet, þe
	G. and D.	as masculine
Plural.	N.	þa, þo, þaie, þe
	G.	þare, þere, þer
	D.	þan, þon, þen, þane, þæn, þeon, þa, þe
	A.	þaie, þo, þe

In the *Ormulum* and other Midland writers the gender of *that* is forgotten, and it is used as a demonstrative pronoun as at present.

In the THIRD PERIOD the article is for the most part flexionless in the singular : though Southern writers, as Robert of Gloucester, Dan Michel (in *Ayenbite*), &c., preserve some of the older forms, as acc. masc. *tha-ne, the-n.*

"Zucche yeares drieuþ *þane* dyevel uram þe herte as þet weter cachcheþ *þane* bond out of þe kechene."—*Ayenbite*, p. 171.[2]

The Kentish of 1340 also preserves the fem. *þo*.

The fem. gen. and dat. *thare* (*ther*) is employed by Shoreham, as "*thare* saule galle" = the gall of the soul (Shoreham's Poems, p. 92); "one *thare* crybbe" (Ib. p. 157).

The old dative *-n* (O.E. *-m*) is preserved in such expressions as "for *the* nonce" (O.E. *for than anes*) : cp. O.E *atten ende* = at then ende (Robt. of Gloucester); "*atter* spousynge" (Shoreham, p. 57); *atter* = *at ther* = at the (fem.).

---

[1] See *Kentish Sermons*, in O.E. Miscellany (ed. Morris).   [2] *herte* is fem.

The plural forms in the THIRD PERIOD are þo, þeo, þa,[1] þai,[1] which are also used for the plural of *that:* e.g. of þo, of þa, to þo = of those, to those.

In the FOURTH PERIOD the plural þo is still in use; but the singular is uninflected.

That, plural *tho* (= those), are demonstratives.

Skelton uses *tho* = those : " Alle *tho* that were on my partye."

þes, þeos, þis, this.

FIRST PERIOD.

		M.	F.	N.
Singular.	N.	þes	þeos	þis
	G.	þises	þisse	þises
	D.	þisum	þisse	þisum
	A.	þisne	þâs	þis
Plural.	N.	þâs		
	G.	þissa		
	D.	þisum		
	A.	þâs		

In the SECOND PERIOD we find the following forms :—

		M.	F.	N.
Sing.	N.	þes, þis	þas, þeos, þis, þos	þis
	G.	þisses, þisse, þis	þissere, þisse	as masc.
	D.	þissene, þissen, þisse	þissere, þisse	,,
	A.	þesne, þisne	þas, þæs	þis

Plural. N. and A. þas, þeos, þos, þes, þese, þis, þise
G. þissere, þisse
D. þissen, þisse, þeos

In the *Ormulum*, *this* has no inflexions except plural *þise*.

In the THIRD PERIOD *this* is flexionless in the singular;[2] we find in the plural *thes*, *this*, *thise*, *these*.

In the *Ayenbite* we find in the singular nom. masc. *this*, acc. masc. *therne* (= *thesne*), acc. fem. *thise*, dat. *thisen*, *thise*.

Shoreham has dat. sing. and pl. *thyssere*.[3]

In the FOURTH PERIOD we have sing. *this*, pl. *thise*, *this*, *thes*, *these*.

---

[1] Northern forms.
[2] We find sometimes *thisne* acc. sing. in some Southern writers.
[3] Trevisa, 1357, has nom. masc. þes, fem. þeos (þues), pl. þeos, þues.

In the Northern dialects we find *ther, thir*, the plural of the Old Norse definite article, used for *these*[1] :—

> " Alle mans lyfe casten may be
> Princip lly in this partes thre,
> That er *thir* to our understandyng,
> Bygynnyng, midward, and endyng.
> *Ther* thre parties er thre spaces talde
> Of the lyf of ilk man yhung and alde."
> HAMPOLE, *P. of C.*

It is used by James I. in his *Essayes in Poesie* (ed. Arber, p. 70) :

" *Thir* are thy workes."

VI. Interrogative Pronouns.

FIRST PERIOD.

Hwa, who.

		MASC. AND FEM.	NEUT.
Singular.	N.	hwa	hwæt
	G.	hwæs	hwæs
	D.	hwam, hwæm	hwæm
	A.	hwone, hwæne	hwæt
	I.	hwî	hwî

GOTHIC.

	MASC.	FEM.	NEUT.
N.	hwas	hwo	hwa
G.	hwis	hwizos	as masc.
D.	hwamma	hwizai	,,
A.	hwana	hwo	hwa
I.	hwe	hwe	hwe

In the SECOND PERIOD we find the following forms :—

		MASC. AND FEM.	NEUT.
Singular.	N.	hwa, whæ, wa, wha, wo	hwat, hwet, what, whæt
	G.	hwas, whes, was, whas	as masc.
	D.	hwam, whan	,,
	A.	hwan, wan, hwam, whan, wham	hwat, whæt, &c. wham

In the *Ormulum* we find *what* used irrespective of gender, as *what* man, *what* thing, &c.

---

[1] In the O.N. pl. *their* (masc.), *thær* (fem.), *thau* (neut.) ; *r* = *s* (sign of plural).

In the THIRD PERIOD the dative replaces the old accusative.

		MASC. AND FEM.	NEUT.
Singular.	N.	wha, who, huo, wo, ho, quo	what, wat, huet, quat
	G.	whas, whos, wos, quas	as masc.
	D.	whom, wham, wom, quam	,,
	A.	whom, wham, won, whan, wan, quam	what, huet

What is used as an adjective without inflexions.

In the FOURTH PERIOD, N. *who, what;* G. *whos, whoos, whose;* A. *whom, what.*

Hwæðer, whether, which of two.

FIRST PERIOD.

		M.	F.	N.
Singular.	N.	hwæðer	hwæðeru	hwæðer
	G.	hwæðeres	hwæðerre	as masc.
	D.	hwæðerum	hwæðerre	,,
	A.	hwæðerne	hwæðere	hwæðer

		M. AND F.	N.
Plural.	N.	hwæðerre	hwæðeru
	G.	hwæðerra	—
	D.	hwæðerum	—
	A.	hwæðere	hwæðeru

Hwilc is declined like the strong declension of adjectives.

SECOND PERIOD.

In Laȝamon we find in Text A:—

		M.	F.
Singular.	N.	whilc, whulc	whulche
	G.	whulches	whulchere
	D.	whulche	whulchere
	A.	whulcne	whulche
Plural.	N.	whulche, &c.	

In Text B we have *woch* (oblique cases *woche*).

In the *Ormulum* we have Sing. N. *whillc*, G. *whillkes*, Plur. N. *whillke*.

In the THIRD PERIOD this pronoun is flexionless; the pl. often has the final e^1:—*whylc, whilch, whilk, wich, wuch, woch, huich;* pl. *whilche, whiche, huiche*.

In the FOURTH PERIOD *the* is joined to *which*, as *the which* (relative).

VII. Relative Pronouns.

FIRST PERIOD.

(1) Se (masc.), seo, sio (fem.), thæt (neut.).

"Caron *se* hæfde eac þrio heafdu and *se* wæs swiðe oreald."—BOETHIUS.
"He hæfde an swiðe ænlice wif *sio* wæs haten Eurydice."—*Ib.*
"Þa næfde he nâ scipa þonne ân *þæt* wæs þeah þre-reþre."—*Ib.*
"*Se* þurhwunað óð ende *se* byð hál."—*Matt.* x. 26.

(2) þe with *se, seo, þæt,* as *se-þe, seo-þe, þæt-þe* (*þæt-te*).

"Is for-þi ân Fæder *se þe* æfre is Fæder."—ÆLFRIC, *De Fide Catholica.*

(3) þe (indeclinable).

"Gesælig bið se mon *þe* mæg geseon."—BOETHIUS.
"Ælc þâra *þe* yfele deð, hatað þæt leoht."—*John* iii. 20.

(4) Se þe . . . se.

"*Se þe* bryd hæfð, *se* is brydguma."—*John* iii. 9.

(5) þe with personal pronouns, as *þe ic* (*ic þe*), *þu þe,* &c.

"Ic eom Gabrihel *ic þe* stand beforan Gode."—*Luke* i. 19.
"Fæder ure, *þu þe* eart on heofonum."—*Matt.* vi. 9.

(6) þe . . . he = who, þe . . . his = whose, þe . . . him = whom.

"*Þe he* sylfa astah ofer sunnan up."—*Ps.* lxvii. 4.
"Þæt næs nâ eôwres þances, ac þurh God *þe* ic þurh *his* willan hider asend wæs."—*Gen.* xlv. 8.

In the SECOND PERIOD we find—

(1) indeclinable þe. (2) *that, thet,* with antecedents of all genders. (3) *þe þe, þeo þe* (= *se þe, seo þe*). Cp.

---

[1] The *Ayenbite* has dative plural in *-en,* as *huichen.*

(1) "Eft *se* þe dælð ælmyssan for his drihtnes lufon *se* behyt his goldhord," &c. —*O.E. Hom.* p. 300.

(2) "Eft þe þe deleð elmessen for his drihtnes luuan : þe behut his goldhord." —*Ib.* p. 109.[1]

(3) þe þe is further changed to þe þat and *he þat* (*he þet*). Cp.

"Se þe[2] aihte wil holde."—*Moral Ode*, l. 55, in *O.E. Hom.* Second Series.
"þe þet," &c.—*Ib.* in *O.E. Hom.* First Series.
"Se þe her doð ani god."—*Ib.* l. 53, in *O.E. Hom.* Second Series.
"þe þe," &c.—*Ib.* in *O.E. Hom.* First Series.
"He þat, &c."—*Ib.* in *O.E. Miscellany*, latter part of thirteenth century.

þe þe is not found in Laȝamon's *Brut*.

In the *Ancren Riwle* þe . . . þet = þe þe . . . þe :

"þe is federleas þet haueð . . . vorlore þene Veder of heouene."
"þeo deð also þeo is betere þen ich am."

That as a relative replaced—(1) the indeclinable þe ; (2) þe in þe þe (*se* þe), &c.

(1) First period—
"On anre dune þe is gehaten Synáy."—ÆLFRIC.

Second period—
"Uppon ane dune þat is þe mont of Synai."—*O.E. Hom.* First Series, p. 86.

(2) First period—
"Swa sceal se láreow dón *se* ðe bið," &c.—ÆLFRIC.

Second period—
"Alswa scal þe larðeu don þe þet bið," &c.—*O.E. Hom.* p. 95

(3) First period—
"An (tyd) is *seo* ðe wæs buten æ."—ÆLFRIC.

Second period—
"On is þet wes buten e."—*O.E. Hom.* p. 89.

In the *Ormulum*, þat replaces þe . . . þe, þe, &c. The pl. þa þat= those that.

---

[1] Extract (1) is from the English of the First period, (2) of the Second period (about 1150).
[2] *Se* þe is borrowed from a version of the First period.

In Chaucer we find *that* . . . *he* = who; *that* . . . *his* = whose; *that* . . . *him* = whom.

> "A worthy man,
> *That* from the tyme that he first began
> To ryden out, *he* lovede chyvalrye."—*Prol.* ll. 43-45.

> "Al were they sore hurte and namely oon
> *That* with a spere was thirled *his* brest boon."
> *Knightes Tale*, ll. 1843-44.

> "I saugh today a corps yborn to chirche,
> *That* now on Monday last I saugh *him* wirche."
> *Milleres Tale.*

For other forms see RELATIVE PRONOUNS.

VIII. Indefinite Pronouns.

(1) **An** (one, a) is declined according to the strong declension.

FIRST PERIOD.

		M.	F.	N.
Singular.	N.	ân	ân	ân
	G.	ânes	ânre	ânes
	D.	ânum	ânre	ânum
	A.	ânne, ænne	âne	ân
	I.	ânê	ânrê	ânê
Plural (of all genders).	N.	âne		
	G.	ânra		
	D.	ânum		
	A.	âne		
	I.	ânum		

In the Second period we find—

		M.	F.	N.
Singular.	N.	an, on, a	an, on, a	an, a
	G.	anes, ænnes, ones	ære, are, ore	as masc.
	D.	ane, anne	are, one	,,
	A.	ænne, enne	ane, æne	an, a

In the Third and subsequent periods it is uninflected.[1]

---

[1] In the *Ayenbite, enne* acc. of *one, ane* acc. masc. and fem. of *an, a;* so *onen* = *anum,* dat. sing. = to *one* (used subst.): see *Ayenbite,* p. 175.

(2) Nán (= ne + an), no, is declined in the same way.
In the Second and Third periods it is for the most part uninflected. In Southern writers we find gen. sing., as *nones kunnes*, of no kind. The *Ayenbite* has acc. *nenne*, dat. *nonen*.

(3) Sum (a, certain, some) is declined in the First period according to the strong declension of adjectives.

In Laȝamon (Second period) we have the following forms:—

		M.	F.
Singular.	N.	sum	sum
	G.	summes	sumere
	D.	summe	sumere
	A.	sumne	sum
Plural.	N. and A.	summe	
	D.	summen	

In the *Ormulum* we find—

N. *sum.* G. *sumess.* Pl. *sume*

In the Third and Fourth periods we find *sum, som, some;* Pl. *sume, summe, some,* used mostly in its modern acceptation.

(4) Man (Ger. *man*), one, is used in the First period only in the nom. In the Second and subsequent periods we find *mon, man,* and *me*[1] used with a verb in the singular.

Traces of this *me* are found in Elizabethan literature:—

" Stop *me* his dice you[2] are a villaine " (LODGE); *i.e.* let any *one* stop his dice, &c.

(5) Ænig (any), negative nǽnig, was declined according to the strong declension.

In the Second period the *g* falls away. The following forms are used by Laȝamon:—Sing. N. *æni, æi, ai, ei;* Gen. *æies, æi;* Dat. *æi;* Acc. *æine, æie.* Pl. *æi.*

In the subsequent periods we find *ani, any, ony, eny,* with Pl. *enie, anie,* &c.

(6) Oðer, one of two, the first or the second.

" Lamech nam twa wif, *oðer* wæs genemned Ada and *oðer* Sella."—*Gen.* iv. 19.

" Sōðlice *oðer* is se Fæder, *oðer* is se sunu."—ÆLFRIC, *De Fide Catholica.*

---

[1] This form is looked upon as a shortened form of *men.*
[2] *You* is used as an indefinite pronoun, cp. " as *you* may say."

In the Second period we find *an oþerr, ani3 oþerr, nan oþerr, sum oþerr*—(*Ormulum*).

In the Third period—*that an, that oon, the ton, the toon* = the one, the first; *that other, thet other* = the other, the second. We also find *thother* = the other.

The pl. of *oðer* is *oðre*. In the Third and Fourth periods we find —*ðre* and *oðer*. In the *Ayenbite* we find pl. *oðren*.

(7) **Wha** (any one) and **whæt** (aught).

"And gif *hwa* to inc *hwæt* cwyð."—*Matt.* xi. 3.

See other examples in INDEFINITE PRONOUNS.

We have also compounds, as *swylces hwæt, hwæt lytles* (in *Ormulum, kittless whatt*), *elles hwæt*.

In the Second period *summwhatt* (*Orm.*) makes its appearance.

(8) **Hwylc** (any one).

"Gif eow *hwylc* segð."—*Mic.* xiii. 21.

Cp. "Þai fande iii crossis; an was þat ilke. Bot wiste þai no3t *quilk* was *quilk*, þe quilk muþt þe þeuis be."—*Legends of Holy Rood*, p. 113.

(9) In all periods *such* is an indefinite pronoun :—

"Be *swilcum*, and be *swilcum* þu miht ongitan," &c. (BOETHIUS) = By such and such thou mayest perceive, &c.
"Whi art thou *swich* and *swich* that thou darst passe the lawe."—*Pilgrimage*, p. 78.

(10) Even *that* becomes an indefinite pronoun :—

"*Swich* a time thou didest thus, *swich* a sonedai, *swich* a moneday thanne thou didest *that* and thanne *that*."—*Pilgrimage*.

Cp.
"Had it been
Rapier or *that* and poniard . . .
. . . I had been then your man."—*A Cure for a Cuckold.*

(11) In "Hakluyt's Voyages" (1589) we find *he* used indefinitely—he . . . he = *one . . . other:* "After comes *hee* and *hee*." Cp. Chaucer's use of *he* in *Knightes Tale*, ll. 1756—1761 :

"*He* rolleth under foot as doth a balle.
He foyneth on his feet with a tronchoun,
And *he* him hurtleth with his hors adoun,
He thurgh the body is hurt, and siththen take,
Maugre *his* heed, and brought unto the stake;
Another lad is on that other side."

IX. Compounds.

(1) Of hwa :—*ge-hwa*, each, every ; *ǽg-hwa* (= *á-ge-hwá*), every ; *elles hwa* (Lat. *ali-quis*), any ; *swá-hwá-swá*, whoso, whosoever ; *hwæt-hwugu* (= *hwigu-húgu*), anything.

In the subsequent periods, *swá-hwá-swá* becomes (1) *hwa-swa*, *hwa-se*, (2) *whoso, whose*.

(2) Of hwæðer :—*á-hwæðer*, anyone ; *áwðer, áðor, áðer* (= *a-ge-hwaðer*), *ǽghwæðer, ægðer, ègðer*, other, either ; *ge-hwæðer*, either ; *n-á-hwaðer, náwðer, nowðer, noðer*, neither.[1]

Later forms are *owwþer, eyþer, ouþer, oþer* = either ; *nouþer, nowwþer, noþer* = neither.

(3) Of hwilc :—*ge-whilc*, anybody ; *æghwilc*, whoever ; *hwilchúgu*, anyone, anything ; *swá-hwilc-swá*, whosoever.
In the Second period we find *ge-hwilc* softened down to *ihwilc*.

(4) Ælc (= *á-ge-líc*), each, all, was declined like *hwilc*.

In the Second period we have the following forms :—

		M.	F.
Singular.	N.	ælc, ech	ælc, ech
	G.	ælches, alches, eches	alchere, elchere
	D.	elchen, alche, eche	alchere, elchere
	A.	ælcne, alcne, echne	elche, eche

We also find *ælcan* = each one, which is uninflected.

In the subsequent periods we find *ilk, ech, uch, ilka, uch a, ech a, ych a.* In the *Ayenbite* we find *echen*, after the prepositions *of, to, in*.

Æuer-ælc (every) was inflected like *ælc*, and in the Third period we find—
   " *Evereches* owe name."—*St. Brandan*, p. 3.

In the *Ayenbite* we find Sing. Acc. *evrinne*, Dat. *evrichen*.

---

[1] From these forms we get *either, other, or, nor*.

CONJUGATION OF WEAK VERBS.

First Period.

PRESENT INDICATIVE.		PRESENT SUBJUNCTIVE.	
Sing.	Pl.	Sing.	Pl.
(1) nerie [1]	neriað	nerie	nerien
sealfie [2]	sealfiað	sealfie	sealfien
nerest	neriað	nerie	nerien
sealfast	sealfiað	sealfie	sealfien
(2) nereð	neriað	nerie	nerien
sealfiað	sealfiað	sealfie	sealfien

INDICATIVE PERFECT.		SUBJUNCTIVE PERFECT.	
Sing.	Pl.	Sing.	Pl.
(1) nerede	neredon	nerede	nereden
sealfode	sealfodon	sealfode	sealfoden
(2) neredest	neredon	nerede	nereden
sealfodest	sealfodon	sealfode	sealfoden
(3) neredede	neredon	neredes	nereden
sealfode	sealfodon	sealfode	sealfoden

IMPERATIVE MOOD.		INFIN.	DAT. INF.
Sing.	Pl.	nerian	to nerienne
(2) nere	neriað	sealfian	to sealfianne
sealfa	sealfiað		

PRES. P.	PASS. P.
neriende	nered
sealfiende	sealfod

GOTHIC.

INDICATIVE PRESENT.		SUBJUNCTIVE PRESENT.	
Sing.	Pl.	Sing.	Pl.
(1) nasja	nasjam	nasjau	nasjai-ma
salbô	salbôm	salbô	salbôma
(2) nasjis	nasjiþ	nasjais	nasjaiþ
salbôs	salbôþ	salbôs	salbôþ
(3) nasjiþ	nasjand	nasjai	nasjaina
salbôþ	salbônd	salbô	salbôna

---

[1] To save. [2] To salve.

STRONG VERBS.

	INDICATIVE PERFECT.		SUBJUNCTIVE PERFECT.	
	SING.	PL.	SING.	PL.
(1)	nasida	nasidêdum	nasidêdjau	nasidêdeima
	salbôda	salbôdêdum	salbôdêdjau	salbôdêdeima
(2)	nasidês	nasidêduþ	nasidêdeis	nasidêdeiþ
	salbôdes	salbôdêduþ	salbôdêdeis	salbôdêdciþ
(3)	nasida	nasidêdum	nasidêdi	nasidêdeina
	salbôda	salbôdêdum	salbôdêdi	salbôdêdeina

	IMPERATIVE.		INFIN.
	SING	PL.	nasjan
(2)	nasei	nasjiþ	salbôn
	salbô	salbôþ	

PRES. P.	PASS. P.
nasjands	nasiþs
salbônds	salbôþs

CONJUGATION OF STRONG VERBS.

FIRST PERIOD.

ACTIVE VOICE.

Niman, to take.

PRES. INF.	PERF.	PL.	P. P.
niman	nam	nâmon	numen

INDICATIVE MOOD.		SUBJUNCTIVE.	

Present (and Future) Tense.

	SING.	PL.	SING.	PL.
(1)	Ic nime	we nimað	Ic nime	we nimen
(2)	þu nimest	ge nimað	þu nime	ge nimen
(3)	he nimeð	hi nimað	he nime	hi nimen

Perfect.

	Sing.	Pl.	Sing.	Pl.
(1)	Ic nam	we nâmon	Ic nâme	we nâmen
(2)	þu nâme	ge nâmon	þu nâme	ge nâmen
(3)	he nam	hi nâmon	he nâme	hi nâmen

INFINITIVE.

	IMPERATIVE.	Simple.	Dative.
(2)	nim nimað	niman	to nimanne

	PRES. P.	PASS. P.
	nimende	numen

GOTHIC.

INDICATIVE PRESENT.   SUBJUNCTIVE PRESENT.

	Sing.	Pl.		Sing.	Pl.
(1)	nima	nimam	(1)	nimâu	nimâi-ma
(2)	nimis	nimiþ	(2)	nimâis	nimâiþ
(3)	nimiþ	nimand	(3)	nimâi	nimâi-na

INDICATIVE PERFECT.   SUBJUNCTIVE PERFECT.

	Sing.	Pl.		Sing.	Pl.
(1)	nam	nêmum	(1)	nêm-jau	nêmeima
(2)	namt	nêmuþ	(2)	nêmjeis	nêmeiþ
(3)	nam	nêmun	(3)	nêmi	nêmeina

	IMPERATIVE.		INFIN.	DAT. INFIN.
	Sing.	Pl.	niman	—
(2)	nim	nimiþ		

	PRES. P.	PASS. P.
	nimand-s	nimiþs

First Period.

(1) Many strong verbs have change of vowel in the second and third persons sing. pres. indic.

(1)	cume (come)	creope (creep)	bace (bake)	feallan (fall)
(2)	cymst	crypst	becst	felst
(3)	cymð	crypð	becð	felð

(2) Some lose their connecting vowel and assimilate the suffix of the second and third persons singular pres. indic. to the root,[1] as :—

(1) ete (eat)   binde (bind)   slea (slay)
(2) ytst   binst   slehst (slyhst)
(3) yt   bint   slehð (slyhð)

(3) Strong verbs have the same vowel-change in the second person perfect indicative as in the plural, as *ïc fand* (found), *þu funde* (= foundest), pl. we *fundon*, &c.

CLASSIFICATION OF STRONG VERBS.
DIVISION I. *Class I.*

	PRES. *a, ea.*	PERF. *eó, é.*	PASS. P. *a, ea.*	
(1)	fealle	feóll	feallen	fall
	wealle	weóll	weallen	well
	fealde	feóld	fealden	fold
	healde (halde)	heóld	healden	hold
	stealde	steóld	stealden	possess
	wealde	weóld	wealden	wield
	banne	bên (beón)	bannen	order
	spanne	spên (speón)	spannen	span
	fange (fó)	fêng	fangen	take, catch
	gange	gêng (geóng)	gangen	go
	hange	hêng	hangen	hang
	PRES. *â.*	PERF. *eó, é.*	P.P. *â.*	
(2)	swâpe	sweóp	swâpen	sweep
	ge-nâpe	geneóp	genâpen	whelm
	for-swâfe	forsweóf	forswâfen	drive
	blâwe	bleów	blâwen	blow
	cnâwe	cneów	cnâwen	know
	crâwe	creów	crâwen	crow
	mâwe	meów	mâwen	mow
	sâwe	seów	sâwen	sow
	þrâwe	þreów	þrâwen	thrown
	wâwe	weów	wâwen	blow
	blâte	blêt (bleót)	blâten	pale
	hâte	hêt (hêht)	hâten	order
	hnâte	hneót (hnêt)	hnâten	knock
	scâde	scêd (sciod, sceod)	scâden	shed, divide
	lâce	leólc (lêc)	lâcen	leap
	PRES. *eâ.*	PERF. *eó.*	P.P. *eá.*	
(3)	heâfe	heóf	heâfen	weep
	hleâpe	hleóp	hleâpen	leap
	â-h-neâpe	a-hneóp	ahneâpen	sever
	heâwe	heów	heâwen	hew
	beâte	beót	beâten	beat
	breâte	breót	breâten	break
	gesceâte	gesceót	gesceâten	fall to
	deâge	deóg	deâgen	dye

[1] Weak verbs are also subject to this assimilation.

	PRES. ǽ.	PERF. eó, é.	P.P. ǽ.	
(4)	slǽpe grǽte lǽte on-drǽde rǽde	slêp grêt leôrt (leôt, lêt) -dreôrd (-drêd) reôrd (rêd, rǽd)	slǽpen grǽten lǽten -drǽden rǽden	sleep greet let dread counsel

	PRES. ó.	PERF. eó, é.	P.P. ó.	
(5)	hrôwe hwôpe blôwe flôwe grôwe hlôwe rôwe swôwe blôte swôge	hreôw hweôp bleôw fleôw greôw hleôw reôw sweôw (swêg) bleôt sweôh (sweôg)	hrôwen hwôpen blôwen flôwen grôwen hlôwen rôwen swôwen blôten swôgen	cry whoop blow flow grow low row speed sacrifice sough

	PRES. é.	PERF. eó.	P.P. é.	
(6)	hrêpe wêpe	hreôp weôp	hrêpen wêpen	cry weep

Geóng was replaced by a weak form *eode* (*eade*) from a root *i*, tr. go.[1]
A weak form *gengde* is also met with.
Slêpde occurs for *slêp* in the Northern dialect.

SECOND PERIOD.

PRES.	PERF.	P.P.	
falle, ualle	ueol, feol, fol, fel	iuallen, iueollen[1]	fall
halde (holde)	heold, held, hæld, huld	ihalden, iholden	hold
falde (folde)	feold	ifolden	fold
walde (welde)	wald, weld	awald	wield
walke	weolk, welk	iwalken	walk
fo (fange)	feng	ifon, ifongen	take
ga (go, gange)	—	igan, igon, gangen	go
hange	heong, heng	hongen, hon	hang
hate (hote)	hahte, hehte, het	ihæten, ihote, ihaten	order
lake	læc	—	leap
blawe (blowe, blæwe)	bleou, bleu, blew, blou	iblowen	blow
cnawe (cnowe)	cneow, cnew, kneu	icnawen	know
sawe (sowe)	seow, sow	isowen, isawen	sow
mawe (mowe)	meow, mew	imowen	mow
þrawe (þrowe)	þreou, þreu	ithrowen	throw
slæpe (slepe)	slæp, sleap	islepen	sleep

[1] The Southern dialects retain the prefix *i* or *y* before the p.p., and frequently drop the final -*n*. The Northern dialects drop the prefixal *i*, but seldom lose the *n*.

STRONG VERBS.

Pres.	Perf.	P.P.	
læpe (lepe)	leop, lep, leup, leoup, lup	ileopen, ileapen	leap
læte (lete)	let	ileten, ilæten	let
wepe (weope)	weop, wep	iwepen	wep
hewe	heow, hew	iheawen, ihéouwen, hæwen	hew
bete	beot, bet	ibeaten, ibæten	beat
rowe	rew, reu	irowen	row
growe	greu, greow	igrowen	grow

Some few perfects have become weak, as :—

læte (lete)	lette (lætte, leatte)[1]	—	let
lepe	leopt[1]	—	leap
slepe	sleapte (slapte)[2]	—	sleep
drede	dredde[3]	adrad[1]	dread
shæde	shadde[3]	shadd[3]	shed

Third Period.

Pres.	Perf.	P.P.	
falle	vil, fel, fil, ful	yfalle, yfallen, yvalle, fallen	fall
halde (holde)	held, hield, huld	yholde, iholden	hold
fange (fo, fonge)	afong, afeng, aveng, avong, veng	yfonge, ifongen, ivongen	take
hange (honge)	heng	yhonge	hang
go	—	ygo, gon, gan	go
hote	het, hight	yhote	call, name
blowe (blawe)	blew	yblowe, yblowen	blow
knowe (knawe)	knew, kneu	yknowen, knawen	know
sow	seu, sew	sowen	sow
þrowe	þrew, þreu	iþrowen	thrown
slepe	slep, sleep, sleop, slup	—	sleep
bete	byet, bet	byeten, ibeten	beat
lete (late)	let	ilate, laten	let
drede	dred	—	dread
lepe	lep, hliep, hlip	—	leap
wepe	wep	—	weep
hewe	hew	ihewen	hew
rowe	rew, row	—	row
growe	grew, greu	igrowen	grow

The following weak forms are to be met with :—

idrad (p.p.), *dradde* (perf.), and *fanged* (perf. and p.p.), *hatte* (p.p.), *shadde* (perf.), *shad* (p.p.), *lette* (perf.), *ilet* (p.p.), *wepte*, *weped* (perf.), ȝede and *wende*, *wente* (perf.), *hanged*, *henged* (p.p.).

---

[1] In Laȝamon. [2] In Laȝamon and *Ormulum*. [3] Iu *Ormutum*.

FOURTH PERIOD.

PRES.	PERF.	P.P.	
falle	fel, ful	fallen	fall
holde	held, huld	holden	hold
walk	welk	—	walk
under-fong	-feng	-fongen	undertake
honge, hange	heng, heeng	hongen	hang
gon, goon, goo, go	—	goon, gon, ygo	go
hote	hight	hoten	call, name
blowe	blew	blowen	blow
knowe	knew	knowen	know
crowe	crew, creew	crowen	crow
growe	grew	growen	grow
sowe	sew, seew	sowen	sow
throw	threw	throwen	throw
slepe	slep, sleep	slepen	sleep
lepe	leep, lep	lopen	leap
lete, late	let, leet	leten	let
hewe	hew, heew	hewen	hew
bete	bet, beet	beten	beat
wepe	wep, weep	wepen, wopen	weep

(1) The following weak forms make their appearance:—

weeldide (p.p. *weeldid*), *walked* (perf. and p.p.), *underfonged* (perf.), *hangide, hongede* (perf.), *hanged, honged* (p.p.), *swepide* (perf.), *isweped* (p.p.), *knowide* (perf.), *sowide* (perf.), *sowid* (p.p.), *leppide, lepte* (perf.), *growed* (perf.), *leppid, lept* (p.p.), *slepte* (perf.), *slept* (p.p.), *dredde, dradde* (perf.), *adred, adrad* (p.p.).

(2) *Held, heng,* are sometimes used for the p.p.

(3) A mute final *e* is often found in the perfect, as *blewe, crewe, leete,* &c.

DIVISION II. Class I.

FIRST PERIOD.

PRES. *e, i.*	PERF. *a (ea, æ).*	PL. *u.*	P.P. *u, o.*	
(1) belle	beall	bullon	bollen	bellow
swelle	sweal (sweoll)	swullon	swollen	swell
helpe	healp	hulpon	holpen	help
delfe	dealf	dulfon	dolfen	delve
melte	mealt	multon	molten	melt
swelte	swealt	swulton	swolten	die
be-telde	teald	tuldon	tolden	cover up
melce	mealc	mulcon	molcen	milk
belge	bealh (bealg)	bulgon	bolgen	be wroth
felge	fealh (fealg)	fulgon	folgen	go into

STRONG VERBS.

PRES. *e, i.*	PERF. *a(ea,æ)*	PL. *u.*	P.P. *u, o.*	
swelge	swealh (swealg)	swulgon	swolgen, swelgen	swallow
gille	geal	gullon	gollen	yell
gilpe	gealp	gulpon	golpen	boast
gilde	geald	guldon	golden	pay

(*a*)
hlimme	hlam	hlummon	hlummen	sound
grimme	gram	grummon	grummen	rage
swimme	swam	swummon	swummen	swim
climbe	clamb, clom	clumbon	clumben	climb
gelimpe	gelamp	gelumpon	gelumpen	happen
gerimpe	geramp	gerumpon	gerumpen	rumple
on-ginne	-gan	-gunnon	gunnen	begin
linne	lan	lunnon	lunnen	cease
rinne(eorne)	ran	runnon	runnen	run
sinne	san	sunnon	sunnen	think
spinne	span	spunnon	spunnen	spin
winne	wan	wunnon	wunnen	fight (win)
stinte	stant	stunton	stunten	stint
þrinte	þrant	þrunton	þrunten	swell
binde	band	bundon	bunden	bind
finde	fand	fundon	funden	find
grinde	grand	grundon	grunden	grind
hrinde	hrand	hrundon	hrunden	push
swinde	swand	swundon	swunden	pine (swoon)
þinde	þand	þundon	þunden	swell
winde	wand	wundon	wunden	wind
crince	cranc	cruncon	cruncen	yield
â-cwince	-cwanc	-cwuncon	-cwuncen	go out (quench)
drince	dranc	druncon	druncen	drink
for-scrince	-scranc	-scruncon	-scruncen	shrink
since	sanc	suncon	suncen	sink
stince	stanc	stuncon	stuncen	stink
swince	swanc	swuncon	swuncen	toil
bringe	brang	brungon	brungen	bring
clinge	clang	clungon	clungen	cling (wither)
cringe	crang	crungon	crungen	cringe, fall
gefringe	-frang	-frungon	-frungen	ask
geonge	gang	gungon	—	go
singe	sang	sungon	sungen	sing
springe	sprang	sprungon	sprungen	spring
stinge	stang	stungon	stungen	sting
swinge	swang	swungon	swungen	swing, beat
geþinge	geþang	geþungon	geþungen	grow
þringe	þrang	þrungon	þrungen	throng
þwinge	þwang	þwungon	þwungen	constrain
wringe	wrang	wrungon	wrungen	wring

PRES. *eo.*	PERF. *ea.*	PL. *u.*	P.P. *o.*	

(3)
georre	gear	gurron	gorren	whirr
meorne	mearn	murnon	mornen	mourn
speorne	spearn	spurnon	spornen	spurn
weorpe	wearp	wurpon	worpen	warp, throw
ceorfe	cearf	curfon	corfen	carve, cut
deorfe	dearf	durfon	dorfen	suffer

ENGLISH ACCIDENCE.

	Pres. *eo.*	Perf. *ea.*	Pl. *u.*	P.p. *o.*	
	hweorfe	hwearf	hwurfon	hworfen	return
	steorfe	stearf	sturfon	storfen	starve, die
	sweorfe	swearf	swurfon	sworfen	cleanse
	weorþe	wearþ	wurdon	worden	become
	sweorce	swearc	swurcon	sworcen	grow faint
	beorge	bearh	burgon	borgen	guard
	feohte	feaht	fuhton	fohten	fight

	Pres. *e.*	Perf. *ea* (*æ*).	Pl. *u.*	P.p. *o.*	
(4)	berste	bearst	burston	borsten	burst
	þersce	þærsc	þurscon	þorscen	thresh
	gefregne	gefrægn	gefrugnon	gefrugnen	ask
	bregde	brægd	brugdon	brogden	braid
	stregde	strægd	strugdon	strogden	strow, sprinkle

SECOND PERIOD.

Pres.	Perf.	Pl.	P.p.	
swelle	swal, swol	swolzen	swollen	swell
ʒelpe	ʒealp, ʒalp	ʒulpen	ʒolpen	yelp
ʒelle	ʒal	ʒullen	ʒollen	yell
helpe	halp, help	holpen	holpen	help
delve	dalf, dolf, delf	dulfen, dulven	dolfen, dolven	delve
ʒelde	ʒeald, ʒald	ʒulden, ʒolden	ʒolden	yield
swelte	swalt	swulten	swolten	swelter, die
belge	balg, bælh, belh, balh	bulʒen	bolʒen, bolwen	be angry, swell
swelʒe	swealh	swolʒen	—	swallow
swimme	swam, swom	swummen	swommen	swim
(bi)-limpe	-lomp, -lamp	-lumpen, -lompen	-lumpen	happen
climbe	clamb, clomb	clumben	clumben	climb
b-linne	blan	blunnen	blunnen	cease
(be)-ginne (a)-ginne	-gan, -gon	-gunnen	-gunnen	begin
(i)-winne	-wan, -won	-wunnen	-wunnen	win
rinne (irne, corne, erne)	ran, ron (orn, arn)	urnen	runnen	run
beorne, berne, brinne	born	burnen	—	burn
binde	band, bond	bunden	bunden	bind
finde	fand, fond, vond	funden	funden	find
grinde	grand, grond	grunden	grunden	grind
swinde	swond	—	—	—
winde	wand, wond	wunden	wunden	wind
winche, swinke	swanc, swonc	swunken	swunken	toil
drinke (drinche)	dranc, dronc	drunken	drunken	drink
stinke	stanc, stonc	stunken	stunken	stink
singe	sang, song	sungen	sungen	sing

STRONG VERBS.

Pres.	Perf.	Pl.	P.P.	
springe	sprang, sprong	sprungen	sprungen	spring
swinge	swang, swong	swungen	swungen	swing
ringe	rang, rong	rungen	rungen	ring
clinge	clang, clong	clungen	clungen	cling
stinge	stang, stong	stungen	stungen	sting
þringe	þrang, þrong	þrungen	þrungen	throng
{ weorpe, worpe, werpe	warp, worp, werp	wurpen	worpen	warp
sterfe	starf, sterf	sturven	storven	die
kerfe	carf, cærf, kerf	curven	corven	cut
wurþe (worþe)	warþ	wurþen	wurþen, worþen	become
breste, berste	brast, barst, borst	brusten, bursten	brosten, borsten, brusten, bursten	burst
þresce	þrash	þrushen	þroshen	thresh
swærce	—	swurken	—	grow faint
fehte	faht, feaht, fogt, feht	fuhten	fohten, fogten	fight
berge	barh, barg	burȝen	borȝen, borwen	protect
{ brede, abrede	braid (breid) abred	bruiden —	— abroden }	braid

(1) Southern English dialects have *o* for the Northern *a* in the perfect, as *fond = fand; stonc = stanc*, &c.

(2) A few verbs have become weak in Laȝamon, as—

mornede (perf.), *murned* (p.p.); *freinede* (perf.), *freined* (p.p.); *barnde* (perf.); *derfde* (perf.), *derved* (p.p.); *clemde* (perf.); *ringede* (perf.). *Fraȝȝnedd* (p.p.) occurs in the *Ormulum*.

THIRD PERIOD.

Pres.	Perf.	Pl.	P.P.	
helpe	help, halp, heolp	holpen	holpen [1]	help
yelpe	yalp	—	yolpen	boast
delve	dalf	dolven	dolven	delve
melte	malt, molt	molten	molten	melt
ȝelde	ȝald, ȝold, ȝeld	ȝolden	ȝolden, yolden	yield
swelȝe	swal	—	—	swell
climb	clam	clomben	clomben	climb
swimme	swam, swom	—	—	swim
ginne	gan, gon	gonnen	gonnen, gunnen	begin
winne	wan, won	wonnen	wonnen	win
rinne, renne	ran, ron	ronnen	ronnen, runnen	run

[1] *n* often dropped in Southern dialects. The Northern dialects prefer *n* in the pl. and p.p.

Pres.	Perf.	Pl.	P.p.	
irne	orn, arn, yarn	—	y-yerne	run
linne, b-linne	blan, lan	blonnen	blonnen	lease
binde	band, bond	bonden, bounden	bonden, bounden, bunden	bind
finde	fand, fond, vond	fonden, founden	fonden, funden, founden	find
winde	wond, wand	wonden	wonden	wind
drinke	drank, dronk	drunken	dronken, drunken	drink
sinke	sank, sonk	sunken, sonken	sonken	sink
stinke	stank, stonk	stonken	stonken	stink
swinke	swank	swonken	swonken	toil
singe	sang, song, zang, zong	songen	zongen, songen, sungen	sing
slinge	slong, slang	slongen	slongen	sling
þringe	þrang, þrong	þrongen	þrungen	throng
springe	sprang, sprong	sprongen	sprongen	spring
ringe	rong, rang	rongen	rongen, rungen	ring
wringe	wrang, wrong	wrongen	wrongen	wring
stinge	stang, stong	stongen	stongen, stungen	sting
swinge	swong, swang	swongen	swungen	swing
kerve	carf, kerf	corven	corven	carve
sterve	starf	storven	storven	starve
werpe	warp	—	worpen	warp
berste, breste	brast, barst, borst	borsten	borsten, bursten	burst
ber3e	bor3	—	bor3en	protect
brede	braid (to-bred)	—	—	braid
worþe	werþ, worþ	worþen	—	become
fi3te	fo3t, faght, vo3t	fo3ten	fo3ten, foughten	fight

Weak perfects replace strong ones, as :—

Clemde (Early Eng. Poems); *swelled* (Tristram); *swalte* (Ayenbite); *swel3ed* (Psalter); *arnde* (Rob t. of Gl.); *helped* is a p.p. in Psalter; *melted; slenget* (Havelok).

Fourth Period.

Pres.	Perf.	Pl.	P.p.	
swelle	swall	swollen	swollen	swell
helpe	halp, holp	holpen	holpen	help
delve	dalf	dolven	dolven, delven	delve
melte	malt, molt	molten	molten	melt
swelte	swelt	—	—	die
3elde, 3eelde	3ald, 3o., 3eld	3olden, 3elden	3olden	yield
swimme	swam, swom	swommen	swommen	swim
climbe	clamb, clomb	clomben, clamben	clomben	climb
biginne	(bi)gan	(bi)gonnen, (bi)gunnen	(bi)gunnen, (bi)gonnen	begin
spinne	span	sponnen	sponnen	spin

STRONG VERBS.

Pres.	Perf.	Pl.	P.p.	
winne	wan, won	wonnen	wonnen	win
renne	ran, ron	ronnen, runnen	runnen, ronnen	run
stinte	—	—	stenten	stint (stop)
binde	bond, boond, bound, band	bounden	bounden	bind
findɔ	fond, foond	founden	founden	found
grinde	grond, grand	grounden	grounden	grind
winde	wond	wounden	wounden	wind
sinke	sank, sonk	sonken	sonken, sunken	sink
drinke	drank, dronk	dronken	drunken	drink
swinke	swank	swonken	swonken	toil
stinke	stank, stonk	stonken	stonken	stink
shrinke	shrank	shronken	shronken	shrink
ringe	rang, rong	rongen	rongen, rungen	ring
singe	sang, soong, song	songen	songen, sungen	sing
singe	stong	stongen	stongen, stungen	sting
springe	sprang, sprong, sproong	sprongen	sprongen, sprungen	spring
thinge	throng	throngen, thrungen	throngen	throng
wringe	wrong, wrang	wrongen	wrongen	wring
kerv	karf	korven	korven	carve
sterv	starf	storven	storven	starve
worth	worth	—	worthen	become
breste	brast, brost, brest, barst, borst	brosten, barsten, borsten	brosten, borsten	burst
threshe	thrasch	throshen	throshen	thresh
breide	(to-)brayd	—	—	braid
fi3te	fa3t, fau3t	fo3ten, fou3tᴇn	fou3ten	fight

(1) Weak perfects—*helpede, delvide, meltide, 3eldide, kervyde, renned, threschide* (Wickliffe), *swymmed* (Allit. Poems).

(2) Weak p.p.—*helped, melted, threshed, bray3ede* (Wickliffe).

Division II. Class II.

First Period.

Pres.	Perf. æ, a.	P.p. u, o.	
1) cwele	cwæl[1]	cwolen	kill
ge-dwe	-dwæl	-dwolen	err
hele	hæl	holen	hide, cover
hwele	hwæl	hwolen	sound
stele	stæl	stolen	st...
swele	swæl	swolen	sw...l
(2) nime	nam (nom)	numen	steal, take
cwime, me	cwam (cwom, com)	cumen	come

[1] Pl. *wælon*. All verbs of this class have a long vowel in plural.

ENGLISH ACCIDENCE. [APP.

	Pres.	Perf.	P.P.	
(3)	bere	bær	boren	bear
	scere	scær	scoren	shear
	tere	tær	toren	tear
	ge-þwere	-þwær	-þworen	weld
	sprece	spræc	sprecen	speak
	brece	bræc	brocen	break

Second Period.

	Pres.	Perf.	P.P.	
(1)	stele	stal (stalen, pl.)	stolen	steal
(2)	nime	nam, nom, næm (nomen, nemen, pl.)	numen, nomen	steal
	come, cume	com (comen, pl.)	cumen, comen	come
(3)	bere	bær, bar, bor, beer (pl. beren, bæren)	boren	bear
	soere, schære	scar, schær	scoren	shear
	tere	tar (toren, pl.)	toren	tear
(4)	break	brac, bræc, breac, brec (brocen, braken, pl.)	broken	break
	speke, spæke	spac, spæc, spec (pl. spæken, speken)	speken, spoken	speak

Weak perfect—*helede* (Laȝamon).

Third Period.

	Pres.	Perf.	P.P.	
(1)	hele, hile	hal	holen	hide
	stele	stel, stal	stolen	steal
(2)	nime	nom, nam	nomen, numen	steal
	come	com, cam	comen, cumen	come
(3)	bere	ber, bar, bor	boren	bear
	schere	scher, schar, schor	schoren, schorn	shear
	tere	tar	toren	tear
(4)	breke	brac, brek	broken	break
	speke	spac, spec	spoken	speak

Fourth Period.

Pres.	Perf.	P.P.	
stele	stal, staal, stol, stel	stolen	steal
nime	nam, nom, nem	nomen	take, tal
come, cume	cam, com	comen, cumen	come
bere	bar, baar, beer, bor (bare)	boren, born	bear

STRONG VERBS.

Pres.	Perf.	P.P.	
schere	schar	schoren	shear
tere (teere)	tar (tare)	toren, torn	tear
breke, breeke	brak (brake), breek	broken	break
speke	spak (spake), spek	spoken	speak

Weak perfects—*hilede* and *terede* (Wickliffe).

Division II. Class III.

First Period.

Pres. *e.*	Perf. *æ* (pl. *ǽ*).	P.P. *a, i.*	
drepe	dræp	drepen	strike, kill
swefe	swæf	swefen	sleep
wefe	wæf	wefen	weave
ete	æt	eten	eat
frete	fræt	freten	eat up
mete	mæt	meten	mete, measure
cnede	cnæd	cneden	knead
trede	træd	treden	tread
cweþe	cwæþ	cweþen	quoth
lese	læs	lesen	gather
ge-nese	-næs	-nesen	recover
wese	wæs	wesen	be (was)
wrece	wræc	wrecen	wreak
wege	wæg	wegen	carry
gife	geaf	gifen	give
(for)gite	-geat	-giten	(for)get
on-gite	-geat	-geten	perceive
seohe (seo)	seah (pl. sǽgon, sáwon)	gesen, gesewen	see
fricge	fræg	gefregen	inquire
licge	læg	legen	lie
þicge	þeah, þah (pl. þǽgon)	þegen	take
sitte	sæt	geseten	sit
bidde	bæd	beden	bid

Second Period.

Pres.	Perf.	P.P.	
drepe	drap	dropen	slay
ȝete	æt, et, at, æat	eten	eat
(under)ȝite, (biȝete)	-ȝæt, -gat, -ȝat -ȝet	-ȝeten,-geten,-ȝiten	perceive
(for)frete	fræt	freten	fret
mete	mæt	meten	mete
trede	træd (pl. treden), trad	treden	tread
queþe	cweþ, quæþ, cwaþ (pl. cwæþen, queþen)	queþen	quoth
—	wæs (pl. weren)	—	was
wreke	wræc, wrec	wreken, wroken	wreak

Pres.	Perf.	P.p.	
ȝife	ȝiaf, ȝaf, ȝef	ȝiven, ȝeven	give
lyge	læi, leai, laȝȝ (pl. ȝeven, læȝen)	leien, laien, leȝen	lie
seo, se	sæh, seih, sag, seg, sah (pl. sæȝen, segen)	seȝen, sen, sogen, sowen	see
sitte	sæt (pl. seten), sat, set	seten	sit
bidde	bæd, bed, bad (pl. bæden, beden, boden)	—	bid

Tredded = trodden occurs in *Ormulum*, l. 5728.

Third Period.

Pres.	Perf.	P.p.	
drepe	drap	—	slay
ete	et	eten	eat
frete	fret	freten	fret
ȝete	ȝat, ȝot, ȝet	ȝeten, ȝiten	get
trede	trad	treden, troden	tread
queþe	quoþ, quaþ, quad	—	quoth
wreke	wrak, wrek	wroken	wreak
ȝive	ȝef, ȝaf	ȝiven, ȝoven	give
ligge, lie	lai, lei, leȝ	leyen, liggen	lie
sitte	sat, zet	seten	sit
bidde	bad, bed	beden	bid
se, seye	say, sau, saw, sagh, sauh, sei	seyen, seien, sewen, zoȝen, zeȝen, seen, sain, sen	see

Fourth Period.

Pres.	Perf.	P.p.	
weve	waf?	woven	weave
ete	et, eet	eten	eat
mete	mat, met	meten	mete
ȝete	ȝeet, ȝat, ȝot	ȝetten, ȝoten	get
trede (treede)	trad (trade)	treden, troden	tread
queþe	quod	—	quoth
wreke	wrak, wrek	wroken	wreak
se	saȝ, say, sei, sagh, saw, siȝ, sih, sauh, saugh	seien, seen	see
ȝife, ȝefe, ȝeve	ȝaf, ȝef, yof	ȝiven, ȝeven, yoven	give
sitte	sat (sate)	sitten, seeten, seten	sit
bidde	bad	—	bid
ligge, lie	lay, ley	leyen, leien	lie

Weak forms—*metide* for *mat* or *met*.

STRONG VERBS.

DIVISION II. Class IV.

FIRST PERIOD.

PRES. *a.*	PERF. *ó* (pl. *ó*).	P.P. *a.*	
(1) ale	ól	alen	shine
gale	gól	galen	sing
fare	fór	faren	fare, go
stape	stóp	stapen	step
scape	scóp	scapen	shape
grafe	gróf	grafen	dig
scafe	scóf	scafen	shave
rafe	róf	rafen	rob
hlade	hlód	hladen	load
wade	wód	waden	wade, go
ace	óc	acen	ache
bace	bóc	bacen	bake
sace	sóc	sacen	fight
tace	tóc	tacen	take
wace	wóc	wacen	wake
wasce	wósc	wæscen	wash
drage	dróh	dragen	drag, draw
gnage	gnóh	gnagen	gnaw
(2) sceaðe	scód	sceaðen	scathe
sceace	scóc	scacen	shake
leahe	lóh	leahen, leán	blame
sleahe	slóh	slagen, sleahhen	slay
þweahe	þwóh	þwegen	wash
weaxe	wóx	weaxen	wax
(3) spane	spón	spanen	allure
stande	stón	standen	stand
(4) swerige, swarie	swór	sworen	swear
hebbe (hafie)	hóf	hafen	heave
hleahhe, hlehhe	hlóh	hleahhen	laugh

SECOND PERIOD.

PRES.	PERF.	P.P.	
gulle, ȝelle	goll (pl. gollen, gullen)	ȝolen	sing, yell
fare	for	faren	go, fare
scape	scop	scæpen, scapen	shape
grave	grof	graven	grave
lade	[lod]	laden	lade
wade	wod	waden	go
wasshe	wesh, weosch, weis, wuesch	washen, waschen	wash
bake	bok, book	baken	bake
(for)sake	-soc	-saken	forsake
take	toc	taken	take
ake	oc	—	ache
wakie, wake	woc	waken	wake

Pres.	Perf.	P.P.	
drage, drawe	droh, drouh, drog, drug (pl. drowen)	dra3en, dragen, drawen, drogen	draw
sle	sloh, slæh, slog, slug, slouh (pl. slowen)	slowen, sla3en, sle3en, sleien, slawen, slagen, slain	slay
fle, fla, flo	flo3	vla3en	flay
waxe	weox, wex, wax	waxen, wexen, woxen	wax
stand	stod	standen	stand
swerie	swor	sworen	swear
stepe	stop	stopen	step
hauve, hefe	heaf, hæf, hef, hof, heof	heoven, hofen, hoven	heave
leh3e	loh	lo3en, lowen	laugh

Weak perfects :—*takede* (La3.) = *toc* ; *hefed* = *hof* (O.E. Hom., Second Series); *wakeden* = *woc* (La3. Text B).

Third Period.

Pres.	Perf.	P.P.	
gale	3al, 3ol	—	sing, yell
stonde	stod	standen, stonden	staud
fare	for	faren	fare
swere	swor, swar	sworen, sworn	swear
schape	schop	schapen	shape
wade	'wed	—	go
washe	wesch, wosch	waschen	wash
schake	schok	schaken	shake
ake	ok	(oken)	ache
forsake	forsok	forsaken	forsake
take	tok	taken	take
wake	wok	waken	wake
drawe	drow, drouh, drew	drawen	draw
waxe, wexe	wax, wex	waxen, woxen	wax
sle, sla, slo	slow, slogh, slouh, slou	slawen, slain	slay
fle, fla, flo, fla3e	flogh, flouh, vlea3	flain, flawen	flay
lighe, lawghe, hle3e	low, low3	—	laugh
stepe	step, stap	stopen, stoupen	step
hefe, hebbe	hof	hoven, heven	heave

Fourth Period.

Pres.	Perf.	P.P.	
stonde, stande	stod, stood	stonden, standen	stand
swere, sweere	swer, swor, swoor	sworen	swear
fare	for	faren, foren	go, fare
shape	shop	shapen	shape
stepe	—	stopen, stoupen	step
heue	haf, hef, hof	hoven	heave
grave	(grof)	graven	grave

STRONG VERBS.

Pres.	Perf.	P.P.	
lade	lade	laden	load
schave	schoof	schaven, schoven	shave
wasche	wesch, wosch	waschen	wash
bake	book	baken	bake
schake	schok, schook	schaken	shake
forsake	forsok	forsaken	forsake
take	tok, took	taken	take
wake	wook	waken	wake
ake, aake, ache	ok	—	ache
draw	droȝ, drow, drowh, drew, drouh	drawen	draw
gnaw	gnew, gnow	gnawen	gnaw
laghe, lawe, leyȝe	low, lowȝ, loȝ, lough, loowȝ	laȝen	laugh
sle, slea, sla	sloȝ, slow, slew, slewȝ	slain, slawen, slawn	slay
fle, flo	flouh	flain	flay
wexe, waxe	wox, wax, wex, wæex	woxen, waxen, wexen	wax

(1) Weak perfects :—ȝollide, ȝellide, shapide, stept, hevede, graved, schaved, waschede, bakede, shockide, shakide, wakide, akide, leiȝede, drawede, waxed.

(2) Weak p.p. :—heved, graved, waischid, waked, shapid, awakid.

Division II. Class V.

First Period.

Pres. i.	Perf. a.	Pl. i.	P.P. i.	
cine	cân	cinon	cinen	split
dwine	dwân	dwinon	dwinen	dwindle
gine	gân	ginon	ginen	yawn
hrine	hrân	hrinon	hrinen	touch
hwine	hwân	hwinon	hwinen	whiz
scine	scân	scinon	scinen	shine
gripe	grâp	gripon	gripen	gripe
nipe	nâp	nipon	nipen	darken
ripe	râp	ripon	ripen	reap
to-slipe	-slâp	-slipon	-slipen	dissolve
be-life	-lâf	-lifon	-lifen	remain
clife	clâf	clifon	clifen	cleave
drife	drâf	drifon	drifen	drive
scrife	scrâf	scrifon	scrifen	shrive
slife	slâf	slifon	slifen	split
swife	swâf	swifon	swifen	sweep, turn
spiwe	spâw	spiwon	spiwen	spew
bite	bât	biton	biten	bite
flite	flât	fliton	fliten	flite, strive
hnite	hnât	hniton	hniten	butt
slite	slât	sliton	sliten	slit

ENGLISH ACCIDENCE.

Pres. *t.*	Perf. *á.*	Pl. *i.*	P.p. *i.*	
smite	smât	smiton	smiten	smite
þwite	þwât	þwiton	þwiten	cut off
wite	wât	witon	witen	see, visit, go
wlite	wlât	wliton	wliten	look
write	wrât	writon	writen	write
bide	bâd	bidon	biden	bide
cide	câd	cidon	ciden	chide
glide	glâd	glidon	gliden	glide
gnide	gnâd	gnidon	gniden	rub
hlide	hlâd	hlidon	hliden	cover
ride	râd	ridon	riden	ride
slide	slâd	slidon	sliden	slide
stride	strâd	stridon	striden	stride
wride	wrâd	wridon	wriden	bud
liðe	lâð	lidon	liden	sail
mide	mâð	midon	miden	hide
scriðe	scrâð	scridon	scriden	go
sniðe	snâð	snidon	sniden	slit
wriðe	wrâð	wridon	wriden	writhe, wreathe
wriðe	wrâð	wriðon	wriðen	bud, grow
â-grise	-grâs	-grison	-grisen	dread
â-rise	râs	rison	risen	rise
blice	blâc	blicon	blicen	shine
sice	sâc	sicon	sicen	sigh
snice	snâc	snicon	snicen	sneak
strice	strâc	stricon	stricen	go
swice	swâc	swicon	swicen	deceive
wice	wâc	wicon	wicen	yield
hnige	hnâh	hnigon	hnigen	nod
mige	mâh	migon	migen	water
sige	sâh	sigon	sigen	sink
stige	stâh	stigon	stigen	ascend
wige	wâh	wigon	wigen	fight
lihe	lâh (lâg)	ligon	ligen	lend, give
sihe (seo)	sâh	sigon	sigen	strain
tihe (teo)	tâh (teâh)	tugon (tigon)	tigen, togen	draw, pull
þihe (þeo)	þâh	(þigon) þugon	þogen	grind
wrihe (wreo)	wrâh (wreâh)	wrigon	wrogen, wrigen	cower

Second Period.

Pres.	Perf.	Pl.	P.p.	
chine	chan, chon	—	chinen	split
scine	scæn, son (= shon)	shinen	shinen	shine
rine	ran	—	rinen	touch
gripe	grap, grop, græp	gripen	gripen	gripe
ripe	rop	ripen	ripen	reap
drive	draf, drof, dræf	drifen	driven, drifen	drive
þrife	þraf	þrifen	þrifen	thrive
bite	bat, bot	biten	biten	bite
schrive	schrof	schriven	schriven	shrive
slite	slat	sliten	sliten	slit
strive	strof	striven	striven	strive

STRONG VERBS.

Pres.	Perf.	Pl.	P.p.	
smite	smat, smot, smæt	smiten	smiten	smite
write	wrat, wrot	writen	writen	write
wite	wat	witen	witen	go
wlite	wlæt	—	—	look
a-bide	-bad, -bod	-biden	-biden	abide
stride	strad	—	—	strive
glide	glad, glæd, glod	gliden	gliden	glide
ride	rad, rod, ræd	riden	riden	ride
gnide	gnad	—	gniden	rub
liðe	lað, læð	—	liðen	sail
sniðe	snæð, snað	sniðen	sniðen	cut
scriðe	scrað, scroð	scriðen	scriðen	go
wriðe	wræð	—	wriðen	writhe
a-rise	-ras, -ros, -ræs	-risen	-risen	rise
a-grise	-gras, -gros	—	-grisen	dread
strike	strak	striken	striken	go
swike	swac	swiken	swiken	deceive
siȝe	sah, seh, soh	siȝen	siȝen	sink
stiȝe	steih, steȝ, stah, stæh	stiȝen	stiȝen, stien	ascend
teo	tah, tæh, teh	tuȝen	toȝen, tuhen	accuse
þeo	þæh, þeg, þeah	þiȝen	þoȝen, þowen	grow, thrive
wreo	wreih	wriȝen, wrien	wriȝen, wrien	cover

Weak forms—*liðede, liðde = lað* (La3.); *bilæfde = belaf* (La3.); *bilefed* (p.p. Orm.); *bilefde* (Ancren Riwle); *ȝeonede, ȝenede* (from *geonian, ginian*, to yawn—a weak verb) occurs in *St. Marherete*.

Third Period.

Pres.	Perf.	Pl.	P.p.	
chine	chon, chan	—	chinen	split
schine	schon	schinen	schinen	shine
ripe, repe	[rop]	—	ropen	reap
gripe	grop	gripen	gripen	gripe
drife, drive	draf, drof	driven	driven	drive
schrive	schrof	schriven	schriven	shrive
(to) rive	-rof	-riven	-riven	rive
þrife, thrive	throf	thrifen	thrifen	thrive
bite	bot, bat	biten	biten	bite
flite	flot	—	—	strive
smite	smat, smot	smiten	smiten	smite
write	wrat, wrot	writen	writen	write
abide	abad, abod	abiden	abiden	abide
ride	rad, rod	riden	riden	ride
—	—	—	chidden	chide
gnide	gnad	gniden	gniden	rub
stride	strad, strod	striden	striden	strive
writhe	wroþ	—	wriþen	writhe
rise	ras, ros	risen	risen	rise
agrise	agros	agrisen	agrisen	dread

Pres.	Perf.	Pl.	P.P.	
strice	strek	—	—	go
stiʒe	steʒ, stegh, stey, steaʒ	—	stiʒen	ascend
teo, te	tey	—	toʒen	draw
wre	wreigh	—	wroʒen	cover

(1) Weak perfects—*gripte, griped, schinde, chidde, biswiked, bilifte, belafte, blefede.*

(2) Some singular forms (especially in Northern writers) have a mute *e*, as *smate, bate, abade, abode.*

(3) Northern writers keep *a* (or *o*) in the plural instead of *i*, as *ras = ris(en).*

Fourth Period.

Pres.	Perf.	Pl.	P.P.	
schine	schon, schoon	shinen	shinen	shine
repe	—	—	ropen	reap
dryve	drof, draf	driven	driven	drive
shryve	shrof	shriven	shriven	shrive
stryve	strof, stroof	striven	striven	strive
thrive	throf	thriven	thriven	thrive
byte	bot, boot, bat	biten	biten	bite
flite	flot	—	—	strive
smyte	smot, smoot, smat	smiten	smiten	smite
wryte	wrot, wroot, wrat	writen	writen	write
thwite	—	—	thwiten	cut
bide	bod, bood, bad	biden	biden	bide
chide	—	—	chidden	chide
glide	glod, glood	gliden	gliden	glide
ryde	rod, rood, rad	riden	riden	ride
slyde	slood	sliden	sliden	slide
stride	strad	—	—	stride
wrythe	wrooth	—	writhen, wrethen	writhe
ryse	ros, roos, ras	risen	risen	rise
(a)grise	-gros	—	-grisen	dread
steʒe, stye	stey, steiʒ, stigh	stiʒen	stiʒen	ascend
wrie	—	—	wrien	cover
tee	tigh	—	towen	draw

Weak perfects—*dwynede, agriside, sykide, stiʒed* (Wickliffe); p.p. *dwined* (Chaucer).

In "Alliterative Poems" we find:—*fine*, to cease, with a strong perf. *fon*; and *trine*, to go (of Norse origin), with perf. *tron*.

Division II. Class VI.

First Period.

Pres. *eo* (*û*).	Perf. *eá*.	Pl. *u*.	P.P. *o*.	
creope	creáp	crupon	cropen	creep
dreope	dreáp	drupon	dropen	drop
geope	geáp	gupon	gopen	take up
slûpe	sleáp	slupon	slopen	dissolve
sûpe	seáp	supon	sopen	sup
cleofe	cleáf	clufon	clofen	cleave
deofe, dûfe	deáf	dufon	dofen	dive
sceofe, scûfe	sceáf	scufon	scofen	shove
leofe	leáf	lufon	lofen	love
reofe	reáf	rufon	rofen	reave
breowe	breáw	bruwon	browen	brew
ceowe	ceáw	cuwon	cowen	chew
hreowe	hreáw	hruwon	hrowen	rue
þreowe	þreáw	þruwon	þrowen	throe
breote	breát	bruton	broten	break
fleote	fleát	fluton	floten	float
geote	geát	guton	goten	pour
greote	greát	gruton	groten	greet
hleote	hleát	hluton	hloten	cast lots
hrûte	hreát	hruton	hroten	snore
lûte	leát	luton	loten	lout, bow
neote	neát	nuton	noten	enjoy
reote	reát	ruton	roten	weep, cry
scote	sceát	scuton	scoten	shoot
þeote	þeát	þuton	þoten	howl
á-þreote	-þreát	-þruton	-þroten	loathe, irk
beode	beád	budon	boden	bid
cneode	cneád	cnudon	cnoden	knot
creode	creád	crudon	croden	crowd
leode	leád	ludon	loden	grow
reode	reád	rudon	roden	redden
strûde	streád	strudon	stroden	despoil
á-breoðe	-breáð	-bruðon	-broðen	to make worse
á-hûðe	-heáð	-hudon	-hoden	spoil
hreoðe	hreáð	hrudon	hroden	adorn
seoðe	seáð	sudon	soden	seethe
ceose	ceás	curon	coren	choose
dreose	dreás	druron	droren	mourn
freose	freás	fruron	froren	freeze
be-greose	-greás	-gruron	-groren	frighten
hreose	hreás	hruron	hroren	rush
for-leose	-leás	-luron	-loren	lose
brûce	breác	brucon	brocen	brook, use
lûce	leác	lucon	locen	lock
reoce	reác	rucon	rocen	reek
smeoce	smeác	smucon	smocen	smoke
sûce	seác	sucon	socen	suck
bûge	beáh	bugon	bogen	bow
dreoge	dreáh	drugon	drogen	suffer
fleoge	fleáh	flugon	flogen	fly

Pres. *eo* (*ú*).	Perf. *eá*.	Pl., *u*.	P.p. *o*.	
leoge	leâh	lugon	logen	lie
smúge	smeâh	smugon	smoger	creep
fleohe (fleô)	fleâh	flugon	flogen	flee
teohe (teô)	teâh	tugon	togen	tug
ðeo	ðeâh	ðugon	ðogen	thrive
wreð	wreâh	wrugon	wrogen	cover

Second Period.

Pres.	Perf.	Pl.	P.p.	
crepe	crap, crep	crupon	cropen	creep
deofe	deæf, def	—	—	dive
scuve	scaf, scæf, scef	scuven, schoven	schoven	shove
cleove	clæf	cluven, clufen	cloven, clofen	cleave
brewe	brew	—	browen	brew
reowe	ræw, rew, reuw, reu	—	—	rue
geote	gæt, get	guten	goten	pour
sceote	sceat, scæt, scheat, schet	scuten	scoten	shoot
vleote, flete	flet, flæt	fluten	floten	float
lute	leat	luten	loten	bow
beode, bede, bidde	bæd, bad, bed, bead	buden, biden	boden, beden, beoden	bid
for-beode	-bæd, -bad, -bead	-buden	-boden	forbid
cheose	chæs, ches	curen, chosen	coren, chosen	choose
frese	—	—	froren	freeze
reose, rese	ræs, res	—	—	rush
leose	læs, les, lees, leas	loren, luren	loren	lose
seoþe	seþ	suden	soden	seethe
luke	læc, lok	luken	loken	lock
suke	sæc, soc	suken	soken	suck
buȝe, buwe	bæh, bah, beh, beih	buȝen	boȝen	bow, bend
driȝe	dreih, dreg	droȝen	droȝen, drohen	suffer
liȝe, leȝe, luȝe	læh, leh	luȝen	loȝen	lie
fleo	flæh, fleh, fleih	fluȝen, fluwen	fluȝen, floȝen	fly
fleo	flæh, fleh, fleah, fleih, flei	floȝen, flowen	floȝen, flowen	flee

(1) Weak perfects : *—losede, boȝede, resden* (La3.) ; *defde* = dived (St. Marherete).

(2) Weak p.p. :—*ilosed* (La3.), *bilefed* (Orm.).

Third Period.

Pres.	Perf.	Pl.	P.p.	
creoe	creap	cropen	cropen	creep
cleve	clef, cleef	cloven	cloven	cleave
brewe	brew	browen	browen	brew

STRONG VERBS.

Pres.	Perf.	Pl.	P.p.	
schete	schet, schot, scheat, sset	schoten	schoten, schotten	shoot
schuve	schef, schof	schoven	schoven	shove
brewe	brew	—	browen	brew
rewe	reu	—	—	rue
3ete	yhet, 3et	3oten	3oten, 3et(en)	pour
loute, lute, lote	leat	louten	louten, loten	bow
flete	flet	—	floten	float
bede	bed, bad	boden	boden, beden	bid
seþe	seþ, seath, sod	soden	soden, sodden	seethe
chese, chese	ches, cheas	chosen	chosen, corn, coren	choose
lese	les, lyeas, lees	lesen, losen, loren	losen, loren, lorn	lose
frese	fres	frosen	frosen, froren	freeze
loke, luke	leac, lok	loken	loken	look
a-bu3e, abowe	-bea3	-bowen	-bo3en, -bowen	bow
li3e	leigh	—	lowen	lie
fle, fli3e	fleh, fley, flegh	flowen	flowen	fly
fle, fle3e	flew, fleu, fley	flowen	flowen	flee
dri3e	dregh	—	—	suffer

Weak forms :—*lost, lest, (bi)louked, bowed, lighed, fled, schette.*

FOURTH PERIOD.

Pres.	Perf.	Pl.	P.p.	
crepe	crop (crope)	cropen	cropen	creep
soupe	soop, sop	—	sopen	sup
clyve, cleve	cleef, clef	cloven, cleven	cloven	cleave
schove	schof	—	schoven	shove
brewe	brew	—	browen	brew
for-bede	-beed, -bad	-beden	-boden, -biden, -beden	bid
sethe	seth	—	soden, sothen	seethe
3eete, yete	3ot	—	3oten	pour
schete	schete	—	schoten	shoot
flete	flet, fleet, flot	—	—	float
chese	ches, chees, chos	chosen, chesen	chosen	choose
frese	frees, fres	frosen	frosen, froren	freeze
leese	les, lees	losen	losen, loren	lose
brouke	broke	—	—	brook (enjoy)
loke	lek	—	loken	lock
li3e, lie	lei3	—	lowen	lie
flee, fle3e, flie3e	flei3, flew, flegh, fleigh	flewen	flowen	fly
flee, fli3he	flei3, flew	flowen	flowen	flee

(1) Weak perfects :—*brewede, sethede, 3etide, 3otte, schotte, fletide, lowtide, cheside, freside, losed, loste, leste, bowide, liede, fledde.*

(2) Weak p.p.:—*schot. cleft, lowtid, lost, lest, lyed, fled, ylokked, bowid, soupide.*

CLASSIFICATION OF WEAK VERBS.

FIRST PERIOD.

Class I.

(1) *Radical short.*—The first class has the connecting vowel *e* (= *i* = *ia*), and contains verbs with short and long radical vowels, as *ner-e-de* (perf.), *ner-e-d* (p.p.).

(2) *Radical long.*—The connecting vowel is lost in the perfects of those verbs with long radicals.

INF.	PERF.	P.P.	
dǣl-an	dǣl-de	gedǣl-ed	divide
mǣn-an	mǣn-de	mǣn-ed	lament
lǣd-an	lǣd-de	lǣd-ed	lead
dêm-an	dêm-de	dêm-ed	deem
fêd-an	fêd-de	fêd-ed	feed
&c.	&c.	&c.	

The perfect and p.p. of the following verbs retain the original radical vowel (*ô*) of the stem :[1]—

| sêc-an | sôh-te | sôh-t | seek |
| rêc-an | rôh-te | rôh-t | reck |

(3) Stems ending in *mn, ng, rm, rn, ld, nd, rd*, lose the connecting vowel *e* in the perfect.

The perfects of stems in *mn* drop *n* before *de*.

nemn-an	nem-de	memn-e-d	name
spreng-an	spreng-de	spreng-e-d	spring
bærn-an	bærn-de	bærn-e-d	burn
styrm-an	styrm-de	styrm-e-d	storm

(4) Stems ending (through gemination) in *ll, mm, ss, dd, cg, cc, pp* (for *lj, mj, sj, dj, gj, cj, pj*), have no connecting vowel in the perfect.

wemm-an	wem-de	wemm-e-d	defile
cenn-an	cen-de	cenn-e-d	bring forth
spill-an	spil-de	spill-e-d	spill
âhredd-an	âhred-de	âhredd-e-d	rescue
lecg-an	leg-de	leg-e-d	lay

---

[1] The *e* is caused by the lost connecting vowel *i* (*o* + *i* = *e*).

WEAK VERBS.

Some verbs in the perfect and p.p. retain the *radical* vowel (*a*) of the stem.

INF.	PERF.	P.P.	
cwell-an	cweal-de	cweal-d	kill
sell-an	seal-de	seal-d, sal-d	sell
tell-an	teal-de	teal-d	tell
recc-an	reah-te	reah-t	reck
strecc-an	streh-te (streahte)	streah-t	stretch
wecc-an	weah-te	weah-t	arouse

In the following verbs (with stems in *ld, nd, rd, nt, rt, ft, st, ht*) the connecting vowel is lost, and the suffix *d* of the perfect is assimilated to the final dental of the stem, so that $d + de = de$.

scild-an	scild-e	scild-ed	shield
send-an	send-e	send-ed	send
gyrd-an	gyrd-e	gyrd-ed	gird
stylt-an	stylt-e	stylt-ed	stand astonished
hyrt-an	hyrt-e	hyrt-ed	hearten
mynt-an	mynt-e	mynt-ed	purpose
hæft-an	hæft-e	hæft-ed	bind
riht-an	riht-e	riht-ed	set right
rest-an	rest-e	rest-ed	rest

D becomes *t* when added to stems ending in *p, t, nc, s, x*.

dypp-an	dyp-te	dypp-ed	dip
sett-an	set-te	sett-ed, set	set
drenc-an	drenc-te	drenc-ed	drink
cyss-an	cys-te	cyss-ed	kiss
lix-an	lix-te	lix-ed	shine

When *t* is added to stems in *cc*, the perf. and p.p. have only a single *h* before the suffix.

recc-an	reah-te	reah-t	reck
wecc-an	weah-te	weah-t	arouse
strecc-an	streah-te	streah-t	stretch

In verbs with long stems ending in a sharp mute, *d* in the perf. becomes *t*, as—

ræp-an	ræp-te	ræp-ed	reap
mêt-an	mêt-te	mêt-ed	meet

C becomes *h* before *t*, as—

tǽc-an	tǽh-te	tǽh-t	teach

Class II.

The second class of weak verbs has *o* for its connecting vowel, as *lufian*, to love; perf. *luf-o-de*; p.p. *luf-od*.

This *o* is weakened to *a*, *u*, and *e*, as :—

    þrowade = *þrow-o-de*, suffered.
    cleopade and *cleopede* = *cleopode*, called.
    singude = *singode*, sinned.

SUBSEQUENT PERIODS.

In the Second and subsequent periods, the two conjugations are mixed up, because the connecting vowel *o* has become *e*.

In the earlier part of this period we find perfects in *-ode*, *-ude*, side by side with *-ede*; they are to be regarded as exceptional forms.

(1) *Radical short.*

SECOND PERIOD.

INF.	PERF.	P.P.	
sweven	swev-e-de	ıswev-ĕd	sleep
þankien	þank-e-de	iþank-ĕd	thank

In the Third and Fourth periods we find *-id* and *-ud* in the perfect tense and passive participle, as well as *-ede*, *-de*.

The Fourth period keeps the connecting vowel *e*, but frequently drops the *e* of the suffix *de*.

(2) *Radical long.*—The connecting vowel disappears in long syllable-stems, and *d* is added immediately to the verbal stem.

SECOND PERIOD.

INF.	PERF.	P.P.	
dælen	dæl-de, del-de	idel-ed	divide
demen	dem-de	idem-ed	deem
lenen	len-de	ilen-ed	lend
heren	her-de	iher-d	hear
leden, læden	led-de	ilæ d, ile-d	lead
feden	fed-de	ifed	feed

Third and Fourth Periods.

Inf.	Perf.	P.P.	
dele	del-de	deled	divide
deme	dem-de	dem-d	deem
lede	led-de, lad-de	led, lad	lead
drede	dred-de, drad-de	dred, drad	dread
&c.	&c.	&c.	

(3) The suffix *d* assimilates to the *d* of the combination *-ld*, *-nd* (*-dd*)[1]; *-rt*, *-st*, *-ht*, *-tt*.

Second Period.

Inf.	Perf.	P.P.	
bulden	bulde	buld	build
senden	sende	isend	send
wenden	wende	iwend[2]	turn
setten	sette	iset	set
resten	reste	irest	rest
hurten	hurte	ihurt	hurt
casten	caste	icast	cast

Third Period.

Inf.	Perf.	P.P.	
bulden	bulde	ibuld	build
senden	sende	isend	send
casten	caste	icast	cast
setten	sette	iset	set
&c.	&c.	&c.	

In Northern writers we find *t* often replacing *d*, as—

sende	sent(e)	sent	send
wende	went(e)	went	wend, go

Fourth Period.

The *d* is now regularly converted into *t*, as—

Inf.	Perf.	P.P.	
blenden	blente, blent	blent	blend

(4) The suffix *-d* is changed into *-t* after *p, f, ch, cch, ss, t ; ch* becomes *h* (3) before *te ; nch* becomes *ng* or is vocalized before *te*.

---

[1] Or we may consider that the *d* of *-ld, -nd*, &c. is dropped.
[2] In verbs of this class Laȝamon often replaces *d* by *t*, as, *wenden, wente, iwent*.

Second Period.

	Inf.	Perf.	P.p.	
(1)	kepen	kepte	ikept	keep
	cussen	custe	icust	kiss
	cutten	cutte	icut	cut
	putten	putte	iput	put
	ræcchen	ræhte, rahte	iraht	explain
	{cacchen	cahte	icaht }	catch
	{kecchen	keihte, cauhte	ikeiht}	
	tæchen	tahte	itaht	teach
	smecchen	smeihte	ismecched	taste, smack
	lacchen	lahte	ilaht	seize
(2)	drenchen	drengte, dreinte	adreint	drench
	mengen	meinde	imeind	mingle

In the following verbs there is a return to the radical vowel of the stem:—

	Inf.	Perf.	P.p.	
(3)	{sæchen	sohte	isoht }	seek
	{sechen	souhte	isouht}	
	recchen	rohte (rehte)	iroht	reck
	{strecchen	streahte (streihte)	istreiht	stretch
	{stræcchen			
	tellen	talde, tolde	itald, itold, teld	tell
	sellen	sælde, salde, solde	iseld, isald, isold	sell

Third Period.

	Inf.	Perf.	P.p.	
(1)	kepen	kepte	ikept, kept	keep
	lefen	lefte (left)	ileft, left	leave
	refen	refte (reft)	ireft, reft	(be)reave
	wefen	wefte (weft)	iweft, weft	weave
	cacchen	ca3te	ica3t, ca3t	catch
	clenchen	cleinte, clente	icleint, iclent	clench
	techen	tau3te, tei3te, tauhte (taght)	itau3t, tau3t	teach
(2)	drenchen	dreynte	dreynt	drown
(3)	sechen	so3te, souhte (souht)	iso3t, so3t	seek
	rechen	ro3te	—	reck
	rechen	rauhte, rei3te, rau3te, raughte	—	reach
	tellen	tolde, tald	itold, told, tald, teld	tell
	sellen	solde	isold, sold	sell

The *Ayenbite* keeps the old *ea*, as:—

telle	tealde	yteald, tald	tell
selle	zealde	yzeald, zald	sell

Fourth Period.

	Inf.	Perf.	Pp.	
(1)	kepen	kepte (kepide)	kept	keep
	leeven, leven	lefte, lafte (laft)	left, laft	leave
	refen	refte, rafte (raft)	raft (refed)	be-reave
	greten	grette	gret	greet
	sweten	swatte, swette	swet, swat	sweat
	meeten	mette	met	meet
	kepen	keste, kiste	kest, kĭst	kiss
	twicchen	twight(e)	twight	twitch
	picchen	pight(e)	pight	pitch
	plicchen	plight(e)	plight	pluck
	techen	touȝte, tauȝte	touȝt, tauȝt	teach
	cacche	cauȝte, caughte	caȝt, cauȝt, caught	catch
	lachen	lauȝte	lauȝt	seize
(2)	blenchen	bleynt(e), blent(e)	—	blench
	quenchen	queinte	queint	quench
	drenchen	dreint(e)	dreint	drench

The *g* in *ng* becomes vocalized before the suffix *d* or *t*.

	Inf.	Perf.	P.p.	
	sprengen	spreynde, spreynte, sprengide	spreynt, spreyned	sprinkle
	mengen	meynde, meynte, myngede	—	mingle
	sengen	(seynde)	seynd, seind	singe
(3)	sechen	souȝte	souȝt	seek
	be-sechen	-souȝte	-souȝt	beseech
	recchen	rouȝte, roughte, rauȝte	rauȝt, rouȝt	reck
	reche	rauȝte	rauȝt	reach
	strecche	strauhte, strauȝte	straught, strauȝt	stretch
	biggen	bouȝte	bouȝt	buy
	smeken	smaughte	—	smack
	tellen	tolde, telde	told, teld, tald	tell
	sellen	soold, selde, solde, salde	sold, seld, sald	sell

Anomalous forms are treated along with their modern representatives; see Anomalous Verbs.

ADVERBS.

I. Substantive.

(a) GENITIVE.

First Period.—*Dæges* (of a day), *forð-dæges* (late in the day), *summeres* and *winteres* (summer and winter), *nihtes* (of a night), *neades* (needs), *soðes* (of a truth), &c.

Second Period.—*Forðdaies, dæies (deies), nihtes,* 'aday and *nyhtes*' (*dæies* and *nihtes*), *lifes* (alive), *deathes* (dead), *nedes* (needs), *winteres, sumeres, willes* (willingly), *waldes* (purposely), *unwaldes* (accidentally), *soðes* (of a truth), his *þonkes* (of his own accord), *hwiles* (*hwils*), the *hwiles, oðerhwiles* (sometimes), *summes weis, oðres weis* (*oðerweis*), *nanes weis, alles weis, allegates* (always), *soðrihtes* (truly), *halfinges* (by half), &c.

Third Period.—*Dayes, nyhtes, ani3tes, þonkes, unþonkes, nedes, hwiles,* &c.

Fourth Period.—*Adayes, nedes, other-weies, algates* (always), *eggelinges, hedlynges* (headlong), *noselynges, sidelonges, grovelonges,* &c.

(b) DATIVE AND INSTRUMENTAL.

First Period.—*Æfre, næfre, heodage* (to-day), *hwilum* (whilom), *stundum* (at times), *dagum* (by day), *nahtum* (by night), *stundmæl-um* (by little times, at spare times), *næhtum* (nightly), &c.; *handlunga* (hand to hand), *bæclinga* (backwards), *sûðan* (from the south), *eástan* (from the east), &c.

Second Period.—*Æfre, efre, næfre, næuere, nede* (of necessity), *whilum* (*hwilem, hwilen, whilen*), *wuke-mælum* (weekly), *drope-mele* (drop-meal), *lim-mele* (limb-meal), *wunder = wundrum* (wonderfully), *nedunga, nedlunge* (of necessity), *ruglinge* (backward), *stundmele, umbstunde* (at intervals), *euerte, neuerte, eauer3ette,* &c.

Third Period.—*Evere, euer, nevere, never, whilom, while, lynmele, pecemele, stundemele, euerte, neuerte, wonder, cuppemele, pounamele, floc-mele* (by companies).

Fourth Period.—*Ever, never, whilom, alleweyes, gobbetmele, pecemel, by peçemele* (piecemeal), *hipyll-melum* (by heaps), *stowndmeel, lynmele, parcel-mele, eggelynge, grovelonge,* &c.

(c) ACCUSATIVE.

First Period.—*Hâm* (home), *eâst, west, sûð, norð, â* (ever), *nâ* (no), *ealne weg* (alway), *þâ hwile* (whilst), *sume hwile* (somewhile), *dǽl, sumne dǽl* (somedeal), *wiht, â-wiht* (something, somewhat), *ôðre wisan* (otherwise), *sume wîsan* (somewise), *sôð* (truth), *nǽnigþing* (nought), &c.

Second Period.—*Ham, hom, norð, east (æst), suð, west, sumedale, sumdel, what-gate, allegate, oþer-gate, þeo hwile* (the while), *otherhwile, sumewhile, oþer* (= *oþerwise*), *fulsoð, o, a, aa* (ever), *eawiht* (aught), &c.

Third Period.—*Hom, norþ, est, west, souþ, a, oo, ay, somdel, oʒt, ilka dele, alwei, alnewey, often-tide, sumhwile, oþerhwile, thus-gate, allegate, swagate,* &c.

Fourth Period.—*Hom, algate (allegate), alway, sometime, somdel, somdele, gretdel, everydel, auʒt, oþerwise,* &c.

(d) PREPOSITIONAL FORMS.

First Period.—*On weg* (away), *on bæc, underbæc* (aback), *on-geân* (against, opposite); *togeânes* (against), *tô-æfenes* (in the evening), *on-dæge* (a-day), *on-niht* (anight), *tô-dæge* (to-day), *tô-nihte* (tonight), *on ærne mergen* (early mornings), *on morgen* (a-mornings), *on midne-dæg* (at mid-day), *âdune* (down), *on midre nihte* (at midnight), &c.

Second Period.—*Umbe-stunde, umbe-hwile* (at intervals); *bysydes, biside, bisiden, bisides; bi-daye, bi-nyhte; bihælves* (beside); *bilife, bilifes* (quickly); *adun* (down), *a-bac, abacch; on-ʒan, aʒæn, aʒein, tô-ʒeines* (against, towards); *adæi, adai, aniht, an-hond, a-efnu* (at eventide); *an-ende, on-ende* (lastly); *a-lyve, a-marwe, a-marʒen, a-morwe, a-morʒe* (a-morrow); *arewen (arow), a seoven nihte* (a sennight); *aslepe, awei, awai* (away); *an erne morew* (on early morrow) *on live, a þes half* (on this side of); *oslæpe* (asleep); *on nihtes, atten ende, at þen ende* (at last); *at morwhen, at morwen, to-marhen, to-morwe, to-marewene, to-niht, to-daie, to-ʒere, to-sumere,* &c., *to-soðe* (truly), *bi dages, bi nyhtes,* &c.

Third Period.—*Abak, adoun, afelde, agrund, alonde, awey, amorwe, anyʒt, awynter, ayen, ayenward, an haste, an hond, on hiʒe, onlive, on niʒtes, on dayes, on morwe, on peces; bilife, bilyve, biside, bysydes, bicas, becas* (accidentally), *attenende, bynorþe, bysouþe, by este, by weste,* *uphap, upon hast, forcas, forsoþe, to-day, to-nyȝt, to-morn, tiι*ч (*to-eve*), *insped* (speedily), *at ese*, &c.

Fourth Period.—*Umbe-stoundes, in-stoundes* (at intervals), *um-hwile, adoun, abak, asyde* (*asidishalf*), *afire, aȝen, amorewe, anight, afote* (*on fote*), *arow, aslope, on egge* (on edge), *onsydes, on sidishand* (aside), *a-dregh, o-dregh, on-dreȝ* (aside); *beforehand, to-morwe, to-morn, to-ȝere*, &c.

II. Adjective.

(1) With final -e.

First Period.—*Fæst-e, hlud-e, biter-lic-e*, &c.

Second Period.—*Feste, lhude, ille, ufele, depe, swiþe, vastliche, bliþe-like, baldeliȝ*, &c.

Third Period.—*Wide, side, dere, depe, harde, uneþe, nobliche*, &c.

In the Northern dialects we find *-like* and *-ly* for *-liche*.

Fourth Period.—*Faste, fulle, righte, hevenlich, hevenliche, scharply, passendli, felendly*, &c.

(2) In the comparative and superlative degrees, adjectives (First period) end in **-or** and **-ost**, without any other inflexion, as *geornor* (more diligent), *fæstor* (faster), *eaðelicor* (more easily), *heardost* (hardest), *eaðelicost* (easiest). Some few comparatives drop the suffix, as *leng* (longer), *bet* (better), *má* (more), *éþ* (easier).

In the subsequent periods, adverbs form their comparatives in **-ere** (**-er, -or, -ur**); superlatives in **-este** (**-est**).

The comparative of words in **-liche** becomes—

(*a*) *-liker, -luker, -loker, -laker*.

(*b*) *-lyer*.

The superlative of adjectives in **-liche** ends in—

(*a*) *-likest, -lukest, -lokest, -lakest*.

(*b*) *-lyest*. Cp. *deþliker, gerenluker, deorluker, bliþeloker, fella-ker* (more fiercely), &c.

In the Fourth period **-lyer** predominates.
We also find as late as Chaucer the shortened comparatives *bet*, *mo. leng*.

(3) Many adjectives are used as adverbs, especially those with irregular comparisons.

First Period.—*Wela, wel* (well), *ufele* (ill), *lytlĕ, lytlum* (little), *micles, miclum* (much), *neáh, nih* (nigh, near), *feor* (far), *forð* (forth), *late, latan* (late), *bet* (better), *þe bet* (the better), *betst* (best), *wyrs* (worse), *wyrst* (worst), *þy læs* (the less), *má* (more), &c.

Subsequent Periods.—*Ufele, uvele, ille* (ill), *lute, lyte, lytyl, bet, best, worse, wurst, lasse, lesse, lest, ma, mare, more*, &c., *fer, neor, ner, nerre, nyʒ, nexst, nest, forth, forther, later, latere, laist, ner þe later, never the later*, &c.

(4) Case-endings :—

(*a*) GENITIVE.

First Period.—*þweorhes* (across), *sones* (soon), *ealles* (altogether), *efnes, emnes* (evenly), *micles* (greatly), *elles* (else), &c.
Adverbs in -*weards* (-wards), &c.

Second Period.—*Alles, elles, rihtes, duvel-rihtes* (with a dive), *adunrihtes, alrihtes, ananrihtes, forðrihtes, þerihtes, upwardes, hiderwardes, forðwardes, eftsones, mucheles, cwices* (alive), *alunges* (altogether), *adunwardes, aʒeinwardes*, &c.

Third Period.—*Alles, elles, eftsones, amiddes, riʒtes, dounriʒtes, awaiwardes* (away), &c.

Fourth Period.—*Elles, unèþes, unwares, hiderwardes, upwardes, forwardes, halfinges, endlonges, afterwardes, towardes, uprihtes*, &c.

(*b*) INSTRUMENTAL.

First Period.—*Geara* (of yore), *sóna* (soon), *geta* (yet).

Second Period.—*ʒore, sone, ʒette, ʒet, eftsone, everʒet, neverʒet*.
Third and Fourth Periods.—*Sone, ʒet, everʒet*.

(*c*) DATIVE.

First Period.—*Lytlum* (little), *miclum* (greatly, much), *wundrum* (wonderfully), *furþum* (even), *dearnunga* (secretly), *eallinga* (wholly), &c.

Second Period.—*Lutlen, lytlen, muchele, forþe, allinge, unmundiunge* (unmindfully), *seldum, selden, selde, ane* (alone), &c.

Third Period.—*Lytlen, muchele, moche, selde, selden, one, ferinkli* (suddenly), *sunderlyng* (separately), &c.

Fourth Period.—*Lytlen, lytlum, muche, muchel, allynge*, &c.

(*d*) ACCUSATIVE.

First Period.—*Ǽr* (ere), *eal* (all), *neâh* (nigh), *nôh, genôh* (enough), *feor* (far), *lyt, lytel, riht;* adverbs in *-weard* (ward), &c.

Second Period.—*Al, ær, er* (ere) ; *a-neoh, neh* (nigh), *inoh* (enough); *hiderward, ӡeondward, binward* (within), *þiderward, forþward, forðriht, anonriht, aweiward, amiddeward*, &c.

Third Period.—*Al ; er, ar, or* (ere) ; *neh, nyӡ, riӡt, fer, ynoӡ, imydward, þiderward, awkeward* (= wrongly), *forðriht*, &c.

Fourth Period.—*Al ; er, or ; negh, nyӡ ; afer, riӡt, ynow ; estward, to-warde*, &c.

(*e*) PREPOSITIONAL.

First Period.—*On-middum* (amidst), *on-efen* (anent), *on-þweorh* (across), *on-geador* (together), *on-îdel* (in vain), *on-sundrum* (asunder), *on-eornost* (in earnest), *tô-middes* (amidst), *tô-weardes* (towards), *tô-gædere* (together), *tô-somne* (together), *ofer-eall* (everywhere), *ætgædere* (together), *be ânfealdum* (singly), &c.

Second Period.—*Amidden* (amid), *amiddes, a-neah* (nigh), *a-wiðere* (against), *an-vest, on-fest, anewist, a-newest* (fast by, near), *ariht, anheh* (on high), *alast, anewe, an-anriht, on wiðere* (against), *on-sunder, on oþer* (otherwise), *on-idel, in-idel, to-samen, to-somne, to-gæderes, togedere; to-gode* (gratuitously), *overal, of lah* (from below), *of feor, of feorren* (afar), *of heh* (from on high), *mid-rihte* (rightly), *atte laste*, &c.

Third Period.—*Alast, alefte, amidde, amiddes, in-middes, anhey, on hie, an heiӡ, on heiӡ, abrod, abroad, on-ferrum, an even* (at last), *anaӡt* (to nought), *to gedere, togedere, togederes, overal, uppon heiӡ, at al, at alle* (in all things = *alles*), *at alle riӡtes, anonriӡtes, to-riӡtes, upriӡtes, at arst, atte fulle, ate laste, atte laste, atte best, ate verst* (at first), *albidene, bydene* (= by that, subsequently), &c.

Fourth Period.—*Abrood, alarge, afer, aferre, anheӡ, in melle, amel* (amid), *on rounde, in myddes, in mydde; in seme* (together), *on riӡt, on-wyde, to-geder, in-idel, aloӡ, at þe fulle; overthwart, endlonge, endlonges*, &c.

III. Numeral.

First Period.—*Æne* (once), *æninga, ân-unga* (once), *on-ân* (continually, once for all), *for ân* (for ever), *on âne* (at same time, together), *twiwa* (twice), *betwih* (between), þrîga, þriwa (thrice), &c.

Second Period.—*Ene, ænes, enes, twies, tweien, tweie, þriȝes, at anes, at eanes, ansiþe* (once), *anan, al onan, a twa, a two, on twinne, on þre, betweonen, betwenen, bitwixen, to þan ane, to þan anes, for þe nanes, for þan one,* &c.

Third Period.—*Ene, ones, enes, anes, twie, thrie, twyes, thries, anon; in on* (continually), *at one, at on, at ene, atwo, a þre, atwinne, asevene, bytweyne, for þe nones,* &c.

Fourth Period.—*Anes, ones, twyes, thries, twye, three, anoon, ato, in two, in on, atone, at ene, after on, bytwene, for þe nones,* &c.

IV. Adverbs formed from Particles.

First Per.	Second Per.	Third Per.	Fourth Per.	
æft, eft	eft	eft	efte, eft	eft, aft
æfter	efter, after	after	aftre, after	after
æfterward	efterward (adv. & prep.)	efterward	—	afterward
—	—	efterþanne	—	after that
æftan	—	nevereft	—	never after
wið-æftan	—	—	—	—
be-æftan	bi-æften, bæftan	—	baft	abaft
bi, big	bi, be	by, bi, be	by, be	by
—	—	—	for-by	past, near
fore	fore	fore	—	before
—	forn-on, forn-an (as before)	—	—	—
toran	foren	—	—	—
be-foran	hi-foren, bivoren	bivoren, biforen, bvfore, beforn	beforn, byfore, biforen	before
tô-foran	—	—	—	(here)to-fore
wið-foran	—	—	—	—
—	avoreward	—	—	forward
forð	forð, vorð	forth, vorth	forth	forth
—	forð-rihte	—	—	forth-right
—	forð-ward	forð-ward	—	forward
—	—	forth-with	—	before
—	swire-forð	—	—	neck-forth
—	for-to, for-te, vorte	forte, fort	—	until
—	—	her-forþ	—	—
—	—	þer-forþ	—	—
—	forðþat	—	—	until
geo, iu	—	—	—	—

First Per.	Second Per.	Third Per.	Fourth Per.	
geond	ȝond	be-ȝende, bi-ȝonde, bi-ȝunde	biȝonde, biȝonden	beyond
—	ȝeondward	yondward		
her	her, here	her, here	her, here	here
hider, hidres	hider	hider, huder	hider	hither
—	hiderward	—		hitherward
{hinan, heonan, heonane, heonone, heona	heonne	henne, hennes	hennen, henen, hennes, henne, hen, hennus, hennis, hens	hence
—	{heþen {heþen-ward	heþen —	heþen —	hence henceforth, henceforward
—	—	fra heþen	fro hennes	from hence
—	heonneuorð, henonforð	—	—	henceforth
hindan, hinder, hindweard	—	hindward	hindeward	hindward
behindan	bihinden	byhynde	behinde	behind
hwæt (what)	mesthwet (almost), alse wat se (as soon as), monihwat	alhuet (until), ney-wat (nearly)	—	many-what
hwar, hwær	hwer, wær, whær, whære	where, were	wher, wore	where
—	—	elles wer	—	elsewhere
—	ichwer	—	—	eachwhere
hwæder, hwider, hwyder	hwuder	wyder, whider	whider, where	whither
—	whiderward	whiderward	—	whitherward
—	elleswhider, elles hwar, other hwar	—	—	elsewhere
hwanan, hwana, æghwonene	wonene, hwenene, wheþen	wanne, wheðen	whennes, whens, from whennes	whence, from whence
—	wheþeuward	—	—	whence-ward
æghwar, âhwar, gehwar, æghweder	eȝȝwhær, aihware, owhar, uwher, ihwer	ouwhar	our whar, owhere, aywhere	anywhere, everywhere
—	—	nour, nowhar	—	nowhere
seld-hwonne	seldhwonne, selden, selde, seldum	selden, selde	selde	seldom
in	in	in, yn	in	in
innan	inne	inne, ine	ine	in
binnan	binnen, binne, bine, an-inne	bin	—	within
—	inwardes	—	—	inward, within

ADVERBS.

First Per.	Second Per.	Third Per.	Fourth Per.	
wiðinnan	wiðinnen, wiðinne, inwið	wiþinnen, wiþinne, inwiþ	wiþinne, inwiþ	within
mid	mid, mide	mid	—	with
midealle	midalle	midalle, wiþalli	wiþal	withal, altogether, wholly
niðor, niðer	neoðer, niðer	neðer	neðer	neither
niðan	neðan	—	—	from beneath
be-nyðan	binoðen, bineðen, bineaðen, bineoðe	beneþe, bineþen, bineþe	bineþen, bineþe, beneþe	beneath
neoðeward	neoþer-ward, neþewarde	—	—	nether-ward
nu	nu	now, nou	now	now
on	on	on	on	on
of	of	of	of	of
swâ	swa, swo, so, se	swa, sa, so, se	so, se	so
eal-swâ	alswa, alswo, also, alse, als	alswa, also, alsa, alse, ase, als	also, als, as	as
swylce (as if)	swilce	—	—	—
to	to, te	to	to	to
—	forto, forte (before infin.)	—	—	for to
—	ever-te (ever-to, ever as yet)	—	—	—
—	never-te (never as yet), never-to	—	—	—
—	—	til and fra	til and fro	to and fro
þær	þer, þar, þor	þer, þere, þar, þore	þere, þare, þer, þar, þore	there
bæder, þider, þiderward, þiderweardes	þider, þiderward	þider, þuder, þiderward	þider, þiderward	thither, thitherward, thitherwards
þanon, þonon	þonene, þanene, þanne	þanne, þannene	þennes	thence
þanne, þonne	þanne, þenne	þenne, þanne	þennes, þenne, þan, þen	then
þâ	þa, þo	þa, þo	þo	then
—	þeþen, þeþensforð	þeþen	þeþen, þien	thence, thenceforth
nuða	nuþe, nuþen	nouþe	nouþe	now, now then
þæs (so, very)	þes	—	—	—
tô þam, tô þon (so, very)	—	—	—	—
þus	þus	þus, þous	þus	thus
þurh	þurh, þurch, þureh	þorh, þorgh, þurf	þorgh, þurgh, þorow	through, thorough, throughout
under	under	under	under, undre, from undre	under, from under
up	up	up	up	up
—	upwardes	—	—	upward

Y

First Per.	Second Per.	Third Per.	Fourth Per.	
—	upward	—	—	upward
ufan	—	—	—	above
ufanan	ovenan	—	—	above
bufan	buven, buve	buve	buve	above
âbufan	abufen, bibufen	aboven, above, abuve	above, aboven	above
wið-ufan	—	—	—	above
on-ufan	—	—	—	above
ufan-ward	—	ovenward	—	above
ufeweard	uveward	—	—	upward
—	—	almest	almost	almost [1]
ofer	over	over	over	over
ût, ûte	ut, ute, uten	out	out	out
—	utwardes	—	—	outward
bûtan	abeoten, abuten, abute	abouten, aboute	abouten, aboute	about
ymb-ûtan	—	—	—	—
ûtan-ymb	—	—	—	—
ûta-ymb	—	—	—	—
—	wið-uten, uten-wið, ute-wið	wiþouten, wiþout, outwith	wiþouten, wiþoute, outwith	without
wið	wið	wið	—	against
wiðer	—	—	wiðer (opposite)	
—	wiþ and wiþ			
þǽr-âbûtan	þær-abuten, þer-abuten	þer-aboute		thereabout
—	þær-binnen	—		therewithin
—	þær-bi, þor-bi	þerbi		thereby
þær-æfter	þer(þar)-æfter, þar-after	þer-after		thereafter
—	—	þer ney, þer neih		there nigh
—	—	þer-afterward		thereafter
—	—	þer biside		there beside
þær-inne	þor-inne, þer-inne, þer-aninne, þer-an, þrin	þer-inne	As in Third Period.	therein
þær-mid	þer-mide, þar-mid	þermid		therewith
þær-of	þer-of, þer-offe, þor-offen	þer-of		thereof
þær-on	þron, þær-on, þar-on, þron	þer-on		thereon
þær-to	þer-to, þor-til	þerto, þer-til		thereto
þær-tôgeânes	þer-aȝen, þar-to-ȝeines, þar-to-yeynes	þer-teyenes		thereagainst
þær-ufan	þer-oven, þer-ufenan	—		thereabove
—	þer-ofer	þerover		thereover
—	þer-upon	þerupon		thereupon
—	þar-vore, þer(þær)-fore	þer-fore, þer-vore		therefore

[1] al-mest = *alre mest* = most of all ; *alre* = gen. pl. of *al*.

ADVERBS.

First Per.	Second Per.	Third Per.	Fourth Per.	
þær-ûte	þor-uten, þer-ute, þar-ute	þer-out, þar-oute		thereout
—	þor-buten	—		therewithout
—	þer-þurh, þar-þurh	þer-þrogh		therethrough
þær-wið	þær-wið, þor-wið	þer-wiþ	As in Third Period.	therewith
—	þar-wyþ-al	þer-wiþal		therewithal
—	þor-under, þer-under	—		thereunder
—	þor-fra, þer-fra, þer-from	ther-fro, þer-fram		therefrom
—	þer-uppe, þruppe	therupon	therupon	there-up
—	þer-at	therat	—	thereat
—	þer-anunder, þor-under	—	—	thereunder
—	þer-imong, þer-among, þor-mong	þeramong	—	there among
—	—	þar-into	—	thereinto
—	—	þer-to-fore	—	theretofore
—	þer-toward	—	—	toward
her-æfter	her-efter, her-bi	her-after	herafter	hereafter
—	her-mid	her-mid, -wiþ	—	herewith
—	her-of, -offe	her-of	herof	hereof
—	her-on	her-on	heron	hereon
—	her-fore	her-for, her-fore	herfore	herefore
—	her-to	—	—	hereto
—	her-ut	her-out	—	hereout
—	her-wiðinnen	her-inne	herin	herein
—	her-þurh	—	—	here-through
—	whar-ine, war-ine	huer-ynne	wherin	wherein
—	quor-at	—	—	whereat
—	whæron	huer-an, huer-on	—	whereon
—	—	huer-of, whar-of	wherof	whereof
—	hwer-wið	huer-mide, hwarwiþ	wherwith	wherewith
—	hwar-to, hwer-to	—	—	—
—	hwar-fore, hwar-þuruh	—	wherfore	wherefore
—	—	huer-by	—	whereby
—	—	huer-onder	—	whereunder
—	—	huer-oppe	—	whereup
why ne	hwi ne	quin, quine, whine	—	O that

PREPOSITIONS.

I. Prepositions Proper.

First Per.	Second Per.	Third Per.	Fourth Per.	
æfter, æft	æfter, æftere, after, efter	after	aftre, after	after
—	efterward	—	—	—
bæftan, be-æftan	bæftan, biaften, baften, bieften	—	baft	behind, after
wið-æftan and	—	—	—	behind with, in
æt	æt, at, et	at	at	at
bi, be	bi, by, be	bi, by, be	bi, by, be	by
for, fore	fore, for, vor	for, vor, fore	for, vor	for
foran	for-bi	—	forbi	before
æt-foran	at-foren, et-foren	atvore	—	before
bi-foran, be-foran	foren, elforan	byforen, bifore, bivore	bifore, before, beforn, beforen	before
on-foran	aforen	—	afore	afore
to-foran	tofore, toforen	tofore, tovore	to fore	before
wið-foran	—	—	—	before
forth (adv.)	forþe (prep. = beyond)	—	without-forth = outside of	forth = forth from (in Shakspeare)
—	—	—	even-forth, em-forth, ferforth (according, to the extent of)	—
fram	from, vrom	from	from	from
fromward	—	—	froward	fromward
—	fro, fra	fro, fra	fro, fra	from
giond, geond	geond, ȝeond, gond	ȝeond	—	through, after
(fram)geondan	—	—	—	from beyond
be-geond, be-geondan	biȝende, biȝonden	biȝonde, biȝende	beȝonde, biȝondis	over, by, beyond
wið-geondan	—	—	—	beyond
be-heonan	—	—	—	this side of
be-hindan	bihinden	behynde	behynde	behind
in	in, innen	inne, ine	in	in
innan	inne, innan	—	—	in, within
b-innan	binnen, bine, binne	bin	—	within
wið-innan	wiþinnen, wiþinne, in-wiþ	wyþinne	withinne, within, in with	within

PREPOSITIONS.

First Per.	Second Per.	Third Per.	Fourth Per.	
—	inne midde-ward	amidward	—	amid
mid	mid	mid	mid	with
—	on-midden	amiddes, imyd, imyddes (in the midst of)	—	in the middle of
neoðan	—	—	—	beneath
be-neoðan	bineoþe, bineþen, binoþen	bineþe, beneþe	beneþe	beneath
under-neoðan of	underneþe of	underneaþe of	underneþe of	underneath from, off
on	on, o (before þe), an, a	on, an, a	on, an, a	on, in
on innon	—	—	—	within, into
inne on	an inne	—	—	within, into
up + on	up on, an uppe	upon	upon, in upon (Wickliffe)	upon [1]
{ oð	aþet = oð þæt (O.E. Hom. 1st Series)	o þat	—	until, unto
{ oð in	forte, fort	forte, fort	—	until
to	to	to, alto (unto)	to	to, for
til (Northumbrian Gospels)	til	til	til	to
—	—	unto	unto	unto
—	forte (forto)	forte, vort, fort	—	until
into	into	into	into	into
—	intil	intil, until	intil, until	into, until
b-ûfan	buuen, boue, bufen, buue	—	buue	above
—	a-bufen	above, aboven, oboune, oboven	above, aboven	above, over
on-ufan	oven an, uuenen, ovenon	—	—	from above, upon, over
—	—	an-oue-ward, an-ou-ward on (at the top of)	—	—
ofer	ofer, over	over	over	over, above
—	—	—	at-over, at-above	beyond, above
up (adv.)	up	up, op	up	up
uppan	uppan, uppen, upen, uppe, uppo, uppon	upe, up, op, ope	upe, up	up (upon, on)
on-uppan	an-uppe, on-uppe, an-uppon	—	—	upon
under	under	under	under	under

[1] *Upon* (prep.) = *up* (adv.) + *on* (prep.), not O.E. *uppan, uppen, uppe.*

First Per.	Second Per.	Third Per.	Fourth Per.	
—	anunder	—	anunder	under
ûtan	ute	out, out-of	out	out of, from out
bûtan (= be-utan)	buten, bute [1]	bute, bote, bot, but	bute, but, bot	but, out of, without, except
on-bûtan	abutan	—	—,	about, around
â-bûtan	abuten	abute, aboute, oboute	boute, aboute	about
wiõ-ûtan	wiõuten, wiõ-ute, utwiþ, utewiþ, wiþutan	withouten, withoute, outwith	withouten, withoute, outwith	without
ymb-ûtan, ûtan-ymbe	—	—	—	about, round about
—	—	ute over (above)	—	—
—	þurh-ut with [2]	thorgh out with	thurȝout with	throughout with
wiõ	forõ-wiõ	forþ-wiþ	—	forthwith
wiõer (against)	—	—	—	—
ymbe, ymb, embe, emb	umben, embe, umbe	embe, umbe, umbe-mong (about, round about)	umbe (about) um- only as prefix to verbs	around, about
þurh	þurh, þurch, þureh	þurh, þoru, þurõ, þurf	thurgh, thorȝ, thorgh, thorow	through
—	—	þoru-out	—	throughout

II. Compound Prepositions.

(a) Substantive.

First Per.	Second Per.	Third Per.	Fourth Per.	
eâc (in addition to)	ek, ec (adv.)	ek, eke (adv.)	eke, ek (adv.)	eke
to-eâcan,	to-eke (adv.), teke (adv.), tekan (adv.)	þerteke (adv.)		thereto
on-gegn, on-gên, on-geân, â-geân, â-gên	on-ȝein, on-ȝæn, on-ȝænes, ȝæn, anȝen, aȝen, oȝen, aȝeines, aȝenes, yeynes	gayn, aȝen, aȝein, aȝeyn, aȝain, aȝaine, ogain, aȝaines, ayen, ayans, aye	aȝen, aȝien, aȝens, aȝeines, ayens, aȝeinst, ayenst	against, towards (opposite)

[1] The O.E. *bute* = without, except.
[2] In the Second period *with* often signifies *from*, *by*, and has also the sense of our *with*. In the Third and Fourth periods it takes altogether the place of the older *mid*. In the First period wiõ = with, opposite, against, from, beside, along, &c.

PREPOSITIONS.

First Per.	Second Per.	Third Per.	Fourth Per.	
—	—	avoreye, avorye (against, towards)	—	over against
tô-gegnes, to-gênes, to-geanes	to-ȝæne, to-ȝenes, to-ȝeines, to-ȝeine, to-yeynes	toyenes, toȝens	to-aȝens	against
ge-mang, on-gmang, on-nang, â-mang	imæng, imong, amang, among, bimong, imang	among, omang, amanges, imang, umbe-mong	among, amonges, immonȝes	among, amongst
be-norðan	—	bynorth	by north	north of
be-eâŝan	bi esten	by este	by este	east of
be-wǫtan	biwesten	by weste	by weste	west of
be-sûan	—	by souþer	—	south of
—	bi-side, bisiden, bisides	bysyde, bysides	byside, bysides	beside, besides
be-helfe	bihalf, bihælves, bihalves	—	—	besides (on this side of), on behalf of
—	—	instude of doun	instede of doun	instead of down, adown
â-dùn	adun, dun þurh dynt (with gen.)	thorgh dynt of, with dynt of	—	with dint of, by dint of
—	—	be wey of	—	by way of
onlyfte (adv.)	o-lofte (adv.)	alofte (adv.)	alofte	aloft (Shakspeare)
-	—	toppe (above)	—	—

(b) Adjective.

ær	ar, er	er, ar, or	er, ere, or	ere, before
feː	—	—	—	far from
unor	—	—	—	not far from
geːnde (p. O.Sax. ⊦handum, hand)	ihende	hende (adv.)	hende, ende	handy to, near to
nea	neh	ney	nyȝ, nygh	nigh, nigh to
ne	—	—	ner, nerre	nearer, nearer to, near, near to
nst	næxt	next, nest	next (= next to)	next, next to
nα-hand early)	—	neihand	ner hond	near

In the provincial dialects we find *besouth, be west*, &c. In the Second period the forms are also used adverbially.

First Per.	Second Per.	Third Per.	Fourth Per.	
neâwiste	aneoweste, aneouste	—	—	by, near
tô-weard	toward, touward	toward	toward	toward
tô-weardes	—	—	towardes	towards [1]
—	adune-ward	—	—	down
—	after-ward	—	—	after
from-ward	frommard, fromword, fraward	framward	fromward	from
—	—	upward	—	(upwards of)
wana	wane, on wane, awane	—	—	minus
and-lang, ond-long	on-longen, an-long, inlanges	endelong, end-lang	along, ende-long, endelonges	along
ge-long, preceded by prep. *on*	ilang, ilong, preceded by *on*	along (on)	along (on)	all 'long of, along of
on middan	on midden, imiddes	—	—	amid
on-middum	amidden, amidde, amideward	amydde, amid, mydde, amidward	amyddis, amyddes, amiddes	amid, amidt
tô-middes on-middele	—	in þe middes of	in þe middis of in þe mydil of, in þe myddylle of	in the mids of in the middle of, by the middle of
—	—	—	amel, ymel,[2] omell, amel	amid
be-twih, be-tweoh, betwuh, betuh (beourhs, betweohs), betweox, betwux	bitwihan, bituhhen, bituhhe, bitwixan, bitwixe, bitwixen, bitwixte, bitwix	betuex, bitwix	bitwixe, betwixen, betwixt, bytwyste	betwixt
—	—	—	—	a-twixt (Spenser)
be-twéonum, be-twýnum	bitweonen, bitwine, bitwene, bitwenen	bytwene	betwen, bytwene	between
efene, efne (adv.), nefne, nemne (except), tô-emnes, tô-efnes (along, evenly)	æfne (upon, even with)	emne, efne, an emn, &c. (adv.)	—	even, evenly

[1] In the Second period we find *towardes* (adv.) = about to come, fure. Shakspeare uses *toward* in the same sense.
[2] O.N. *á medel, a milli*; Dan. *imellem*; Swe. *emillem*.

First Per.	Second Per.	Third Per.	Fourth Per.	
on-efn, on-emn	on efn (adv. in La3.), anundes, anont, onont, on-onde, onefent	onence, anente, anende3	anent, anens,[1] anentis, anemptis, anentist, aneynst, anende	anent
—	—	—	em forþ	according to
—	—	—	eveneforþ[2] (adv.)	according to
on-fæst	onfest, onfast, anfest, faste bi	—	faste by	fast by
—	suþþe, siþþe þwer-t-ut (O.N. þvert)	suþþe, siþe —	siþe, sin, sen —	since athwart, thwart
þwyrs, þwirhes, þweorh, þwer, on þweorh (adv.)				
—	—	overþwert	over þwart	athwart, thwart
—	þwertover	—	—	athwart
—	onward	—	—	instead of
—	inward	—	—	within

CONJUNCTIONS.

I. Pronominal.

First Per.	Second Per.	Third Per.	Fourth Per.	
and	and	and	and	and
ono	an, and	and, an	and, an	an, if, an if
nu	nu	now, now	now	now
ne...ne	ne...ne	ne...ne	ne...ne	neither...nor
eâc, êc	ek, eke, ok	ek, eke	eke, eche	also, eke
ac, ach, ah	ah, auh, ec, ach, ok	ac	ac	but
swa	swa, so, sua, swo	sa, swa, sa, so	so	so
eal-swa	alswa, alswo, also, alse, ase	also, alswa, alse, ase	as, also	also, as
—	sum	som, sum	som, sum	as
swa hwær-swa	whær-swa	wher-as	wheras	whereas
swylce	swulc, alse, ase	—	—	as if
gif	3if, gif, yef	3if, yif	3if, if	if

[1] *Anon to* = even to (*anent* in the Third period); cp.
    "Alle (h)is cloþes caste of -verichen
    Anon to is scerte."—*Legends of Holy Rood*, pp. 54, 55.

[2] *Evenforþ* became *evene aboute* in later writers; used as an adv.

First Per.	Second Per.	Third Per.	Fourth Per.	
þý	þi	þi	—	therefore
aþý (þe)	—	—	—	so much the ...as
þýlæs, þy-læs þe, þelæste þe	lest, leoste	leste, laste	lest	lest
þæs	—	—	—	so far, thus
þæsþe	—	—	—	whereby
—	þes	—	—	therefore
þon, þonne	þænne, þanne, þenne, þonne	þanne, þan, þenne, þonne	þanne, þan	then
þonne	þene, þanne, þonne, þan	þenne, þanne, þan	þan, þen	than, since
—	—	—	als, bot	than
þa	þa, þo	þo, þa	þa, þa	then
þa þa	þa, þo	þo	þo, þo þat	when that
þeâh	þæh, þah, þoh, þeh, þaih, þauh, þeih, þeyh	þe3, þei, þof	þou3, þogh, þeigh, þei	nevertheless, though
—	—	—	alle þoughe	although
swa þeâh	þoh-swa-þoh	—	—	nevertheless (though)
þanon	—	—	—	thence
þær, þær þær	þer, þær þær	þer	þer, þeras	there, where
—	þer-fore, þær-fore	þerfore	þerfore	therefore
þenden	þende	—	—	whilst
for þý	forði	for thy	for thy	therefore (*for thy* is used by Spenser)
þæt	þat, þet	þet, þat, at	þat, at	that, in order that, on purpose that
ǽr (þæt)	ær, er, ar	ar, or, er	ar, er, or	ere, or (ever)
ǽr þam þæt, ǽr þam þo	ær þan, er þan	er þan	erthen, erst then, or that	ere that
—	after þat	after that	after that	after
—	—	—	—	during, whilst
—	biforen þat	bifore þat	before þat	before, afore
—	imong þat	—	—	while that
bûtan (þæt), bûtan	bute, buten	bute, bote, bute þat	but, bot	but, but that
—	—	—	no but, no bot	only
—	but 3if	but-3if, but-gif	but 3if	but...if (unless)
—	—	bi þat	bi þat	until, by that
bi þam þe	—	—	—	by this that, as
for þan þæt, for þon þe, for þam þe, for þan þe	for þon þat, for þon, for þi þat, to-for, forþi	for þat, for	for because that, for this that	because that, seeing that, therefore (*for that, for because,* are archaic)

First Per.	Second Per.	Third Per.	Fourth Per.	
—	for	for	for	for, because
—	—	—	for al	for all (notwithstanding)
—	—	—	—	for and (and moreover)
—	fra þat	from þat, fram þat	—	since, from that (time)
—	iþat þat	—	—	in that
mid þam þe, mid þŷ þe	—	—	—	with that, when, while
ncfne, nemne, nymŏe	—	—	—	unless
ŏŏ þæt	a þet, forto, forte, vorte, fort, þat, wat	al huet, fort, forte	—	until
of þon (= syŏŏan, since)	of þat (when that)	—	—	—
siŏŏan (= siŏþam þat)	onȝæn þat seoŏŏen	seþþe, sen	siþen, siþ, siþens, sins, sin þat	against since, sith that (Spenser), sithens (Ib.), sithence, since that (Shaksp.)
—	—	fraþat	froþat	since
—	til þat	tille, til, to	til, unto, to	till, until
—	forte þat, forŏ þat, forte	forto, forte	—	until, till that
wiŏ þon þe	wiŏ þon þe, wiþ þan-þe	wiþ þe þat, wiþ þat	with that	provided
{tŏ þam þæt, tŏ þe þæt, tŏ þŷ þæt}	to þan þat	—	—	to the end that
—	—	—	wiþouten	unless that, except, without
—	þurh þat, þurh þat þat	—	þurȝ þat, þurȝ þat þat, ther thurȝ þat (because that)	through that
—	—	—	—	besides that
—	—	—	—	notwithstanding that
—	—	—	by þe cause þat, because þat	because that
—	—	—	for because þat no but, no but ȝif, but	for because (vulgar) except that, except, excepting that
—	—	save	save that, saf only that	save, save only that

First Per.	Second Per.	Third Per.	Fourth Per.	
—	—	on lesse	—	saving, unless
sam...sam, same...same	sam...sam	—	—	whether...or
ge	—	—	—	and
ge...ge	ge...ge	—	—	both...and
ge...and	ga þa...ga þa	—	ye boþ, ya boþe...and	both...and
ge	ʒe	ʒe	ʒe (ʒhe)	even, yea, nay, nay even, ay
git, get	ʒet, ʒette	ʒet	ʒet	yet
—	hwet...hwet	wat...wat, what...what	what...what, what...and what, what ...and	what...what, what...and
hwonne	wenne, whan, whanne, wane (þonne þanne)	wan, wanne, huen	whan, when, when that	when, when so, when as, whensoever
hwar, huer, swâ huer	hwar	wher, huer, whar	wher, whar	where
—	ware so, hwære-swa, war-swa, wer-swa, whær-swa-se, whær-sum	—	—	whereso
—	—	war-by	wherby that, wherefore that	whereby, wherefore
—	—	wher-with[1]	—	where-with
—	—	war-þoru	—	where-through
—	whuder	whider	whider	whither
swa-hwider-swa	wuder-swa	whider-ever	—	whithersoever
—	woder þat	—	—	whither that
hwæðer...þe	wheþer...oþer, whether...þe	—	whether...or, wher...wher	whether...or, whether, or whether
hwæðer...oððe, oððe...oððe	—	—	—	whether...or
—	þe	—	—	or
swa-þeah-hwæðere	—	þogh-queþer, thogh-whether	the quether	nevertheless, yet
ǣgðer...ge, ǣgðres...ge	eʒðer...ʒe, æiðer...and, eʒþer...and, boðe...and	—	either...and	both...and
—	—	—	eyþer...or, eþer...or	either...or, either, or else
âðor (âðer) ...oþþe	oðer...oðer	oþer...or	oþer...or	either...or
—	—	—	eþer...or	either...or

[1] See Adverbs.

First Per.	Second Per.	Third Per.	Fourth Per.	
—	—	—	eyþer...or, or...ouþer	either...or
—	oþer	oþer, or	or...or	or...or
—	neoðer...ne,	noþer...ne,	oþer, or	or
nâðor...ne	neoðer...na,	nouþer...ne	neiþer...ne,	neither...nor
	nowþer...ne		noþer...ne,	
			neyþer...ne	
—	—	—	nouþer...ne,	neither...neither,
			neþer...neþer,	nor...nor
			neiþer...	
			neiþer	

II. Numeral.

an...sum, sum...sum	sum...sum	som...som, som...and som	som...som, oon...anoþer, oon...and oon, oþer...oþer, on...oþer	one(some)...some, one...another, other...some, one...other
begen¹...and	baðe...and, ba...and	boþe...and	bothe...and	both...and
ǽrest... siþþan...æt nextan	erst...siþþen, et nexten (rare)	first...siþþen (siþþe)	first...and siþþen	first...after wards, ...at last
—	—	—	first...after, „ ...eft, „ ...afterward, „ ...after þat, „ ...ferthermore, „ ...also, „ ...thanne, „ ...than, „ ...finally	first, secondly, lastly, finally, &c.

III. Adjective (Adverbial).

on êfne	an æfne	evene	—	even, even to
eornostlice	—	—	therfore	therefore
for þon	—	—	therefore	therefore
sóðlice	—	—	forsoþe lo! sooþly, soþly	truly
witoðlice	—	—	indeed, forsoþe	truly
elles	and ælles	—	and elles, elles, or elles	else, or else
gelice, gelice-swa, on-lice	iliche (alike)	(an-liche)	—	like as, likewise, alike...and

¹ It was inflected.

First Per.	Second Per.	Third Per.	Fourth Per.	
—	—	—	furthermore	furthermore
—	—	—	furtherover	further
—	—	—	moreover	moreover
—	—	as	—	where that
—	—	as ver forþ as	as fer forþ	as far as

IV. Substantive.

hwilum... hwilum	while (wile)... while (wile)	—	whilom...and whilom	awhile...awhile, sometimes... sometimes, at times...at times
— — þâ hwile þe þa hwile —	— þeonne...þenne þeo while þe þa while þat þe while þe, whil þat, hwils	— — — the while þat the while, while, whiles þat, to while þat, to whils	now...now — — — while that, the while, whils, whiles	now...now now...now the while that the while that while, whilst, the while (the whiles), while that, whilst that, during the while that
— on þæt gerâd	— —	for þe case þat —	in case if —	in case, in case that on condition that

V. Prepositional.

See *ær, æfter, biforan, bûtan, bi, for, from, in, mid, nemne, oð, of, ongeân, sîð, til, tô, wið, wiðutan, þuruh*, &c. These forms are generally followed by *þæt, þe* (*that*).

VI. Verbal.

| — | — | to iwiten | — | to wit |

VII. Compounds.

nâlæs þæt an ...ac eâc	—	no3t one...ac	not only...but, not only... but eke, not only... but and	not only...but, not merely... but

First Per.	Second Per.	Third Per.	Fourth Per.	
nâ þýlæs,	noþelæs,	noþeles,	neverþeles,	nathless,[1]
nâ þe læs	no þe later,	neverþeles,	naþeles,	nevertheless
	neuer þe later	never þe later,	neþeles,	
		ner þe later	never þe later	
ac nâ þê mâ	—	naþemo	—	nathemore (nevertheless)
þæt is	þat is, þet is	þat is	þat is	that is
—	—	that is at say	that is to seye, that is to seie	that is to say
nǣre (newære) þæt	—	warne, warn	warne, warn na war	were it not that
—	—	—	alle be it that, be so it be, by so, were it so that	were it so, be it so, albe, albeit
—	—	—	though so be that, sith that, so is that	how be it

INTERJECTIONS.

eâ	a	a	a A! A! A! (Wickliffe, *Jer.* xiv. 13.)	ah!
—	--	aha	aha	aha
eâ-lâ [2]	—	alas, allas	alas, allas	O, alas, alas the day
—.	—	—	fy allas	alack, lackaday
—	—	—	—	bah (O.F. *bah*)
—	—	—	ey	eh (O.F. *eh*), ay
—	—	fyadebles (= fie a devils)	vath or fie to thee, fyȝ (vath) thou, fy	fie (O.F. *fi*)
—	—	—	vah (vath)	foh, fah, faugh
hig	—	—	—	heigh, hey, heyday
hû	—	—	—	how
hû lâ	—	—	—	how now
hwý	—	—	why	why
lâ	la, lo, lour	lo	lo, loo	lo! la! O la!
—	o	o	ow, ou	O, oh
—	—	—	a	O, O me!

Ne for thi, nat for thi occur in the Third and Fourth periods for *nevertheless*.

[2] Eâ-la seems to be mixed up with F. *hé-las* (Lat. *lassus*, weary), hence *alas!* *alack*

First Per.	Second Per.	Third Per.	Fourth Per.	
—	—	—	te he [1]	aha'!
—	—	—	weu	aha !
—	—	—	—	ugh !
hwæt	—	what	what	what !
wa	wa, wo	wo	woo, wo	woe !
wâ-la	wola, wallan, wela, weolla, wele	—	—	alas !
—	—	—	alas	alas !
wû lâ wâ	ah wala wa, walɔwa, wolawo, wæila, wæi, weilawei	weȝlaway, weilawey	wa la wa	ah, well-a-day, well away
—	awæi, awei, aweih	awei, awey, wei	—	alas ! O woe ! ay me ! aye !
—	—	—	harow	harrow !
—	—	—	whist	whisht ! hush !
—	—	onȝ	—	God's wounds = zounds
—	heil (be þou)	—	—	hail ! al hail !
—	—	—	baw, bawe	bow-wow
—	—	—	heit now	gee
—	—	—	jossa	whoa
—	—	—	avoy (O. Fr. avoi)	fie

In the Second period we find *witicrist, wot Crist* = Christ knows, by Christ !

In the Third period we find (1) *deus, douce* = the deuce; (2) *daþeit, dahet* (O. Fr. *deshait, dchait, dehet*) = ill betide. In subsequent writers it became *daþet*, which has given rise to *dase you ! dise you ! dash you !* (3) *goddot, goddoth* = God wot, God knows. It occurs also in the subsequent period.

Peter = St. Peter, is a common interjection in the Third and Fourth periods, like *Marry !* [2] (= the Virgin *Mary*) in later times.

Bi Crist, for God, Lorde, &c. occur in the Third and Fourth periods.

---

[1] Denotes mocking laughter.
[2] *Seinte Marie !* occurs as interjection in the Second period.

APPENDIX III.

WORDS OF NORMAN-FRENCH ORIGIN IN THE ENGLISH LANGUAGE BEFORE 1300.

I. IN the "*Saxon Chronicle*," before 1200 :—
1086. dubban, dubben, to dub.
1135. pais.
1137. tresor, prisun, justise, rente, privileges, miracles.
1138. standard.
1140. emperice, cuntesse, tur.
1154. curt, processiun.

II. "*Lambeth Homilies*" ("O.E. Hom.," First Series), ed. Morris, for E.E.T. Society, before 1200 :—

Castel, processiun (p. 3), palefrai, saltere, prophete (5), fructe, messe (10), munte (11), asottie (17), rubbere (19), sottes, iugulere (29), meister (41), merci (43), manere, sacremens, ureisuns (51), riche, lechurs, blanchet (53), parais (61), elmesse, cherite (69), salm, font (73), sermonen, ewangeliste (81), liureisun (85), ioffred (87), cachepol (97), passiun (119), crunede (129), seinte (131), clerk (133), flum (141), erites (= heretics), munek, elmesful, poverte, large, prude, spus-had (143), sauter (155), fou, cuning, ermine, ocquerin, sabeline (181), servise, prut.

III. "*Trinity College Homilies*" ("O.E. Hom.," Second Series), ed. Morris, for E.E.T. Society,[1] before 1200 :—

Clerc (9), chastren, custume (11), gestninge, spuse (13), penance (17), richeise, lechure (29), orgele, barun (35), miseise (43), aisie, poure, candel, taper (47), religiun, turtle (49), mesure (55), minster, penitence, roberie (61), meister, onur (83), munt, palm, olive (89), calice, messe, sepulcre (91), crisme-cloth (95), maisterlinges (111),

---

[1] In the Press.

olvente, languste (locust), prisune, marbreston, salm, prophete, turnde, oregel, underplanter, underplantede, tur, corporeals, caliz, bispused, almes, archebissopes, sole, chemise, albe, sol, saffran, fustane, mentel, burnet, sergantes, acheked, martirs, confessors, patriarche, virgines, calch, waferiht, strect.

IV. Words from La3amon's "*Brut*," ed. Madden (?1205) :—

In the first text—achaped, ascaped, admirail, armite, appostolie, archen, astronomie, avallen, balles, barun, biclusen, bounie, bolle, brunie, burne, iburned, bunnen, cacchen, canele, cantelcope, cathel (chattels), cheisil, cludina (or cuiress), clusden (closed), comp (= camp), coriun (musical pipe), crune, cruneden, cros, crucche, dotie, dubben, duc, dus3e-pers, eastresse, falsie, flum, ginne, hardiliche, hiue (hue and cry), hose, hune (topmast?), ieled (anointed), hurte, ire, kablen, lac, lavede, latimer, legiun, licoriz, liun, lof (luff), machunes, mahun, male, mantel, martir, messagere, mile, montaine, munstre, munt, must, nonne, olifantes, pal, paradis, peytisce (= of Poitou), pilegrim, pouere, pore, porz (ports), postes, processiun, puinde, putte, quecchen (= quasser, casser?), riche, riches (= richesse), salmes, salteriun, scærninge, scare, scarn, scornes, sceremigge (scrimmage), scole, scurmen, seælled, senaht, senaturs, seint, servise, servinge, sire, sot, sumunde, talie (?), temple, timpe, toppe, tumbel, tunne, tur, turne, vlette (flat, floor), warde, weorre (war), werre,(to war, ravage), ymages.

In the later text we find the additional words—abbey, anued, aspide (espied), atyr, canoun, changede, chapel, chevetaine, chowles (jowls), cloke, conseil, contre (country), cope, cri, delaie, dosseperes, eyr, failede, fol, folie, gile, gisarme, grace, granti, guyse, harsun (arçun), heremite, honure, hostage, manere, marbre-stone, nonnerie, note, paide, pais, paisi, parc, passi, pensiles, porses, prisune, rollede, route, sarvi, scapie, seine (ensign), siwi (follow), soffri, istored, tavel, tresur, truage, tumbe, urinal, usi, waiteth.

V. (1) "*Seinte Marharrete*," ed. Cockayne, for E.E.T. Society, about 1220 :—

Seinte, passiun, crunede, font, martir (1), grace, prince (2), merci, chevese, changede (3), salve, samblant (5), liun (6), mantles (7), warant (8), bascin (9), drake (10), crauant, crune, castel (11), ibreuet (16), taperes (18), fontstan (19), chapele, lampe (20), martirdom, turnen (21), grandame, prisun (23).

(2) "*On Ureisun*," &c. in Lambeth MS. and Cotton MS. Nero, A. xiv. ("O.E. Hom.," First Series), about 1220 :—

Privite, medicine, cunfort, fals (185), delit, unsauuet (187), salvi, abandun (189).

(3) "*On God Ureisun*," Cotton MS. Nero, A. xiv. (" O. E. Hom.," First Series) :—
Paradise, servise, ciclatune, ikruned, krune (193), munuch, cherite (199).

(4) " *On Lofsong of ure Lefdi* " (Ib.) :—
Passiun, prude, pris (205), bufettunge, crununge, sacrement, sacreð, grace (207).

(5) " *On Lofsong of ure Louerde*" (Ib.):—
I-sacred, merci, ewangeliste (209), merciable, warant (211), turnen, obedience (213), sawter, seruunge, of-seruunge, unofserued (215).

(6) "*Soules Warde*" (Bodl. MS. 34, Royal MS. 17, A. 27, Ib.) :—
Semblant, irobbet, tresur, tresor, castel, meistreð, cunestable, meistre, meosure, cruneð (247), preouin (249), mealles (253), mesure (255), meoster, icheret, aturnet (257), keiseres, trones, cunfessurs (261).

(7) " *Wohunge of ure Louerd* " (Cotton MS. Titus, D. 18, Ib.) :—
Druð, largese, noblesce, debonairte (269), large, druri, hardi (271), praie, robbedes, prisun, noble, gentile, gentiller, gentileste (273), deboneirschipe, grace, passiun, calenges (275), spuse, pouerte, strete, poure, beast (277), mesaise, treitur, tresun, ribauz (279), buffet, prince, piler, crune (281), munt, schurges, lettres (283), dol, derennedes, chaumbre, paie (285), prei, eise, carpe (287).

(8) "*Hali Meidenhad*," (Ib.) ed. Cockayne :—
. Eise (1), servise, chaunger, confort, grace, delit, serven (7), cuntasse, treitre, gentil (9), leccherie, tresor, acovered, coveringe, meistre (11), uerte, estat, beast, basine, prophete (13), dignete, irobbed, chaisteð, crunen (19), weimeres, chaste (21), aturn, icruned, gerlaunde, flurs, degrez, preoueð (23), haunteð, heritage (25), un-coverlich, acoveringe, vanite (27), sauuure, trubuil, seruise (29), richesce, huler, semblaund (30), greue, prisun, cuncweari, puisun, cangun (33), suleð, turnunge, angoise (35), adamantine stan, nurice (37), laumpe, paraise (45), prokie, asailʒet (47).

(9) "*Ancren Riwle*," ed. Morton, for Camden Society :—
Spus, riwle (3), riwlen, religiun (4), chaungunge, chaungen, clergesse, ures, manere, professiun, obedience, chastete (6), cherite, penitence, riwlunge, seint, ordre, descriued, canoniel (8), recluses, prelaz, prechures, religiuse, maten (10), abit, scandle, prophete,

gile, seruien, distinctiuns (12), seruise, cheapitres, sauter, kunfort, saluen (14), crucifix, auez, relikes (16), creviz, collecte, vers, salme, crede, prime (20), eise, silence, lescuns, feste, cumplie, anniversaries, ureisuns, letanie, observaunce, trinite (24), servie (26), verset, merci (30), prisun, prisune, temptaciuns (32), igranted (34), antefne (36), verslunge, meditaciuns (44), uenie, clauses (46), parlures, unseaueliche, creoice, chastite (50), preoue, deliten, point (52), kalenge, parais, feble (54), cope, sleve, mesur, treisun, speciale (56), lecheries, folherdi, asaileð, quarreaus, castel, weorreur, cwarreaus, kerneaus, kernel, ancheisuns, sacrement, kurteisie, creoisen, duble, advent, parten, blamen, preisen, fantesme (62), sot, pris, keccheð, noise (64), mercer, salve (66), preche, prechen, counsail, semblaunt, chastiement, cluse (72), mesure (74), noces, reisun, autorite, turnes, spice (78), eresie, nurice (82), charoines, corbin, mesteres, menestraus, preisunge (84), rob, poure (86), chere, bisaumpleð, grace, rikelot (88), gelus, gelusie (90), chaumbre (92), crune, anui (94), pleinte (96), cauncre, sauuen, propreliche (98), scorn (100), cumfort (102), joie, wardeins (104), trufles, bitrufleð, munt, buffeten (106), dangerus, schaundle, meseise, ipaied, mesterie (108), bi-clusinge, anguise (110), anguisuse, largeliche, asaumple, tendrust, fefre, berebarde (112), reisuns, diete, presente, pitaunce (114), eaise, gibet (116), pellican, juggen, juggement (118), leun, unicorne, versalie, remedies, unstable (120), raunsun, ransun, dette, detturs, acwiten (124), cwitaunce, purgatorie, andetted, persun, persone (126), cul, simple, ipocrite, gilen (128), achate, defautes, regibbeð, disciplines, sacrifise, sacrefises, sauur, ikupled, paien (138), ameistren, dignite, cwointe, cwiver, meistrie (140), i-ancred, ancre (anchor), cuntinuelement, contemplaciun (142), ipreised (144), priuement (146), leprus, figer, despoiled (148), frut, figes, tresor, robbares, muchares (150), mercer, riche, celles, aromaz (152), present, priuite, sturbinge, turne, baret (154), auaunceþ, barain, ymne, suiilede, ancheisun (158), baptiste, priuilege, prechur, merit, astaz, preeminces, preofunge (160), disturben, licur, bame, chaste, medicine (164), hurlunge, noble, gentile, noblesce, largesce, itrussed (166), trusseaus, purses, burgeises, renten, larger, relef, genterise, richesses, familiarite, prive, presse (168), sepulcre, bi-barred (170), fol, peis (172), entermeten, preouen, awaitie (174), orhel (176), itempted, puffes (178), pacience, meister (180), grucche, debonere (186), crununge, pilere (188), messager (190), cwite (192), treitre, plenté, adversité, prosperité, lecherie, glutunie, salue (194), aspieden, propre, assauz (196), liun, unicorn, scorpiun, mis-ipaied, chastiement, inobedience, prelat, paroschian, blasphemie, impacience, continaunce, riote (198), rancor (200), tricherie, simonie (202), stat, incest, waite, gigge (204), presumciun, accidie, terme (208), kurt, iuglur (210), angoise, skirm (212), augrim, kuuertur, glutun, manciple, celere, neppe (214), lechur, vileinie, eremite (216), tentaciun, akointed, miracle (218), adote, chetel (222), ampuiles (226), tur, tenten, asailen, cite, weorrur, kunscence, tempti (228), dialoge, greueu, dame (230), feblesce (232), baban (234), champiun (236), trone, prokie (238), armes, peinture, sauuaciun, pope, sucurs, efficaces (246), ape, ape-ware (248), cwaer, departunge, driwerie, spitel (250), attente, deskumfit (252), recorde, misericorde (256), turnen, capitalen, garcen, skurgen (258), palm, despuiled (260), sponge, mistrun, unsauure, articles, sulement, iturpled (266), sacrament, sacreð, messeð, trublen, dewleset (268), amased, bimased, maseliche (272), rosen (276), ignorance (278), haunche (280), ameistre, quaer (282), afeited (284), robben, pagine (286), cogitaciun, affectiun, creaunt (288), lettre, passiun (292), recoilen, gunfaneur (300), urnemenz, eritage (302), belami, weorrede, chaunge (312), sarmun, totages, circumstances, cause (316), munuch, clerk (318), flatterunge (320), trussen, torplen (322), sol, sutare (324), harloz, festre (328), truwandise, cancre (330), arche (334), baundune (338), iflured, flures, abstinence, delices, auenture (340), ipocrisie (342), enbreued, sire, absoluciun, remissiun (346), sentence, pilegrimes (348), rute, spense, isonted, untrussed (350), jurneie, vilte, asperete (354), harlot, glorie, seinte, gredil, sotschipe, pilche (362), sabraz, akoveren (364), deuociun, ungraciuse, feblie (368), fisiciens, spices, gingiuere, gedewal, cloudegelofre, letuarie (370), mirre, aloes, perfectiun, tures (372), devot (376), reclus (378), ententes, testament, saluz, destruied, beaubelet (388), debonerte, turnement (390), peintunge (392), giwerie, depeinten, passen (396), tribulaciuns (402), failede, piment (404), chaumberling, kunsiler (410), seruen, deinte, assumciun, nativite (412), potage, rentes, kurtesie, gingiure (416), vestimenz, stamin (418), vaumpez, ilaced, veiles, atiffen, broche (420), obedient, hesmel (424), aturn (426), isturbed, servant (428).

VI. (1) *O.E. "Bestiary,"* in "An O.E. Miscellany," ed. Morris, for E.E.T. Society, about 1240:—

Leun, funt-fat, crede, grace, venim, poure, capun, market, cethegrande, cete, elpe, mandragores, turtre, spuse, panter, dragun, robbinge, simple.

(2) *"Genesis and Exodus,"* ed. Morris, for E.E.T. Society, about 1240:—

Aucter, auter, astronomige, arsmetrike, bigamie, crisme, charité, canticle, circumcis, corune, crune, desert, graunte, gruchede, holocaust, hostel, iurnes, iusted, lecherie, lepre, munt, mester, meister, offiz, pais, plente, pore, present, pris, prisun, promissioun, prophet, roche, sacrede, cite, spirit, spices, suriun, swinacie, serue, service, ydeles, ydolatrie.

(3) "*Old Kentish Sermons*," in "An O.E. Miscellany," about 1240 :—

Seinte, aperen, conseil, anuri, onuri, aparailen, anud, somoni, glorius, miracle, ensample, cuuenable, sacrefyse, verray, signefien, suffri, amunteð, defenden, cors, pelrimage, visiti, poure, amonestement, signefiance, urisun, ofserven, cite, auenture, sergaunz, ydres, seruen, religiun, custome, contrarie, commencement, natureliche, lecherie, roberie, spusbreche, orgeilus, umble, lechur, chaste, folies, vertu, montayne, sarmun, leprus, onure, lepre, iwarised, maladie, glutunie, desevird, compainie, asoiled, perissi, peril, merci, acumbri, marcatte, travail, commandement, isauued, deliuri, seruise, paie, gruchche, serui, aresunede, diuers, nature, grante.

(4) "*Owl and Nightingale*," ed. Stratmann, 1244 :—

Plaid, plaiding, ipeint, dahet, faucun, castel, acorde, plaidi (6), grante, afoled (7), schirme (10), weorre (12), barez, grucching (13), plaites, riche, povre, cundut (15), ginne (21), purs (22), clerkes, munekes, canunes, pope (23), manteine (24), fitte (23), mester (29), gelus (33), merci (34), spusing (41), sot (42), spus-bruche (42), sothede (46), sputing (47), pais (54), rente, maister (55).

(5) "*Jesus Poems*," in "An O.E. Miscellany," about 1244 (MS. written after 1250) :—

Duzeper, turnen, flum, seruy, prechi, bitrayen, fowe, robe, palefray, temple, prute, maystres, feste, askape, munt, prysune, calehe, trayen, hardy, mantel, cendal, dute, princes, kustume, crune, quyte, croyz, cheysil, sepulchre, mercy, prechen, prechynge, turn, ofseruie, pouernesse, playdurs, drywories, spusynge, lecherye, sermonye, laced, warantye, poure, flur, kastel, spis, amatiste, grace, calcydone, lectorie, tupace, iaspe, saphir, sardone, smaragde, beril, crisopace, amur, symonye, clergie, weorreþ, crysme-child, prynce, sermun, barun, scarlat, rencyan, russet, meyné, reyne, fyn, culur, buffet, gayhol, curteys, skarlet, palle, persones, matines, quiten, nappes.

VII. "*Havelok the Dane*," ed. Skeat, for E.E.T. Society, about 1280 :—

Fyn (1), barun, robberes (2), pouere, ayse, preyse, menie (3), merci, large, eyr (4), pleinte, poure, preyden, turnen (5), preye, payed, messe-bok, caliz, messe-gere, corporaus (6), curteysye, luuedrurye, tendre, arke (7), catel, sauteres, sayse (8), fey, justises, grith-sergeans, gleyues, cri, beste (9), chaste, datheit, sire, trayson, traytur (10), pourelike, feble, chanounes (11), auter, castel, feblelike (13), malisun, kopes, hermites, trechery, felony (14), waiten (16), anker, riche (17), poke, croune, leoun, best (18), cerges (19), pastees, flaunes (20), chartre (21), traytour, doutede (22), flote, sturgiun, turbut (23), tumberel, paniers, gronge, laumprei, wastels, simenels (24), gruched (25), mester (26), segges (28), parlement, chaumpioun (31), baroun (32), traysoun (33), maugre, grauntede (35), spusing, spusen (36), ioie, syre (37), uoyz, croiz (39), closede, trone, corune, burgeys (40), prey (41), iustise (44), storie (45), curt (46), seinte, beneysun, veneysun, pyment, plente (47), gleiues, chinche, supe, ioupe (48), barre (49), asayleden, leun (51), allas, ribbe (52), sergaunz, baret (53), sleues, frusshe (55), trusse, mayster (56), couere, dubbe, mele, palefrey, seriaunz, warant (57), glotuns, serganz, serges, pappes (59), gent, charbucle (60), saue (62), per (63), conestable (64), taleuaces, hasard, romanz, tabour (65), cauenard (67), blame (68), leteres (70), seysed (71), desherite, gisarm, aunlaz (72), runci, priorie, nunnes (73), noblelike, wade (75), pateyn (77), eritage, utrage, feyth, conseyl (81), curteyse, spuse (82), curteys, rose, roser, flour (83), barnage, coruning, parted (84), tresoun, felonnye (85).

VIII. (1) "*King Horn,*" ed. Lumby, for E.E.T. Society, before 1300 :—

Flur, colur, rose, payn, serue, roche, admiral, arive, galeie, mestere, seruise, curt, squiere, spusen, dubbing, gegours, crune, gestes, proue, manere, prowesse, grace, bataille, denie, maister, assaille, auenture, turne, homage, enuye, folye, couerture, messaventure, lace, place, graunt, iarmed, paynyme, prime, compaynye, scaped, rengne, rente, devise, enemis, bigiled, spuse, posse, ankere, palmere, ispused, castel, deole, chaunge, sclavyne, scrippe, colmie, bicolmede, ture, pure, squier, galun, glotun, disse, pilegryn, damesele, preie, bitraie, palais, chaere, blame, heritage, baronage, crois, passage, banere, chapeles, roch, serie, cosin, ginne, gravel.

(2) "*Assumpcioun,*" in the volume containing "King Horn :"—

Lescoun, assompcion, temple, serui, poure, mester, messager, frut, palm, meigne, belamy, chauntre, gile, bitraie, space, amendy, parchement, seruise, chere.

(3) "*Florice and Blauncheflur,*" in "King Horn" :—

Date, grace, place, departe, chaumberlein (51), marchaunt, semblaunt (52), mariner, largeliche, parais, baruns, cite, paleis (53), riche, ioie, meniuier, pane, burgeis, curtais (54), ginne, pirate, porter, marbelston (55), sopere, marchaundice, curties, gref (56), entermeten, aquite, tures, plenere, kernel, crestele, charbucle (57), lampe, torche, lanterne, barbecan, culuart, felun, areisun, seriauns, stage, parage (58), capun, cristal, cler, saphir, flur, onur (59), chaunge, pris, coniureson, chauntement, ginnur, squire, schauntillun, mascun (mason), culvert, felun, resun, felonie, spie (60), esceker, covetus, envius, preie, grante, angussus, coveitus, honure (61), compaygne, druerie, parte, cunsail (62), fin (end), chaumbre (63), crie, par amur (64), art, part (65), certes, merci, crien, pité, dute, pal, admiral (66), tur, towaille, bacin, pcire, oresun, passiun, sire, demure (67), piler, chamberlayn (68), belamy, hardy, barnage, iugements, prison, palais, barons, deshonur, accupement (69), suffre, tendep, parting (70), quite (71), engin, granti, igranted (72), mainé, dubbede, spusen (73).

IX. "*Kyng Alixaunder,*" ed. Weber, before 1300 :—

Divers, defaute, poverte (3), flour, annye, maner, fool, duyk, pris, desireth, solas, cas, ribaudye, joye, baret, pais, jeste, maister (4), deliciouse (5), clerk, maistrie (6), ars, planet, chaunce, baroun, popet, bat (stick), enemye, chain, conjureson, asaied, regioun, assaile, puyr, bataile, cler, nacioun, dromoun, batayling, y-chaunged (8), ymage, basyn, distinctioun, weorre, disgysed, sojournyng, cité, anoyed, distryed (9), iniquité, saun fable, table, astromyen, astronomye, nygremauncye, discrye (10), justes, turnay, jay, accord[e] (11), jolif, feste, honeste, burgeys, jugoleris, mesteris, desirith, los, praisyng, folie, dame, gentil, face, marchal, atire, damoselis, delis, muyle (12), orfreys, roite (= rute), swte (= sute), trumpes, orgles, tymbres, carolying, champion, skyrmyng, lioun, chas, bay, baudekyn, pres, sengle, mantal-les, crounc (13), atyred, gentil, gent, faile, mervaile, contray, abasched, leisere (14), y-chaste (15), undur-chaumburleyn, by-cache, jugge, matynges, pryveté, madame, heygh-maister (16), sacrefying, chaisel, place, certes, ars-table, cours, colour, cristal, propre, nature, saffer [saphir] (18), irrous, herbes, herber, stamped, morter, virgyn, charmed, conjuryng, dragon, covertour, preost [= pressed] (19), messanger, pallis, riche, chaumbre, voidud, aspyed (20), refuse, maisterlyng, conqueren, charmyng, aferis (21), mesanter, desirous, repentyng, solace, losynger (22), priveté, gileful, suspecioun (23), galopith, encheson, hardy, chere, powere, comburment, fruyt, comforted, sorcerye, dressed, pavyloun (25), best (26), greved, ameye, semblaunt, gentil-men (27), drake, pray (= prey), faukon (28), strete, dotaunce, signifiaunce, signifyng, estellacioun, signefieth, sourmouncie (29), poisond, return, traitour, dragonet, resset, gynne, cowart, feynt (30), planete, werryour, hardyest(e), norice (31), geste, dosayn, afatement, demayne, skyrme, pars, romaunce, storie, disraying, justyng, (a)sailyng, defendyng, reveryng (32), playn, chayn, presented, perce, cheyn (33), firmament, verrament, tresond, afaunce, quyt (34), part, art, failith, sclaundre, aire [heir] (35), soun, stable, monteth, reyne, demeynith, aforced (36), reverence, crouned (37), somound, roune (38), issue, dubbed, servise, dubbyng, plenté, deynté, tresoreris [treasurers], someris, comaundement, present, departed, botileris, jogoleris, page (39), y-greved, manas, trussed, barge, olifauns, camelis, vitailes, armes (40), party, savage, asteynte [?] (41), ascaped, gage, maltalent, ire (42), departyng, armed, trumpyng, laboryng, demaynyng, baner, ynde [blew], asaied, launce, armures, yperced (44), amoure [lover], socour, scoumfyt, damage, grevaunce (45), visage, rage, pité, spoile, perile, duk, delivered, liversoon, foisoun, skarsliche, counsail, spouse, grauntid, counsailyng, spoused, message, flores (47), samytes, cortined, gardynes, people, harneys, prynce, nobles, sytolyng, carolyng, turneieyng, tour (48), arived, paleis (49), praised, y-crouned, chaunge, anired, coup (50), maigné, aschape, purveyede, contek, prison (51), à reson, to reygne, male ese, acorded, gestnyng (52), defende, veynes, deray, amende, olifaunt, sones, prest, batail, boceleris, forkis (53), touched, y-siwed, mangnelis, alblastres, engyn, myne, mynoris (54), poraile, apertelche, pore, sire, pes, ese, 'countryng, to hardye, talant, trouage, usage, anoied, truage (58), daunte, manace, rent, deliverid (59), to dres[se], presentis, compissement, verament, noise, cry, richely, treson, siwith, palfrey (61), coroune, feute, parted, tresour, nobleye, noumbre, ancres, acise (= asise), mariners, vigor, bac[h]elur, sojour[n], encresed (63), lettres, renoun, honour, seignour, weorriour (64), senas (senates), assentyn, servisd, distruyed (65), chivalrie, castel, seignorie, sojornith, temple, market, purtreyed (66), curteis (67), travaile, vestement, sacrifise, sacrefyeng, besans (68), peoren (peers), ribaud, (69), jewelis, empire, barbicans, mayntenid, quarellis, Dieu mercy, trappen (70), travailled, cors, launceynge, peys, metal, fronst, tolonst (71), assaut, solaced, angwysch (72), trowage, salved, distrene (? derreyne), parlement, comune, assent (73), braunche, scourge, haumudeys, paramours, neyce, cosynes, governor, robbour, coinoun (74), outrage, peer, pautener (75), amayed, doute, round (76), amiraylis, chast[e], purs (77), chaunselere, frusche, appertenaunce (78), amye (friend), mercye, trespas, juggement, acordement (80), verreyment, 'carole, tent, entent, justis, ven(e)sounes (81), bikir, bocher, lyon, mace (82), pleynt, soudan, verger, long-berdet (83), counselers, matere, ost, messantour (84), gonfanoun, sendel, siclatoun, joly, perceyved (85), standard, orgulous (86), conseillynge, arme, ordeyn, astore, apaied, graunt, covenaunt, y-pavylounded, prechid (87), honourith, kourith, coward (89), siwen (90), menage, compaignye, samyt, delyt, ches [chess] (91), warante, akedoun, tronchon, certe(s), melodye, crye, labour (93), assaylyng, bray, poudré, quarel, aspieth (94), destuted, autour, conceyved, drewery (96), basnet, gysarme, peces, saun faile, saun dotaunce (99), ypreost, arsoun, weilyng, mason, hawberk, vertuous, socoure (101), passed, veyne, batelynge, nobleys (= noblesse), acost, croupe, batalye, aperte (103), defoille, boyle, corour (104), raundoun, asiweth, curtesye, vylanye, garsounes, comunes (105), pellis, harneys, quystron, warysom, castles, arayed, assailed, valoure, parforce, ascapith, pavelounes (107), spoil, payed, deol, turneth, sojorneth, avauncement, amour (109), chevalry, messangers, justices, alblastreris, defence, dispence, vygoure, noble (112), barounye, bachelrye, fortresses, segedyn, aviroun, asawt, gyse, pencil (113), avetrol, justyng, acorde, y-foiled, emperour, armure (115), berfreyes, quarelis, hurdices, dismayng (117), coyntise (118), favour, nortoure, adaunt, preche (119), venyme, cleir (120), flourith, pertyng [parting] (122), homage, feuté, lewté, servys, marchauns, clergie, acord, parage (124), dispised (125), pyrie (jewels), unplye, palys, acoste (126), tence, distroied, rebel, chast, almatour, quoynte, coragous, trayed (127), busard, povert, lynage, servage (128), reherce (129), paye, norysched, baronage, plas (place), chesse (131), avowe, crount, raunsoun, soffraunce, amendement, haven, cheventeyn, asoyne, gay, geaunt (133), magnelis, rowte, torellis (134), pypyn (pipe), male-aperte, duyre, hast, tayl, gonnes (135), dure, speciale, gyle (136), person, rybaud, verger, velasour, swyer (137), harlot, cowardieth, continaunce, hardieth, rente, by-lace, dosseyn (139), pays, travaille, soudans (140), ordeyne, dragman (= interpreter), flum, maugre, camailes, dromedaries, somers, justers (141), trappe, croper, queyntise, laboures, trumpours, jangelours, route, robbedyn, tresours, corant, palfray, amblant, sergant, serjans, asemblaye, gylyng (145), ficicion (146), pocions, lettrure, aprise, spies (147), proferid, scareliche, perage (= parage), cage, corage, forest, sodeynliche (148), hardinesse, prowesse (149), chaunse, defendit, entraile, gargaze, gorger, joster (151), mace, lyoun (152), pesens (154), faynt, flank, launche (155), weorryours, meschef, agref, asay (157), pray, favasour, slyces (158), amy, voys (159), deshonour, descharged, aquyted, asyghe (= essay), oncas, antoure, lechour, traytour, aliene (161), aventure, victorie, chesoun, acoysyng, amiture (163), traytory, pere, preoire, glove (164), honest, cure, entermetyd, dispoyled, joyned (165), tastyng, feyntise, corsour (166), trouble (168), aspye, tyffen, pryveliche (169), contynaunce, demorrance, peolure, destrere (170), perlement, message (171), fable, pyment, botileir, vengaunce, laroun, usage, court, richesse, répentand (173), vysage (174), auntred, keoverid, folye (175), eschape (176), dragoun, failleth (178), constable, ostage, ape, scape (180), disray, pomon, arsun (181), soket, perced (182), pryvé, vygour, antur, assoyne (185), tressours, autors, peyn, autorité, salueth (186), purchas, discryve (187), posterne (188), norische, medlay (189), tyger, spirit, vaite (190), amended, gentiliche, bawmed, schryne, entaile, fyne (191), maried, ystabled, avaunce, baudry, keouere, harnesche (192),

NORMAN-FRENCH WORDS. 347

gybet, dispit, noyse, bailifs (193), siweye, jolifliche, partie, ylis, afyhe (197), botemeys, merveille (198), desert, apert (199), memorie, sklaunder (200), gyoures, peryl, straungest, lessoun, mountayne, engyneful, avenaunt, asperaunt, conquerrende, jugge (203), fest, joliffe, damoysel, haunteth (205), garnement, penaunce, discipline, medecyne (206), palmer, ermine, skarlet, pers, furchures (207), couloure, malicious (209), pleyne, laak, tryacle (210), charrey, astrangled, magnels (211), nombre (212), oost, mangenils, aketoun, plate, gaumbisoun, meschaunce, greuance (213), ypotame, semblabel, reisyn (214), purchacyng, pas, mendyng, soiournyng (215), tornay, dauncen, leopardes, unces, baneret (217), beef, motoun, venysoun, seysouns, sopere, charbokel, laumpe, aveysé, scorpion, bugle, cheyne, glotoun, fuysoun, meyntenaunt (218), lake (220), saven, loos, mounde (221), tressed, pecock (223), envenymed, molest, perch, saumoun, foysoun (225), estre, robe, furred, menevere, tabard, borel (227), scarseté, mantel (228), ennesure, defyeaunce, chaumpe, defendynge, assailynge, pardé (230), merveilynges, ymages, pure, stage, conquerde (231), envenymen, gorgen (232), dromuns, barge, spyces (233), faas, preciouse, conceyveth (234), jacynkte, piropes, crisolites, safyres, smaragdes, margarites, terrene, fourmed, doloure, remenaunt (235), cokedrill, monecros (236), vitailles (237), yportami, entreden, fygeres (238), delited, tempestes, entree, rekowered, duzeyn (241), tourment (242), doutaunce (244), consent (246), mynstral, juwel, sumpteris (250), lumbars, cayvars (251), ryvage, vysite, mont (252), hurdles, strayte, greven, anoye, vermye (253), destruye, sacrefyse, queyntaunce, yle, syment, pyrates (255), power, mountaunce, purveyed, y-changed (256), tempreth, muray, koyntise (258), merveillouse, robbery (259), lecherie, pasture, furchur, sustinaunce, honouryng, archeris, panter (260), nobleyse (262), fame, langage, encence, flum (263), arnement (264), carayne, unhonest (266), rinocertis, hont, medli, monoceros, marreys, front, rasour (270), noriceth, delfyns, valour (271), treble (272), enbrace (273), tenour (274), desyre, caries (carats), chargen, perdos, unycornes (275), ceptres, mester, cortesy (276), delit, solasying, aresoned (277), sakret, notemugge, sedewale, wodewale, canel, licoris (278), gilofre, quybibe, gynger, comyn, odour, delices, spices, broches (280), destenyng (281), largenesse, prowes[se] (282), fairye, comforte (283), creature (284), poysond, amonestement, certeyn, dysours, dalye (286), tressen, sygaldrye, emeraundis, peopur (288), soffred, mesureabele, bonere, assise, marchaunt, baudekins, pelles (290), latimer, rocher, distresse, teste [head], counseiler, enherit, hostel, lyvereyng (293), defyghe, vawte, alouris, corner (295), preove, dette, atyr, defyeng, deffyeng (297), demere, seynory, chalangith (298), blamed, affye, dereyne, afeormed (300), acount (301), malese, devyse (302), reremayn, spye, gangle [jangle] (303), discoverte, covenaunt, glorious, warentmentis (304), batest, abatest, tyranné (306), amendyng, pilgrimage, chalenge (307), to coverye, tapnage (308), demayn, paleys, qweynte (311), certyn, esteris, evorye (312), ymagour, disseyte, losenger, konioun (315), trace (316), reirwarde (317), remuwing, depose, encombrement (318).

X. A. "*Lives of Saints*," &c., in "Early English Poems," ed. Furnivall, for Philological Society, about 1295 :—

(1) St. Dunstan.—Miracle, doute, manere, sodeynliche, taper (34), crouning, norischi, crede, uncle, ioye, deynté, grauntede, abbei, ordeynour, rente, ordre, monek (35), cordeyned, amende, privei, celle, oreisouns, servie, poure, enuye, treoflinge (36), contrai, pose, poer, consailler, abbey, sojournede, sire, grace, folliche (37), blamie, persoun, persones, lecherie, maistres, preveie, place, aperteliche, priveite, masse (38), kirileyson, solaz, joyfulle, anteyn, specials, servede, trespas, assoillede, freres (39).

(2) An Oxford Student.—Madame (40), scole, penance, repentant, iserved (41), onoury, servise, privé, clerk, onourede, priveiliche, cors (42).

(3) The Jews and the Cross.—Sacring, trecherie (42), forme, vylté, priveité (43).

(4) St. Swithin.—Confessour, turnde, seint (43), chiefe, consail, heir, norissie, portoure, ioyous, bobaunce, squiers, bost, amendede (44), masoun, ribaudie (45), ischryned, doutest, poynt, signe, iolyf, igreved, honer, assignede, consayl (46), sumnede, oreisouns, irevested, devocioun, processioun, schrine, noble (47).

(5) St. Kenelm.—Abbai, principales (48), departed (49), accountes, folie, enuye, heritage, outrage, purveide, felonye, poisoun, ymartred, ambesas, wardeyn, traitour, trecherie, frut (50), deol, priveite, norice, tendre (51), travaillest, iugement, valleye, vers, cumpaignye, martirs (52), honury, seisi (53), larder, awaitede, lettres, diverse (54), nobliche, relike, noblerere, feste, messager (55), conteckede, pees, for-travailed, sauf, suy, bigyled, chapel (56), sautere, sauvoure, attefyne, schryne (57).

(6) St. James.—Isued, preisi, beau, membre, pelegrim, cas, bitraye, queyntise, bigyli, resoun (58), justise, dulfulliche, merci, doutede, agyled (59).

(7) St. Christopher.—Melodie, iugelour, firce, beau sire, delyvri (60), poer, mester, croiz, croice, ipassed, turnede, hermyte [here-

myte, ermyte] (61), prechi, confortie, tourment (62), virtu, preching, tourne, yarmed, cowardz (63), icristned, cristnede, sige, prisoun, itournd (64), gridire, roste, piler, arblestes, angusse, feble, clere (65).

(8) The 11,000 Virgins.—Virgines, fame, queynte, noblei, spouse, Marie, heir, destruye, message, deol, paye, grante, certeyn (66), honoure, servie, cristenie, priveite, preisi, tresches, sustenance, aryve, damaisele, aryvede, honourede, dignete (68), chast, baptize, ibaptised, suffrie, suede, cride, creatoure, gent(r)ise (69), nonnerie, granti, martyrs, enclynede, covent, tumbe, abbesse, honoury, chere (70).

(9) St. Edmund the Confessor.—Confessour, seint, isoilled, ordre, nonnes, hauberk, spense, scole (71), usede, grace, signe, grevy (72), yused, grevede, ensentede, chastete, ymage, pryveiliche, spoushode, mariage, ostesse, febliche (73), discipline, fyne (end), chaste, catel, flour, porveide (74), symonye, desire, priorasse, quitoure, itourmentede, tuochi (75), confort, oreisoun, custume, lessoun, pamerie (76), contynuelliche, profound, arsmetrike, cours, figours, numbre, visciun, entende, paume, rounde, cerclen, trinité, divinité, chanceler, alosed, université, pitousliche, religioun, desputede, scolers (77), savour, clergie, magesté, stat, desputie, studie, delyvre (78), prechour, croserie, procuracies, persones, largeliche, pouere, prechede (79), merci, roveisouns, baners, desturbie, desturbi, grevede (80), canoun, seculer, tresourer, avanced, sojournede, defaute, abbod, disciple, comun, ellectioun, messager (81), chamberlayn, archebischop, maistrie, messagers, semblant, lettres, chapitre, plener, queor, consailli, certes, obedience (82), ioyful, pité, heriet, deolfulliche, meseise, best (83), envie, contek, grandsire, legat, acordi, ensample, werrie, franchise, payest, amende, sentence, stabliche (84), anuy, isustened, ancestres, amendement, feble, soiourny (85), ipreched, minstre, faillede, ischryned (86).

(10) St. Edmund the King.—Hardie,ʼ corteys, quoynte, robbede (87), bisigede, scourgen, tourmentours (88), pitousliche, suede, pelrynage, honoury, noble (89).

(11) St. Katherine.—Artz, emperour, gywise, sacryfyse, temple, reisouns, preotlede, queyntise (90), justise, gent, preise, blame, veyne glorie, resoun, maister, maistrie, sustenie (91), desputi, plaidi, preovie, falliest (92), philosophe, iscourged, prophete, traitours, conforti (93), apeired, paleys, blandisinge, tourmentz, scourges, turne, prisoun, emporice, privei (94), prisones, ibaptized, turmente, tourment, iugement, gentrise, emperesse (95), rasours, mossel-mele, turmende (96), preyere, igranti (97), iourneyes, nobliche, oylle (98).

(12) St. Andrew.—Pur, doutede (99), folie, itournd, doutie, scourgi, tourmentours, preciouses (100).

(13) Seinte Lucie. — Grevous, fisciciens, ispend, meneisoun, amende, tuochede, presse, tuochinge (102), igranted, norice, que(y)nteliche, spere, lechour (103), comun, bordel, defouled, sauter, aprochi, enchantours, enchantementz (104), tendre (105).

(14) St. Edward.—Blame, aventoures, pore (106).

(15) Judas Iscariot.—Norischie, barayl (107), hurlede, bicas, heire, privite, ichasted, awaitede (108), maugre, anuyed, peren [pears] (109), repentant, purs-berer, susteynie, oignement, keoverie (110), baret.

(16) Pilate. — Spousbreche, norisschi (111), hostage, truage, faillede, queyntere, gyle, peer, chasteþ, duri, enquerede, yle (112), amaistrede, ascapede, crede, felonie, tresour, baillie, trecherie, accountie, bitrayd, acorded (113), repentede, keverchief, face, defaute, forme (114), assentede, tempest (115), swaged, iuggede, enqueste, destruyde, passede (116), passi, gailer, gentrice, curteisie, aventoure, atroute (117), roche, dulfol (118).

(17) The Pit of Hell (in "Fragments of Popular Science," ed. Wright).—Cours, cler, candle, firmament, planéte, frut, diverse, glotouns, qualité, crestal (133), balle, elementz, rounde, eir [air] (134), post, noyse, pur (135), debrusede, turment, tempest, mayster (136), occian (ocean), veynes, bal, boustes (? boustus), debonere, bosti, hardi, lecherie, temprieth, entempri (138), change, turneth, maner, norisschinge (139), purveide, forme, resoun, departi, attefyne, angusse, iclosed, i-strei3t, semblant, signes (140).

X. B. "þe Holy Rode" (in "Legends of the Holy Rood"), ed. Morris, for E. E. T. Society :—

Parais, valeie, envie (18), failede, anuyd, oile (20), defaute, doute (22), delit, ioie, floures, frut, maner, place (24), stat, prophete, trinyté, honur, confermy (26), power, cercle, honured (28), lecherie, penaunce, sauter, temple, noble, carpenters (30), defoulede, grace, destrued, vertu (32), croys, paynym (34), batail, fyn, lettres, signe, maister, enquerede (36), baptizen (37), conseil, somounce, amounty, enqueri, comun (38), sepulcre, prechede, debrusede (40), prison, cristeny, hasteliche, icristened (42), chere, fourme, servy, paie (44), treson, procession, ibaptised, scryne, presiouse (preciouses), desirede (46), ahansed, feste, partie, presious, queyntise (48), sege, trone, cok, bast (bastard), emperour, dedeyned (50), baundone, sivy, mark, sertes (52), honur, pascion, nobleic, feble (54), scivede, price, contreie, honouri, save, companye, offring, melodie (56), prechede, turne, gredice, rosti, gynne, honure (58), deboner, caudron, tormentynge (60).

XI. "*Robert of Gloucester's Chronicle*," ed. Hearne, about 1295 :—

Yle, doute, fruyt, parkes, ryveres, plenté (1), defaute, maystres (2), emperoures, worrede, destruiode, maystrie (4), chase, metel (6), clos, stret, pleyn, gyn, pek (7), pur, amende (8), age, transmigracion, incarnacion, bataile (9), enchantement, passe, enchaunterye (10), trauayl, deolful, servage, ostage, prowes, stat, power, noble (11), ost, pryson, chaunce, enhaunce, oblige, prys (12), store, messager, chargede, delyverede, deol, cryede (13), comfortede, change, y-armed, contre, temple, bestes, astore, offrede, honourede, place, ymage (14), geandes, geant, sovereyn, acoyntede, company (15), porchase, pes, hardi, solas, peses, robbery, strange, robbede (16), prest, percede, maister (17), batail, chateus, ystored, cheson, castel, despit, armeþ, armede, departede, partyes (18), ordeynede, bisegede, posterne, neueu, of-scape, quoyntise, faileth, honour, tabernacle, cité, pais, havene, ariruede (20), geand, to-raced, roches (22), aspiede, esé, plenteus, prince (23), for þe cas (because), astorede, damyseles, cheventeyn, pere, colour, maner, gent, spouse, bitraye (24), of-scapie, spousede, coynteliche, priveliche, prive, privité, sacrifise, sposhed, poer, spousebruche (26), concubine, attefine, diverse, letre (27), fame, veyn, close, cacheth, enchanter, chauntement (28), eir, crie, regned, hautinesse (29), Marie, noblest, bacheler, richesse (30), despisest, mariage, unmaried, graunt (31), tresour, entisede, spene, playnede, amendement (32), serve, grace, poverté, joiful (33), myseise, meseise, asayed, noblei (34), ensample, symple, antres, ma dame (35), siwte, arayed, false (36), aunte, prison, part (37), cosyn, nobliche, prophecie (38), feyntyse, koyntise, porveyede, truage, route (39), condyt (40), occean, companye, cler, sustynance (41), ese, eritage, rage, siwede (42), bi-cas, towchyng, venymed (43), amendede, governede (45), messingeres, homage, destruye, defoule, gentrise, couetyse, nobleye (46), franchise, conseleres, pavelon, ordeyned, quareles, mace, awatede (49), maistry, corteysie, joye (50), portes, ronde, ambes, atyr, y-osted, certeyn (52), menstrales, carole, bacheleres, anyed, court, asise, fest, siwie, juggement (53), abaty, sawve, stable, conseil (= council), vilenye, undeserved (54), sire, treson, bysegede, valei (55), tricherie, defendede, defaut, ascapede (56), amendy, preyse, pees, lyon, cruel (57), vncle, merci, ysuffrede, trespas, forme, acordede (58), cas (59), descrivyng, messageres, paide, noumbre (60), adauntede (61), aryvede (62), felonye, partye, ynorisched, trecherus, yserved, hardynesse (64), anauntre, acordþ, perauntre, acordy, spousyng, nobleste, damesel, alied (65), purliche, yspoused (66), evangelist, preche (67), chaumbre, blamede, fey, ficicianes (68), norische, gynne, langage, feble, chef (69), suffre (70), martri, joyned (71), temprede, rebel, emperie, quoynte (72), miracles, lettres, hastiliche, archetemples (74), eyr, bachelerie, bachiler, avaunsed, cartre, purchas (77), daungere, delivere (78), quoyñteliche, bytraide (79), egre, torment, conquerede, croys (82), crowne, grantede (83), ycrowned (84), deserite, deserites, enlegeance, firmament (85), baptize, pur mesel, baptizing, ybaptized (86), mastling (87), joyful (88), counseileres, spousi, aliance, avys (89), destourbede, contek (90), spousedest, (atte) fyn (91), warnesture, wardeynes, robboures (94), simpler, acente (96), robby (97), obligi, werrours, recet (98), hamer, marchandise, hauberk (99), travail, turnede, squiers (100), a-stored, destruyeth (101), armes (102), sacryng, governe, trayson, sustene, purchace (108), hastiues, ycompaced, large, poynte (109), glose, susteynede (110), arivede, choys (111), powers, servise, honoureth, planetes (112), chatews, covenaunt (113), rentes, wareson, privete (114), graunte, apayed (117), vassayl, paith, prechoures, lechour, lecheri, paynen (119), prechede, porpos (121), poyson, apoysnede (122), stabliche, payns [pagans] (123), ypayd, bitray(e), vilanye (124), semble, pay, barons (125), mantel, defoulede (126), ofserved, conselers (127), enchanters, morter (128), nonnery, semblant (129), philosophie, enchantoures [enchanters] (130), fundement, dragon, asailede (131), seynorie, change, digne, sege (132), asaile (133), chaste, corteys (134), savede (135), outrage, faylede (136), joustes, tornemens, lance, meschance (137), armour, comforted, siwe, ordeyne (139), entente, fynede (140), verdyt, peces (141), pyte, destresse, prisones (143), defende, treche, medycine, vertu (147), leveres, cables, enchantery (148), chauntiment (149), abyt (150), spycery, fsyik, noyse, yformed (151), branches (152), cors, mynstre (154), monteynes (155), delaye, demayde (156), contasse, parlemente, despyte, anguyssous, entre, folye (158), porter, privey (159), compas, febliche (162), feblor, feblesse, pouere, aspyed (165), debonere, gentyl, meyné (167), biseged (168), mercy (170), encented (171), armeth, dedeyn (172), purlyche, asoiled, prechynge (173), ypeynt, toret (174), asaut (175), afayted, prelats, processyon, anguysse, relykes (177), plente (180), largesse, storys, sumny (181), maynage (183), pas, dure, atyled (184), keverede, frount (185), clery (186), rounde, dossepers, fers (188), los (189), paleys (190), ermyne, boteler, suwyte, botelerye, druery, yproved, chastore (191), preve, tables, chekere, alurs (192), senatour, reverye, auncetres (193), mandement (194), taverne, hasarderye (195), descord (196), honoury (197), anhansy (198), archers (199), veage, conquery (200), jugede, pavylous, gleyve (203), hardyssy, pitos (204), mysaventure, pece, noryse (205), comforty, yspyted, spyte, rostede, astoned (207), governy (209), byturnde, despoylede, condut (212), seyngnerye (213),

NORMAN-FRENCH WORDS. 353

defense, recetted, conseyly, dureynede (214), pece-mele (217), byclosede (218), passy, cheance, spousbreche (220), anguysous (222), traytor, coler, souple, scapye, yperysed (226), cell (233), entyced, ermytes (235), yconfermed (237), norysynge, norysede, masse (238), sauflyche, ensenten (239), susteyny (240), chantement, porchacy, veneson, best (243), yrosted (244), playnte (252), deserte (253), poueral, avysyon, prophecye, regnede (254), dyscordyng, penance (255), conteked (259), scourged, crounement (263), cacchynge (265), spousy, fol, delyt, encheson (268), blamede (272), scaubert, preste (273), noblyliche, tresorye (274), relygion, spence (275), prioryes, abbeys (276), chartre, confermyng, pytoslyche, arysed (277), mescheance (278), apeyrede, kalangede (279), tempest (281), cathedral, ferce, ssryne (282), terme, envye (284), ysaved, bycas (288), porveyde (289), sacring, crouny (290), repentant, bastard (295), raymson, debrusede (298), cancrefrete (299), partede (302), yordeyned, soffry (303), coveyteth (306), partyner, desyry (309), gyle, foundement, ypoynted (310), avanced, avancement (312), scarlet, taylor, tour (313), assygned, glosyng (314), alyance, tendre, norysy (315), restorede (319), caroyne (320), enresonede, chacre (321), almesse, peryl, rose, acording (331), sclaundre, contenance (333), vengeance, desyre (334), orysons, feynede (336), trone, apoysony, perysy (337), wympel, myracle (338), delyvery (340), mossel, poudre, jugged (345), baronye, conferment (349), conseyly, peraventer (358), conseylede, corageus (359), glotonye (360), targe (361), vantward, valeye (362), keverynge, vysyon (363), largelyche, canons (364), streytlyche (373), tyrant, raunsom (374), apertelyche, myscheving, mysauntre (375), arblaste (377), dyverse (378), largylyche (383), omage (387), spenynge, follarge (389), say, belamy (390), sauf, quyt, creyserye, creysede (393), magnales (394), armure (397), potage (404), devocyon, revested (406), amyrayl, garyson, besans (409), renable, hastyf, secund (414), conseylers (417), forest (419), clergye (420), hardyssede (426), destourbaunce, chasty (428), assyses, mesures (429), waryson (431), damascle (432), gentryse (434), dystourbed (436), emperesse, lampreye (442), pryncypal (446), meseyse (450), calangy, conseyly (451), ordeyne, hardy (452), percy, resun (453), taper, offrynge, sygne (456), lyge, fol-hardy, porueance, leon (457), anhansyeth (458), socour (462), emprisonede, despyt, asoyly (464), improued (466), chaunceler (468), ordeinour (469), custome, costome (470), playdinge, patron, voweson (471), purchasy, bailifs, vacauns, prelat, chapele (472), ercedekne, plaininge, amendi, citacion, felon, bulle, desordeini (473), crouni (474), marbreston, paviment, cardinals (476), patriarc (480), presauns, presant (485), croyserye, delivery (487), annyd, trossi, romance (487), broche, calis (489), palefrey, chamberlein (490), mareshal, pitous, quarel (491), contesse (492), seisede, chaunge, isacred, covent (493), sousprior, arivi (494), general, passion, pitosliche (495), jus-

A A

tizes, principals (496), specialliche, graunti, paiden, defendi, sosteini (498), forester (499), demande, relesi, entredit, commune (500), apert, chasti (501), avauncieth (503), sentence (504), gywel (508), unstable (510), destance (511), delaied (513), legat (514), sinkpors, scarseliche (515), meschaunce (516), prieueliche (518), sacri (522), acused, prise, faile (523), prechors, concentede (528), freres (530), pleinede, porveance (533), hauntede, tornemiens (534), borgeis, portreven (541), viniterie, dosils (542), unarmed, attired, conteini (547), defensables, mangenel (549), procurede, banerets (551), solaci (552), reverence (553), remuede (555), demembred (559), sodeinliche (560), diner, grevede, suspendede (563), saut, gout (564), constable (565), closi, cope, cirurgian (566), deserited (567), somenie, despepled, feblede (568), assumption (570).

XII. *Harl. MS.* 2253.

(1) Proverbs of Hendyng, 1272—1307 (in "Specimens of Early English").—Servys, warysoun, fule, tempred, sot, male, gyleth.

(2) Lyric Poetry (ed. Wright, for Percy Society).—Soteleth, sotel, poure (23), siwith (24), flour, feynt, beryl, saphyr, jasper, gernet, ruby, onycle, diamaunde, coral (25), emeraude, margarite, charbocle, chere, rose, lilye-white, primerols, passeth, parvenke, pris, Alisaundre, ache, anys, coynte, columbine, bis, celydoyne, sauge, solsicle, papejai, tortle, tour, faucoun, mondrake, treacle, trone, licoris, sucre, saveth (26), gromyl, quibibe, comyn, crone, court, canel, cofre, gyngyvre, sedewale, gylofre, merci, resoun, gentel, joyeth, baundoun (27), bounte (29), richesse, reynes (31), croune, serven (32) noon, spices, romaunz (34), parays, broche (35), gyle, grein (38), chaunge (40), non, pees (42), doute, bref, notes (43), mandeth [mendeth] (44), tricherie, trichour (46), asoyle, folies, 'wayte glede' (watch-ember), goute (48), glotonie, lecherie, lavendere, coveytise, latymer (49), frount, face, launterne, fyn, graciouse, gay, gentil, jolyf, jay (52), fi(th)ele, rubie, baner, bealte, largesse, lilie, lealté, poer, pleyntes, siwed, maistry (53), engyn, preye, fourme (59), fyne, joie (60), peyne (62), duel (dole), lykerusere, alumere (68), servyng, preie (69), grace (72), graunte (73), soffrede (83), compagnie, scourges (84), blame, virgyne, medicyn, tresor, piete, jolyfte, floures, honoures (89), par-amours (91), flur, crie, soffre, cler, false (93), solas, counseileth, presente, encenz, sontes (96), ycrouned (98), vilore, dempned (100), feble, porest, eyse (102), maister, precious (103), counsail (104), palefrey, par, charité, tressour (105), champioun (106), trous, forke, frere, caynard (110), maystry, bayly (111), preide (112).

For the list of words from the "Saxon Chronicle" and Laȝamon's "Brut" I am indebted to Mr. Joseph Payne. See his list of Norman-French words used by Laȝamon, in *Notes and Queries*, No. 80, Fourth Series, July 10, 1869.

For Norman-French loans after 1300, see Marsh's "The Origin and History of the English Language," and Dr. Latham's "English Language."

INDEX.

INDEX.[1]

(The numerical references are double; the *former* number of each pair denoting the *page*, the *latter* denoting the *section*.)

A, prefix, 34, 31.
  for *he, she, it, they*, 119, 157.
  for *o*, 44, 37; into *e*, 49, 41.
  into *o* in strong verbs, 165, 273.
  into *u* in past tense, 160, 269.
  how produced physiologically, 58, 47.
  different sounds of, 61, 51; 63, 52.
  before verbs = *on, in*, &c., 179, 292.
  adverbial prefix, 194, 311.
  = *of*, 223, 323 (note).
  Teutonic prefix, 224, 324.
  Romance prefix, 243, 325.
Ab, Romance prefix, 243, 325.
Abbott, Shakespearian Grammar, 56, 44; 140, 216 (note).
  on *thou, you*, 118, 153.
  his for *its*, 124, 172 (note).
  on infinitive in *ing*, 178, 291 (note).
  on gerundial infinitive, 179, 292 (note).
Ablative case, ending of, 101, 96.
Able, suffix, 234, 325.
  Romance suffix, 40, 33.
About, compound preposition, 204, 314.
Above, compound preposition, 204, 314.
Absolute case, 103, 102.
Ac, ace, suffix, 238, 325.
Accent, definition of, 74, 54.
  in Old English, 74, 54.
  after Conquest, 74, 54.
  in Chaucer, Spenser, &c., 74, 54.

Accent, in Shakespeare, Milton, &c., 75, 54.
  on final syllables, 75, 54.
  in Elizabethan period, 75, 54.
  Latin, Greek, French influence on, 75, 54.
  distinguishes verb from noun, 76, 55.
  influence of, 76, 57.
Accoutre, 244, 325.
Accusative case, ending, 101, 96.
  in modern English, 101, 97.
  adverbs from, 194, 311; 196, 311.
Ad, Romance prefix, 243, 325.
Adder, 72, 53.
Ade, suffix, 239, 325.
Adjectival adverbs, 196, 311.
  suffix, 212, 321; 219, 322.
  compounds, 223, 323.
Adjective, in N. and S. dialects, 45, 37.
  changes in, 50, 41; 52, 41; 53, 41.
  distinguished by accent, 76, 55.
  uses as substantive, 99, 90; 100, 94.
  classified as noun, 79, 60.
  definition of, 80, 60.
  comparison of, 105, 108; 107, 115.
  numerals, 110, 127.
  indefinite article, 115, 137.
  indefinite numerals, 115, 138.
  uninflected in modern English, 104, 103.
  inflected in Chaucer's time, 104, 105.

---

[1] This Index (compiled by Mr. John Eliot, student in the Evening Department of King's College, London) does not include the Appendices.

INDEX.

Adjectives of Romance origin, 104, 105.
   used as substantives, 105, 106.
Adverb, ending in *e*, 55, 43.
   indeclinable, 79, 59.
   definition, formation, 80, 63.
   definition of, 193, 310.
   of place, time, &c., 193, 310.
   substantive, 193, 311.
   adjectival, 196, 311.
   numeral, 197, 311.
   from participle, 197, 312.
   pronominal, 198, 312.
   prepositional, 197, 312.
   compound, 201, 313.
Adverbial terminations, *ly*, *ment*, 80, 63.
   prefix, 80, 64; 247, 325.
   suffix, 220, 322.
African, South, dialects of, 12, 15.
After, prefix, 40, 33; 227, 324.
   comparative preposition, 204, 314.
   adverb, 197, 312.
Again, against, preposition, 205, 314.
Age, suffix, 39, 33; 237, 325.
Agglutinative language, 2, 6; 12, 15.
Ain, suffix, 235, 325; 236, 325.
Ajar, 68, 53.
Al, prefix, 34, 31; suffix, 233, 325.
Alatian languages, 11, 15.
Alfred, treaty with Danes, 29, 23.
All, prefix, 227, 324.
   indefinite numeral, 115, 138.
   used with *some*, 142, 218.
Alms, 99, 91; 99, 92.
Along, preposition, 205, 314.
Alphabet, 57, 45.
   spoken and written, 58, 46.
   elementary sounds in, 61, 51.
   inconsistent, 62, 52.
   imperfect, redundant, 62, 52.
Also, 200, 312.
Amb, Romance prefix, 243, 325.
American words in English, 33, 29.
Amid, amidst, preposition, 205, 314.
Among, compound preposition, 204, 314.
An, suffix, 235, 325; 236, 325.
   = *if*, 207, 317.
   plural termination, 95, 80.
   infinitive suffix, 176, 290.
Analytical language, English, 48, 40.
   form of denoting tense, 191, 309.
Ance, Romance suffix, 39, 33.
Ancestor, 243, 325.
Anent, 128, 181 (note); 206, 314.
Angeln, 27, 20.

Angles invade England, 27, 20.
   Teutonic tribes before them, 28, 20.
   distinguished from Jutes, Saxons, &c., 41, 34.
   Anglian dialect, 41, 34; (*see also* Dialects).
Anon, 197, 311.
Another, 150, 245.
   preceded by *one*, 150, 246.
Ante, Romance prefix, 243, 325.
Any, 147, 236.
   compounded, 147, 237.
   old negative of, 147, 237.
   joined to *whit*, 146, 233.
Aphæresis, 76, 57.
Apocope, 76, 57.
Apostrophe in genitive case, 102, 100.
Apron, 236, 325.
Arabic, Semitic language, 11, 14.
   words in English, 32, 29.
   influence on Europe, 33, 29.
Are, 30, 24; 42, 34; 53, 41; 182, 195.
Armour, 240, 325.
Article, definite, in Scandinavian, 6, 11.
   in First Period, 48, 40.
   in Second Period, 51, 41; 53, 41.
   in Third Period, 54, 42.
   definite, in North and South dialects, 45, 37.
   indefinite, 111, 128; 115, 137.
   definite, 121, 161; 125, 178.
   definite, in O.E., 130, 188.
Articulation, physiology of, 58, 46.
Ary, suffix, 232, 325.
Aryan, origin of name, 7, 12.
   Indo-European languages, 7, 12.
   comparison of languages, 106, 112.
   strong verbs, 155, 264.
As, used with *such*, 135, 206; 135, 207.
   = *that*, 133, 198.
   used with *what*, 134, 205.
   compounded with *so*, 135, 206.
   also, 200, 312.
Ass, suffix, 236, 325.
Asunder, 200, 312.
At, before infinitive, 46, 37; preposition, 203, 314.
Ate, suffix, 238, 325.
Atic, suffix, 237, 325.
Athwart, preposition, 206, 314.
Ative, Romance suffix, 40, 33.
Aught, etymology of, 146, 233.
Aunt, 84, 72.
Ay, aye, 201, 312.

INDEX. 361

B, change into *p*, 25, 18; 63, 53.
  inserted into words, 25, 18; 63, 53.
  change into *p*, *v*, *m*, 63, 53.
Bachelor, 84, 72.
Bad, 107, 117.
Bain on use of *that*, 132, 197 (note).
Bake, 6, 11.
Barley, 24, 18; 68, 53; 219, 322.
Barn, 218, 322.
Bask, 30, 24.
Basque, 12, 15.
Battledoor, 239, 325.
Be, prefix, 34, 31; 40, 33; 225, 324.
  verb *to be*, 180, 294.
  in Milton's time, 182, 295.
  Norse influence, 182, 295.
Bee, 88, 72.
Behight, 156, 266.
Beornicia, kingdom of, 28, 20.
Bet, better, best, 107, 116.
Bis, Romance prefix, 243, 325.
Bitch, 88, 72; 92, 74.
Blame, 32, 28.
Ble, suffix, 113, 134; 234, 325.
Boar, 87, 72; 92, 74.
Boisterous, 220, 322.
Bondman, 86, 72.
Born, borne, 161, 270.
Both, 113, 135.
Bound, 30, 24.
Boy, 84, 72.
Breaths, how produced physiologically, 59, 49.
Brethren, 96, 80.
Bridal, 222, 323.
Bride, 86, 72.
Bridegroom, 83, 71; 86, 72.
Bring, brought, 172, 281.
Brother, 83, 72.
Buck, 87, 72; 92, 74.
Bull, 87, 72.
Burial, 216, 321.
But, 81, 65.
  compound preposition, 204, 314.
Buy, bought, 172, 218.
By, in distributives, 113, 133.
  preposition, 197, 312; 203, 314.

C changed to *ch*, 50, 41.
  = *k* and *s*, 61, 50.
  = *k*, 63, 53.
  in Romance suffixes, 236, 325.
Can, 183, 298; 192, 309.
Canterbury, etymology of, 78, 57.
"Canterbury Tales," accent in, 75, 54.
Cardinal numbers (*see* Numerals).

Case, in First Period, 48, 40.
  in Second Period, 50, 41.
  -endings, 100, 95.
  Max Müller on, 100, 95.
  six cases in O. E., 100, 96.
  Possessive, 101, 97.
  absolute, 103, 102.
Castra, 29, 22.
Catch, caught, 171, 280.
Caxton, influence of printing, 56, 44.
Celtic (*see* Keltic).
Certain, indefinite pronoun, 151, 251.
Ch for *k*, 44, 37; 50, 41.
  = *c*, *dg*, *sh*, *tch*, 69, 53.
Chaffare, 25, 18.
Chariot, 239, 325.
Chaucer, wrote in East Midland dialect, 47, 39.
  influence, 47, 39.
  accent in, 74, 54.
  plural endings, 93, 76.
  genitive case, 102, 99.
  adjective inflexions, 104, 104; 105, 106.
  comparative of adjectives, 106, 110.
Checks, how produced physiologically, 59, 49.
Children, 96, 80.
Chinese language, 2, 6; 12, 15.
  words in English, 33, 29.
Christianity introduced into England, 28, 22.
Chum, 78, 57.
Circum, Romance prefix, 243, 325.
Clad, 171, 281.
Classical words in English, 34, 30.
  learning, revival of, 56, 44.
Classification of consonants, 60, 49.
Clemde, 160, 269.
Clothe, clad, 171, 281.
Coalition; verbs with pronouns, &c., 46, 38.
Cobweb, 25, 18.
Cock, 88, 72; 92, 74.
Colt, 88, 72; 92, 74.
Com, Romance prefix, 243, 325.
Comparative Sounds, Table of, 13, 16.
  degree, 105, 109; 106, 112.
Comparison, English, past and present, 48, 40; 50, 41.
  of adjectives, 105, 108.
  Marsh on, 105, 108.
  degrees of, 105, 109.
  double, 106, 111.
  strengthened by adverbs, 106, 112.
  irregular, 107, 115.

Comparison with *m* and *most*, 109, 123; 110, 124.
English and Romance words, 35, 31.
Composition, words formed by, 221, 323.
 with Teutonic particles, 224, 324.
 of Romance roots, 242, 325.
 Romance particles in, 243, 325.
Compound words, plural of, 95, 78.
 genitive of, 102, 101.
 adverbs, 201, 313.
 prepositions, 204, 314.
 conjunctions, 208, 317.
 words, Romance, 242, 325.
 substantive, 222, 323.
 adjectival, 223, 323.
 verbal, 224, 323.
 (*See also under* Composition.)
Con for *can*, 184, 298.
 Romance prefix, 243, 325.
Conjunction, indeclinable, 79, 59.
 origin of, 81, 65.
 divisions of, &c., 207, 316.
Conquest, Norman, effects on English, 49, 41.
 effects on accent, 74, 54.
 change at, 179, 292.
Consonant endings, 230, 325.
Consonants, two together, 25, 18.
 Grimm's law, 13, 16.
 in Indo-European languages, 57, 45.
 how produced physiologically, 59, 49.
 classification of, 59, 49.
 table of, 60, 49.
 equivalents of, *c, g, q, x*, 61, 50.
 various sounds of, 62, 52.
 inconsistent use of, 63, 53.
 labials, 63, 53.
 dentals, 64, 53.
 sibilants, 66, 53.
 gutturals, 68, 53.
 liquids, 71, 53.
 changed before *s* in plural, 94, 78.
 infixed in verb, 158, 268.
 as suffixes, 213, 321.
Contra, Romance prefix, 244, 325.
Cornish, Keltic language, 7, 12.
Cost, 244, 325.
Couch, 32, 28.
Counter, Romance prefix, 244, 325.
Countess, 85, 72.
Cow, 87, 72.
Coy, 32, 28.
Cumberland, Danes in, 29, 23.
Cunning, from *can*, 184, 298.

Curry, 244, 325.
Curse = *kers* = *cress*, 201, 312.
Cutlass, 237, 325.

D for *th*, 25, 18; 217, 321.
 inserted into words, 25, 18.
 inserted, cast off, &c., 64, 53.
 in past of weak verbs, 155, 263; 174, 286; 168, 276.
 in *mind*, 190, 306.
Daisy, 77, 57.
Dame, used by Spenser, 87, 72.
Dandelion, 243, 325.
Danes invade England, 29, 23.
Danish, branch of Scandinavian, 5, 9.
 grammatical peculiarities, 6, 11.
 allied to English, 30, 24.
 words of, in English, 30, 24.
 terms in Northern dialect, 41, 34.
 invasion, effects on language, 49, 41.
Dare, 184, 299; 185, 299.
Dative case, Second Period, 52, 41.
 Third Period, 54, 42.
 effects on plural, 96, 80.
 case, ending of, 101, 96.
 case, absolute, 103, 102.
 infinitive, 177, 290; 178, 291.
 adverbs formed from, 194, 311; 196, 311.
Daughter, 84, 72.
De, Romance prefix, 244, 325.
Decay, phonetic, 24, 18.
Deer, used by Shakespeare, 87, 72.
Definite article (*see* Article).
Degrees of comparison, 105, 109.
Demonstrative pronoun, forms in Northern and Southern dialects, 45, 37.
 changed into adverbs, 80, 63.
 in nominative case-ending, 101, 96.
 in genitive case-ending, 101, 96.
Dentals, 26, 18; 64, 53.
 how produced physiologically, 59, 49.
Derivation, 79, 58; 211, 319.
Di, dis, Romance prefix, 244, 325.
Dialectic growth, 24, 17.
 peculiarities, 24, 17.
Dialects, definition of, 1, 2.
 modern provincial Keltic element, 28, 20.
 Northern English Scandinavian element, 30, 24.
 corrupt Norman-French, 31, 25.
 before Conquest, Northern and Southern, 41, 34.

INDEX. 363

Dialects, in thirteenth and fourteenth centuries, 42, 35.
  two forms of Midland, 44, 36 ; 46, 38.
  in A. D. 1589, 47, 39.
  in Second Period, 53, 41.
  in Fourth Period, 54, 43.
  gender distinctions, 82, 68.
  Northern, gender suffix, 90, 73.
  ordinals in, 114, 136.
  concerning possessives, 125, 177.
  provincial, strong verbs, 157, 267.
  strong verbs, 161, 270.
  Northern, 182, 295.
  West Saxon, 182, 295 (note).
  Southern, Midland, and Northern, 173, 283 ; 175, 289 ; 180, 293.
Did, exhibiting reduplication in past tense, 156, 266.
Different = sundry, 151, 250.
Digraphs, 62, 52.
Diphthongs, how produced physiologically, 59, 48.
  different sounds of, 61, 51.
Dis, Romance prefix, 40, 33.
Distaff, 223, 323.
Distract, distraught, 171, 280.
Distributives, numeral, 113, 133.
Divers = sundry, 151, 250.
Do, suffix, weak verbs, 168, 276 ; 173, 283 ; 192, 309.
  = to cause, 192, 309.
  in *how do you do*, 191, 308.
Doe, 87, 72.
Dog, 88, 72 ; 92, 74.
Dom, nominal suffix, 84, 31.
  English suffix, 40, 33.
Doom, 218, 322.
Dor, door, dore, suffix, 239, 325.
Double forms from Latin, 82, 28.
  form of past participle, 168, 271 ; 164, 272.
  forms, 77, 57.
  feminine forms, 90, 73.
  form of weak verbs, 169, 279 ; 170, 279 ; 171, 280.
  plural forms, 97, 83.
  plural forms of foreign words, 98, 84.
  plural forms with two senses, 98, 85.
  meaning, singular and plural, 99, 89.
  comparisons, 106, 111.
Dowdy, 86, 72 (note).
Drake, 88, 72.
Drofe, 88, 72.
Dual number, First Period, 48, 40.
  Second Period, 52, 41.

Dual number, Third Period, 54, 42.
  in English, 93, 75.
  in pronouns, 117, 150.
Duchess, 92; 73.
Duck, 88, 72.
Dutch, branch of Low German, 4, 9.
  words in English, 33, 29.

E, between root and suffix in verbs, 168, 278.
  connecting root and suffix of verbs in Chaucer, 174, 283.
  suffix of adverbs, 196, 311.
  Romance prefix, 244, 325.
  for *a, o, u*, 49, 41.
  different sounds of, 61, 51.
  adjective termination, 104, 104.
Each, 118, 133 ; 147, 238.
  used as *every*, 148, 238.
  used as *both*, 148, 239.
  followed by *an, a, on,* &c., 148, 240.
Ean, suffix, 236, 235.
Earl, 85, 72.
East Anglia, 29, 23.
East Midland dialect, 44, 36 ; (*see also* Dialects.)
Eaves, 100, 92.
Ecclesiastical influence on English, 29, 22.
Edward III., act concerning French, 31, 25.
Ee, suffix, 238, 325.
Eer, suffix, 232, 325.
Ed, suffix, 238, 325.
Egyptian, Hamitic language, 11, 14.
  hieroglyphics, 57, 45.
Eight, 111, 127 (note); 111, 128.
Eighth, 114, 136.
Eign, suffix, 236, 325.
Either, 149, 242.
El, suffix, 238, 325.
Elbow, 77, 57.
Elder, eldest, 107, 115.
Elementary sounds in English, 61, 51.
Eleven, 112, 128.
Eleventh, 114, 136.
Elizabethan period, use of writers in, 90, 73 ; 91, 73 ; 102, 99 ; 160, 269 ; 170, 279 ; 195, 311 ; 196, 311 ; 228, 323 (note).
Elra, 150, 247 (note).
Else, 81, 65 ; 150, 247 ; 151, 247.
Em, Romance prefix, 40, 33 ; 245, 325.
En, Romance prefix, 40, 33 ; 245, 325.
  suffix to denote gender, 89, 73.
  plural termination, 95, 80.

INDEX.

En, adjectival and verbal suffix, 34, 31.
  or *ene*, 102, 98; 176, 289.
  adjective termination, 104, 104.
  for *him* or *hine*, 120, 157.
  suffix, 235, 325; 236, 325.
Ence, ent, suffix, 241, 325.
Endings (*see* Termination, Suffixes).
English language, branch of Low German, 5, 9.
  came from Continent, 27, 19.
  influences of invasions, 27, 20; 28, 22; 29, 23; 30, 24.
  effect on, of political events, 31, 25.
  number of words in, 34, 30.
  hybrids in, 39, 33.
  elementary sounds, 61, 51.
" English, Past and Present," Trench, 91, 73.
Enough, enow, 147, 325.
Er, suffix for comparative, 105, 109.
Ere, in compound adverbs, 202, 313.
  adjectival preposition, 205, 314.
Erel, suffix, 233, 325.
Ern, suffix, 236, 325.
Errand, 216, 321.
Erse, Keltic language, 7, 12.
Es, suffix of genitive singular, 101, 98.
  a distinct syllable, 102, 99.
  suffix to denote plural, 93, 76.
  reduced to *s*, 94, 78.
  suffix, 244, 325.
Ese, ess, suffix, 231, 325.
Esque, suffix, 237, 325.
Ess, Romance suffix, 40, 33.
  to denote gender, 90, 73.
Et, Romance suffix, 40, 33; 239, 325.
Ete, suffix, 238, 325.
Etymology, definition of, 79, 58.
  division of, 79, 58.
  parts of speech, 79, 59.
Euphonic changes, 24, 18; 25, 18; 26, 18; 44, 37; 63, 53.
Every, 113, 133.
  used as *each*, 148, 238.
  = *ever each*, 148, 241.
  compounded, 149, 241.
  use in sixteenth century, 149, 241.
Evil, 107, 117.
Ewe, 87, 72; 92, 74.
Ex, Romance prefix, 244, 325.
Extra, Romance prefix, 245, 325.
Ey, suffix, 242, 325.

F sound for *th*, 25, 18.
  for *v*, 44, 37; 63, 53.
  cast off, lost, &c., 63, 53; 230, 325.

Far, farther, farthest, 109, 122.
Fashion, 32, 28.
Fast by, adjectival preposition, 206, 314.
Father, 88, 72.
Fela = many, 115, 140.
Female, 92, 74 (*see* Gender).
Feminine gender, 83, 69; 102, 98 (*see also* Gender).
Few, 115, 141.
Fifth, 114, 136.
Filly, 88, 72; 92, 74.
First, 109, 123; 113, 136.
Five, 111, 128; 111, 127 (note).
Flat sound, how produced physiologically, 59, 49.
Flexionless neuter nouns, 96, 81.
Foal, 88, 72.
Fold, suffix, 113, 134.
For, prefix, 34, 31; 40, 33; 225, 324.
  related to dative case, 101, 96.
  adverb, 197, 312.
  preposition, 203, 314.
Fore, Teutonic prefix, 226, 324.
Foreign words naturalized, 32, 29.
  plural, how formed, 97, 84; 99, 90.
  used only in plural, 98, 86.
  take plural in English, 99, 87.
Formation of words, 211, 319.
Former, 109, 123.
Forswear, 225, 324 (note).
Forth, prefix, 227, 324.
  preposition, 203, 314.
Forthi = therefore, 199, 312.
Forwhy = wherefore, 199, 312.
Foster, 26, 18.
Four, 110, 127 (note); 111, 128.
Fourth, 114, 136.
Franks, Teutonic influence on French, 31, 26.
French, Italic language, 7, 12.
  possessions lost to England, and wars with, 31, 25.
  influence of Franks, 31, 26.
  words in English, 33, 29.
  words, accent of, 74, 54.
  (*See also* Norman-French.)
Friar, 85, 72.
Frisian branch of Low German, 4, 9.
  invasion of England, 27, 20.
Fro, 30, 24.
  prefix, 227, 324.
From, preposition, 203, 314.
  Teutonic prefix, 227, 324.
Froward, 30, 24

INDEX.   365

Ful, adjectival suffix, 84, 31.
  prefix, 34, 31.
Full, English suffix, 40, 33.
  suffix, plural of, 95, 78.
Future tense in First Period, 49, 40.
  in Second Period, 52, 41.

G, sound of, into *j*, 25, 18 ; 61, 50.
  into *y* and *w*, 50, 41 ; 186, 301.
  hard, softened, cast off, &c., 68, 53.
Gaelic, Keltic language, 7, 12.
Gain Teutonic prefix, 226, 324.
Gan = *did*, 192, 309.
Gander, 88, 72.
Gates, adverbial suffix, 194, 311.
Ge, prefix, 49, 40 ; 53, 41.
Gender in First Period, 48, 40.
  in Second Period, 52, 41 ; 53, 41.
  in Third Period, 54, 42.
  of substantives, 82, 66.
  grammatical, lost in English, 82, 67.
  distinctions, 83, 70—92, 74.
  in pronouns, 116, 144 ; 119, 156.
Genitive case, 54, 42 ; 101, 96.
  Max Müller on, 101, 96.
  case-ending, 102, 98.
  case in *his*, 102, 100 (note).
  case in compound words, 102, 101.
  of personal pronouns, 123, 171.
  suffix *n* and *r*, 123, 170 ; 123, 171.
  partitive of *one*, 144, 125.
  case, adverbs formed from, 193, 311 ; 196, 311.
Geographical limits of Northern, Midland, and Southern dialects, 42, 35.
  of East Midland and West Midland dialects, 44, 36.
  names plural in form, 100, 94.
German, origin of name, 3, 8.
  Low, 4, 9.
  Low, Grimm's Law, 13, 16.
  High, 4, 9.
  Old High, 5, 9.
  Old High, Grimm's Law, 13, 16.
  Middle, 5, 9.
  Modern, 5, 9.
  Modern, Grimm's Law, 13, 16.
  Low, Elements in English, 34, 31.
  words in English, 33, 29.
Gerundial infinitive, 177, 290 ; 178, 291.
Girl, 84, 72.
Go, 173, 283.
Good, 107, 116.

Goose, 88, 72.
Gospel, 26, 18 ; 65, 53.
Gossip, 26, 18 ; 63, 53.
Gothic, branch of Low German, 4, 9.
  literature, 4, 9.
  Grimm's Law on, 13, 16.
  comparison of adjectives in, 106, 112.
  past tense a reduplication, 156, 264.
  three conjugations of weak verbs, 168, 277.
Gower wrote in East Midland dialect, 47, 39.
Gradation of vowels, 58, 47.
Gramercy, 243, 325.
Grammar, use of, 1, 3.
  descriptive, 1, 4.
  comparative, 1, 4.
  English, unmixed, 34, 30.
Greek, ancient, Hellenic language, 7, 12.
  modern, Hellenic language, 7, 12.
  Grimm's Law in, 13, 16.
  words in English, 32, 28.
  plural, how formed, 98, 84 ; 99, 88 ; 99, 90.
  comparison of adjectives, 106, 112.
  past tense formed by reduplication, 155, 264 ; 156, 266.
Grimm's Law, 13, 16—23, 16.
  not the law of all changes, 24, 18.
Growth, dialectic, 24, 17.
Gutturals, softening of, 24, 18.
  changes of, 25, 18 ; 44, 37.
  how produced physiologically, 50, 49.
  changes in, 68, 53.

H disappears before *l, n, r*, intruded, cast off, changed, 70, 53.
Hamitic languages, 11, 14.
Hart, 87, 72.
Hautboy, 67, 53.
Have, had, 172, 281 ; 191, 309.
  Whitney on, 191, 309.
He, adverbial stem, 119, 156 ; 119, 157 ; 196, 312.
  and *she* used as nouns, 92, 74.
  prefix denoting gender, 92, 74.
  represented by *a*, 119, 157
  expressed by *one*, 144, 223.
Hebrew, Semitic language, 11, 14.
  words in English, 32, 29.
  words in English, plural of, 98, 84.
Heifer, 87, 72.

Hellenic languages, 7, 12.
 of Indo-European family, 7, 12.
Hen, 88, 72.
 prefix denoting gender, 92, 74.
Hence, 199, 312.
Her, 120, 158; 123, 172.
Here, 199, 312.
Hers, 125, 177.
Hext, superlative of *high*, 108, 120.
High German (*see* German).
Hight, exhibiting reduplication in past tense, 156, 266.
Him (dative), 119, 157.
 (accusative), 120, 157.
 represented by *en*, 120, 157.
Hind, 87, 72; 197, 312.
Hindu words in English, 33, 29.
His, 123, 172.
 sign of genitive case, 102, 100 (note).
Hither, 199, 312.
Hood, nominal suffix, 34, 31.
 English suffix, 40, 33.
Horse, 88, 72.
Hound, 88, 72.
How, 199, 312; 202, 313.
Huckster, 90, 73.
Hundred, 112, 131.
Husband, 86, 72.
Huzzy, 86, 72.
Hybrids, English and Romance, 39, 33.
 words, 90, 73; 217, 320.

I, for *u*, 44, 37.
 how produced physiologically, 58, 47.
 different sounds of, 61, 51.
 concerning, 57, 45.
 Teutonic prefix, 226, 324.
 (the pronoun), 116, 144—116, 146.
Ible, suffix, 234, 325.
Ic, suffix, 236, 325.
Icelandic language, 5, 9.
Icicle, 69, 53; 222, 323.
Id, suffix, 238, 325; 240, 325.
Ier, suffix, 232, 325.
Il, ile, suffix, 233, 325.
Ilk, 127, 179.
Ill, 30, 24; 107, 117.
In, before verbal nouns, 179, 292.
 adverb, 197, 312.
 preposition, 203, 314.
 Teutonic prefix, 228, 324.
 Romance prefix, 245, 325.
 suffix, 235, 325.

Indefinite article (*see* Article).
Indo-European languages, 6, 12; 9, 13; 10, 13; 27, 19; 57, 45; 106, 112.
Ine, suffix, 235, 325.
 Romance suffix denoting gender, 90, 73.
Infinitive mood, in First Period, 49, 40.
 in Second Period, 52, 41.
 in Fourth Period, 55, 43.
Inflectional or polysyllabic languages, 2, 6; 11, 14.
Inflections in English, Danish influence on, 30, 24.
 plural, verbal, comparative, 34, 31.
 of dialects (*see* Dialects).
 all significant at one time, 79, 58.
 denoting gender, 82, 67.
 verbal, 172, 282.
 neuter nouns not having, 96, 81.
 in genitive singular feminine nouns, 102, 98.
 to form genitive case, 101, 97.
 in oblique case of adjectives lost, 104, 103.
 of adjectives in Chaucer's time, 104, 104.
Ing, nominal suffix, 34, 31.
 = *ung, ende, inde*, 177, 291.
 in participles, 180, 293.
Instrumental case, 101, 96.
 adverbs formed from, 194, 311; 196, 311.
Inter, Romance prefix, 245, 325.
Interjection, 79, 59.
 definition of, 209, 318.
 as onomatopœia, 210, 318.
Intro, Romance prefix, 245, 325.
Introductions into English through Norman-French, 32, 28.
 direct from Latin, 32, 28.
 by Romance languages, 34, 31.
Invading tribes into England, 27, 20.
Invasion, Norman, A.D. 1066, 30, 25.
Ion, suffix, 236, 325.
Irish, Keltic language, 7, 12.
Irregular comparisons, 107, 115.
Is, auxiliary verb, 191, 309.
Ise, ize, suffix, 242, 325.
Ish, adjectival suffix, 34, 31.
 English suffix, 40, 33; 242, 325.
Ism, suffix, 234, 325.
Isolating or monosyllabic languages, 2, 6; 12, 15.
Issa, Mediæval Latin suffix, 91, 73.
Ist, suffix, 240, 325.
It, 119, 156; 120, 159.

INDEX.   367

It, also *hit*, 124, 173.
   also *its*, 124, 172.
Italian, Italic language, 7, 12.
   words in English, 33, 29.
Ite, suffix, 238, 325; 240, 325.
Ity, Romance suffix, 39, 33.
Ive, suffix, 230, 325.
Ix, Romance suffix, denoting gender, 90, 73.

J, 57, 45.
Jackanapes, 195, 311.
Japanese language, 12, 15.
   dialect of Loochoo, 12, 15.
   alphabet, 57, 45.
Jingo, 210, 318 (note).
Jutes, invade England, 27, 20.
   distinguished from Angles, 41, 34.

K, changed to *t*, 25, 18.
   for *ch*, 44, 37; 50, 41.
   for *c*, 61, 50; 68, 53.
   loss of, in *made*, 172, 281.
Keltic languages, 7, 12.
   elements in early, modern, and provincial English, 28, 21.
   words in French, 31, 26.
   population displaced, 27, 20.
   word *bachelor*, 84, 72.
Kent invaded, A.D. 449, 27, 20.
   dialects of, 83, 68.
Kerchief, 242, 325.
Kid, 87, 72.
Kin, nominal suffix, 34, 31.
   English suffix, 40, 33.
Kine, plural of cow, how formed, 95, 80.
King, 85, 72.
Knowledge, 219, 322.
Knowlech = acknowledge, 192, 309.
Koch, on *those*, 126, 178 (note).

L, weakened into *u*, cast off, changed to *r*, *n*, intruded, 71, 53.
   in *could*, not radical, 183, 298.
   in Romance suffixes, 238, 325.
Labial, aspirate, 25, 18.
   how produced physiologically, 59, 49.
   changes in, 63, 53.
Lad, 86, 72.
Lady, 86, 72.
Laminas, 77, 57; 222, 323.
Landscape, 219, 322.

Language, definition of, 1, 1.
   parts of speech, 79, 59.
Languages, classification of, 2, 5.
   morphological, 2, 6.
   monosyllabic, 2, 6; 12, 15.
   agglutinative, 2, 6; 12, 15.
   Semitic inflectional, 11, 14.
   polysyllabic, 2, 6.
   polysynthetic, 12, 15.
   genealogical, 3, 7.
   Indo-European, 6, 12.
   Basque, 12, 15.
   synthetic, 48, 40.
   analytical, 48, 40.
Lass, 86, 72.
Last, 109, 122.
Late, later, latest, 109, 122.
Latin, Grimm's law in, 13, 16.
   in English, 32, 28.
   in English, through Norman-French, 32, 28.
   words of Second Period, 29, 22.
   introduced by ecclesiastics, 29, 22.
   words of First Period, 29, 22.
   Third Period, 31, 26.
   Fourth Period, 31, 27.
   accent of, in English, 75, 54; 76, 55.
   words in English, plural, how formed, 97, 84; 99, 88.
   comparison of adjectives in, 106, 112.
   past tense, reduplication, 155, 264; 156, 266.
   prepositions in English, 206, 315.
Law, Grimm's, 13, 16.
   other laws of change, 24, 18.
Lay, laid, 172, 281.
Le, suffix, 233, 325.
Least, 108, 119.
Less, English suffix, 40, 33; 108, 119.
Less, least, 108, 119.
Lesser, 108, 119.
Lest, 199, 312.
Let, suffix, 40, 33; 239, 325.
Letters, 25, 18.
   definition, use, origin of, 57, 45.
   written and spoken, 58, 46.
   vowels, 57, 45; 58, 47; 61, 51; 62, 52.
   consonants, 59, 49; 61, 50; 63, 53.
Lic, suffix = *like*, 127, 179.
Lif, suffix = *ten*, 112, 128.
Ling, nominal suffix, 34, 31.
Linguals, how produced physiologically, 59, 49.
Liquids, changes in, 71, 53.

INDEX.

Literature of English language, 48, 40.
Little, 108, 119.
Littus Saxonicum, 28, 20.
Livelihood, 219, 322.
Locative case, 101, 96.
Long, adverbial suffix, 194, 311.
Lord, 64, 53; 86, 72.
Low German (*see* German).
Luther, effect on High German, 5, 9.
Ly, adjectival suffix, 34, 31.
   English suffix, 40, 33.
   adverbial suffix, 80, 63.

M, lost, weakened, changed, 71, 53.
   suffix of first person in verbs, 175, 289.
   in superlatives, 109, 123.
   in *from*, 203, 314.
   in Romance suffixes, 234, 325.
Ma, old superlative suffix, 107, 114.
Madam, 87, 72.
Maid, 84, 72; 92, 74.
Make, made, 172, 281.
Mal, Romance prefix, 248, 325.
Malay language, 12, 15.
   words in English, 33, 29.
Male, 92, 74.
Maltese language, 11, 14.
Mamma, 84, 72.
Man = *one*, 144, 224; 143, 222.
   men into *me*, 144, 222 (note).
   O. E. word for, 83, 71; 86, 72.
   in composition, 83, 71.
   denoting gender, 92, 74.
Many, 108, 118; 115, 139.
Manx, Keltic language, 7, 12.
March, on comparison of adjectives, 105, 108; 106, 110.
Marchioness, 92, 73.
Mare, 88, 72.
Mareschal, 89, 73.
Marsh, 231, 325 (note).
   reference to, 54, 42; 92, 74.
   on accent, 74, 54.
   on gerundial infinitive, 179, 292 (note).
Masculine gender, 83, 69.
Max Müller on Chinese, 2, 6.
   on consonants, 24, 17.
   on dialectic growth, 24, 17.
   on phonetic decay, 24, 18.
   on case, 100, 95.
   on Greek adjective, 101, 96.
   on word *genitive*, 101, 96.
   on *ing*, in infinitive, 178, 291.

Max Müller on *not a thread*, 201, 312 (note).
May, might, 186, 301.
Me, 117, 147.
   dative with impersonal verbs, 117, 147.
   as an expletive, 117, 147.
   from *men*, 144, 222 (note).
Meal, adverbial suffix, 194, 311.
Megrim, 242, 325.
Men becomes *me*, 144, 222 (note).
Ment, suffix, 39, 33; 80, 63; 235, 325.
Middle German (*see* German).
Midland counties, peopled by Angles, 28, 20.
   dialect (*see* Dialects).
Milter, 88, 72.
Milton, accent, 75, 54.
   case absolute, 103, 102.
   use of verb *to be*, 182, 295.
Minchen, 85, 72.
Mind, 190, 306.
Mine, 123, 171; 125, 176.
Mis, Teutonic prefix, 226, 324.
   Romance prefix, 245, 325.
Mistress, 92, 73.
Mo = *more*, 108, 118.
Modern High German (*see* German).
Modification of vowels, 58, 47.
   of diphthongs, 59, 48.
   of consonants, 63, 53.
Mole, 222, 323.
Monk, 85, 72.
Monosyllabic language, 2, 6; 12, 15.
Monosyllables in English, 34, 31.
Mony, suffix, 235, 325.
Mood, defined, 154, 259.
   indicative, 173, 283; 174, 285.
   subjunctive, 174, 284; 175, 288.
   infinitive, 176, 290.
   infinitive and verbal nouns, 177, 291.
   participle, 180, 293.
   imperative, 175, 288.
More, 108, 118; 106, 110.
Morphological language, 2, 6.
Morrice dance, 237, 325.
Most, 108, 118; 106, 110.
   suffix for *mest*, 110, 124.
Mot = *must*, 189, 304.
Mother, 83, 72.
Much, 108, 118.
Müller (*see* Max Müller).
Must, 156, 266; 189, 304.
Mutes, how produced physiologically, 59, 49.
My, mine, 123, 171; 125, 176.

N, lost, intruded, changed, &c., 72, 53.
   genitive suffix, 123, 170.
   suffix in past participles, 155, 263.
   infixed, 153, 268.
   falling off in p. part., 161, 270; 162, 271.
   falling out before dental, 203, 314.
   lost before *d*, 211, 319 (note).
   in Romance suffixes, 235, 325.
Na, adverbial stem, 200, 312.
Nag, 72, 53.
Nam, 182, 297.
Names, geographical, personal, 100, 94.
Nasals, how produced physiologically, 59, 49.
Naturalized words in English, 33, 29; 208, 315.
Naught, naughts, 147, 234.
Ncy, suffix, 241, 325.
Nd, suffix, 241, 325.
Near, 108, 120; 108, 121.
Neath, 197, 312.
Negative form of *yes*, 200, 312.
   form of verbs, 183, 297.
   form of will = nill, 187, 302.
Neither, 149, 243.
   used with plural verb, 150, 243.
Nephew, 85, 72.
Ness, nominal suffix, 34, 31.
   English suffix, 40, 33.
Nether, Teutonic prefix, 226, 324.
Neuter gender, 83, 69. (*See also* Gender.)
News, 99, 91 (note).
Newt, 64, 53; 72, 53.
Next, 108, 120.
Niece, 85, 72.
Nill, negative of *will*, 187, 302.
Nim = to take, 161, 270
Nine, 111, 128; 111, 127 (note).
Ninth, 114, 136.
No, 115, 137.
   used adjectively, 145, 229.
   = *not one*, 146, 230.
   -other = *none other*, 146, 230.
   used with *one*, 146, 231.
Nominal words, 79, 58.
Nominative case, ending of, 101, 96.
   in modern English, 101, 97.
   absolute, 103, 102.
Non, Romance prefix, 248, 325.
Nonce, in *for the nonce*, 197, 311.
None, 115, 137.
   used substantively, 145, 229.
   = *not one*, 146, 230.
   followed by *other*, 146, 230.

None = *no*, 146, 230.
Norman-French invasion, 30, 25.
   effects of, 49, 41; 54, 41; 82, 67; 93, 76; 218, 321.
   not spoken by the people, 31, 25.
   coalesces with English, 31, 25.
   corrupted, 31, 25.
   Latin words through, 32, 28.
   conquest, effect on accent, 74, 54.
   suffix to denote gender, 89, 73.
   adjectives in plural, 104, 105.
   influence on comparison of adjectives, 106, 110.
Normandy, loss of, 31, 25.
Norse, old, 5, 9.
North of England, Scandinavian influence, 30, 24.
Northern dialect, Scandinavian forms in, 46, 37. (*See also* Dialects.)
Northmen (*see* Danes), in North of France, 31, 26.
Northumbria, Danes in, 29, 23.
Nostril, 66, 53; 77, 57; 222, 323.
Not, 201, 312.
Nothing, 146, 232.
Nought, 201, 312.
Noun, in Northern and Southern dialects, 44, 37.
   genitive, 45, 37.
   in First Period, 48, 40.
   Second Period, 50, 41.
   Third Period, 54, 42.
   distinguished by accent, 76, 55.
   inflectional, 79, 59.
   substantive and adjective, 79, 60.
   verbal, in infinitive, 177, 290; 178, 291.
   as a suffix, 212, 321; 218, 322.
Now, 200, 312.
Nt, suffix 241, 325.
Number (*see* Dual and Plural).
Numbers, etymological origin of, 110, 127 (note).
Numerals, 110, 127—115, 138.
   used with some, 138, 214.
   one, 142, 219.
   adverbs, 197, 311.
Nun, 85, 72.

O for *a*, 44, 37.
   changed into *e*, 49, 41.
   different sounds of, 61, 51.
   changed into *ou*, 161, 269.
   for *a* in strong verbs, 166, 273.
Ob, Romance prefix, 246, 325.

Object to transitive verbs, 153, 252.
  cognate, 153, 256.
Oc, suffix, 236, 325.
Ock, nominal suffix, 34, 31.
Of, preposition, in adverbs, 194, 311;
  197, 312; 203, 314.
  Teutonic prefix, 228, 324.
Off, Teutonic prefix, 228, 324.
Old, 107, 115.
Old English dialects (*see* Dialects).
Old High German (*see* German).
Old Norse, 5, 9.
Old Saxon, branch of Low German, 4, 9.
  literature, ninth century, 4, 9.
Om, on, suffix, 241, 325.
On, suffix, 236, 325.
  prefix, 34, 31; 228, 324; 197, 312.
  preposition, 203, 314.
Once, 113, 134; 197, 311.
One, 110, 127; 115, 137; 111, 128; 142, 219.
  used for *self*, 123, 169; 142, 219.
  used with *some*, &c., 141, 217.
  various meanings of, 143, 220; 145, 228.
  used with *another*, 150, 246.
  used with *no*, 146, 231.
Onomatopœias, 210, 318.
Oon, suffix, 236, 325.
Or, suffix denoting gender, 90, 73.
Orchard, 25, 18; 69, 53; 77, 57; 221, 323; 222, 323.
Ordinal numbers (*see* Numerals).
Orm wrote in East Midland dialect, 47, 39.
Orthŏepy, definition of, 62, 52.
Orthography, English, 49, 41.
  definition of, 62, 52.
  inconsistency of, 62, 52.
Ose, suffix, 230, 325.
Other for *second*, 114, 136; 150, 244.
  used with *some*, 142, 217.
  genitive form, 150, 244.
  preceded by *each*, 150, 246.
Ought, 156, 266; 189, 303.
Our, 124, 175.
  suffix, 231, 325.
Ous, Romance suffix, 40, 35.
  suffix, 230, 325.
Out, prefix, 34, 31; 40, 33; 193, 312.
  preposition, 203, 314.
  Teutonic prefix, 228, 324.
Outrage, 247, 325.
Over, 110, 125; 197, 312.
  prefix, 34, 31; 40, 33; 228, 324.
  preposition, 204, 314.

Owe, ought own, 188, 303.
Own, 123, 168; 124, 174; 189, 303; 191, 307.
Ox, 87, 72.
Oxen, a plural in *en*, 95, 80.

P, changed into *b*, 25, 18.
  represented by *v*, inserted between *m* and *t*, 63, 53.
Pain, 99, 91 (note).
Palatals, how produced physiologically, 59, 49.
Papa, 84, 72.
Pardon, 246, 325.
Parliament, records in French, 30, 25.
  act concerning French, 31, 25.
Parsley, 242, 325.
Participle, in Northern and Southern dialects, 45, 37.
  present in *ind*, *and*, 45, 37.
  in *ende*, 49, 40.
  passive with prefix *ge*, 49, 40.
  in Second Period, 52, 41.
  in Third Period, 54, 42.
  in Fourth Period, 55, 43.
  a mood, 154, 259.
  of strong and weak verbs, 155, 263.
  unchanged in root vowel, 157, 267.
  changed in root vowel, 158, 269.
Particles, Teutonic, in composition, 224, 324.
  Romance, in composition, 243, 325.
Parts of speech, 79, 59.
Peas, 97, 83.
Pellucid, 246, 325.
Pen, Romance prefix, 248, 325.
Per, Romance prefix, 246, 325.
Periods of English language :—
  First Period, 450—1100, 48, 40.
  Second, 1100—1250, 40, 41.
  Third, 1250—1350, 54, 42.
  Fourth, 1350—1460, 54, 43.
  Fifth, 1460 to present, 56, 44.
Periods of introducing Latin :—
  First or Roman, 27, 22.
  Second, or Ecclesiastical, 28, 22.
  Third, or French, 31, 26.
  Fourth at revival of learning, 31, 27.
Permutation of consonants :—
  Grimm's Law, 13, 16.
  Whitney on, 24, 17.
  other laws than Grimm's, 24, 17.
  in English, 59, 49; 63, 53.
Persian language, 9, 12.
  words in English, 33, 27.
Person, in pronouns. 116, 144.
  in verbs, 155, 262.

Person-endings in verbs, 173, 282; 175, 289; 181, 295; 182, 296.
   changes in fourteenth century, 175, 287.
   m in first person, and *s*, *st*, in second, 175, 289.
   in past of strong verbs, 183, 298.
   th, *s*, in third person, 176, 289.
   en in plural, 176, 289.
Personal name, 100, 94.
   pronoun, dual, 93, 75.
Phonetic, decay, 24, 18.
   principles in alphabet, 62, 52.
Phonology, 57, 45.
Physiology of speech, 58, 46.
   of vowels, 58, 47.
   of diphthongs, 59, 48.
   of consonants, 59, 49.
Pickaxe, 67, 53.
Pig, 87, 72.
Pilgrim, 246, 325.
Ple, suffix, 113, 134.
Plural, in nouns, Second Period, 52, 41.
   in nouns, Third and Fourth Periods, 54, 42—55, 43.
   endings, 93, 76.
   change of consonant in, 94, 78.
   of compound words, 95, 78; 100, 94.
   change of vowel in, 95, 79.
   formed in *en*, 95, 80.
   of neuter words, 96, 81.
   of collective substantives, 97, 82.
   double forms, 97, 83—98, 85.
   of naturalized words, 97, 84.
   words only used in, 98, 86.
   formation of, 99, 88—99, 91.
   forms treated as singular, 99, 91.
   singular forms treated as plural, 99, 92.
   singular forms having the appearance of plural, 100, 93.
   of proper names, 100, 94.
   genitive of, 102, 98.
   of adjectives, 104, 104—105, 107.
Political events, effects on language, 31, 25.
Polysyllabic languages, 2, 6; 11, 14.
Portuguese language, 7, 12.
   words in English, 33, 29.
Position, words signifying, 79, 58.
Post, Romance prefix, 246, 325.
Præ, Romance prefix, 246, 325.
Prefixes, purely English, 34, 31.
   Romance, 40, 33.
   English, 40, 33.
   ge to p. participle, 49, 40; 53, 41.
   denoting gender 92, 74.

Prefixes, *a*, in *a-day*, &c., 194, 311.
   to, 195, 311.
   Teutonic particles, 224, 324.
   Romance particles, 243, 325.
Preposition, 49, 40; 203, 314.
   indeclinable, 79, 59.
   definition of, &c., 80, 64.
   to, for, in, &c., 101, 96.
   removed from relative, 153, 198.
   to before infinitive, 177, 290.
Preter, Romance prefix, 246, 325.
Printing, influence of, 56, 44.
Priscian on interjection, 209, 318 (note).
Pro, Romance prefix, 246, 325.
Pronominal adverbs, 198, 312; 201, 313.
Pronoun, reflex in Scandinavian, 6, 11.
   coalescing, 46, 38.
   dual number of, 48, 40.
   forms in First Period, 48, 40.
   forms in Second Period, 52, 41.
   forms in Third Period, 54, 42.
   forms in Fourth Period, 55, 43.
   forms in Fifth Period, 55, 43.
   inflectional, 79, 59.
   definition of, 80, 62.
   Whitney on, 80, 62.
   personal, dual, 93, 75.
   personal, 116, 144.
   demonstrative, 125, 178.
   interrogative, 128, 182.
   relative, 130, 188.
   indefinite, 136, 211.
   substantive, 116, 144.
   of first person, 116, 144.
   has dual number, 117, 150.
   reflexive, 121, 162.
   adjective, 123, 170.
   in person-endings, 173, 282; 181, 295.
   in imperative mood, 175, 288.
Pronunciation, changes in, 63, 52.
Proper names, plural of, 100, 94.
   used with *one*, 145, 226.
Provincial English, plural in *en*, 95, 80.
Proxy, 77, 57.
Pullet, 239, 325.
Pure English, 34, 30.
   tables of words, 35, 31.
   words with Romance suffixes, 39, 33.
   words with Romance prefixes, 40, 33.
Puttenham, Geo., refers to three dialects in England in 1589, 47, 39.
   quotations from, 47, 39 (note).

B B 2

Q, equal to *kw*, 61, 50.
Quality, words significant of, 79, 58.
    adjectives, 79, 60.
Quash, 244, 325.
Queen, 85, 72.
Quell = kill, 161, 270.
Quoth, 162, 272.

R, representing disappears, intruded, 73, 53.
    genitive suffix, 123, 172; 124, 175.
    in Romance suffixes, 230, 3 25.
Radical part of a word, 79, 58; 211, 319
Rally, 246, 327
Ram, 87, 72.
Rather, 109, 122.
Re, Romance prefix, 40, 33; 246, 325.
Red, Romance prefix, 246, 325.
Reduplication of present to form the past tense, 155, 264.
Reeve, 88, 72.
Reflective verbs, 154, 258.
    Scandinavian, 154, 258.
Rel, suffix, 233, 325.
Relational words, 79, 58.
Revival of learning, 31, 27; 56, 44.
Retro, Romance prefix, 246, 325.
Riches (note), 99, 91; 100, 92.
Rick, English suffix, 40, 33; 88, 72 (note).
Riddle, 67, 53; 216, 321.
Righteous, 220, 322.
Robert of Brunne wrote in East Midland dialect, 47, 39.
Robert of Gloucester, accent, 74, 54.
Roe, 87, 72.
Roman influence on English, 29, 22.
Romance dialects, 7, 12.
    words in English, 34, 31.
    table of words, 35, 31 *et seq.*
    words with English suffixes and prefixes, 40, 33.
    suffixes to denote gender, 90, 73.
    word, plural how formed, 94, 78; 98, 84.
    origin, adjectives of, 104, 105.
    prepositions, 206, 315.
    suffixes, 229, 325.
    roots, compound, 242, 325.
    particles in composition, 243, 325.
Root of a word, 79, 58.
    and suffix connected in verbs, 174, 283.
Roots, definition of, 211, 319.
Ruff, 88, 72.

Runic letters, 57, 45.
Ry, Romance suffix, 39, 33; 233, 325.

S, changed into *st*, 26, 18.
    for *z*, 44, 37.
    allied to *r*, represented by *c*, 66, 53.
    changes in, intruded, 66, 53.
    plural suffix, 93, 77; 94, 78.
    suffix to singular words, 99, 92 100, 93.
    genitive case-ending, 102, 100.
    forming plural of adjectives, 104, 105.
    in second person of verbs, 175, 289.
    in third, 176, 289.
    before a dental, 217, 321.
    in Romance suffixes, 230, 325.
    for *t*, 238, 325.
Sam, adverbial stem, 200, 312.
Same, 127, 180.
    = *one*, 145, 228.
Sand, Teutonic prefix, 226, 324.
Sandblind, 226, 324.
Sanskrit, 8, 12.
    Grimm's Law in, 13, 16.
    comparison of adjectives in,106,112.
    past tense formed by reduplication, 155, 264; 156, 266.
Saxon, branch of Low German, 4, 9.
    literature in ninth century, 4, 9.
Saxons, 41, 34.
    invade England, 27, 20.
Say, said, 172, 281.
Scandinavian (*see also* Danes)—
    language, 4, 9.
    dialects, 5, 9.
    compared with other Teutonic languages, 6, 11.
    definite article in, 6, 11.
    pronoun reflexive, 6, 11.
    influence on English, 30, 24.
    local names, &c., 30, 24.
    words in English, 30, 24.
    words in Norman-French, 31, 26.
    influence on *they*, 120, 160.
    forms in Northern dialect, 46, 37.
    origin of *slyk*, *sli*, &c., 127, 179.
    influence on *same*, 127, 180.
    origin of *are*, 182, 295.
Scarce, 238, 325; 244, 325.
Scourge, 244, 325.
Se, Romance prefix, 246, 325.
Sed, Romance prefix, 246, 325.
Second, 114, 136; 211, 325.
    = *other*, 150, 244.

Self, reflex pronoun, 121, 162.
  adjective = *same*, 122, 164.
  prefixed with personal pronoun, 122, 165.
  various uses of, 122, 166.
  used with *own*, 123, 168.
  represented by *one*, 123, 169.
Semitic languages, 11, 14; 57, 45.
Seneschal, 89, 73.
September, 197, 311 (note).
Ser, sere = sundry, 151, 250.
Seven, 111, 128.
Seventh, 114, 136.
Several, 151, 249.
Sexton, 77, 57.
Shall, 185, 300; 191, 309.
  = to owe, 185, 300.
Shamefaced, 219, 322.
Shakespeare, accent, 74, 54.
Sharp sound, how produced, physiologically, 59, 49.
She, 92, 74; 119, 156; 120, 158; 121, 161.
Sheriff, 77, 57.
Ship, nominal suffix, 34, 31.
  English suffix, 40, 33.
Si, adverbial stem, 200, 312.
Sibilant, for two dentals, 26, 18.
  changes in, 66, 53.
Sik, 6, 11 (note).
Since, adjective preposition, 206, 314.
Sinden, 182, 295.
Sine, Romance prefix, 248, 325.
Singular, like plural, 96, 81.
  some words none, 98, 86.
  distinct meaning from plural, 99, 89.
  use of plural nouns, 99, 91.
  form as plural, 99, 92.
  form with the appearance of plural, 100, 93.
  genitive of, 101, 98.
Sion, suffix, 241, 325.
Sire, 87, 72.
Sister, 83, 72.
Six, 111, 127 (note): 111, 128.
Sixth, 114, 136.
Slattern, 86, 72.
Sloven, 86, 72.
Slut, 86, 72.
Sneeze, 67, 53.
So = O.E. *swa*, 128, 182.
  compounded, 135, 206.
  with *swyle*, 136, 207.
  with *also*, 200, 312.
Softening gutturals:—
  end of word, 24, 18.

Softening gutturals:—
  into labial aspirate, 25, 18.
  until quite lost, 25, 18.
  g into *j*, 25, 18.
  initial letter, 25, 18.
  k into *ch*, 44, 37.
Some, adjectival suffix, 34, 31.
  English suffix, 40, 33.
  other uses, 138, 214; 139, 215; 142, 217; 142, 218.
Somdel, 142, 217.
Son, 84, 72.
Songster, 90, 73.
Sor, suffix, 240, 325.
Sory, suffix, 240, 325.
Sounds, division of, 13, 16.
  Grimm's Law on, 13, 16.
  f for *th*, 25, 18.
  p into *b*, 25, 18.
  neighbouring, influence of, 25, 18.
  two consonants assimilated, 25, 18.
  s into *st*, 26, 18.
  assimilating of, 26, 18.
  t for *k*, 25, 18.
  d for *th*, 25, 18.
  physiology of vocal organs, 58, 46—59, 49.
  elementary, in English, 61, 51.
  number of, in English, 62, 52.
  change in (*see* Vowels, Consonants).
Sovereign, 235, 325; 247, 325.
Sow, 87, 72; 92, 74.
Spanish, 7, 12.
  words in English, 33, 29.
Spawner, 88, 72.
Speech, physiology of, 58, 46.
  parts of (*see* Parts of Speech).
Spelling, changes in, 63, 52.
Spirants, how produced physiologically, 59, 49.
Spoken alphabet, 58, 46.
Ss, suffix, 239, 325.
St = *s*, 26, 18.
Stag, 87, 72.
Stallion, 88, 72.
Stem (*see* Theme).
Ster, suffix to denote gender, 89, 73.
  denoting also contempt, 90, 73.
Stevedore, 239, 325.
Steward, 222, 323.
Strong verbs, 155, 263—166, 274.
  now strong, once weak, 167, 275.
  letter infixed, 158, 268.
Sub, Romance prefix, 247, 325.
Substantive (*see also* Noun)—
  gender of, 82, 66.
  number of, 93, 75.

374 INDEX.

Substantive, case of, 100, 75.
 plural of (see Plural).
 neuter, 96, 81.
 from adjective, 105, 106.
 adverbs, 193, 311.
 as suffix, 212, 321; 218, 322.
 compounds, 222, 323.
Subter, Romance prefix, 247, 325.
Such, 127, 179.
 used with *as*, 135, 206; 135, 207.
Suffixes, plural, comparative, 34, 31.
 nominal, 34, 31.
 adjectival, 34, 31.
 verbal, 34, 31.
 Romance, 39, 33.
 English, 40, 33.
 iy, ment, 80, 63.
 denoting gender, 82, 67; 83, 70; 90, 73; 91, 73.
 rick, 88, 72 (note).
 en, to denote feminine, 89, 73.
 ster, ess, to denote feminine, 89, 73; 217, 321; 91, 73.
 denoting plural, 93, 76.
 s, denoting plural, 93, 77; 94, 78.
 en, denoting plural, 95, 80.
 denoting case, 101, 96.
 n, in adjectives, 101, 96; 104, 104.
 es, genitive singular, 101, 98; 102, 99.
 ene, genitive plural, 102, 98.
 s, plural adjectives, 104, 105.
 er, comparative degree, 105, 109.
 est, superlative degree, 105, 109.
 m, superlative, 215, 320.
 ma, old superlative ending, 107, 114.
 most, 110, 124.
 lif, 112, 128.
 teen, 112, 129.
 ty, 112, 130.
 fold, ple, 113, 134.
 dja, tha, in ordinals, 114, 136.
 n, genitival, 123, 170.
 r, genitival, 123, 172; 124, 175.
 lic, 127, 179.
 d, t, in past part., 155, 263; 171, 279.
 n, in past part., 161, 270.
 denoting mood and tense, 172, 282.
 denoting person, 173, 283.
 how connected with root in verbs, 174, 283.
 an, en, e, infinitive, 176, 290.
 ung, ing, infinitive, 177, 291.
 ing, inde, &c. participles, 180, 293; 214, 320.

Suffixes, *t* in *might*, 186, 301.
 long, gates, meal, in adverbs, 219, 322; 194, 311.
 e, ly, in adverbs, 196, 311.
 ber in *September*, 197, 311 (note).
 m in *from*, 203, 314.
 once independent words, 211, 319.
 in word formation, 211, 320.
 of Teutonic origin, 212, 321.
 vowel, 212, 321.
 consonantal, 213, 321.
 being nouns, 212, 321; 218, 322.
 being adjectives, 219, 322.
 adverbial, 220, 322.
 verbal, 220, 322.
 in compound words, 221, 323.
 of Romance origin, 229, 325.
 ther, 218, 321.
Summons, 100, 93.
Sundor, adverbial compound, 200, 312.
Sundry, 151, 248.
 = *divers, different, sere*, 151, 250.
Super, Romance prefix, 247, 325.
Superlative degree in *est*, 105, 109.
 degree in *most*, 106, 110; 110, 124.
 in Aryan languages, 106, 112.
 in *ma*, 107, 114.
 containing *m*, 109, 123.
 for South, East, West, 110, 126.
 used with *one*, 145, 225.
Sure, suffix, 240, 325.
Surplice, 237, 325.
Sweetheart, 219, 322.
Swine, 87, 72.
Swylc, 135, 207.
Syllabic language, 57, 45.
Syllable, recipient of accent, 74, 54.
 weakening, and casting off of, by accent, 76, 57.
 list of accented terminations, 74, 54 (note).
Synonyms, 32, 28; 39, 32.
Synthetic language, English in first period, 48, 40.

T, represented by *d*, cast off, inserted, &c., 65, 53.
 suffix in past tense, 155, 263; 174, 286.
 = *d* = *do*, suffix to weak verbs, 168, 276.
 changed to *s* (note), 174, 286; 190, 305.
 in *might*, 186, 301.
 sound of *k*, 25, 18.
 in Romance suffixes, 238, 325.

Table of comparative sounds, 13, 16.
    of synonyms, 39, 33.
Tadpole, 222, 323.
Teen, suffix, 112, 129.
Teu, 112, 128.
Tense, defined, 154, 260.
    emphatic, intentional, 155, 261.
    past, in strong and weak verbs, 155, 263.
    past, formed by reduplication, 155, 264; 174, 285.
    past, change of vowel in, 157, 267; 158, 269.
    past, formed with *d*, *t*, 168, 276; 174, 286.
    present, 173, 283; 174, 284.
    present participle, 180, 293.
    formed by composition, 191, 309.
    denoted analytically, 191, 309.
Tenth, 114, 136.
Ter, suffix, 239, 325.
Terminations (*see* Suffixes).
Tery, suffix, 241, 325.
Teutonic, origin of name, 3, 8
    groups of dialects, 4, 9.
    elements in English, 4, 9.
    of Indo-European family, 6, 12; 7, 12.
    group, English from, 27, 19.
    people, invaders of England, 27, 20.
    tribes in England before the Angles, 28, 20.
    suffixes, 212, 321.
    particles as prefixes, 224, 324.
Th becomes *d*, *t*, *s*, cast off, &c., 66, 53.
    in third person of verbs, 176, 289.
    for *d*, 25, 18.
    nominal suffix, 34, 31.
That-thæt = *that which*, 133, 200.
That, 45, 37; 126, 178; 132, 197; 133, 198.
    in Second Period, 53, 41.
    used with *what*, 134, 204.
    replaced by *as*, 133, 198.
    followed by preposition, 133, 198.
    used for *what*, 133, 199.
    used with *that*, 133, 200.
    definite article, 121, 161.
The, 125, 178; 132, 197; 133, 198.
    stem of pronominal adverbs, 198, 312; 199, 312.
Thee, 118, 154.
Their, 121, 161; 124, 175.
Them, 121, 160; 121, 161.
    em, used for, 121, 160.
Theme, definition of, 211, 319.
    how formed, 211, 320.
Then, 198, 312.

Thence, 198, 312.
Ther, old comparative suffix, 106, 113.
    used with *inne*, 133, 198.
There, 198, 312.
Thes, 126, 178.
These, 126, 178.
They, 120, 160; 121, 161.
Thi, instrumental case of *the*, 127, 179.
Thilk, 126, 178; 127, 179.
Thine, 123, 171; 125, 176.
Thing = *one*, 143, 221.
Think, thought, 172, 281
Third, 114, 136.
Thirteen, 112, 129.
Thirteenth, 114, 136.
This, thas, those, 126, 178.
Thither, 198, 312.
Thorn letter, 57, 45.
Thorough, Teutonic prefix, 228, 324.
Those, 126, 178.
Thou, 118, 152.
    changed to *you*, 118, 153.
Thousand, 112, 132.
Three, 110, 127 (note); 111, 128.
Threshold, 77, 57.
Thresum, 139, 214.
Thrice, 197, 311.
Through, thorough, compar. preposition, 204, 314.
    root of, 106, 113; 197, 312.
    Teutonic prefix, 228, 324.
Thus, 199, 312.
Thy, thine, 123, 171; 125, 176.
Ticket, 77, 57.
Tig, ty, suffix, 112, 130; 239, 325.
Tike for *dog*, 88, 72; 180, 293.
Till, 30, 24; 205, 314.
Tion, suffix, 241, 325.
Tmesis, 133, 198; 136, 208; 142, 218; 205, 314.
To, before infinitive, 49, 40; 54, 42; 177, 290.
    related to dative case, 101, 96.
    adverb, 197, 312.
    adverbial prefix, 195, 311.
    preposition = *for*, 204, 314.
    Teutonic prefix, 226, 324.
To wit = *namely*, 190, 305.
Too, preposition, 204, 314.
Tor, suffix, 239, 325.
Tory, suffix, 240, 325.
Toward, towards, 205, 314.
Tramway, 78, 57.
Trans, Romance prefix, 247, 325.
Treen, plural of *tree*, 96, 80.
Trench, " English Past and Present," 91, 73.

INDEX.

Trills, how produced physiologically, 59, 49.
Trix, suffix, 240, 325.
Tude, suffix, 239, 325.
Ture, suffix, 240, 325.
Turkish language, 11, 15.
  words in English, 33, 29.
Twain, 111, 128.
Twasum, 139, 214.
Twelfth, 114, 136.
Twelve, 112, 128.
Twentieth, 114, 136.
Twenty, 112, 130.
Twice, 197, 311.
Two, 111, 128 (note); 110, 127.
Ty, tig, suffix, 112, 130; 239, 325.

U for i, 44, 37.
  for e, 49, 41.
  concerning u and v, 57, 45.
  how produced physiologically, 58, 47.
  different sounds of, 61, 51.
  from a in past tense, 160, 269.
  = v, 230, 325.
Uc, suffix, 236, 325.
Ultra, Romance prefix, 247, 325.
Un, uni, Romance prefix, 247, 325.
  English prefix, 40, 33.
  Teutonic prefix, 226, 324.
Uncle, 84, 72.
Und, suffix, 241, 325.
Under, prefix, 34, 31; 40, 33; 228, 324.
  adverb, 197, 312.
  preposition, 204, 314.
Ung, infinitive termination, 177, 291; 180, 293.
Until, 30, 24.
  compound preposition, 204, 314.
Unto, compound preposition, 204, 314.
Up, prefix, 40, 33; 228, 324.
  adverb, 197, 312.
  preposition, 203, 314.
Urn, suffix, 236, 325.
Us, 117, 149.
Ut, Teutonic prefix, 228, 324.
Utter, preposition, 203, 314.

V, 57, 45.
  for f, 44, 37.
  represented by ph, w, m, 64, 53.
  = u, 230, 325.
  in Romance suffixes, 230, 325.
; Vagabond, 241, 325.

Ve, suffix, 230, 325.
Verb, distinctions of, in O.E. dialects, 41, 34—45, 37.
  coalesces with pronoun, 46, 38.
  forms in First Period, 49, 40.
  forms in Second Period, 53, 41.
  strong and weak, Second Period, 53, 41.
  strong and weak, Third Period, 54, 42.
  in Fourth Period, 55, 43.
  distinguished from noun by accent, 76, 55.
  inflectional part of speech, 79, 59.
  definition, formation of, 80, 61.
  classification, 153, 252.
  transitive, 153, 253; 153, 255.
  intransitive, 153, 254.
  intransitive, with cognate object, 153, 256.
  reflexive, 153, 253; 153, 255.
  reciprocal, 153, 283.
  causative, 153, 254.
  passive, 153, 255.
  impersonal, 153, 257.
  voice, mood, tense of, 153, 258.
  number, person of, 155, 262.
  conjugation of, 155, 263.
  strong, weak, 155, 263.
  elements of, 172, 282.
  inflexions of, 172, 282.
  present indicative, 173, 283.
  present subjunctive, 174, 284.
  past indicative, 174, 285.
  past subjunctive, 175, 288.
  person-ending, 175, 289.
  infinitive mood, 176, 290.
  present participle, 180, 293.
  anomalous, 180, 294 *et seq*.
  verbal nouns, 177, 291.
  negative forms of, 183, 297.
  auxiliary, 191, 309.
  intransitive and transitive, from same root, 221, 322.
Verbal nouns, 177, 291.
  suffixes, 220, 323; 242, 325.
  compounds, 224, 323.
  endings, 242, 325.
Verjuice, 242, 325.
Viand, 241, 325.
Vice, Romance prefix, 247, 325.
Vinegar, 242, 325.
Vixen, 89, 73; 216, 320 (note).
Vocabulary, English, 34, 30.
  no foreign elements in, in the First Period, 48, 40.
  changes, Second Period, 54, 41.

INDEX.

Vocabulary, changes, Third Period, 54, 42.
  changes, Fifth Period, 56, 44.
  changes by influence of printing, &c., 56, 44.
Vocal organs, physiology of, 58, 46.
Vocative case, 100, 96.
Voice, human, physiology of, 58, 46.
  active, passive, 154, 258.
Vowel, change in *elder*, 107, 115.
  change in strong verbs, 155, 263.
  change in past tense, 157, 267; 158, 269.
  between root and suffix in weak verbs, 168, 277; 168, 279.
  radical, in weak verbs, 169, 279.
  change in weak verbs, 171, 279.
  original of verbal stems, 171, 279 (note).
  connecting root and suffix, 172, 282; 173, 283; 174, 285; 175, 288.
  suffixes, 212, 321; 229, 325.
Vowels, how produced physiologically, 58, 47.
  gradations, modifications of, 58, 47.
  modification into diphthongs, 59, 48.
  different sounds of, 61, 51.
  various sounds of, in English, 62, 52.
  long and short, how represented in spelling, 63, 52.
  changed to form plural, 95, 79.

W for *g*, 50, 41.
  cast off, inserted, *wh* = *hw*, 64, 53.
Wan = *whan*, 131, 192.
  Teutonic prefix, 226, 324.
Wanton, 227, 324.
Ward, adjectival suffix, 34, 31.
Was, 182, 296; 162, 271.
We, 117, 148.
Weak verbs, 168, 276.
  in Gothic, 168, 277.
  in Old English, 168, 278.
  in Modern English, 168, 279.
  radical vowel in, 169, 279; 171, 279.
  suffix *d* unused, 170, 279.
  exceptional forms, 171, 280; 172, 281.
Wên letter, 57, 45.
Wench, 84, 72.

Welsh, origin of name, 3, 8.
  Keltic language, 7, 12.
Went, from *wend*, 172, 281.
West Midland dialect (*see* Dialects).
Wether, 67, 72.
Whan or wan, 131, 192.
What, whatever, 128, 183; 129, 184; 133, 201.
  replaced by *that*, 133, 199.
  archaic use of, 134, 202.
  vulgar use of, 134, 203.
  used with *that*, 134, 204.
  used with *as*, 134, 205.
  used for *whatever*, 136, 209.
  = *something*, 137, 213.
  aneshwæt, swilceshwæt, 137, 213.
What for a = *what sort of a*, 129, 185.
Whatso, 136, 208.
Whatsoever, whatasever, whatever, 136, 210.
When, 199, 312.
Where, 199, 312.
Whether, whethersoever, 128, 183.
  = which of the two, 129, 186.
Which, whichsoever, 128, 183; 130, 189; 131, 195; 133, 197; 136, 208.
  O.E. *hwilc*, &c., 130, 187.
  whichever, 136, 210.
  with *the, that*, &c., 131, 196.
Whit, 146, 233.
Whither, 199, 312.
Whitney, account of Indo-Europeans, 10, 13.
  on Grimm's Law, 24, 17.
  on laws other than Grimm's, 24, 17.
  on syllables, 57, 45.
  on orthography, 63, 52 (note).
  on pronouns, 60, 62.
  on prepositions, 80, 64.
  on verb *have*, 191, 309.
Who, whoever, 128, 183; 130, 188; 130, 189; 130, 190; 133, 197; 136, 210.
  = *any one, some one*, 137, 212.
  joined to *some*, 140, 217.
  adverbial stem, 199, 312.
Whom, 128, 183.
  with *the*, 131, 193.
Whose, 128, 183.
  with *the, that*, 131, 193.
Whoso, whosoever, 136, 208.
Wickliffe wrote in East Midland dialect, 47, 39.
  case absolute, 103, 102.
Wife, 83, 71 (note); 86, 72.
Wig, 237, 325.

Wight, 146, 233.
Will, auxiliary verb, 191, 309.
  also *wol*, 187, 302.
Wind (a horn), 261, 269.
Windsor, 78, 57.
Wit, 190, 305.
Witch, 85, 72.
With, wither, preposition, 204, 314.
  Teutonic prefix, 226, 324.
Wizard, 85, 72.
Wolen, as infinitive, 187, 302.
Words, definition of, 1, 1.
  naturalized in English, 33, 29.
  number of, in English, 84, 30.
  pure and classical, 84, 30.
  vocabulary of English, 34, 30.
  Romance, in English, 34, 31.
  meaning of, distinguished by accent, 76, 56.
  denoting quality, position, 79, 58.
  as parts of speech, 79, 59.
  used to denote gender, 92, 74.
  naturalized, plural of, 97, 84; 99, 90.
  used only in plural, 98, 87.
  compound, genitives of, 102, 101.
  compound, 221, 323.
  formation, roots of, 211, 319.
Work, wrought, 172, 284.
World, 222, 323.
Worse, worst, 107, 117.
Written alphabet, 58, 46.

X, equivalent to *ks* or *gs*, 61, 50.

Y, for *g*, 50, 41 : 186, 301.
  Teutonic prefix, 226, 324.
  in Romance suffixes, 229, 325.
Ye, 118, 155; 200, 312.
Yea, 200, 312.
Yes, 200, 312.
Yesterday, 200, 312.
Yet, 200, 312.
Yon, yond, yonder, 125, 178; 128, 181.
York, 78, 57.
You, 118, 155.
  used for *thou*, 118, 153.
  used for *ye*, 118, 155.
Your, 124, 175.
Youth, 216, 321.

Z, for *s*, 44, 37.
  for *s*, *c*, intruded, changed, 67, 53.

Þ (thorn letter), 57, 45.

Ƿ (wên letter), 57, 45.

Ð, ð, 57, 45.

THE END.

www.ingramcontent.com/pod-product-compliance
Lightning Source LLC
Chambersburg PA
CBHW032013220426
43664CB00006B/228